HIGHLAND COUNTY VIRGINIA

DEATH RECORDS

1853–1898

Transcribed by
Woodrow Clay Hamilton, Jr.

HERITAGE BOOKS
2010

HERITAGE BOOKS
AN IMPRINT OF HERITAGE BOOKS, INC.

Books, CDs, and more—Worldwide

For our listing of thousands of titles see our website
at
www.HeritageBooks.com

Published 2010 by
HERITAGE BOOKS, INC.
Publishing Division
100 Railroad Ave. #104
Westminster, Maryland 21157

Copyright © 2010 Woodrow Clay Hamilton, Jr.

All rights reserved. No part of this book may be reproduced or transmitted in any form or by any means, electronic or mechanical, including photocopying, recording or by any information storage and retrieval system without written permission from the author, except for the inclusion of brief quotations in a review.

International Standard Book Numbers
Paperbound: 978-0-7884-5042-6
Clothbound: 978-0-7884-8296-0

TABLE OF CONTENTS

Introduction v

Archaic Medical Terms vii

1853 1	1877 96
1854 5	1878 98
1855 7	1879 100
1856 10	1880 103
1857 14	1881 108
1858 18	1882 111
1859 21	1883 116
1860 24	1884 121
1861 26	1885 126
1862 38	1886 135
1863 57	1887 142
1864 57	1888 149
1865 63	1889 155
1866 66	1890 160
1867 68	1891 167
1868 70	1892 174
1869 73	1893 182
1870 75	1894 189
1871 78	1895 196
1872 82	1896 202
1873 84	1897 209
1874 87	1898 215
1875 90	
1876 92	

Index 220

INTRODUCTION

This volume reproduces the major portion of Highland County, Virginia's death records—some forty-five years worth. It does not include deaths recorded from 1912-1917.

Readers will note the large number of deaths in 1862. This is the result of two factors. In 1861 and 1862, a diphtheria epidemic swept Highland and surrounding counties. In Highland in 1862, 122 deaths were attributed to diphtheria and typhoid alone. The epidemic was devastating—in some cases killing all the children in a family group. Also adding to this large number was the recordation of Highland soldiers killed outside the county during the war. These records also note the pre-emancipation deaths of some sixty slaves. Of these, four entries name one of the deceased slave's parents.

Recently, death records spanning twenty-seven years (1871-1898), were discovered in a hidden cabinet in the Highland County Circuit Clerk's office in Monterey, Virginia. The records had been out of public view and public use for perhaps as many as forty years. Moreover, these records were only recently microfilmed by the Library of Virginia and have never been privately copied by anyone.

Highland County was formed in late 1847. In 1853, when Virginia mandated the recordation of births and deaths, Highland officials purchased large registers in which to enter this information. However, soon after the Civil War, county officials apparently concluded that the old registers, which contained column headings to record the births and deaths of slaves and the names of slave owners, should be replaced by new ones.

The new registers were put into service during 1870 and entries continued through 1898—two years longer than the law required. These registers remained in public use until the late 1960s or early 1970s. The then Clerk apparently directed the now damaged and worn birth and death registers be unbound and retired and the data copied onto blank pages of the 1853-era registers—still in good condition from lack of use.

The births were copied into the old register (except 1898) but the death records were not. Instead, the unbound pages of the original death records were rolled, wrapped, tucked away, and forgotten. In 1981, when other Highland County records were collected for microfilming by the Library of Virginia, the 1871-1898 death records were not included.

Death records for 1870 through 1874 were compiled separately by the various assessors of the three Highland County townships—Blue Grass, Monterey, and Stonewall—and were styled according to the whims of the assessor. Beginning in 1875, one county-wide record was compiled by the Commissioner of the Revenue according to the new ordinance of 1873. But, here too, the compilers styled their entries according to whim.

The death records are not complete. One quarter sheet of the 1897 death list is missing—affecting both sides. Of the seventy-five death entries for this year, the first seventeen lines of information are missing as are the first seventeen names of the *deceased on the reverse, from entries thirty-seven through fifty-four. Also, entries at the bottom of a few other pages are damaged and only partially readable. Such missing data are represented by dashes (----). Information never recorded on the original ledger sheets is represented by a solid line (____).*

The transcriber has adhered to the spellings and language used on the original ledger sheets and, where appropriate, has explained anomalies, double entries, and confusing data in footnotes. Where the informant was unable to provide the name of the decedent (or an infant was not yet named) an upper case dash (____) has been inserted. This is reflected in the index for unnamed decedents, and unnamed spouses.

Preceding the death records is a list, with definitions, of some of the more archaic and obscure medical terms.

Although every effort has been made to avoid errors in transcribing, some may have successfully eluded detection. These errors are mine and mine alone.

                                                                      Clay Hamilton
                                                                      Hightown, Virginia
                                                                       January 2009

Some Archaic Medical Terms Associated with Causes of Death

Arthemia: loss of strength—a general debility.

Apoplexy: most commonly a brain hemorrhage or stroke.

Billious: excessive secretions of bile—disordered liver function.

Catarrah: inflammation of the muscous membranes, especially in the air passages.

Consumption: pulmonary tuberculosis.

Delirium tremens: delirium and tremors induced by excessive and prolonged use of alcohol.

Dropsy: swelling or edema, often associated with congestive heart failure.

Dyspepsia: acute indigestion.

Erysipelas: streptococcal infection of the blood.

Flux: profuse discharge of fluids from the body, especially uncontrolled diarrhea.

Gravel: calcareous accretions in the urinary tract, most often kidney stones.

Hysteritis: inflammation of the uterus.

La Grippe: influenza.

Phthisis: pulmonary consumption characterized by emaciation.

Puerperal fever: infection of the placenta or uterus often leading to blood poisoning.

Pyaeria: probably pyorrhea, an inflammation of the periodontium (gums) with discharge of pus and loosening of teeth.

Pyemia: probably pyaemia, or blood poisoning with multiple abscesses and toxemia.

Quinsy: bacterial infection of the throat and tonsilar area with swelling and inflammation.

Scrofula: tuberculosis of the lymph nodes especially in the neck.

Thrush: fungal disease of the mouth and throat especially in infants.

Veneral: various infections contracted through sexual intercourse.

White swelling: tuberculosis of the bones and joints.

1853

Delord, John, WM, **d. 12 Dec.** in Highland of phthesis, age,____.
      parents, ____ **&** ____. born ____. occ. shoemaker. unmarried.
      info, William C. Jones, physician.

Lantz, Jonas, WM, **d. 17 July** in Highland of gastro ontritis, age, ____,
      parents, ____ **&** ____. born ____. occ. farmer. consort of ____.
      info, William C. Jones, physician.

Brown, Margaret, WF, **d. 11 Aug.** in Highland of dyspepsia, age, ____.
      parents, ____ **&** ____. born ____. occ. house keeper. unmarried.
      info, William C. Jones, physician.

Pullin, Margaret, WF, **d. 28 Aug.** in Highland of apoplexy, age, ____.
      parents, ____ **&** ____. born Highland. occ. house keeper.
      consort of ____, info, William C. Jones, physician.

McCluster, Martin, WM, **d. 4 Aug.** in Highland of peritonitis, age, ____.
      parents, Franklin McCluster. born____. occ. farmer. unmarried.
      info, William C. Jones, physician.

Killingsworth, Margaret, WF, **d. 20 Oct.** in Highland of phthisis, age,____.
      parents, ____ **&** ____. born ____. occ. ____. unmarried.
      info, William C. Jones, physician.

Woods, Martha, WF, **d. 20 April** in Highland of typhoid fever, age, ____.
      parents, James & Polly Woods. born Pendleton & Augusta Co.,*
      occ. farmer. consort of ____. info, William C. Jones, physician.

Allen, Hannah, WF, **d. 31 March** in Highland of puerperal fever, age, ____.
      parents, Adam Rexrode. born Pendleton Co. occ. ____.
      consort of ____. info, William C. Jones, physician.

Armstrong, Hanson, WM, **d. 10 April** in Highland of peritonitis, age,____.
      parents, Eleanor Armstrong. born Pendleton Co. occ. farmer.
      unmarried. info, William C. Jones, physician.

Jones, Joseph, WM, **d.14 Nov.** in Highland of dropsy, age,____.
      parents, ____ **&** ____. born Pendleton Co. occ. farmer.
      consort of ____. info, William C. Jones, physician.

---

* May reflect parents' birthplaces.

Jones, Sarah, WF, **d.** ____ **June** in Highland of ericipelas, age, ____.
        parents, ____ **&** ____. born Pendleton Co. occ. ____.
        consort of ____. info, William C. Jones, physician.

Peck, Andrew J., WM, **d.** ____ **April** in Highland of scarlatina, age,____.
        parents, ____ **&** ____. born Pendleton Co. occ. farmer. unmarried.
        info, William C. Jones, physician.

_____, WM, **d.10 July** in Highland of cholera infantum, age, ____.
        parents, Abraham Peck. born Pendleton Co.
        occ. farmer. unmarried. info, William C. Jones, physician.

Gum, Leonard, WM, **d.** ____ in Highland of peritonitis, age, ____.
        parents, John & Mary Gum. born Bath Co. occ. farmer.
        consort of Mary Gum. info, George N. Kinney, physician.

Hidy, Jacob, WM, **d.** ____ **Jan** in Highland of peritonitis, age, ____.
        parents, ____ **&** ____. born Pendleton Co. occ. farmer.
        consort of Catherine Hidy. info, George N. Kinney, physician.

Wright, Christopher G., WM, **d. 25 Feb.** in Highland of pneumonia, age, ____.
        parents, Robt. & Susan Wright. born Bath Co.
        occ. storekeeper. consort of Elvina Wright.
        info, George N. Kinney, physician.

Matheny, Silas B., WM, **d.** ____ in Highland of pneumonia, age, ____.
        parents, Levi Matheny. born Bath Co. occ. farmer. unmarried.
        info, James H. Byrd, physician.

Bird, Frederick, WM, **d.** ____ in Highland of paralysis, age, ____.
        parents, ____ **&** ____. born Bath Co. occ. farmer. consort of ____.
        info, James H. Byrd, physician

Gwin, Eliza, WF, **d. 18 July** in Highland of acute entritis, age, ____.
        parents, Jas. & Rachel Gwin. born Bath Co. occ. house keeper.
        unmarried. info, James H. Byrd, physician.

Hiner, Eliza J., WF, **d. 12 June** in Highland of hysteria, age, ____.
        parents, ____ **&** ____. born Pendleton Co. occ. house keeper.
        consort of William Hiner. info, James H. Byrd, physician.

Wiley, Robert, WM, **d. 18 Feb.** in Highland of pneumonia, age, ____.
        parents, Jas. & Nancy Wiley. born Bath Co. occ. farmer.
        consort of Susan Wiley. info, James H. Byrd, physician.

Wiley, John, WM, **d. 16 May** in Highland of pneumonia, age, age, ____.
  parents, Jas. & Nancy Wiley. born Bath Co. occ. farmer.
  consort of Elizabeth Wiley. info, James H. Byrd, physician.

Fleming, Margt. L., WF, **d. 6 March** in Highland of hysteritis, age, 38yrs.
  parents, ____ & ____. born Virginia. occ. house keeper.
  consort of Wm. W. Fleming. info, James H. Byrd, physician.

Hardway, Elizabeth, WF, **d. 15 Sept.** in Highland of hydrops, age, ____.
  parents, ____ & ____. born Virginia. occ. house keeper.
  consort of ____. info, James H. Byrd, physician.

Slaven, Mary & child, WF, **d. ____ March** in Highland of hysteritis & chepuriche, age, ____. **parents, Samuel Vance.** born Bath Co. occ. housekeeper.
  consort of James Slaven. info, James H. Byrd, physician.

Chesnut, Mary, WF, **d. ____** in Highland of acute enteritis, age, ____.
  parents, ____ & ____. born Highland Co. occ. ____. unmarried.
  info, James H. Byrd, physician.

Kinkead, John J., WM, **d. ____** in Highland of pneumonia, age, ____.
  parents, Thomas Kinkead. born Pendleton Co.
  occ. farmer. unmarried. info, James H. Byrd, physician.

Stephenson, Elizabeth, WF, **d. ____ July** in Highland of erisepelas, age, ____.
  parents, ____ & ____. born Virginia. occ. house keeper.
  consort of ____. info, James H. Byrd, physician.

Wilson, Elizabeth, WF, **d. 10 July** in Highland of pneumonia, age, ____.
  parents, ____ & ____. born Virginia. occ. house keeper.
  consort of Samuel Wilson. info, Samuel Wilson, husband.

Davis, Harvey W., WM, **d. 5 June** in Highland of ____, age, ____.
  parents, ____ & ____. born Highland Co. occ.____. unmarried.
  info, Mr. Davis, father.

McDaniel, Mary E., WF, **d. 3 June** in Highland of ____, age, ____.
  parents, ____ & ____. born Highland Co. occ. ____. unmarried.
  info, Mr. McDaniel, father

Kincaid, Nancy, WF, **d. ____** in Highland of ____, age, ____.
  parents, ____ & ____. born Highland Co. occ. ____, unmarried.
  info, ____.

Kincaid, Sarah J., WF, **d. 16 April** in Highland of ____, age, ____.
        parents, ____ & ___. born Highland Co. occ. ____. unmarried. info, ____.

Gwin, Rachel, WF, **d. 10 May** in Highland of ____, age, ____.
        parents, ____ & ____. born Highland Co. occ. house keeper. unmarried. info, ____.

Gwin, Mary, WF, **d. 23 May** in Highland of ____, age, ____.
        parents, ____ & ____. born Highland Co. occ. house keeper. unmarried. info, ____.

Johns, Sarah, WF, **d. 10 Feb.** in Highland of ____, age, ____.
        parents, ____ & ____. born Highland Co. occ. house keeper. unmarried. info, ____.

Rexrode, John L., WM, **d.** ____ in Highland of ____, age, ____.
        parents, ____ & ____. born Highland Co. occ. farmer. consort of ____. info, ____.

Jones, Mary A., WF, **d. 9 June** in Highland of ____, age, ____.
        parents, ____ & ____. born Highland Co. occ. ____. unmarried. info, ____.

Swecker, Levi, WM, **d. 10 March** in Highland of typhoid fever, age, ____.
        parents, Benjamin Swecker. born Highland Co. occ. farmer. unmarried. info, Benj. Swecker. father.

Swecker, Jeremy, WM, **d. 11 March** in Highland of typhoid fever, age, ____.
        parents, Benjamin Swecker. born Highland Co. occ. farmer. unmarried. info, Benj. Swecker, father.

Swecker, Cain, WM, **d. 14 March** in Highland of typhoid fever, age, ____.
        parents, Benjamin Swecker. born Highland Co. occ. farmer. unmarried. info, Benj. Swecker, father.

Nicholas, Catherine J., WF, **d.** ____ in Highland of ____, age, ____.
        parents, ____ & ____. born Virginia. occ. house keeper. consort of ____. info, ____.

Rexrode, John, WM, **d. 15 May** in Highland of ____, age, ____.
        parents, ____ & ____. born Pendleton Co. occ. farmer. consort of ____. info, Benjamin Rexrode, son.

Stephenson, Jane, WF, **d. 3 March** in Highland of pneumonia,
  age, 73yrs, 3mos, 21 dys. **parents, Wm. & Margaret Greene.**
  born, Bath Co. occ. house keeper. consort of ____.
  info, Adam Stephenson, son.

Slave Philip, of John B. Slaven, M, **d.** ____ in Highland of ____, age, ____.
  parents, ____ & ____. born, Highland Co. occ. farmer.
  consort of ____. info, John B. Stuart, Master.

Slave Sarah, of Rebecca G. Hamilton, F, **d.** ____ in Highland of ____, age, ____.
  parents, ____ & ____. born, Highland Co. occ. house keeper.
  consort of ____. info, Rebecca G. Hamilton, ____.

Slave William, of Robert Lockridge, M, **d.** ____ in Highland of ____, age, ____.
  parents, ____ & ____. born, Highland Co. occ. farmer.
  consort of ____. info, Robert Lockridge, Master.

Smith, Eliza & child, WF, **d.** ____ in Highland of ____, age, ____.
  parents, ____ & ____. born, Highland Co. occ. house keeper.
  consort of ____. info, ____.

1854

Bird, Eleanor, WF, **d. 21 Oct.** on Back Creek of consumption, age, ____.
  parents, David & Eliz. Bird. born, Bath Co. occ. ____. unmarried.
  info, David H. Bird, friend.

Chesnut, Thos. A., WM, **d. 3 May** on B. Creek of ____, age, ____.
  parents, John F. & Elizi Chesnut. born, Bath Co.
  occ. ____. unmarried. info, John F. Chesnut, father.

Simmons, Malinda, WF, **d. 14 Sept.** on B. Creek of ____, age, ____.
  parents, Peter Michael. born, Rockingham Co. occ. ____.
  consort of ____. info, John Simmons, husband.

Hevener, George W., WM, **d. 4 Nov.** in Highland of ____, age, ____.
  parents, Wm. & Jane Hevener. born, Pendleton Co. occ. farmer.
  unmarried. info, Wm. Hevener, father.

Kramer, Wellington, WM, **d. 3 Sept.** in Highland of ____, age, ____.
  parents, Conrad & B. Kramer. born, Pendleton Co. occ. farmer.
  unmarried. info, Conrad Kramer, father.

Rexrode, Margaret, WF, **d. 14 March** in Pendleton Co. of ____, age, 83yrs, 9mos.
    parents, Jacob & Barbara. born, ____. occ. farmer. unmarried.
    info, Benj. Rexrode, son.

Lane, John R., WM, **d. 3 Sept.** in Highland of ____, age, ____.
    parents, Harvey & Lucinda Lane. born, Highland Co. occ. farmer.
    unmarried. info, Lucinda Lane, mother.

Kitz, Dorothy, WF, **d. 7 Dec.** in Highland of ____, age, 92yrs.
    parents, ____ & ____. born, ____. occ. farmer. unmarried.
    info, Joseph Varner, friend.

Slave Mary A. of Rebecca G. Hamilton, F. **d. 23 May** in Highland of ____,
    age, 14yrs, 12mos. **parents, ____ & ____.** born, Bath Co.
    occ. farmer. unmarried. info, James Wright, ____.

Johns, Mary, WF, **d. 13 Nov.** in Highland of ____, age, 56yrs.
    parents, Wm. & Mary Wilson. born, B. & Pen. Co. occ. farmer.
    unmarried. info, Wm. Johns (of Jr.), ____.

Chew, Silas N., WM, **d. 20 June** in Highland of ____, age, 15yrs.
    parents, Jesse & Mar. Chew. born, B. & Pen. Co. occ. farmer.
    unmarried. info, Jesse Chew, father.

Mozingo, Wm. H., WM, **d. 20 July** in Highland of consumption, age, 35yrs.
    parents, Robt. & Cath. Mozingo. born, Culpeper Co.
    occ. shoe maker. consort of ____. info, Louisa E. Mozingo, widow.

Botkin, Sarah M., WF, **d. 23 Aug.** in Highland of ____. age, 1yr, 8mos.
    parents, Saml & Barbara Botkin. born, Pendleton Co. occ. farmer.
    unmarried. info, Samuel Botkin, father.

_____, WM, **d. 23 Aug.** in Highland of ____, age, ____.
    parents, Robert C. & Mary M. Masters. born, Highland Co.
    occ. ____. consort of ____. info, Robert C. Masters, father.

Rexrode, Amos, WM, **d.** ____ in Highland of ____, age, ____.
    parents, Henry A. Rexrode. born, ____. occ. ____
    consort of ____. info, Jesse Rexrode, ____.

Slave John Letcher of George H. Benson, M, **d.** ____, in Highland of ____, age, ____.
    parents, ____ & ____. born ____. occ. ____. consort of ____. info, ____.

Slave Rachel of Wm K. Gwin, F, **d. 1 May** in Highland of ____, age, ____.
    parents, ____ & ____. born, ____.occ. ____. consort of ____. info, ____.

Slave James of Moses Gwin, M, **d. 13 Oct.** in Highland of ____, age, ____.
parents, ____ & ____. born ___. occ. ___. consort of ___. info, ___.

Slave Hannah of John B. Steuart, F, **d. 10 June** in Highland of ____, age, ____.
parents, ____ & ____. born ___. occ. ___. consort of ___. info, ___.

1855

Slave ____ of Jacob W. Stuart, M, **d.** ____ in Highland of ____, age, ____.
parents, ____ & ____ born Highland Co. occ. farmer.
consort of ____. info, Jacob W. Stuart, owner.

Wade, Matilda, WF, **d. 20 Nov.** in Highland of ____, age, 62yrs, 18dys.
parents, Stuart & Isabella Slaven. born Bath Co. occ. ____
consort of John Wade. info, John Wade, husband.

Campbell, Azanah P., WM, **d. 17 Sept.** in Highland of ____, age, 27yrs.
parents, Alexr. & Mary Campbell. born Pendleton Co. occ. ____.
unmarried. info, Saml B. Campbell, relation.

Waggoner, Joseph, WM, **d. 8 March** in Highland of ____, age, 17yrs, 4mos.
parents, Sampson & Barbara Waggoner, born Pendleton Co.
occ. ____. unmarried. info, Sampson Waggoner, father.

Slave James of George Hammer, M, **d.** ____ **Dec.** in Highland of ____, age, 3mos.
parents, ____ & ____. born ____. occ. ____. consort of ____.
info, George Hammer, owner.

Rough, George A., WM, **d.** ____ **May** in Highland of ____, age, 7yrs.
parents, J. & L. Rough. born Highland Co. occ. ____. unmarried.
info, J. Rough, father.

Waggoner, Benj. A., WM, **d.** ____ in Highland of ____, age, 8yrs, 11mos.
parents, Jacob & Eliz Waggoner. born Highland Co. occ. ____.
unmarried. info, Jacob Waggoner, father.

Rymer, Martha J., WF, **d. 7 June** in Highland of ____, age, 2yrs, 10mos, 19dys.
parents, George & Sarah Rymer. born Highland Co. occ. ____.
consort of ____. info, George Rymer, father.

Helmick, E. C., WF, **d. 27 Aug.** in Highland of ____, age, 2mos, 24dys.
parents, Philip & M. Helmick. born Highland Co. occ. ____.
unmarried. info, Philip Helmick, father.

Varner, Morgan, WM, **d. 22 Feb.** in Highland of ____, age, 14yrs, 2mos, 23dys.
   parents, Joseph & Mary Varner. born Highland Co. occ. ____.
   unmarried. info, Mary Varner, mother.

_____, WM, **d. 15 March** in Highland of ____, age, ____.
   parents, Michael & Sarah Rexrode. born Highland Co. occ.____.
   unmarried. info, Sarah Rexrode, mother.

Hull, Morgan W., WM, **d. 21 May** in Highland of ____, age, 13yrs, 5mos.
   parents, F. K. & Mary E. Hull. born Highland Co. occ. ____.
   unmarried. info, Benj. Fleisher, relation.

McCoy, Cynthia A., WF, **d. 6 May** in Highland of ____, age, 22yrs.
   parents, John & Mary Malcom. born Highland Co. occ. ____.
   consort of Benj. McCoy. info, And. J. McCoy, relation.

McCoy, Margaret, WF, **d. 27 June** in Highland of ____, age, 76yrs, 8mos, 9dys.
   parents, Henry Jones. born Pendleton Co. occ. ____.
   consort of ____. info, Henry C. Jones, relation.

Ruleman, Christian W., WM, **d. 9 Jan.** in Highland of ____, age, 9yrs, 10mos, 18dys.
   parents, Henry & Sarah Ruleman. born Pendleton Co. occ.____.
   consort of ____. info, Henry Ruleman, father.

Fleisher, John H. A., WM, **d. 20 Sept.** in Highland of ____, age, 6yrs, 6mos, 27dys.
   parents, Henry J. & Barbara Flesher. born ____. occ.____.
   consort of ____. info, Henry J. Fleisher, father.

Smith, Barbara, WF, **d. 16 Dec.** in Highland of ____, age, 50yrs, 11mos, 14dys.
   parents, Christina & Henry Smith. born Pendleton Co. occ. ____.
   unmarried. info, Christina Smith, mother.

Jones, Mary, WF, **d. 26 May** in Highland of ____, age, 67yrs, 3mos, 12dys.
   parents, Hannah & Thomas Eureto. born Pendleton Co.
   occ. ____. consort of Thos. Jones. info, Henry C. Jones, relation.

Smith, Henry, WM, **d. ____ June** in Highland of cancer, age, 55yrs.
   parents, Jno. & Catherine Smith. born Pendleton Co. occ. ____.
   consort of ____. info, not recalled.*

Brown, Elizabeth, WF, **d. 12 Dec.** on South Fork of ____, age, 67yrs.
   parents, Mary & David Dick. born Alfred Co., Maryland.**
   occ. ____. consort of Thos. Brown. info, Thomas Brown, husband.

---

*Apparently the clerk neglected to record the informant and could not later recall the name.   ** likely Harford Co., Maryland

Slave James M. of Moses Gwin, M, **d. 31 May** on Cowpasture of ____, age, ____.
        parents, ____ **&** ____. born Highland Co. occ. ____.
        consort of ____. info, Moses Gwin, owner.

Slave Alice of Peter Hupman, F, **d.** ____ **Sept.** on C. Pasture of ____, age, ____.
        parents, ____ **&** ____. born Highland Co. occ. ____.
        consort of ____. info, Peter Hupman, owner.

_____, WM, **d.** ____ **Dec.*** on B. Pasture of ____, age, ____.
        parents, Jno. A. & E. A. Cobbs. born Highland Co. occ. ____.
        consort of ____, info, John A. Cobbs, father.

_____, WM, **d.** ____ **Dec.*** on B. Pasture of ____, age, ____.
        parents, Jno. A. & E.A. Cobbs. born Highland Co. occ. ____.
        consort of ____. info, John A. Cobbs, father

Eagle, Sarah, WF, **d. 1 Oct.** on B.Pasture of ____, age, 47yrs, 2mos.
        parents, ____ **&** ____. born Highland Co. occ. ____.
        consort of Benj. B. Eagle. info, Benj. B. Eagle, husband.

_____, WF, **d. 31 Dec.** on B. Pasture of ____, age, 1yr.
        parents, John Carlisle. born Highland Co. occ. ____.
        consort of ____. info, Christopher Carlisle, relation.

Carlisle, Rachel, WF, **d. 20 May** on B. Pasture of ____, age, 74yrs.
        parents, Christopher & Jane Graham. born Highland Co. occ.____.consort of ____. info, Christopher Carlisle, relation.

Jones, Mary, WF, **d. 20 May** on Bullpasture Mt. of ____, age, 100yrs.
        parents, ____ **&** ____. born Germany. occ. ____.
        consort of ____. info, Mrs. Gwin, friend.

Steuart, Thercey, WF, **d. 26 May** on Bullpasture River of ___, age, 47yrs, 1 mo, 24dys.
        parents, Wm. & Nancy Douglass. born Bath Co. occ. ____.
        consort of Charles Steuart. info, Charles Steuart, husband.

Campbell, Robert, WM, **d. 10 Oct.** on B. Creek of ____, age, ____.
        parents, Father, James Campbell, born ____. occ. ___. unmarried.
        info, Wm M. Campbell, friend.

---

*Two entries suggest twin males, stillborn.

_____, WM, **d. ____ June** on B. Creek of ____, age, ____.
        parents, Father, James Trimble. born Highland Co. occ. ____.
        consort of ____. info, James Trimble, father.

Stephenson, Emma V., WF, **d. 5 June** at Monterey of ____, age, 3yrs, 8mos, 12dys.
        parents, Adam & Sarah C. Stephenson. born Highland Co.
        occ. ____. consort of ____. info, Adam Stephenson, father.

Wolf, Martenella, WF, **d. 8 Oct.** in Highland of ____, age, 1mo, 21 dys.
        parents, Josiah & Sarah E. Wolf. born Highland Co.
        occ.____. consort of ____. info, Josiah Wolf, father.

1856

Colaw, Elizabeth, WF, **d. 17 Dec.** in Highland of apoplexy, age, 65yrs.
        parents, Henry & Catherine Wimer. born Pa. occ. house keeper
        consort of George Colaw. info, George Colaw, husband.

Grogg, John, WM, **d. 8 Feb.** in Highland of unknown, age, 88yrs.
        parents, Henry & unknown Grogg. born Rockingham Co.
        occ. farmer. consort of Sophia Grogg. info, Henry Grogg, son.

Grogg, Martha J., WF, **d. 28 March** in Highland of jaundice, age, 5mos.
        parents, Adam & Charlotte Grogg. born Crab Bottom. occ. ____.
        consort of ____. info, Adam Grogg, father.

Swecker, John Hannan, WM, **d. 25 April** in Highland of hepatitis,
        age, 1yr, 5mos, 25dys. **parents, David W. & Cecilia Swecker.**
        born Crab Bottom. occ. ____. consort of ____.
        info, David W. Swecker, father.

Hevener, Jno., WM, **d. 26 Aug.** in Highland of dropsy, age, 76yrs.
        parents, ____ & ____. born ____. occ. ____.
        consort of Eleanor Hevener. info, Wm. Hevener, son.

No name, WF, **d. 6 Jan.*** on Back Creek of unknown, age, 1dy.
        parents, Jno. & Lucinda Simmons. born Back Creek occ. ____.
        consort of ____. info, John Simmons, father.

No name, WF, **d. 6 Jan.*** on Back Creek of unknown, age, 1dy.
        parents, Jno. & Lucinda Simmons. born Back Creek. occ.____.
        consort of ____. info, John Simmons, father.

---

* Two identical entries suggest twins.

Halterman, Ambe S., WM, **d. 12 Feb.** on Straight Creek of scarlet fever,
    age, 10mos, 2dys. **parents, Joseph & Elizabeth Halterman.**
    born Straight Creek. occ. ____. consort of ____.
    info, Joseph Halterman, father.

Peck, Ann, WF, **d. 18 April** on Straight Creek of sudden death, age, 74yrs.
    parents, Martin & Ann Life. born Pendleton Co.
    occ. house keeper. consort of Jacob Peck. info, Abraham Peck, son.

No Name, WF, **d. 11 Aug.** on Straight Creek of unknown, age, 1mo, 3dys.
    parents, Jacob & Lucy Sprouse. born Straight Creek.
    occ. ____. consort of ____. info, Jacob Sprouse, father.

Hill, Lucy R. A., WF, **d. 24 Feb.** in Monterey of convulsion, age, 5mos.
    parents, Jacob J. & S. C. Hill. born Monterey. occ. ____.
    consort of ____. info, Jacob J. Hill, father.

Beverage, Robert, WM, **d. 13 April** on Straight Creek of dropsy, age, 64yrs.
    parents, Jno. & Elizabeth Beverage. born Pendleton Co.
    occ. farmer. consort of Elizabeth Beverage.
    info, Thomas Beverage, nephew.

Varner, Joseph, WM, **d. 2 Jan.** on Straight Creek of pleuorsa, age, 38yrs, 7mos.
    parents, Peter & Ann Varner. born Pendleton Co. occ. farmer.
    consort of Mary Varner. info, Mary Varner, wife.

Wade, Emma E., WF, **d. 3 Sept.** on Back Creek of ____, age, 2yrs, 8mos, 15dys.
    parents, Anson O. & Adella Wade. born Back Creek occ.____.
    consort of ____. info, A. O. Wade, father.

Briscoe, Sarah, WF, **d. 13 Oct.** on Back Creek of ____, age, 57yrs.
    parents, Saml & Mary Woods. born Bath Co. occ. house keeper.
    consort of Jacob Briscoe. info, J. Briscoe, husband.

Sheridan, Francis, WM, **d. 4 Aug.** on Jacksons River of murdered by Sam, age, 23yrs.
    parents, ____ & ____. born ____.
    occ. ____. consort of Elizabeth Sheridan. info, ____, ____.

Kinkead, David H. A., WM, **d. 28 Nov.** on Jacksons River of ____, age, 2yrs, 3mos.
    parents, David G. & Mary Kinkead. born Jacksons River.
    occ. ____. consort of ____. info, David G. Kinkead, father.

Reed, Mary, WF, **d. 23 May** in Jacksons River Valley of influenza, age, 77yrs.
    parents, Richard Foutess. born Louisa Co. occ. house keeper.
    consort of Alexr Reed. info, James Reed, son.

Wright, George, WM, **d. 15 July** on Jacksons River of scarlet fever, age, 11yrs.
        parents, Elisha & Nancy Wright. born Jacksons River. occ. ____.
        consort of ____. info, Elisha Wright, father.

No name, WM, **d. 11 May** on Jacksons River of croup, age, 15dys.
        parents, Jesse & Lucinda Robertson. born Jacksons River.
        occ. ____. consort of ____. info, Jesse Robertson, father.

Davis, Phebe C., WF, **d. 2 Dec.** on Bullpasture, of scarlet fever, age, 3yrs, 2dys.
        parents, Harvey S. & Nancy Davis. born Bullpasture. occ. ____.
        consort of ____. info, H. S. Davis.

Steuart, Jacinthia, WF, **d. ____ June** on Bullpasture of consumption, age, 42yrs.
        parents, Jas. & Isabella Bradshaw. born Bath Co.
        occ. house keeper. consort of Jacob W. Steuart.
        info, J. W. Steuart, husband.

Hupman, Rebecca, WF, **d. ____ July** on Bullpasture of consumption, age, 21yrs.
        parents, Jacob & Jacinthia Steuart. born Bullpasture.
        occ. house keeper. consort of J. W. Hupman.
        info, J. W. Steuart, father.

Steuart, Hannah, WF, **d. ____ Jan.** on Bullpasture of old age, age, 90yrs.
        parents, Jno. & Jane Hicklin. born Bath Co.
        occ. house keeper. consort of John Steuart.
        info, Edward Steuart, son.

Steuart, Thomas, WM, **d. ____ Aug.** on Cowpasture of ____, age, 1yr, 6mos.
        parents, Chas. & Eliz. Steuart. born Cowpasture. occ. ____.
        consort of ____. info, Charles Steuart, son.

Beathe, Mary A., WF, **d. 29 March** on Crab Run of pleurrisa, age, 4yrs, 4mos.
        parents, Jas. & Margt. Beathe. born Crab Run. occ. ____.
        consort of ____. info, Jas. Beathe, father.

Killingsworth, Mary S., WF, **d. ____ Sept.** on Bullpasture of scarlet fever,
        age, 2yrs, 4mos. **parents, John & Jane Killingsworth.**
        born Bullpasture. occ. ____. consort of ____.
        info, Jane Killingsworth, mother.

Wilson, Isaac B., WM, **d. 20 Feb.** on Bullpasture of inflammation of brain, age, 2yrs.
        parents, Eli & Maoma[sic] Wilson. born Bullpasture. occ. ____.
        consort of ____. info, John M. Wilson, brother.

No name, WF, **d. 22 Nov.** on Bullpasture of ____, age, 1dy.
    parents, Isaac N. & Mary A. Botkin. born Bullpasture
    occ.____. consort of ____. info, Isaac N. Botkin father.

Siple, Martha, WF, **d. 1 May** on Bullpasture of scarlet fever, age, 2yrs, 11mos.
    parents, Joel & Marg. Siple. born Bullpasture. occ. ____.
    consort of ____. info, Margaret Siple, mother.

No name, WM, **d. 22 Jan.** on Bullpasture of croup, age, 5mos, 20dys.
    parents, Saml & Polly Armstrong. born Bullpasture.
    occ.____. consort of ____. info, Saml Armstrong, father.

Jordan, Peter, WM, **d. 18 Dec.** on Spring Run of scarlet fever, age, 7yrs, 4mos.
    parents, Sampson Jordan & Nancy Jordan. born Spring Run.
    occ. ____. consort of ____. info, Nancy Jordan, mother.

Jones, Martha M., WF, **d. 14 May** on Cowpasture of scarlet fever, age, 5yrs.
    parents, Henry C. & Victoria Jones. born Cowpasture. occ. ____.
    consort of ____. info, Henry C. Jones, father.

Chew, Milton E., WM, **d. 12 March** at Monterey of scarlet fever, age,5mos, 4dys.
    parents, Wm. M. & Susan Chew. born Monterey. occ. ____.
    consort of ____. info, Wm M. Chew, father.

Slave Lucinda, of _____, F, **d.** ____ **Aug.** at Monterey of croup, age, 6mos.
    parents, Slave Milla born ____. occ. ____.
    consort of ____. info, Wm J. Noel, hirer.

Seybert, Jacob, WM, **d. 20 March** on Straight Creek of affection of heart, age, 82yrs.
    parents, Henry & Rachel Seybert. born Maryland. occ. farmer.
    consort of Mary Seybert. info, Henry Seybert, son & Exr.

Beverage, Mary, WF, **d. 17 Jan.** on Straight Creek of unknown, age, 54yrs.
    parents, Jno. & Ann McGlaughlin. born Bath Co.
    occ. house keeper. consort of Wm Beverage.
    info, Wm. Beverage, companion.

Slave Charles of Solomon Fleisher, M, **d.** ____ **April** on South Branch of pneumonia,
    age, ____. **parents, Slave Sarah.** born ____. occ. ____.
    consort of ____. info, Solomon Fleisher, owner.

Brantner, Sarah M., WF, **d. 26 May** at Crab Bottom of affect. of liver, age, 1yr, 3mos.
    parents, Saml & Sarah J. Brantner. born Crab Bottom.
    occ. ____. consort of ____. info, Samuel Brantner, father.

Ervin, Robert P., WM, **d. 19 Feb.** on Back Creek of from hurt, age, 16yrs.
  parents, Benj. & Nancy Ervin. born Back Creek.
  occ. farmer. unmarried. info, Benj. Ervin, father.

Ervin, Jarucia E., WF, **d. 7 Sept.** on Back Creek of scarlet fever, age, 11yrs.
  parents, Benj. & Nancy Ervin. born Back Creek. occ. ____.
  unmarried. info, Benj. Ervin, father.

Doyle, Sarah M., WF, **d. ____ Aug.** on Back Creek of scarlet fever, age, 11mos.
  parents, Jno. & Catherine Doyle. born Bath Co. occ. ____.
  consort of ____. info, Jacob C. Doyle, grandfather.

Doyle, Jacob J., WM, **d. 10 Oct,** on Jacksons River of dropsy, age, 1yr, 9mos.
  parents, Wm. & Lucy A. Doyle. born Jacksons River. occ. ____.
  consort of ____. info, Jacob C. Doyle, grandfather.

Gum, Mary P. C., WF, **d. 2 June** on Back Creek of scarlet fever,
  age, 3yrs, 4mos, 12dys. **parents, Abm. & Mary Gum.**
  born Back Creek. occ. ____. consort of ____.
  info, Abraham Gum, father.

1857*

Patterson, Rebecca A., WF, **d. 15 Nov.** on Back Creek of consumption,
  age, 19yrs, 9mos,9dys. **parents, Reuben & Becca A. Slaven.**
  born Back Creek. occ. house keeper. consort of J. H. Patterson.
  info, Reuben Slaven, father.

Slaven, Jacob O., WM, **d. ___ Aug.** in Pocahonats Co. of scarlet fever, age, 3yrs, 7mos.
  parents, Jesse B. & Mary P. Slaven. born Back Creek
  occ. ____. consort of ____. info, Reuben Slaven, grandfather.

Stephenson, Luella H., WF, **d. 14 Sept.** on Back Creek of flux, age, 10yrs.
  parents, Jas. & Lucinda Stephenson. born Back Creek.
  occ. ____. consort of ____. info, James Stephenson, father.

Floid, Virda A., WF, **d. 30 May** on Jacksons River of scarlet fever, age, 4yrs, 1mo.
  parents, Edward M. Floid & Polly M. Floid. born Jacksons River.
  occ. ____. consort of ____. info, Ed M. Floid, father.

---

* The original ledger carries no date for this page. Judging from the number of deaths in 1855, 1856 and 1859, this transcriber believes these deaths occurred in 1857.

White, Louisa C., WF, **d. 20 Aug.** at Crab Bottom of inflamation,
  age, 7yrs, 11mos, 20 dys. **parents, Henry & Sabina White.**
  born Crab Bottom. occ. ____. consort of ____.
  info, Henry White, father.

Slave Betta of Jno. Sitlington, F, **d. 28 March** at Crab Bottom of from burn, age, 104yrs.
  parents, ____ & ____. born ____. occ. ____.
  consort of ____. info, Jno. Sitlington, owner.

Trimble, Sarah, WF, **d. 17 Feb.** on Jacksons River of consumption, age, 31yrs, 1mo.
  parents, Leonard & Phebe Harper. born Pendleton Co.
  occ. house keeper. consort of Wm. Trimble.
  info, Wm Trimble, companion.

Folks, Jno. W., WM, **d. 26 Dec.** on Jacksons River of scarlet fever, age, 9yrs.
  parents, Valentine Folks & Mary Folks. born Jacksons River.
  occ. ____. consort of ____. info, Mary Folks, mother.

Slave Amanda of Wm. S. Thompson, F, **d. 28 Feb.** on Jacksons River of bronchitis,
  age, 16yrs. **parents, ____ & ____.** born ____. occ. ____.
  consort of ____. info, Wm. S. Thompson, owner.

Stephenson, Sarah E., WF, **d. 14 April** in Jacksons River Valley of cold, age, 23yrs.
  parents, Wm. & Nancy Stephenson. born Jacksons River Valley.
  occ. ____. unmarried. info, Wm. Stephenson, father.

Slave Mahala of Edward M. Steuart, F, **d. ____ Aug.** on Bullpasture of unknown,
  age, 45yrs. **parents, ____ & ____.** born ____. occ. ____.
  consort of ____. info, Ed M. Steuart, owner.

Slave Madora of Edward M. Steuart, F, **d. ____ Nov.** on Bullpasture of cold, age, 4yrs.
  parents, ____ & ____. born ____. occ. ____. consort of ____.
  info, Ed M. Steuart, owner.

Steuart, Eliza, WF, **d. __ June** on Bullpasture of consumption, age, 18yrs.
  parents, Jacob W. & Jacintha Steuart. born Bull Pasture.
  occ. ____. unmarried. info, Jacob W. Steuart, father.

Steuart, Hulda, WF, **d. ____ April** on Bullpasture of consumption, age, 16yrs.
  parents, Jacob W. & Jacintha Steuart. born Bull Pasture.
  occ. ____. unmarried. info, Jacob W. Steuart, father.

Mullinax, Hannah, WF, **d. 28 Jan.** on South Branch of apoplexy, age, 65yrs, 8mos.
  parents, George Arbogast & Catherine Arbogast.
  born Pendleton Co. occ. house keeper. consort of Jacob Mullinax,
  info, Jno. Mullinax, son.

Steuart, Mary J., WF, **d. 1 July** on Bull Pasture of affection of lungs, age, 21yrs.
    parents, Lewis & Sarah A. Davis. born Bull Pasture.
    occ. house keeper. consort of Gilson Steuart.
    info, Lewis Davis, father.

Byrd, Alice, WF, **d. 27 Oct.** on Jacksons River, of consumption, age, 43yrs.
    parents, Jno. & Rebecca Byrd. born Greenbrier Co.
    occ. house keeper. consort of James H. Byrd.
    info, Jas. H. Byrd, companion.

Slave Lucy of James H. Byrd, F, **d. ____ June** on Jacksons River of poison, age, ____.
    parents, ____ & ____. occ. ____. consort of ____.
    info, Jas. H. Byrd, owner.

Wilson, Martha E., WF, **d. 27 April** on Bull Pasture of scrofula, age 15yrs.
    parents, Eli H. & Maoma Wilson. born Bull Pasture.
    occ. ____. unmarried. info, Eli H. Wilson, father.

Siron, Thomas L., WM, **d. 25 March** on Bull Pasture of consumption, age, 13yrs.
    parents, Joseph & Jane Siron. born Bull Pasture.
    occ. ____. consort of ____. info, Joseph Siron, father.

Steuart, Jno. B., WM, **d. 25 May** on Bull Pasture of cronic rumatism, age, 59yrs.
    parents, James & Jane Steuart. born Bath Co. occ. farmer.
    consort of Margaret Steuart. info, Margaret Steuart, companion.

Armstrong, Nancy J., WF, **d. ____ Aug.** on Cow Pasture of cholera morbus,
    age, 1yr, 4mos. **parents, Mahlon & Louisa F. Armstrong.**
    born Cow pasture. occ. ____. consort of ____.
    info, Mahlon Armstrong, father.

Wilson, Sarah M., WF, **d. 30 March** on Shaws Fork of affection of lungs,
    age, 1yr, 8mos. **parents, Wm. & Martha A. Wilson.**
    born Shaws Fork. occ. ____. consort of __. info, Wm. Wilson, father.

Slave Hiram of Geo. H. Benson, M, **d. ____ April** on Cow Pasture of pneumonia,
    age, 40yrs. **parents, ____ & ____.** born ____. occ. ____.
    consort of ____. info, Geo. H. Benson, owner.

Slave Charlotte of Geo. H. Benson, F, **d. ____ May** on Cow Pasture of consumption,
    age, 25yrs. **parents, ____ & ____.** born ____. occ. ____.
    consort of ____. info, Geo. H. Benson, owner.

Steuart, Wm. B., WM, **d. 15 May** on Cow Pasture of yellow jaundice, age, 28yrs.
    parents, Wm. R. & Elizabeth Steuart. born Cow Pasture.
    occ. ____. unmarried. info, Wm. R. Steuart, father.

Rexrode, Robert T., WM, **d. 26 June** on Bull Pasture of from hurt, age, 9yrs, 11mos. **parents, Andrew & Mary A. Rexrode.** born Bull Pasture. occ. ____. consort of ____. info, Andrew Rexrode, father.

Whitelaw, Alexander, WM, **d. 17 Jan.** at Monterey of apoplexy, age, 66yrs, 8mos. **parents, unknown.** born Orange Co. occ. land lord. consort of Lucy Whitelaw info, Nicholas A. Whitelaw, son.

Strickler, Mary B., WF, **d. 20 Sept.** at Monterey of flux, age, 3yrs, 2mos, 18dys. **parents, Jacob P. & E. M. Strickler.** born Monterey. occ. ____. consort of ____. info, J. P. Strickler, father.

Slaven, Edwin, WM, **d. 22 April** at Monterey of scarlet fever, age, 3yrs, 3mos. **parents, Thos. H. & Margaret Slaven.** born Monterey. occ. ____. consort of ____. info, Thos. H. Slaven, father.

Gum, Adam, WM, **d. __ March** at Crab Bottom of typhoid fever, age, ____. **parents, Adam & Susan Gum.** born Crab Bottom. occ. farmer. consort of Lucinda Gum. info, Lucinda Gum, companion.

Coil, Jno., WM, **d. __ Jan.** on Straight Fork of consumption, age, ____. **parents, unknown.** born Pendleton Co. occ. farmer. consort of Dorothy Coil. info, Henry Life, doct.

Slave Sarah E. of Mary Ann Sitlington, F, **d. 15 April** at Crab Bottom of unknown, age, 1yr, 6mos. **parents, Slave Catherine.** born Crab Bottom. occ. ____. consort of ____. info, Mary Ann Sitlington, owner.

Fleisher, Elizabeth C., WF, **d. 26 Nov.** in Alemarle Co. of eryseplas, age, 27yrs. **parents, Joseph Dettor & Margaret Dettor.** born Alemarle Co. occ. house keeper. consort of Henry H. Fleisher. info, Henry H. Fleisher, companion.

Campbell, Elizabeth, WF, **d. 2 June** on Back Creek of consumption, age, 56yrs. **parents, Steuart & Isabella Slaven.** born Bath Co. occ. house keeper. consort of Thomas Campbell. info, Thos. Campbell, companion.

Dunlap, Archibald, WM, **d. ____ Oct.** on Bull Pasture of from stab, age, ____. **parents, ____ & ____.** born Augusta Co. occ. farmer. consort of Julian Dunlap. info, Wm. C. Jones, physician.

1858

Rexrode, Sarah, WF, **d. 14 April** at Crab Bottom of congestion of lungs, age, 51yrs.
    parents, Wm. & Barbara Hoover. born Pendleton Co.
    occ. house keeper. consort of Benj. Rexrode.
    info, Benj. Rexrode, husband.

Colaw, Catherine E., WF, **d. 16 Dec**. at Crab Bottom of affection of heart,
    age, 11mos, 27dys. **parents, Cyrus & Lucinda Colaw.**
    born Crab Bottom. occ. ____. consort of ____.
    info, Cyrus Colaw, father.

No name, WF, **d. 1 Dec** at Crab Bottom of unknown, age, 1mo, 3dys.
    parents, James & Alcinda Arbogast. born Crab Bottom.
    occ. ____. consort of ____. info, James Arbogast, father.

Spencer, George W., WM, **d. 10 July** at H. Jacksons River* of disease of bowels,
    age, 4mos, 4dys. **parents Jno. H. & Frances Spencer.**
    born H. Jacksons River. occ. ____. consort of ____.
    info, Jno. H. Spencer, father.

Gum, Jesse McBride, WM, **d. 22 July** at Crab Bottom of inflammation of brain,
    age, 12yrs, 2mos, 2dys. **parents, McBride & Elcy Gum**
    born Crab Bottom. occ. ____. consort of ____.
    info, McBride Gum, father.

Slave Adam of Jacob Hevener, M, **d.** ____ **Feb**. at H. Jacksons River, of from burn,
    age, 10mos. **parents,** ____ **&** ____. born H. J. River. occ. ____.
    consort of ____. info, Jacob Hevener, owner.

Lightner, Mary D., WF, **d. 11 Oct**. on Back Creek of consumption, age, 45yrs, 11mos.
    parents, Charles & Elcy Hamilton. born Back Creek.
    occ. house keeper. consort of Wm. Lightner.
    info, Wm. Lightner, husband.

No name, WF, **d. 8 July** on Back Creek of unknown, age, 1dy.
    parents, Jno. V. B. & Mahala Wade. born Back Creek.
    occ. ____. consort of ____. info, Jno. V. B. Wade, father.

Gum, Wm. H. P. WM, **d. 19 Jan**. on Back Creek of unknown, age, 1yr, 7mos, 19dys.
    parents, Abraham W. & Margaret A. Gum. born Back Creek.
    occ. ____. consort of ____. info, Abm. W. Gum, father.

---

* Head of Jacksons River.

Puffenberger, Sarah, WF, **d. 9 Feb.** on Straight Creek of obstruction of bowels,
>age, 15yrs, 8mos, 9dys. **parents, Job & Elizabeth Puffenberger.**
>born South Fork. occ. ___. unmarried. info, Job Puffenberger, father.

Murphy, Mary, WF, **d. 15 Jan.** on Bull pasture of flux, age, 47yrs.
>**parents, Peter & Ann Raugh.** born Augusta Co.
>occ. house keeper. consort of Jno. Murphy.
>info, Jno. Murphy, husband.

Slave Andrew of David Gwin, M, **d. 1 Sept.** on Jacksons River of pneumonia,
>age, 2yrs. **parents, ___ & ___.** born ___. occ. ___.
>consort of ___. info, David Gwin, owner.

Stephenson, Washington, WM, d. 30 May on Jacksons River of typhoid fever,
>age, 45yrs. **parents, Jno. & Jane Stephenson.** born Bath Co.
>occ. farmer. consort of Susan E. Stephenson.
>info, David Stephenson, brother of decd.

Oaks, Thomas, WM, **d. 19 June** on Bull pasture of Af. of bowels, age, 73yrs.
>**parents, Jno. & ___ Oaks.** born Orange Co. occ. farmer.
>consort of Malinda Oaks. info, Wm. R. Oaks, son.

Steuart, Warwick, WM, **d. ___ July** on Bull pasture of consumption, age, 26yrs.
>**parents, Jacob & Jacintha Steuart.** born Bull Pasture.
>occ. farmer. unmarried. info, Jacob W. Steuart, father.

Wright, Susan, WF, **d. 29 June** on Bull pasture of ___, age, 68yrs.
>**parents, Christopher Wright & Jane Graham.** born Bath Co.
>occ. house keeper. consort of Robert Wright.
>info, James Wright, son.

Slave Charlotte of Robert Lockridge, F, **d. 29 March** on Bull pasture of dropsy,
>age, 30yrs. **parents, ___ & ___,** born ___. occ. ___.
>consort of ___. info, Robert Lockridge, owner.

Steuart, Elizabeth, WF, **d. 11 Nov.** on Cow pasture of palpitation of heart, age, 58yrs.
>**parents, Ferdinand Kincaid & Margaret Kincaid.**
>born Bath Co. occ. house keeper. consort of Wm. R. Steuart.
>info, Wm. R. Steuart, husand.

Rodgers, Mary, WF, **d. 19 April** on Shaws Fork of consumption, age, 35yrs.
>**parents, Jacob & ___ Keishear.** born Augusta Co.
>occ. house keeper. consort of Wm. L. Rodgers.
>info, Wm. L. D. Rodgers, husband.

Wilson, Martha A., WF, **d. 25 Aug.** on Shaws Fork of consumption, age, 25yrs.
  parents, Jno. & Margaret Devericks. born Pendleton Co.
  occ. house keeper. consort of Wm. Wilson.
  info, Wm. Wilson, husband.

Wilson, Sarah M., WF, **d. 8 March** on Shaws Fork of consumption, age, 2yrs.
  parents, Wm. & Martha A. Wilson. born Shaws Fork.
  occ. ____. consort of ____. info, Wm. Wilson, father.

Morton, James, WM, **d. __ Feb.** on Shaws Fork of consumption, age, 38 yrs.
  parents, James & Sarah Morton. born Pendleton Co.
  occ. farmer. consort of Mary J. Morton.
  info, Jno. Devericks, father-in-law.

Morton, Mary J., WF, **d. __ Aug.** on Shaws Fork of consumption, age, 30yrs.
  parents, Jno. & Margaret Devericks. born Shaws Fork.
  occ. house keeper. consort of James Morton.
  info, Jno. Devericks, father.

Morton, Robert B., WM, **d. __ Nov.** on Shaws Fork of consumption, age, 4yrs.
  parents, James & Mary J. Morton. born Shaws Fork.
  occ. ____. consort of ____. info, Jno Devericks, grandfather.

Ervin, Benja. C., WM, **d. 15 Sept.** on Cow pasture of pneumonia, age, 37yrs, 10mos.
  parents, Wm. & Frances Ervin. born Cow Pasture.
  occ. farmer. consort of Sarah Ervin. info, Wm. Ervin, father.

Fleisher, Rachel P., WF, **d. 30 July** Bull pasture of consumption, age, 35yrs.
  parents, Wm. & ____ Keer. born Pocahontas Co.
  occ. house keeper. consort of Joseph Fleisher.
  info, Joseph Fleisher, husband.

Fleisher, Rachel, WF, **d. 28 June** on Bull pasture of consumption, age, 1mo.
  parents, Joseph & Rachel P. Fleisher. born Bull pasture
  occ. ____. consort of ____. info, Joseph Fleisher, father.

Wilson, Eli H., WM, **d. 1 Sept.** on Bull pasture of affection of lungs, age, 51yrs.
  parents, Eli Wilson & Elizabeth Wilson. born Pendleton Co.
  occ. farmer. consort of Maoma Wilson. info, Maoma Wilson, wife.

Bashaw, Cuthbert, WM, **d. ____ April** on Bull pasture of lung disease, age, 68yrs.
  parents, unknown, born unknown. occ. Doct. consort of ____.
  info, Saml. C. Eagle, neighbor.

Bird, Andrew J., WM, **d. 18 July** at Monterey of typhoid fever,
age, 31yrs, 9mos, 11dys. **parents, Jno & Margaret Bird**.
born Pendleton Co. occ. Sheriff. consort of Emily Bird.
info, Jno. Bird, father.

Mullenax, Charity, WF, **d. ____ March** on Jacksons River of infirmity, age, 80yrs.
parents, unknown. born unknown. occ. house keeper
consort of Saml. Mullenax. info, Jno. Bird, neighbor.

Noel, Wm. J., WM, **d. 6 Oct.** at Monterey of consumption, age, 41yrs.
parents, Jno. & Elizabeth Noel. born Fluvanna Co. occ. joiner.
consort of Mary E. Noel. info, Mary E. Noel, wife.

No name, WM, **d. __ June** at Monterey of unknown, age, 1mo.
parents, James & Sarah Kincaid. born Monterey.
occ. ____. consort of ____. info, James Kincaid, father.

Grove, Hannah M., WF, **d. 2 April** on Jacksons River of unknown, age, 3yrs, 6mos.
parents, David & Genetta Groves. born Jacksons River.
occ. ____. consort of ____. info, David Groves, father.

Weiland, Mary M., WF, **d. 21 Sept.** at Crab Bottom of from burn, age, 3yrs.
parents, Thos. & Christina Weiland. born Crab Bottom.
occ. ____. consort of ____. info, Thomas Weiland, father.

Arbogast, Sarah, WF, **d. 8 June** at Crab Bottom of cholera morbus, age, 65yrs.
parents, Nathaniel & Elizabeth Swecker. born Rockingham Co.
occ. house keeper. consort of Daniel Arbogast.
info, Benj. Swecker, brother.

1859

Bowyer, Sarah S. J., WF, **d. 4April** on Back Creek of scarlet fever,
age, 1yr, 10mos, 15dys. **parents, W. C. & Mary J. Bowyer**.
born Back Creek. occ. ____. consort of ____.
info, W. C. Bowyer, father.

No name, WM, **d. 30 Aug.** on Back Creek of unknown, age, 1dy.
parents, Jno. & Olive Bird. born Back Creek. occ. ____.
consort of ____. info, Jno. Bird, father.

No name. WM, **d. ____ Sept.** on Back Creek of unknown, age, 28dys.
parents, Jno. & Olive Bird. born Back Creek, occ. ____.
consort of ____. info, Jno. Bird, father.

No name, WF, **d. 30 Sept.** on Crab Bottom of unknown, age, 1dy.
        parents, Danl H. & Barbara Rexrode. born Crab Bottom.
        occ. ____. consort of ____. info, Benj. Rexode, G----.

McCarty, Justin, WM, **d. 12 Sept** on Back Creek of flux, age, 11yrs, 8mos.
        parents, Catherine McCarty. born Back Creek. occ. ____.
        consort of ____. info, Jno. Bird, -----.

Matheny, Mary, WF, **d. 19 April** on Back Creek of typhoid fever, age, 64yrs.
        parents, Robert & ____ Haslet. born Augusta Co.
        occ. house keeper. consort of Levi Matheny.
        info, Adam Lightner, -----.

Clendenen, Steuart, H. A., WM, **d. 9 June** on Back Creek of flux, age, 14yrs, 10mos.
        parents, Jacob & Cath. Clendenen. born Pocahontas Co.
        occ. ____. consort of ____. info, Jacob Clendenen, father.

Bowyer, Rachel, WF, **d. 1 Aug.** on Back Creek of flux, age, ____.
        parents, ____ & ____. born ____. occ. house keeper.
        consort of Leonard Bowyer. info, Chas. Wade, neighbor.

Wade, Electa E., WF, **d. 21 April** on Back Creek of croup, age, 1yr, 11mos, 10dys.
        parents, Chas. & Cath. Wade. born Back Creek. occ. ____.
        consort of ____. info, Chas. Wade, father.

Dever, Jackson, WM, **d. 24 Dec.** on back Creek of consumption,
        age, 33yrs, 8mos, 25dys. **parents, Jno. & Eliza Dever.**
        born Back Creek. occ. farmer. unmarried. info, John Dever, father.

Vance, Charles H., WM, **d. 26 March** at Crab Bottom of spasms, age, 8mos, 21dys.
        parents, George & Susan M. Vance. born Crab Bottom.
        occ. ____. consort of ____. info, George Vance, father.

Vance, Wm. H., WM, **d. 8 Oct** at Crab Bottom of disease of head, age, 34yrs.
        parents, Christian Vance & Sarah Vance. born Rockingham Co.
        occ. farmer. consort of Alcinda Vance, info, Alcinda Vance, wife.

No name, WF, **d. 29 Aug.** on Straight Fork of unknown, age, 21dys.
        parents, Esau & Eley Ketterman. born Straight Fork.
        occ. ____. consort of ____. info, Esau A. Ketterman, father.

Marshall, Sarah E., WF, **d. 19 Aug.** on Straight Fork of flux, age, 3yrs, 9mos.
        parents, Wm. & Phebe Marshall. born Straight Fork.
        occ. ____. consort of ____. info, Wm. Marshall, father.

Nicholas, Annie, WF, **d. 22 April** at Crab Bottom of unknown, age, 13dys. **parents, Sol. & Jane Nicholas.** born Crab Bottom. occ. ____. consort of ____. info, Jane Nicholas, mother.

Waggy, Mahala, WF, **d.** ____ on Jacksons River of pneumonia, age, 21yrs. **parents, Abm. & Susan Waggy.** born Jacksons River. occ. ____. unmarried. info, Abraham Waggy, father.

Stephenson, James B., WM, **d. 15 Aug.** on Jacksons River of flux, age, 1yr, 3mos, 15dys. **parents, Jas. & Lucinda Stephenson.** born Jacksons River. occ. ____. consort of ____. info, Lucinda Stephenson, mother.

Sharp, Elizab. M., WF, **d. 25 Dec.** on Dry Branch of infirmity, age, 96yrs. **parents, Richd. & ____ Curry.** born Ireland. occ. house keeper. consort of Jno. Sharp. info, John Sharp, husband.

Williams, Mary, WF, **d.** ____ on Bullpasture of infirmity, age, 75yrs. **parents, ____ & ____.** born ____. occ. house keeper. consort of Thos. Williams. info, T. Williams, grandson.

Hicklin, George, WM, **d. 16 Sept.** on Bullpasture of dropsy, age, 80yrs, 2mos. **parents, Jno. & Jane Hicklin.** born Bullpasture. occ. far. consort of Elizabeth Hicklin. info, Harvey Hicklin, son.

Kincaid, Charles L., WM, **d. 13 Nov.** on Cowpasture of consumption, age, 39yrs. **parents, Charles & Nancy Kincaid.** born Cowpasture. occ. far. consort of Amanda E. Kincaid. info, Saml. M. Marshall, brother-in-law.

Morton, Jno. T., WM, **d. 25 Nov.** on Shaws Fork of consumption, age, 27yrs. **parents, Jas. & Sarah Morton.** born Cowpasture. occ. far. unmarried. info. Ed. D. Morton, brother.

No name, WF, **d. 8 Aug.** on Cowpasture of hives, age, 1dy. **parents, H. W. & Margt. M. Wilson.** born Cowpasture. occ. ____. consort of ____. info, Henry W. Wilson, father.

No name, WM, **d. 3 Jan.** on Bullpasture Mt. of unknown, age, 7mos. **parents, J. & Savina Armstrong.** born B. P. Mt. occ. ____. consort of ____. info, Saml. E. Armstrong, grandfather.

Siron, Martha J., WF, **d. 9 Oct.** on Bullpasture Mt. of consumption, age, 74yrs. **parents, Jacob & Lavina Siron.** born Bullpasture. occ. ____. consort of ____. info, Jacob Siron, father.

McGlaughlin, Jane, WF, **d. 9 April** on Jacksons River of ____, age, 26yrs, 8mos.
        parents, ____ & ____. born ____. occ. house keeper.
consort of James M. McGlaughlin.
info, Jas. M. McGlaughlin, husband.

Fleisher, Rachel H., WF, **d. 5 Nov.** at Monterey of consumption, age, 37yrs.
        parents, Reuben &Bexe*Slaven. born Bath. occ.housekeeper.
consort of Adam H. Fleisher. info, Adam H. Fleisher, husband.

1860

Jack, John, WM, **d. 22 Aug.** at Crab Bottom of apoplexy, age, 72yrs.
        parents, Jno. & Sarah Jack. born unknown. occ. farmer.
consort of Sarah Jack. info, Jacob Jack, son.

Kramer, Margaret E., WF, **d. ____ Aug.** at Crab Bottom of coup, age, 4yrs.
        parents, Conrad & Barbara Kramer. born Crab Bottom.
occ. ____. consort of ____. info, Conrad Kramer, father.

Rymer, Thomas, WM, **d. 12 May** on Straight Creek of pneumonia, age, 75yrs.
        parents, George & Ellen Rymer. born Pendleton Co.
occ. farmer. consort of Elizabeth Rymer. info, Thos. J. Rymer, son.

Gum, Alice, WF, **d. 15 Dec.** at head of Jacksons River, of from cold, age, 78yrs, 8mos.
        parents, Jno. & Mary Gum. born Bath Co. occ. house keeper.
consort of McBride Gum. info, John Gum, son.

Slave Harriet of Thos. Campbell, F, **d. 11 Aug.** on Back Creek of childbirth, age, 34yrs.
        parents, ____ & ____. occ. ____. consort of ____.
info, Thomas Campell, owner.

May, Reuben A., WM, **d. 26 April** on Bull Pasture of fall from horse, age, 28yrs.
        parents, Jacob May & Rachel May. born Bath Co. occ. farmer.
consort of Margaret J. May. info, Jas. M. May, brother.

Campbell, Wm. T., WM, **d. 1 April** on Jacksons River of from burn, age, 4yrs, 2mos.
        parents, Austin W. & Susan M. Campbell. born Jacksons River.
occ. ____. consort of ____. info, Austin W. Campbell, father.

Beverage, Rufus, WM, **d. ____ Nov.** at Crab bottom of consumption, age, 20yrs, 8mos.
        parents, Geo. & Hannah Beverage. born Crabbottom.
occ. farmer. unmarried. info, George Beverage, father.

---

*Rebecca.

Sipes, Alice C., WF, **d. 7 Dec.** at Crab bottom of febry *[sic]*, age, 1yr, 2mos.
    parents, Jno. E. & Mary A. Sipes. born Monterey. occ. ____.
    consort of ____. info, John E. Sipes, father.

Rauch, David, WM, **d. 7 March** at Crab bottom of hives, age, 3mos.
    parents, Joseph & Lucinda Rauch. born Crab Bottom occ. ____.
    consort of ____. info, Joseph Rauch, father.

Doyle, Michael, WM, **d. 20 April** on Jacksons River of unknown, age, 81yrs.
    parents, Michael & ____ Doyle. born Ireland. occ. farmer.
    consort of Ann Doyle. info, Sarah Doyle, daughter.

Carpenter, Martha A., WF, **d. 29 Nov.** in Jacksons River Valley, of unknown,
    age, 5yrs. **parents, Jno. M. & Rebecca Carpenter.**
    born Jacksons River Valley. occ. ____. consort of ____.
    info, Jno. M. Carpenter, father.

Slave Israel of Edward Steuart, M, **d. ____ April** on Bull Pasture of ____, age, 60yrs.
    parents, ____ & ____. born ____. occ. ____. consort of ____.
    info, Ed Steuart, owner

Bradshaw, Isabella, WF, **d. 25 April** on Bull Pasture of unknown, age, 69yrs.
    parents, Robt. & ____ Stephens. born Greenbrier Co.
    occ. house keeper. consort of Jas. Bradshaw.
    info, Franklin Bradshaw, son.

Gwin, Wm. K., WM, **d. 29 Sept.** on Cow Pasture of consumption, age, 60yrs.
    parents, James & Mary Gwin. born Augusta Co. occ. farmer.
    consort of Jane Gwin. info, Wm. A. B. Gwin, brother-in-law.

Botkin, Jacob. T., WM, **d. 17 Dec.** South Fork of unknown, age, 1yr, 10mos.
    parents, James & Susan Botkin. born South Fork. occ. ____.
    consort of ____. info, Susan Botkin mother.

Armstrong, Esther C., WF, **d. 18 May** on Bull Pasture of inflamation of bowels,
    age, 4yrs. **parents, Allen & Martha E. Armstrong.**
    born Bull Pasture. occ. ____. consort of ____.
    info, Allen Armstrong, father.

Pullin, Theodore N., WM, **d. 20 March** Bull Pasture of unknown, age, 10mos.
    parents, Saml. & S. E. Pullin. born Bull Pasture. occ. ____.
    consort of ____. info, Saml. S. Pullin, father.

Bowers, Alzina, WF, **d. 5 July** on Straight Creek of infla bowels, age, 17yrs, 7mos.
    parents, Wm. & Margt. Bowers. born Straight Creek. occ. ____.
    unmarried. info, Margaret Bowers, mother.

Benson, Alles S., WF, **d. 20 July** on Jacksons River of croup, age, 5dys.
      parents, Wm. W. & Rebecca A. Benson. born Jacksons River.
      occ. ____. consort of ____. info, Wm. W. Benson, father.

Slave Zechariah of Rebecca G. Hamilton, M, **d. 3 March** on Bull Pasture of dropsy,
      age, 11yrs, 7mos. **parents, ____ & ____.** born Bull Pasture
      occ. ____. consort of ____. info, Rebecca G. Hamilton, owner.

Meadows, Nancy, WF, **d. 16 April** on Bull Pasture of unknown, age, 80yrs.
      parents, Lewis Davis & Sarah Davis. born Alemarle Co.
      occ. house keeper. consort of Jacob Meadows
      info, Thomas J. Meadows, son.

Slave Andrew of D. V. Ruckman, M, **d. ___ July** on Back Creek of unknown, age, 2yrs.
      parents, ____ & ____. born ____. occ. ____. consort of ____.
      info, David V. Ruckman, owner.

Slave no name of Adam Stephenson, **d. 20 Feb.** at Monterey of ____, age, 1mo.
      parents, ____ & ____. born ____. occ. ____. consort of ____.
      info, A. Stephenson, owner.

Pullin, Jesse, WM, **d. 13 Feb.** on Bull Pasture of pneumonia, age, 63yrs.
      parents, Thos. & Jane Pullin. born Bath Co. occ. farmer.
      consort of Catherine Pullin. info, Henry Pullin, brother.

Pullin, Loftus, WM, **d. 16 March** on Bull Pasture of pneumonia, age, 62yrs.
      parents, Saml. & ____ Pullin. born Bath Co. occ. farmer.
      consort of Francis Pullin. info, Balser H. Pullin, son.

1861

Chew, Jno. H. WM, **d. 9 Oct.** at Crab Bottom of typhoid fever, age, 37yrs.
      parents, Ezekiel & Christn. Chew. born Pendleton Co.
      occ. farmer. consort of Lavina Chew. info, ____.

Chew, Susan, WF, **d. 9 Sept.** at Crab Bottom of affection of head, age, 55yrs.
      parents, Ezekiel & Christn. Chew. born Pendleton Co.
      occ. housemaid. unmarried info, ____.

Waggoner, Barbara, WF, **d. 8 July** at Crab Bottom of yellow jaundice, age, 67yrs.
      parents, Joseph & Susan Lantz. born Pendleton Co.
      occ, house keeper. consort of Henry Waggoner,
      info, Henry Waggoner, husband.

Waggoner, Solomon WM, **d. 6 Oct.** at Crab Bottom of typhoid fever, age, 31yrs.
parents, Henry & Barb. Waggoner. born Pendleton Co.
occ. farmer. consort of Lucinda Waggoner.
info, Henry Waggoner, father.

Jack, Jacob, WM, **d. 29 Nov.** at Crab Botton of typhoid fever, age, 20yrs.
parents, David & Mary Jack. born Highland Co.
occ. farmer. unmarried. info, David Jack, father.

Swecker, Saml. C. E WM, **d. 19 Sept.** at Crab Bottom of fever, age, 7yrs, 6mos, 1dy.
parents, David W. & Celia Swecker. born Highland Co.
occ. ____.consort of ____. info, David W. Swecker, father.

Rough, Joseph, WM, **d. 23 Sept.** at Crab Bottom of typhoid fever, age, 45yrs.
parents, George & Sally Rough. born Augusta Co.
occ. farmer. consort of Lucinda Rough.
info, David W. Swecker, neighbor.

Page, Mary J., WF, **d. 13 Sept.** at Crab Bottom of flux, age, 46yrs.
parents, James & Nancy Smith. born Amherst Co.
occ. house keeper. consort of Joel Page. info, Joel Page, husband.

Brantner, Martha B., WF, **d. 27 Oct.** at Crab Bottom of inflame of stomach,
age, 8mos, 15dys. **parents, Saml. & Sarah Brantner.**
born Highland Co. occ. ____. consort of ____.
info, Saml. Brantner, father.

Hull, Jacob, WM, **d. 27 Nov.** at Crab Bottom of pneumonia, age, 55yrs.
parents, Adam & Esther Hull. born Pendleton Co. occ. farmer.
consort of Mahala Hull. info, F. K. Hull, brother.

Beverage, Charles E., WM, **d. 11 Aug.** at Crab Bottom of typhoid fever,
age, 3yrs, 7mos, 2dys. **parents, Harvey & Lucinda Beverage.**
born Highland Co. occ. ____. consort of ____.
info, Harvey Beverage, father.

Slave Clarke of Saml. B. Campbell, M, **d. 15 Jan.** on Jacksons River of diptheria,
age, 17yrs. **parents, ____ & ____.** born ____. occ. ____.
consort of ____. info, Saml. B. Campbell, owner.

Gardner, Jno. H., WM, **d. 20 Nov.** on Back Creek of unknown, age, 1dy.
parents, S. H. & Naomi Gardner. born ____. occ. ____.
consort of ____. info, Saml. H. Gardner, father.

McCarty, Amanda K. WF, **d. 20 Dec.** on Back Creek of diptheria, age, 5yrs, 6mos. **parents, Jestin & Jane McCarty.** born Bath Co. occ. ____. consort of ____. info, Jestin McCarty, father.

Doyle, Admison W., WM, **d. 7 Oct** on Back Creek of measels, age, 8yrs, 6mos, 24dys. **parents, Eli & Mary Doyle.** born Upshur Co. occ. ____. consort of ____. info, Eli Doyle, father.

Lockridge, Wm. H., WM, **d. 17 Oct** on Bull Pasture, of dropsy, age, 6yrs. **parents, Robt. C. & Lidda Lockridge.** born Ill[inois] occ. ____. consort of ____. info, Robt. C. Lockridge, father.

Townsend, Kinney, WM, **d. 17 Oct,** on Back Creek of hoping cough, age, 2yrs, 6mos. **parents, Jno. & Mary Townsend.** born Back Creek. occ. ____. consort of ____. info, Jno. Townsend, father.

Slave Emiline of Jno. G. Matheny, F, **d.** ____ on Back Creek of breast compt., age, 28yrs. **parents,** ____ **&** ____. occ. ____. consort of ____. info, Jno. G. Matheny, owner.

Clendenen, Catherine, WF, **d. 23 Aug.** on Back Creek of flux, age, 59yrs, 5mos. **parents, Jacob & Catherine Seebert.** born Pocahontas Co. occ. house keeper. consort of Jno. Clendenen. info, J. M. Clendenen, son.

Wade, Paul A., WM, **d. 26 Dec** on Back Creek of measles, age, 6yrs, 5mos. **parents, Chas. & Cath. Wade.** born Back Creek. occ. ____. consort of ____. info, Chas. Wade, father.

Gilmor, Jesse S., WM, **d. 26 Sept.** on Back Creek of typhoid fever, age, 23yrs, 6mos. **parents, Alex. & Sally Gilmor.** born Back Creek. occ. merchant. unmarried. info, S. Gilmor, mother.

Bird, Sarah A., WF, **d. 5 Dec.** on Back Creek of diptheria, age, 7yrs, 11mos. **parents, Valentine & Esther Bird.** born Back Creek occ. ____. consort of ____. info, Valentine Bird, father.

Bird, Nancy E., WF, **d. 8 Dec.** on Back Creek of diptheria, age, 13yrs, 6mos. **parents, Valentine & Esther Bird.** occ. ____. consort of ____. info, Valentine Bird, father.

Chesnut, Joseph G., WM, **d. 28 Dec.** on Back Creek of typhoid fever, age, 43yrs. **parents, Jno. & Nancy Chesnut.** born Bath Co. occ. farmer. consort of Eliza C. Chesnut. info, Wm. G. Chesnut, brother.

Chesnut, Joseph D., WM, **d. 8 Aug.** on Back Creek of flux, age, 2yrs, 3mos.
    parents, Jno. F. & Elizth. Chesnut. born Back Creek.
    occ. ____. consort of ____. info, Jno. F. Chesnut, father.

Woods, Jno., WM, **d. 7 Oct.** on Back Creek of typhoid fever, age, 52yrs.
    parents, Saml. & Catharine Woods. born Bath Co. occ. farmer.
    consort of M. L. Woods. info, D. Woods, son.

Woods, Jno., A., WM, **d. 24 July** on Cht. Mtn.* of shot by Yankee, age, 21yrs.
    parents, Jno. & M. L. Woods. born Bath Co. occ. farmer.
    unmarried. info, D. Woods, brother.

Gum, James E., WM, **d. 29 Oct.** on Back Creek of T. fever, age, 24yrs, 4mos.
    parents, Isaac & Mary Gum. born Bath Co. occ. farmer.
    consort of Elizabeth A. Gum. info, Isaac Gum, father.

Woods, James, WM, **d. 20 Oct.** on Back Creek of T. fever, age, 58yrs, 6mos.
    parents, Saml. & Mary Woods. born Bath Co. occ. farmer.
    consort of Mary Woods. info, T. J. Woods, son.

Hull, Jno., WM, **d. 20 Nov.** on Jacksons River of measles, age, 65yrs.
    parents, Adam & Esther Hull. born Pendleton Co.
    occ. farmer. consort of Margaret Hull. info, Robert Hull, son.

Slave Sylvester of Mary More, M, **d. 25 Nov.** on ____ of fever, age, 17yrs.
    parents, ____ & ____. occ. ____. consort of ____.
    info, Jno. Lightner, owner.

Slave Eliza of David Lockridge, F, **d. ____ Sept.** on ____ of fever, age, 15yrs.
    parents, ____ & ____. born ____. occ. ____. consort of ____.
    info, Jno. Lightner, owner.

Waggy, Wm. C., WM, **d. 22 Aug.** on Alleghany Mt. of measles, age, 3yrs.
    parents, Jacob & Mariah Waggy. born Crab Bottom.
    occ. ____. consort of ____. info, J. Waggy, father.

Waggy, Lavina, WF, **d. 15 Oct.** on South Branch of fever, age, 6yrs.
    parents, Jacob Waggy & Mariah Waggy. born ____. occ. ____.
    consort of ____. info, J. Waggy, father.

Slave no name of A. Stephenson, F, **d. 9 Dec.** on J. River of unknown, age, 1yr.
    parents, ____ & ____. born ____. occ. ____. consort of ____.
    info, A. Stephenson, owner.

---

*Cheat Mountain

Waggy, Abraham, WM, **d. 15 Sept**. on J. River of fever, age, 47yrs.
       parents, unknown, born unknown, occ. farmer.
    consort of Susan Waggy. info, Susan Waggy, wife.

Waggy, Crawford, WM, **d. 18 March** on J. River of fever, age, 18yrs.
       parents, Abrm. Waggy & Susan Waggy. born Pendleton Co.
    occ. farmer. unmarried. info, Susan Waggy, mother.

Gwin, James K., WM, **d. 13 Aug.** on J. River of cholera morus, age, 2yrs, 6mos.
       parents, James Gwin & Mahala Gwin. born Jacksons River.
    occ. ____. consort of ____. info, Jas. Gwin, father.

Thompson, Margaret, WF, **d. 30 May** on J. River of consumption,
       age, 28yrs, 3mos, 22dys. **parents, Jacob & Cynthia Steuart.**
    born Bath Co. occ. house keeper. consort of Wm. S. Thompson.
    info, Wm. S. Thompson, husband.

Robertson, W., WM, d. ____ Nov. in J. River Valley of diptheria, age, 6yrs, 1mo.
       parents, Jesse & Lucinda Robertson. born Big Valley, J. R.
    occ. ____. consort of ____.info, Wm. Hicks, neighbor.

Robertson, Walter, WM, d. ____ Nov. in J. River Valley, of diptheria, age, 1yr, 5mos.
       parents, Jesse & Lucinda Robertson. born Big Valley, J. R.
    occ. ____. consort of ____. info, Wm. Hicks, neighbor.

Houdyshell, Rebecca E., WF, **d. 10 Sept.** in J. River Valley of measles, age, 1yr, 6mos.
       parents, Jno. & Lidda Houdyshell. born J. River.
    occ. ____. consort of ____. info, Lidda Houdyshell, mother.

Wolf, Wm. W., WM, **d. 22 Oct.** on J. River of fever, age, 17yrs, 7mos.
       parents, Jno. & Margaret Wolf. born Augusta Co.
    occ. farmer. unmarried. info, Jno. Wolf, father.

Slave Pegga of David Stephenson, F. **d. 1 Oct.** on J. River of measles, age, 48yrs.
       parents, ____ & ____. occ. ____. consort of ____.
    info, D. Stephenson, owner.

Fox, Asiriah M., WM, **d. 16 Nov.** in Big Valley J. R. of diptheria,
       age, 10yrs, 4mos, 27dys. **parents, Jared M. Fox & H. Fox**
    born Big Valley J. R. occ. __. consort of __. info, J. M. Fox, father.

Wright, Louisa, WF, **d. 6 Nov.** in Big Valley J. R. of diptheria, age, 17yrs.
       parents, Elisha & Nancy Wright. born Big Valley J. R.
    occ. ____. unmarried. info, E. Wright, father.

Wright, Lorra T., WF, **d. 7 Nov.** in Big Valley J. R. of diptheria, age, 13yrs, 6mos.
   parents, Elisha & Nancy Wright. born Big Valley J. R.
   occ. ____. unmarried. info, E. Wright, father.

Wright, Albert C., WM, **d. 24 Nov.** in Big Valley J. R. of diptheria, age, 22yrs, 1mo.
   parents, Elisha & Nancy Wright. born Big Vally J. R.
   occ. farmer. unmarried. info, E. Wright, father.

Sharp, Daniel K., WM, **d. 10 Aug.** on Dry Branch of measles, age, 4yrs, 6mos.
   parents, John & Betty Sharp. born Dry Branch occ. ____.
   consort of ____. info, John Sharp, father.

Sharp, Mary K., WF, **d. 11 Aug.** on Dry Branch of measles, age, 22yrs.
   parents, John & Betty Sharp. born Dry Branch.
   occ. ____. consort of ____. info, John Sharp, father.

Sharp, Rice, WM, **d. 1 Sept.** on Dry Branch of measles, age, 5yrs.
   parents, John & Betty Sharp. born Dry Branch.
   occ. ____. consort of ____. info, John Sharp, father.

Davis, Wm. P., WM, **d. 20 Sept** on Bull Pasture of measles, age, 15yrs.
   parents, Lewis & Sarah A. Davis. born Bull Pasture.
   occ. farmer. unmarried. info, Lewis Davis farmer.

Church, Jno., WM, **d. 30 July** on Bull pasture of hoping cough, age, 3yrs.
   parents, Wm. Church & Eliza Church. born Bull Pasture.
   occ. ____. consort of ____. info, Lewis Davis, neighbor.

Williams, Margaret, WF, **d. 20 Nov.** on Bull Pasture of fever, age, 4yrs.
   parents, P. D. & Elizth. Williams. born Bull Pasture.
   occ. ____. consort of ____. info, P. D. Williams, father.

Slave Bill of P. D. Williams, M, **d. 30 Dec.** on Bull Pasture of fever, age, 8yrs.
   parents, ____ & ____. born ____. occ. ____. consort of ____.
   info, P. D. Williams, owner.

Beathe, Saml. W., WM, **d. 20 Sept.** in Pocahontas Co. of fever, age, 1yr, 11mos.
   parents, Jno. & Martha Beathe. born Pocahontas Co.
   occ. ____. consort of ____. info, Jno. Beathe, father.

Pullin, Jno. H., WM, **d. 7 Sept.** on Bull Pasture of pneumonia, age, 60yrs.
   parents, Saml. Pullin & Sarah Pullin. born Bath Co.
   occ. farmer. unmarried. info, Henry Pullin, cousin.

Moyers, Nickson S., WM, **d. 1 Sept.** on Bull Pasture of measles, age, 2yrs.
        parents, James & Rachel Moyers. born Bull pasture
        occ. ____. consort of ____. info, Saml. Moyers, uncle.

Carroll, Wm. K., WM, **d. 19 Oct.** on Bull Pasture of unknown, age, 51yrs.
        parents, Wm. & Mary Carroll. born unknown. occ. farmer.
consort of Lavina Carroll. info, Charles Carroll son.

Horn, Elizabeth, WF, **d. 13 July** on Bull Pasture of consumption, age, 31yrs.
        parents, Jno. Merrett & Elizth. Merrett. born Augusta Co.
occ. house keeper. consort of Jefferson Horn.
info, Jeff Horn husband.

Slave Adaline of Rebecca G. Hamilton, F, **d. 8 Feb.** on Bull Pasture of unknown,
        age, 9yrs. **parents, ____ & ____.** born ____. occ. ____.
consort of ____. info, Rebecca G. Hamilton, owner.

Slave Ru of Rebecca G. Hamilton, M, **d. 30 May** on Bull Pasture of old age, age, 78yrs.
        parents, ____ & ____. born ____. occ. ____. consort of ____.
info, Rebecca G. Hamilton, owner.

Slave Esteline of James Wright, F, **d. 10 May** on Bull Pasture of unknown, age, 2yrs.
        parents, ____ & ____. born ____. occ. ____. consort of ____.
info, James Wright, owner.

Hooks, Adison, WM, **d. 12 May** on Cow Pasture of fever, age, 16yrs.
        parents, Geo. W. & Mary Hooks. born Bull Pasture.
occ. farmer. unmarried. info, J. S. Hooks, uncle.

Gwin, John. C., WM, **d.17 May** on Cow Pasture of affec. of head, age, 77yrs.
        parents, Joseph & Mary Gwin. born Cow Pasture. occ. farmer.
consort of Rachel Gwin. info, Hamilton Gwin, son.

Johns, Mary A., WF, **d. 15 Nov.** on Shaws Fork of typhoid fever, age, 13yrs.
        parents, Saml. & Martha Johns. born Shaws Fork. occ. ____.
consort of ____. info, Margaret Johns, step mother.

Johns, Samuel, WM, **d. 18 Dec** on Shaws Fork of typhoid fever, age, 32yrs.
        parents, Wm. & Mary Johns. born Shaws Fork. occ. farmer.
consort of Margaret Johns. info, Margaret Johns, wife.

Johns, Wm. W., WM, **d. 16 Sept** on Shaws Fork of typhoid fever, age, 36yrs.
        parents, Wm. & Mary Johns. born Shaws Fork. occ. farmer.
consort of Lucinda Johns. info, Lucinda Johns, wife.

Jones, Wilbur K., WM, **d. 26 Aug.** at Monterey of diptheria, age, 2yrs, 10mos, 3dys. **parents, Wm. C. & Mary A. Jones.** born Monterey. occ. ____. consort of ____. info, Wm. C. Jones, father.

Jones, Lilia F., WF, **d. 26 Aug.** at Monterey of diptheria, age, 8yrs, 4mos. **parents, Wm. C. & Mary A. Jones.** born Monterey. occ. ____. consort of ____. info, Wm. C. Jones, father.

Jones, Carter M., WM, **d. 31 Aug.** at Monterey of diptheria, age, 4yrs, 3mos, 8dys. **parents, Wm. C. & Mary A. Jones.** born Monterey. occ. ____. consort of ____. info, Wm. C. Jones, father.

Jones, Wm. E., WM, **d. 3 Sept.** at Monterey of diptheria, age, 10yrs, 10mos. **parents, Wm. C. & Mary A. Jones.** born Monterey. occ. ____. consort of ____. info, Wm. C. Jones, father.

Jones, Caroline H., WF, **d. 3 Sept.** at Monterey of diptheria, age, 12yrs, 9mos. **parents, Wm. C. & Mary A. Jones.** born Monterey. occ. ____. consort of ____. info, Wm. C. Jones, father.

Devericks, John, WM, **d. 20 Oct.** on Shaws Fork of consumption, age, 65yrs. **parents, Jno. & Mary Devericks.** born Shaws Fork. occ. farmer. consort of Margaret Devericks. info, Allen Devericks, son.

Morton, Margaret E., WF, **d. 20 Aug.** on Shaws Fork of consumption, age, 23yrs, 6mos. **parents, Ed & Sarah Morton.** born Cowpasture. occ. ____. unmarried. info, Edwd D. Morton, brother.

Michael, George, WM, **d. 27 Dec.** on South Fork of diptheria, age, 3yrs, 2mos. **parents, David & Martha Michael.** born South Fork. occ. ____. consort of ____. info, David Michael, father.

Jordan, Sampson, WM, **d. 8 June** on Spring Run of shot, age, 56yrs. **parents, Andrew & Lotta Jordan.** born South Fork. occ. farmer. unmarried. info, Jno. Jordan, son.

Simmons, Geo. A., WM, **d. 16 Dec.** on Bull Pasture Mt. of fever, age, 21yrs. **parents, Christian & Laney Simmons.** born Bull Pasture Mtn. occ. farmer. unmarried. info, Christian Simmons, father.

Armstrong, Louisa, WF, **d. 13 Oct.** on Bull Pasture of measles, age, 35yrs. **parents, Jane Devericks.** born Shaws Fork. occ. house keeper. consort of Mahlon Armstrong. info, Mahlon Armstrong, husband.

Matheny, Martin M., WM, **d. 1 Sept.** on Cow Pasture of measles, age, 8yrs.
    parents, Reuben & Frances Matheny. born Dry Fork. occ. ____.
consort of ____. info, Reuben Matheny, father.

Jones, Susan E., WF, **d. 22 Oct.** on Cow Pasture of typhoid fever, age, 13yrs.
    parents, Decatur H. & Jane Jones. born Cowpasture. occ. ____.
consort of ____. info, D. H. Jones, father.

Church, Elizth., WF, **d. 15 June** on Bull Pasture of typhoid fever, age, 24yrs.
    parents, Wm. & Eliza Church. born Shaws Ridge.
occ. ____. unmarried. info, Wm. Church, father.

Chew, Jno. W., WM, **d. 4 Nov.** on Straight Fork of diptheria, age, 21yrs, 8mos.
    parents, Joseph L. Chew & Polly Chew. born Straight Fork.
occ. farmer. unmarried. info, Jos. L. Chew, father.

Hidy, Wm. J., WM, **d. 4 Oct.** at Crabbottom of typhoid fever, age, 23yrs.
    parents, Jno. & Matilda Hidy. born Crab Bottom occ. farmer.
unmarried. info, Jno. Hidy, father.

Arbogast, Jonathan, WM, **d. 30 July** on South Branch of rheumatism, age, 66yrs.
    parents, Jno. Arbogast & Hannah Arbogast. born Pendleton Co.
occ. farmer. consort of Catherine Arbogast.
info, Catherine Arbogast, wife.

Peck, Morgan, WM, **d. 22 Sept.** on Straight Creek of typhoid fever,
age, 17yrs, 11mos, 15dys. **parents, Jno. & Susan Peck.**
born Straight Creek. occ. farmer. unmarried.
info, Jno. Peck, father.

Bowers, Jr., Joseph, WM, **d. 10 Aug.** on Straight Creek of measles,
age, 20yrs, 11mos, 20dys. **parents, Wm. & Margt. Bowers.**
born Straight Creek. occ. farmer. unmarried.
info, Margt. Bowers, mother.

Varner, Andrew, WM, **d. 3 Sept.** on Straight Creek of diptheria, age, 13yrs, 6mos.
    parents, Joseph & Mary Varner. born Straight Creek.
occ. farmer. unmarried. info, Mary Varner, mother.

Varner, Harvy F., WM, **d. 6 Sept.** on Strt Creek of diptheria, age, 13yrs, 6mos.
    parents, Joseph & Mary Varner. born Str. Creek occ. ____.
consort of ____. info, Mary Varner, mother.

Varner, Mary S., WF, **d. 10 Sept.** on Strt. Creek of diptheria, age, 9yrs, 4mos.
    parents, Joseph & Mary Varner. born Str. Creek. occ. ____.
consort of ____. info, Mary Varner, mother.

Varner, Wm. H., WM, **d. 14 Sept.** on Strt. Creek of diptheria, age, 6yrs.
    parents, Joseph & Mary Varner. born Str. Creek occ. ____.
consort of ____. info, Mary Varner, mother.

Varner, Sarah K., WF, **d. 25 Sept.** on Strt. Creek of diptheria, age, 16yrs.
    parents, Joseph & Mary Varner. born Str. Creek occ. ____.
unmarried. info, Mary Varner, mother.

Varner, Joseph S., WM, **d. 3 Oct.** on Strt. Creek of diptheria, age, 12yrs.
    parents, Joseph & Mary Varner. born Str. Creek occ. ____.
unmarried. info, Mary Varner, mother.

Bowers, Joseph, WM, **d. 18 Oct.** on Strt. Creek of typhoid fever, age, 72yrs.
    parents, Jno. & Lucy Bowers. born Pendleton Co. occ. farmer.
consort of Barbara Bowers. info, Solomon Bowers, son.

Vance, Susan M., WF, **d. 26 Nov.** on Bull Pasture of from cold, age, 28yrs.
    parents, James & __ Kiter. born Frederick Co. occ. house keeper.
consort of Geo. Vance. info, George Vance, husband.

Vance no name, WF, **d. 30 Nov.** on Bull Pasture of croup, age, 14dys.
    parents, Geo. & Susan Vance. born Bull Pasture. occ. ____.
consort of ____. info, George Vance, father.

Ervin, Ebeline E., WF, **d. 8 Oct.** on Cow pasture of childbirth, age, 25yrs.
    parents, Jno. & Sarah Reynolds. born Augusta Co.
occ. house keeper. consort of Jared D. Ervine.
info, J. D. Ervin, husband.

Rexrode, Barbara, WF, **d. 15 Aug.** on St. Creek of unknown, age, 60yrs.
    parents, Jno. & Margt. Rexrode. born Pendleton Co.
occ. house keeper. consort of Leond. Rexrode
info, L. Rexrode, husband.

Wilfong, Joseph, WM, **d. 16 Aug.** on Alleghany Mt. of measles, age, 1yr, 9mos.
    parents, Elias & Sabina Wilfong. born Alleghany Mt. occ. ____.
consort of ____. info, E. Wilfong, father.

Pence, Angeline, WF, **d. 6 Mar.** at Crabottom of diptheria, age, 9yrs, 8mos.
    parents, Reuben & Mary Pence. born Augusta Co.
occ. ____. consort of ____. info, R. Pence father.

Colaw, Lee, WM, **d. 6 June** at Crabbottom of fever, age, 2yrs.
    parents, Allen & Roxana Colaw. born Crabbottom. occ. ____.
consort of ____. info, Allen Colaw, father.

Trimble, James A., WM, **d. 21 Aug.** on Straight Creek of measles, age, 4yrs, 27dys. **parents, Harvey & Elizth. Trimble.** born Str. Creek occ. ____. consort of ____. info, Elizth. Trimble, mother.

Seybert, Andrew, WM, **d. 4 Sept.** at Monterey of typhoid fever, age, 58yrs. **parents, Jacob & Mary Seybert.** born Str. Creek. occ. farmer. consort of Leah Seybert. info, Leah Seybert, wife.

Grogg, Adam, WM, **d. 28 Feb.** at Crabbottom of killed by waggoner, age, 46yrs. **parents, Philip & ____ Grogg.** born Pendleton Co. occ. farmer. consort of Charlotte Grogg. info, Jno. Grogg son.

Beathe, Wm. C., WM, **d. 26 Nov.** on Crab Run of typhoid fever, age, 30yrs. **parents, Jos. & Mary Beathe.** born Pendleton Co. occ. farmer. consort of ____. info, Jas. A. Beathe, brother.

Beathe, Jas. M., WM, **d. 17 Oct.** on Crab Run of typhoid fever, age, 48yrs. **parents, Jos. & Mary Beathe.** born Pendleton Co. occ. farmer. consort of M. J. Beathe. info, Jas. A. Beathe. brother.

Beathe, E. J., WF, **d. 25 Oct.** on Crab Run of pneumonia, age, 27yrs. **parents, Jos. & Mary Beathe.** born Pendleton Co. occ. ____. unmarried. info, Jas. A. Beathe, brother.

Slave Grace of Ewin Dever, F, **d. 26 March** on Bull Pasture of pneumonia, age, 7yrs, 6mos. **parents, ____ & ____.** born ____. occ. ____. consort of ____. info, Ewin Dever, owner.

Pullin, Jno. H., WM, **d. 26 Aug.** on Bull Pasture of unknown, age, 60yrs. **parents, Saml. & ____ Pullin.** born Bath Co. occ. farmer. unmarried. info, Ewin Dever, neighbor.

Steuart, Harriett, WF, **d. 29 Nov.** on __ of consumption, age, 14yrs, 10mos. **parents, Jac. & Cynthia Steuart.** born Bull pasture. occ. ____. consort of ____. info, J. W. Steuart, father.

Slave Nancy of J. W. Steuart, F, **d. 29 Sept.** on Bull Pasture of diptheria, age, 10mos. **parents, ____ & ____.** born ____. occ. ____. consort of ____. info, J. W. Steuart, owner.

Hull, Felix H., WM, **d. 30 Oct.** on Bull Pasture of typhoid fever, age, 38yrs. **parents, Peter & Rachel Hull** born Pendleton Co. occ. farmer. consort of Elizabeth Hull info, Eliz. Hull, wife.

Pullin, Saml. S., WM, **d. 9 Dec** on Bull Pasture of typhoid fever, age, 39yrs.
       parents, Loftus & Fr. Pullin. born Pendleton Co. occ. farmer.
consort of Susan E. Pullin. info, S. E. Pullin, wife.

Seybert, Mary, WF, **d. 5 Oct.** on Strt. Creek of typhoid fever, age, 83yrs, 7mos. 18dys.
       parents, Isaac & Martha Gum. born Pendleton Co.
occ. house keeper. consort of Jacob Seybert.
info, Henry Seybert, son.

Puffenbarger, Martha, WF, **d. 10 Dec.** on Strt. Creek of typhoid fever,
       age, 18yrs, 5mos, 3dys. **parents, Job & Elizth. Puffenbarger.**
born Str. Creek. occ. ___. unmarried. info, Job Puffenarger, father.

Campbell, James B., WM, **d. 4 Aug.** on Jacksons River of diptheria,
       age, 8yrs, 3mos, 36dys. **parents, Edgar & Elizth. Campbell.**
born J. River. occ. __. consort of __. info, Edgar Campbell, father.

Slave Emaline of Edgar Campbell, F, **d. 18 Sept.** on Jacksons River of typhoid fever,
       age, 19yrs. **parents, ___ & ___.** born ___. occ. ___.
consort of ___. info, Edgar Campbell, owner.

Hull, Jacob, WM, **d. 27 Nov.** at CrabBottom of pneumonia, age, 57yrs, 6mos, 27dys.
       parents, Adam & Hester Hull. born Pendleton Co. occ. farmer.
consort of Mahala Hull info, Mahala Hull, wife.

Seiver, Robt. M., WM, **d. 19 April** at CrabBottom of diptheria, age, 5yrs, 1mo, 16dys.
       parents, Jas. W. & Martha K. Seiver. born Crabbottom.
occ. ___.consort of ___. info, J. W. Seiver, father.

Seiver, Henry S., WM, **d. 8 May** at CrabBottom of diptheria, age, 2yrs, 2mos, 15dys.
       parents, Jas. W. & Martha K. Seiver. born Crabbottom.
occ. ___. consort of ___. info, J. W. Seiver, father.

Lantz, George W., WM, **d. 19 Oct.** at CrabBottom of typhoid fever, age, 21yrs, 6mos.
       parents, Benj. & Jemima Lantz. born Crabbottom. occ. farmer.
unmarried. info, Cyrus Lantz, brother.

Arbogast, Mary E., WF, **d. 8 April** at CrabBottom of diptheria, age, 1yr, 10mos, 8dys.
       parents, Jno. W. & Amanda M. Arbogast. born Crabbottom.
occ. ___. consort of ___. info, John W. Arbogast, father.

Arbogast, Cora A., WF, **d. 31 Aug.** at CrabBottom of diptheria, age, 7mos. 24dys.
       parents, Jno. W. & Amanda M. Arbogast. born Crabbottom.
occ. ___. consort of ___. info, John W. Arbogast, father.

1862

Kinkead, Virginia E., WF, **d. 30 Sept.** at Crab Bottom of diptheria, age, 9yrs, 4mos, 19dys. **parents, Wm. P. & H. Kinkead.** born Crabbottom. occ. ____. single. info, W. P. Kinkead, father.

Slave Lucinda of Wm. P. Kinkead, F, **d.** ____ **Sept.** at Crab Bottom of diptheria, age, 36yrs. **parents** ____ **&** ____. born Pendleton Co. occ. ____. consort of ____. info, W. P. Kinkead, master.

Slave Geo. Washington of Wm. P. Kinkead, M, **d.** ____ **Sept.** at Crab Bottom of diphtheria, age, 20yrs. **parents,** ____. born Crab Bottom. occ. ____. consort of ____. info, W. P. Kinkead, master.

Miller, Mary M., WF, **d. 12 Jan.** at Crab Bottom of fever & pneumonia, age, 59yrs, 29dys. **parents, Balser & E. Hammer.** born Pendleton Co. occ. ____. consort of A. G. Miller. info, A. G. Miller, husband.

Snyder, Sally WF, **d.** ____ **May** on Jacksons River of unknown, age, 17yrs. **parents, Saml. & Polly Snyder.** born Pendleton Co. occ. ____. consort of ____. info, E. Campbell, E. Campbell.

Snyder, Lucinda, WF, **d. 9 Aug.** on Jacksons River of unknown, age, ____. **parents, Saml. & Polly Snyder.** born Pendleton Co. occ. ____. consort of ____. info, E. Campbell, E. Campbell.

Ervin, Jno. P WM, **d. 26 Feb.** in Bath Co. of pneumonia, age, 40yrs, 5mos. **parents, Robt. & Phebe Ervin** born Bath Co. occ. farmer. consort of Elizth. W. Ervin info, E. W. Ervin, wife.

Ervin, Saml. R., WM, **d. 22 Aug.** in Bath Co. of diptheria, age, 14yrs, 1mo, 7dys. **parents, Elizth. R. & J. P. Ervin.** born Highland Co. occ. ____. single. info, E. R. Ervin, mother.

Ervin, R. A., WM, **d. 15 Aug.** in Bath Co. of diptheria, age, 12yrs, 1mo, 28dys. **parents, Elizth. R. & J. P. Ervin.** born Bath Co. occ. ____. single. info, E. R. Ervin, mother.

Ervin, D. W., WM, **d. 9 Sept.** in __. of diptheria, age, 5yrs, 5mos, 11dys. **parents, Elizth. R. & J. P. Ervin.** born Bath Co. occ. ____. single. info, E. R. Ervin, mother.

Matheny, Araminta, WF, **d. 3 Aug**. in Green Valley of diptheria, age, 5yrs.
        parents, J. G. & M. J. Matheny. born Highland Co.
        occ. ____. consort of ____. info, J. G. Matheny, father.

Matheny, Saml. R., WM, **d. 5 Aug**. in Green Valley of diptheria, age, 2yrs.
        parents, J. G. & M. J. Matheny. born Highland Co.
        occ. ____. consort of ____. info, J. G. Matheny, father.

Lightner, Jno. H., WM, **d. 26 Nov**. in Frederick Co. of pneumonia,
        age, 28yrs, 7mos, 23dys. **parents, Adam & Eleanor Lightner**
        born Pendleton Co. occ. farmer. single. info, A. Lightner father.

Townsend, Kenny, WM, **d. __ Oct**. in Highland Co. of hoping cough,
        age 2yrs, 6mos, 5dys. **parents, Jno. & Mary Ann Townsend**.
        born Highland Co. occ. ____. consort of ____.
        info, Jno. Townsend, father.

Wade, Isaac N., WM, **d. 23 Dec**. in Highland Co. of diptheria, age, 14yrs, 11mos.
        parents, Chas. & C. Wade. born Highland Co. occ. ____.
        consort of ____. info, C. Wade, father.

Bird, Aaron, WM, **d. 25 Sept**. in Maryland of died from wound, age, 31yrs.
        parents, Val & Nancy M. Bird. born ath Co. occ. farmer.
        consort of M. J. Bird. info, Val Bird, father

Dever, Jno., WM, **d. 10 Feb**. at Green Hill of pneumonia, age, 63yrs, 9mos. 25dys.
        parents, John & Peggy Dever. born Rockingham Co.
        occ. farmer. consort of Eliza Dever. info, E. Dever, wife.

Bird, Frances, WF, **d. 7 June** at Green Hill of diptheria, age, 16yrs, 9mos, 18dys.
        parents, P. H. & S. Bird. born Bath Co. occ. ____. single.
        info, P. H. Bird, father.

Bird, David H., WM, **d. 22 Feb**. at Green Hill of eresypilas, age, 57yrs, 11mos, 18dys.
        parents, J. & S. Bird. born Bath Co. occ. farmer.
        consort of S. A. Bird. info, C. A. Bird, son.

Bird, Anson G., WM, **d. 9 June** at Port Republic of killed in battle,
        age, 20yrs, 4mos, 19dys. **parents, D. H. Bird & S. A. Bird.**
        born Bath Co. occ. farmer. single. info, C. A. Bird, brother.

Bird, Morgan S., WM, **d. 18 July** at Staunton of died from wound,
        age, 18yrs, 3mos, 5dys. **parents, D. H. & S. A. Bird.**
        born Bath Co. occ. farmer. single. info, C. A. Bird, brother.

Chesnut, Virginia, WF, **d. ____ Sept.** at Green Hill of diptheria, age, 3yrs, 6mos. **parents, Wm. G. & S. A. Chesnut.** born Highland Co. occ. ____. consort of ____. info, Wm. G. Chesnut, father.

Chesnut, N. J., WF, **d. ____ Sept.** at Green Hill of diptheria, age, 14yrs, 6mos. **parents, Jos. & Eliza Chesnut.** born Highland Co. occ. ____. consort of ____. info, Wm. G. Chesnut, uncle.

Chesnut, Jac. N., WM, **d. ____ Sept.** at Green Hill of diptheria, age, 11yrs. **parents, Jos. Chesnut & Eliza Chesnut.** born Highland Co. occ. ____. consort of ____. info, Wm. G. Chesnut, uncle.

Chesnut, Alice, WF, **d. ____ Sept.** at Green Hill of diptheria, age, 7yrs. **parents, Jos. & Eliza Chesnut.** born Highland Co. occ. ____. consort of ____. info, Wm. G. Chesnut, uncle.

Chesnut, Wm. H., WM, **d. ____ Oct.** at Green Hill of diptheria, age, 3yrs. **parents, Jos. & Eliza Chesnut.** born Highland Co. occ. ____. consort of ____. info, Wm. G. Chesnut, uncle.

Bird, Laura J., WF, **d. 1 Oct.** at Green Hill of diptheria, age, 13yrs, 8mos, 22dys. **parents, Wm. C. & S. M. Bird.** born Bath Co. occ. ____. consort of ____. info, Wm. C. Bird, father.

Bird, Jesse F., WM, **d. 20 Dec.** at Green Hill of diptheria, age, 6yrs, 8mos, 9dys. **parents, Wm. C. & S. M. Bird.** born Highland Co. occ. ____. consort of ____. info, Wm. C. Bird, father.

Curry, Medda, WF, **d. 7 Feb,** in Bath Co. of dropsy in head, age, 9mos, 17dys. **parents, A. & S. Curry.** born Bath Co. occ. ____. consort of ____. info, A. Curry, father.

Kirkpatrick, Geo. D., WM, **d. 3 July** in Highland Co. of diptheria, age, 14yrs, 1mo, 19dys. **parents, J. & N. Kirkpatrick.** born Pocahontas Co. occ. ____. consort of ____. info, J. Kirkpatrick, father.

Kirkpatrick, Adam B., WM, **d. 18 June** in Highland Co. of diptheria, age, 10yrs, 6mos. **parents, J. & N. Kirkpatrick.** born Highland Co. occ. ____. consort of ____. info, J. Kirkpatrick, father.

Kirkpatrick, Naomi J., WF, **d. 28 June** in Highland Co. of diptheria, age, 9yrs. **parents, J. & N. Kirkpatrick.** born Highland Co. occ. ____. consort of ____. info, J. Kirkpatrick, father.

Gum, Jas. B., WM, **d. 31 May** in Highland Co. of fever, age, 21yrs, 11mos, 13dys.
        parents, Abraham & M. Gum. born Bath Co. occ. farmer.
        single. info, Abrm. Gum, father.

Gum, Abraham R., WM, **d. 11 June** in Highland Co. of diptheria,
        age, 10yrs, 8mos, 21dys. **parents, Abraham & M. Gum.**
        born Highland Co. occ. ____. consort of ____.
        info, Abrm. Gum, father.

Gum, Margt. C., WF, **d. 17 Sept.** in Highland Co. of diptheria,
        age, 16yrs, 4mos, 14dys. **parents, Isaac & Mary Gum.**
        born Bath Co. occ. ____. consort of ____. info, I. Gum, father.

Gum, Mary E., WF, **d. 17 Sept.** in Highland Co. of diptheria, age, 12yrs, 6mos, 15dys.
        parents, Isaac & Mary Gum. born Highland Co. occ. ____.
        consort of ____. info, I. Gum, father.

Slaven, Alice V WF, **d. 12 Jan.** in Highland Co. of consumption,
        age, 17yrs, 9mos, 27dys. **parents, Jacob & E. Slaven.**
        born Pocahontas Co. occ. ____. single. info, Mrs. Patterson, sister.

McNulty, Danl WM, **d. 25 Feb.** in Highland Co. of fever, age, 44yrs, 3mos, 10dys.
        parents, J. & M. McNulty. born Pocahontas Co. occ. farmer.
        single. info, F. McNulty, brother.

Hull, John A., WM, **d. __ March** in Highland Co. of boll hives, age, 2mos, 20dys.
        parents, M. H. & A. Hull. born Highland Co. occ. ____.
        consort of ____. info, M. H. Hull, father.

Snyder, Jno., WM, **d. 14 Nov.** in Highland Co. of unknown, age, 70yrs, 11mos, 19dys.
        parents, J. Snyder & S. Snyder. born Pendleton Co. occ. farmer.
        consort of Elizth. Snyder. info, E. Snyder, wife.

Folks, Adam, WM, **d. 23 Jan.** in Highland Co. of tiford pneumonia,
        age, 56yrs, 4mos, 26dys. **parents, M. & C. Folks.**
        born Pendleton Co. occ. farmer. consort of M. Folks.
        info, E. Folks, daughter.

Folks, Wm., WM, **d. 29 July** at Staunton of unknown, age, 24yrs, 1mo, 19dys.
        parents, H. & M. Folks. born Pendleton Co. occ. farmer. single.
        info, E. Folks, sister.

Bird, Jacob, WM, **d. 15 June** at Mt. Meridian of apoplexy, age, 24yrs, 6mos, 26dys.
        parents, J. & M. Bird. born Pendleton Co. occ. farmer. single.
        info, Jno. Bird, father.

Bird, Jr., David, WM, **d. 16 Aug.** in Orange Co. of apoplexy, age, 30yrs, 8mos, 2dys. **parents, J. & M. Bird.** born Pendleton Co. occ. merchant. consort of Isabella Bird. info, Jno. Bird, father.

Campbell, Ananais, WM, **d. 15 April** in Augusta Co. of tiford fever, age, 23yrs, 11mos, 14dys. **parents, S. B. & J. Campbell.** born Pendleton Co. occ. farmer. single. info, S. B. Campbell, father.

Slave Clarke of S. B. Campbell, M, **d. 15 Jan.** in Highland Co. of diptheria, age, 16yrs. **parents, ____ & ____.** born ____. occ. ____. consort of ____. info, S. B. Campbell, master.

Gum, Matilda, WF, **d. 12 Dec.** in Highland Co. of tyford fever, age, 42yrs. **parents, McB. & A. Gum.** born Pendleton Co. occ. ____. single. info, J. Gum, brother.

Gum, Josiah, WM, **d. 11 June** at Port Republic of from wound, age, 29yrs, 2mos, 22dys. **parents, Jno. E. & J. Gum.** born Pendleton Co. occ. farmer. single. info, Jno. E. Gum, father.

Mauzy, Jemima, WF, **d. 2 June** in Highland Co. of diptheria, age, 24yrs, 4mos, 3dys. **parents, D. L. & M. Mauzy** born Pendleton Co. occ. ____. single. info, D. L. Mauzy, father.

Sommers, Saml., WM, **d. 11 Feb.** in Highland Co. of eresypelas, age, 61yrs, 1mo, 11dys. **parents, M. & M. Sommers.** born Shenandoah Co. occ. farmer. consort of S. Sommers. info, W. M. Sommers, son.

Hevener, Mary, WF, **d. 13 Feb.** in Highland Co. of eresypelas, age, 60yrs. **parents, ____ & ____ Stone** born Pendleton Co. occ. ____. consort of Jacob Hevener. info, W. M. Sommers, Wm. M. Sommers.

Williams, Margt. F., WF, **d. ____ June** in Highland Co. of tiford fever, age, 5yrs. **parents, P. D. & E. Williams.** born Highland Co. occ. ____. consort of ____. info, P. D. Williams, father.

Williams, Jas. W., WM, **d. ____ Sept.** in Highland Co. of diptheria, age, 3yrs. **parents, P. D. & E. Williams.** born Highland Co. occ. ____. consort of ____. info, P. D. Williams, father.

Slave Bill of P. D. Williams, M, **d. ____ Dec.** in Highland Co. of tiford pneumonia, age, 8yrs. **parents, ____ & ____.** born Highland Co. occ. ____. consort of ____. info, P. D. Williams, master.

Stephenson, Mary T., WF, **d. 12 Sept.** in Highland Co. of diptheria, age, 8yrs. **parents, A. C. & V. Stephenson.** born Highland Co. occ. ____. consort of ____. info, A. C. Stephenson, father.

Stephenson, Harriet E., WF, **d. 27 Sept.** in Highland Co. of diptheria, age, 6yrs. **parents, A.C. & V. Stephenson.** born Highland Co. occ. ____. consort of ____. info, A. C. Stephenson, father.

Hiner, Rachel, WF, **d. 17 Jan.** in Highland Co. of pneumonia, age, 52yrs, 7mos, 12dys. **parents, Jas. & R. Gwin.** born Bath Co. occ. ____. consort of Jno. Hiner. info, Jno. Hiner, husband.

Kinkead, Wm. F., WM, **d. __ June** in Highland Co. of consumption, age, 21yrs. **parents, D. G. & M. A. Kincaid.** born Bath Co. occ. ____. single. info, D. G. Kincaid, father.

Varner, Danl., WM, **d. 20 Nov.** in Highland Co. of typhoid pneumonia, age, 23yrs, 2mos, 20dys. **parents, Jos. &. M. Varner** born Pendleton Co. occ. farmer. consort of M. H. Varner. info, H. L. Varner, bro.

Bird, Andrew H., WM, **d. 16 Sept.** in Highland Co. of consumption, age, 73yrs. **parents, Jno. & Mary Byrd.** born Bath Co. occ. farmer. consort of E. Byrd. info, Jno. T. Byrd, son.

McCoy, Henry, WM, **d. 10 Nov.** in Highland Co. of small pox, age, 59yrs, 3mos, 7dys. **parents, Benj. & Mary McCoy.** born Pendleton Co. occ. farmer. consort of M. A. McCoy. info, M. A. McCoy, wife.

Beverage, Andrew, WM, **d. 9 May** at Staunton of tifoid fever, age, 20yrs, 7mos, 9dys. **parents, Peter & P. Beverage.** born Pendleton Co. occ. farmer. single. info, Jas. Shineberry, uncle.

Simmons, Sarah F., WF, **d. 29 Oct** in Highland Co. of diptheria, age, 17yrs, 10mos, 8dys. **parents, Wm. & R. Simmons.** born Pendleton Co. occ. ____. single. info, Wm. Simmons, father.

Simmons, ____, WM, **d. 11 July** in Highland Co. of unknown, age, 2dys. **parents, J. W. & A. Simmons.** born Highland Co. occ. ____. consort of ____. info, J. W. Simmons, father.

Simmons, ____, WF, **d. 7 Sept.** in Highland Co. of unknown, age, 1mo, 28dys. **parents, J. W. & A. Simmons.** born Highland Co. occ. ____. consort of ____. info, J. W. Simmons, father.

Grogg, Wm., (of H), WM, **d. 27 Aug.** in Faquier Co. of killed, age, 20yrs, 3mos, 15dys.
    parents, H. & C. Grogg. born Pendleton Co. occ. farmer.
single. info, H. Grogg, father.

Grogg, Wm., (of A), WM, **d. ____ June** in Richmond, of killed, age, 23yrs, 10mos.
    parents, A. & C. Grogg. born Pendleton Co. occ. farmer. single.
info, C. Grogg, mother.

Keller, Eline, WF, **d. 21 Nov.** in Highland Co. of diptheria, age, 13yrs, 8mos, 20dys.
    parents, A. & M. L. Keller. born Randolph Co. occ. ____.
consort of ____. info, A. Keller, father.

Jack, Cain, WM, **d. 20 Jan.** in Pocahontas Co. of apoplexy, age, 21yrs, 9mos.
    parents, D. & M. Jack. born Pendleton. occ. farmer. single.
info, D. Jack, father.

Jack, Harman, WM, **d. 20 Jan.** in Highland Co. of tifoid fever, age, 17yrs, 7mos, 12dys.
    parents, D. & M. Jack. born Pendleton Co. occ. farmer. single.
info, D. Jack, father.

Varner, Susannah, WF, **d. __ March** in Highland Co. of diptheria, age, 24yrs.
    parents, D. & M. Varner. born Pendleton Co. occ. ____. single.
info, David Varner, father.

Varner, Martha J., WF, **d. __ Sept.** in Highland Co. of diptheria, age, 11yrs.
    parents, D. & M. Varner. born Highland Co. occ. ____.
consort of ____. info, David Varner, father.

Gwin, Andrew S., WM, **d. 17 Oct.** in Highland Co. of diptheria, age, 6yrs, 2mos, 3dys.
    parents, H. F. Gwin & J. Gwin. born Highland Co. occ. ____.
consort of ____. info, Susan Chew, aunt.

Trimble, G. W., WM, **d. 8 July** in Augusta Co. of from wound, age, 32yrs, 5mos.
    parents, James & C. Trimble. born Pendleton Co. occ. farmer.
single. info, Jno. Trimble, brother.

Eagle, Jane, WF, **d. ____ March** in Highland Co. of fever, age, 80yrs.
    parents, Paul & ____ Cook. Born Augusta Co. occ. ____.
consort of Christian Eagle. info, Geo. Eagle, son.

Eagle, Jane, WF, **d. ____ Jan.** in Highland Co. of tifoid fever, age, 48yrs.
    parents, C. & J. Eagle. born Augusta Co. occ. ____.
single. info, Geo. Eagle, bro.

Eagle, Christian, WM, **d. ____Feb.** in Highland Co. of fits, age, 37yrs.
parents, C. & J. Eagle. born Pendleton Co. occ. ____.
single. info, Geo. Eagle, bro.

Folks, Wm. A., WM, **d. 24 June** in Charlottesville of tifoid pneumonia,
age, 33yrs, 10dys. **parents, Jno. & E. Folks.** born Pendleton Co.
occ. farmer. consort of Levina Folks. info, L. Folks, wife.

Beathe, Peter H., WM, **d. 24 June** in Rockingham of from wound, age, 29yrs.
parents, Jas. & M. Beathe. born Pendleton Co.
occ. farmer. single. info, Jas. A. Beathe, bro.

Church, Mary E., WF, **d. 1 Aug.** in Highland Co. of scarlet fever, age, 7yrs.
parents, Wm. & E. Church. born Highland Co. occ. ____.
consort of ____. info, Wm. Church, father.

Vance, Margaret J., WF, **d. 24 July** in Highland Co. of diptheria, age, 19yrs.
parents, Wellington & B. Vance. born Augusta Co. occ. ____.
single. info, Geo. Vance, uncle.

Vance, Eliza, WF, **d. 2 Aug.** in Highland Co. of diptheria, age, 17yrs.
parents, Wellington & B. Vance. born Augusta Co. occ. ____.
single. info, Geo. Vance, uncle.

Vance, Mary E., WF, **d. 10 July** in Highland Co. of diptheria, age, 2yrs, 3mos.
parents, Geo. & S. M. Vance. born Highland Co. occ. ____.
consort of ____. info, Geo. Vance, father.

Steuart, Jno., WM, **d. 12 May** at Lynchburg of ereypelas, age, 19yrs.
parents, J. W. & J. Steuart. born Bath Co. occ. farmer. single.
info, J. W. Steuart, father.

Slave Nancy Jane of J. W. Steuart, F, **d. 11 March** in Highland Co. of diptheria,
age, 1yr. **parents, ____ & ____.** born Highland Co. occ. ____.
consort of ____. info, J. W. Steuart, master.

Slave Moses of Andrew Kinkead, M, **d. ____ Aug.** in Highland Co. of diptheria,
age, 14yrs. **parents, ____ & ____.** born Highland Co. occ. ____.
consort of ____. info, Wm. M. McClung, Wm. M. McClung.

Bradshaw, Robt. H., WM, **d. 9 June** at Port Republic of killed in battle,
age, 24yrs, 5mos, 9dys. **parents, Jno. & Eliza J. Bradshaw.**
born Pendleton Co. occ. school teacher. single.
info, Eliza J. Bradshaw, mother.

Slave Henry of Geo. Revercomb, M, **d. 12 Feb.** in Highland Co. of consumption,
   age, 16yrs. **parents,** ____ **&** ____. born Bath Co. occ. ____.
   consort of ____. info, Geo. Revercomb, master.

Slave Ellen of Geo. Revercomb, F, **d. 14 March** in Highland Co. of consumption,
   age, 12yrs. **parents,** ____ **&** ____. born Bath Co. occ. ____.
   consort of ____. info, Geo. Revercomb, master.

Slave Ellis of Rebecca Hamilton, F, **d.** ____ **Sept.** in Highland Co. of unknown,
   age, 50yrs. **parents,** ____ **&** ____. born Bath Co. occ. ____.
   consort of ____. info, R. Hamilton, mistress.

Slave ____ of Rebecca Hamilton, F, **d.** ____ **Aug.** in Highland Co. of unknown,
   age 3mos. **parents,** ____ **&** ____. born Highland Co. occ. ____.
   consort of ____. info, R. Hamilton, mistress.

Slave ____ of Rebecca Hamilton, F, **d.** ____ **June** in Highland Co. of unknown,
   age, 1dy. **parents,** ____ **&** ____. born Highland Co. occ. ____.
   consort of ____. info, R. Hamilton, mistress.

Steuart, Joanna S., WF, **d.** ____ **June** in Highland Co. of diptheria, age, 35yrs.
   parents, Geo. & Deborah Ervin. born Pendleton Co. occ. ____.
   consort of J. M. Steuart. info, J. M. Steuart, husband.

Steuart, Barbara A., WF, **d.** ____ **June** in Highland Co. of diptheria, age, 4yrs.
   parents, J. M. & J. Steuart. born Highland Co. occ. ____.
   consort of ____. info, J. M. Steuart, father.

Steuart, Jared M., WM, **d.** ____ **July** in Highland Co. of diptheria, age, 6yrs.
   parents, J. M. & J. Steuart. born Highland Co. occ. ____.
   consort of ____. info, J. M. Steuart, father.

Rough, Delila, WF, **d.** ____ **July** in Highland Co. of diptheria, age, 22yrs.
   parents, Jno. & Isabella Rough. born Bath Co. occ. ____.
   single. info, J. M. Steuart, J. M. Steuart.

Slave Rachel of Matilda Kincaid, F, **d. 1 July** in Highland Co. of consumption,
   age, 41yrs. **parents,** ____ **&** ____. born ____. occ. ____.
   consort of ____. info, M. Kincaid, mistress.

Slave Rachel Ann of Wm. Kincaid, F, **d. 1 March** in Highland Co. of hooping cough,
   age, 2yrs. **parents,** ____ **&** ____. born Highland Co. occ. ____.
   consort of ____. info, Wm. Kincaid, master.

Gwin, Elizabeth, WF, **d. 18 April** in Highland Co. of unknown, age, 75yrs.
        parents, T. & J. Kincaid. born Augusta Co. occ. ____.
consort of M. Gwin. info, M. Gwin, husband.

Slave Margaret of H. Benson, F, **d.** ____ **Aug.** in Highland Co., of fever, age, 18yrs.
        parents, ____ **&** ____. born Bath Co. occ. ____. consort of ____.
info, H. Benson, master.

Brown, Thos., WM, **d. 5 April** in Highland Co. of dropsy, age, 88yrs.
        parents, ____ **&** ____ **Brown.** born Italy. occ. farmer.
consort of E. Brown. info, M. Brown, daughter-in-law.

Brown, Winfield, WM, **d. 5 Aug.** in Highland Co. of scarlet fever, age, 6yrs, 11mos.
        parents, J. & M. Brown. born Highland Co. occ. ____.
consort of ____. info, M. Brown, mother.

Gwin, Margaret A., WF, **d.** ____ **Aug.** in Highland Co. of consumption, age, 41yrs.
        parents, Wm. & M. Johns. born Pendleton Co. occ. ____.
consort of O. Gwin. info, J. G. Wilson, J. G. Wilson.

Page, Malvina J., WF, **d. 10 July** in Highland Co. of scarlet fever, age, 23yrs.
        parents, S. & A. Wilson. born Pendleton Co. occ. ____.
consort of J. W. Page. info, J. G. Wilson, bro.

Page, Emma S., WF, **d. 6 July** in Highland Co. of scarlet fever, age, 4yrs.
        parents, J. W. & M. Page. born Highland Co. occ. ____.
consort of ____. info, J. G. Wilson, uncle.

Johns, Wm. W., WM, **d. 28 Sept.** in Highland Co. of tifoid fever, age, 35yrs.
        parents, W. & M. Johns. born Pendleton Co. occ. farmer.
consort of Lucinda Johns. info, J. W. Johns, bro.

Johns, Saml., WM, **d. 28 Dec.** in Highland Co. of tifoid fever, age, 53yrs.
        parents, Wm. & M. Johns. born Pendleton Co. occ. farmer.
consort of Margaret Johns. info, J. W. Johns, bro.

McQuain, Hugh, WM, **d. 30 Sept.** in Mississippi of diarrhea, age, 19yrs, 1mo, 2dys.
        parents, Jno. & ____ **McQuain.** born Pendleton Co. occ. farmer.
single. info, E. Vint, aunt.

Price, Wm., WM, **d.** ____ **Aug.** in Highland Co. of consumption, age, 2yrs.
        parents, ____ **&** ____ ____. born Highland Co. occ. ____.
consort of ____. info, S. M. Marshall, master.*[sic]*

Deal, Hannah, WF, **d. ____ April** in Highland Co. of unknown, age, 68yrs. **parents, P. & M. Young.** born Maryland. occ. farmer. consort of Jno. Deal. info, Amos Deal, son.

Erwin, Fanny, WF, **d. ____ Sept.** in Highland Co. of diptheria, age, 7yrs. **parents, Benj. & S. Erwin.** born Pendleton Co. occ. ____. consort of ____. info, Wm. Erwin, grandfather.

Jones, John W., WM, **d. 31 July** in Albemarle Co. of tifoid fever, age, 22yrs. **parents, Decatur H. & Jane Jones.** born Pendleton Co. occ. farmer. single. info, D. H. Jones, father.

Jones, Thos. H., WM, **d. 30 Nov.** in Highland Co. of diptheria, age, 17yrs, 6mos. 11dys. **parents, A. J. & J. Jones.** born Pendleton Co. occ. farmer. single. info, A. J. Jones, father.

Jones, Elizth. E., WF, **d. 11 Dec.** in Highland Co. of diptheria, age, 11yrs, 11mos, 4dys. **parents, A. J. & J. Jones.** born Highland Co. occ. ____. consort of ____. info, A. J. Jones, father.

Euritt, Nancy, WF, **d. 13 Jan.** in Highland Co. of lung disease, age, 62yrs. **parents, Thos. & H. Euritt.** born Winchester. occ. ____. single. info, H. C. Jones, nephew.

Jordan, Geo. W., WM, **d. 27 Feb.** in Highland Co. of diptheria, age, 6yrs. **parents, Sampson & N. Jordan.** born Highland Co. occ. ____. consort of ____. info, Nancy Jordan, mother.

Jordan, Barbara Ann, WF, **d. ____ March** in Highland Co. of diptheria, age, 2yrs. **parents, Sampson & N. Jordan.** born Highland Co. occ. ____. consort of ____. info, Nancy Jordan, mother.

Jordan, John, WM, **d. ____ March** in Highland Co. of diptheria, age, 20yrs. **parents, Sampson & N. Jordan.** born Pendleton Co. occ. ____. single. info, Nancy Jordan, mother.

Jordan, Abraham, WM, **d. ____ March** in Highland Co. of diptheria, age, 13yrs. **parents, Sampson & N. Jordan.** born Highland Co. occ. ____. consort of ____. info, Nancy Jordan, mother.

Jordan, Wm. F., WM **d. ____ March** in Highland Co. of diptheria, age, 8yrs, **parents, Sampson & N. Jordan.** born Highland Co. occ. ____. consort of ____. info, Nancy Jordan, mother.

Jordan, Elizth., WF, **d. ____ April** in Highland Co. of diptheria, age, 4yrs. **parents, Sampson & N. Jordan.** born Highland Co. occ. ____. consort of ____. info, Nancy Jordan, mother.

Jordan, Nancy C., WF, **d. ____ April** in Highland Co. of diptheria, age, 10yrs. **parents, Sampson & N. Jordan.** born Highland Co. occ. ____. consort of ____. info, Nancy Jordan, mother.

Wine, John, WM, **d. 10 June** in Highland Co. of diptheria, age, 9yrs. **parents, Geo. & Mary Ann Wine.** born Highland Co. occ. ____. consort of ____. info, Geo. Wine, father.

Wine, Jos., M., WM, **d. 23 June** in Highland Co. of diptheria, age, 2yrs. **parents, Geo. & Mary Ann Wine.** born Highland Co. occ. ____. consort of ____. info, Geo. Wine, father.

Wine, Susannah, WF, **d. 27 June** in Highland Co. of diptheria, age, 15yrs. **parents, Geo. & Mary Ann Wine.** born Rockingham Co. occ. ____. single. info, Geo. Wine, father.

Wine, Barbara, WF, **d. 29 June** in Highland Co. of diptheria, age, 13yrs. **parents, Geo. & Mary Ann Wine.** born Highland Co. occ. ____. consort of ____. info, Geo. Wine, father.

Wine, Geo. W., WM, **d. 1 July** in Highland Co. of diptheria, age, 5yrs. **parents, Geo. & Mary Ann Wine.** born Highland Co. occ. ____. consort of ____. info, Geo. Wine, father.

Wine, Solomon, WM, **d. 18 July** in Highland Co. of diptheria, age, 11yrs. **parents, Geo. & Mary Ann Wine.** born Highland Co. occ. ____. consort of ____. info, Geo. Wine, father.

Wine, ____, WF, **d. 30 Aug.** in Highland Co. of diptheria, age, 15dys. **parents, Geo. & Mary Ann Wine.** born Highland Co. occ. ____. consort of ____. info, Geo. Wine, father.

Whistleman, Danl., WM, **d. 25 Feb.** in Highland Co. of diptheria, age, 9yrs. **parents, Geo. & Jain Whistleman.** born Highland Co. occ. ____. consort of ____. info, Geo. Wine, Geo. Wine.

Whistleman, ____, WM, **d. 25 Feb.** in Highland Co. of diphtheria, age, 14dys. **parents, Jno. & S. Whistleman.** born Highland Co. occ. ____. consort of ____. info, Geo. Wine, Geo. Wine.

Whistleman, Wm., WM, **d. 28 Feb.** in Highland Co. of diptheria, age, 12yrs. **parents, Geo. & Jain Whistleman.** born Highland Co. occ. ____. consort of ____. info, Geo. Wine, Geo. Wine.

Whistleman, Geo., WM, **d. 5 March** in Highland Co. of diptheria, age, 17yrs. **parents, Geo. & Jain Whistleman.** born Pendleton Co. occ. ____. single. info, Geo. Wine, Geo. Wine.

Whistleman, Sarah, WF, **d. 7 March** in Highland Co. of diptheria, age, 15yrs. **parents, Geo. & Jain Whistleman.** born Highland Co. occ. ____. consort of ____. info, Geo. Wine, Geo. Wine.

Wilfong, Emanuel, WM, **d. 7 March** in Highland Co. of diptheria, age, 20yrs. **parents, Jos. & ____ Wilfong.** born Pendleton Co. occ. ____. consort of L. Wilfong. info, Geo. Wine, Geo. Wine.

Crummet, Sarah, WF, **d. 9 March** in Highland Co. of diptheria, age, 24yrs. **parents, Henry & S. Crummet.** born Pendleton Co. occ. ____. single. info, Geo. Wine, Geo. Wine.

Wilfong, Lydia, WF, **d. 13 March** in Highland Co. of diptheria, age, 22yrs. **parents, Henry & S. Crummet.** born Pendleton Co. occ. ____. consort of E. Wilfong. info, Geo. Wine, Geo Wine.

Wilfong, ____, WF, **d. 15 April** in Highland Co. of diptheria, age, 1mo. **parents, E. & L. Wilfong.** born Highland Co. occ. ____ consort of ____. info, Geo. Wine, Geo. Wine.

Michael, Jno., WM, **d. 4 Jan.** in Highland Co. of diptheria, age, 5yrs. **parents, David & Martha Michael.** born Highland Co. occ. ____ consort of ____. info, Geo. Wine, Geo. Wine.

Siple, Margaret, WF, **d. 10 Jan.** in Highland Co. of diptheria, age, 26yrs. **parents, Jno. & Polly Botkin.** born Pendleton Co. occ. ____. consort of Conrad Siple. info, Geo. Wine, Geo. Wine.

Botkin Laban, WM, **d. 20 Jan.** in Highland Co. of diptheria, age, 10yrs. **parents, Margaret Botkin.** born Highland Co. occ. ____. consort of ____. info, Geo. Wine, Geo. Wine.

Hiner, Chas. P., WM, **d. 3 March** in Highland Co. of diptheria, age, 7yrs, 5mos, 16dys. **parents, Jos. & M. M. Hiner.** born Highland Co. occ. ____. consort of ____. info, Joseph Hiner, father.

Armstrong, Gideon, WM, **d. 1 March** in Highland Co. of diptheria,
    age, 22yrs, 10mos, 10dys. **parents, A. H. & M. A. Armstrong.**
    born Pendleton Co. occ. ____. single
    info, M. A. Armstrong, mother.

Armstrong, Wm. H., WM, **d. 8 June** at Port Republic, of killed, age, 20yrs, 11mos.
    parents, A. H. & M. A. Armstrong. born Pendleton Co.
    occ. ____. single. info, M. A. Armstrong, mother.

Armstrong, Geo., WM, **d. 5 March** in Highland Co. of diptheria,
    age, 10yrs, 4mos, 18dys. **parents, Saml. E. & Polly Armstrong.**
    born Highland Co. occ. ____. consort of ____.
    info, Saml. Armstrong, father.

Armstrong, Jared, WM, **d. 15 March** in Highland Co. of diptheria,
    age, 28yrs, 6mos, 2dys. **parents, Saml. E. & Polly Armstrong.**
    born Pendleton Co. occ. ____. consort of Savina Armstrong.
    info, Saml. Armstrong, father.

Armstrong, Robert, WM, **d. 7 April** in Highland Co. of diptheria,
    age, 4yrs, 2mos, 25dys. **parents, Jared & S. Armstrong.**
    born Highland Co. occ. ____. consort of ____.
    info, Saml. E. Armstrong, grandfather.

Wilson, Saml., WM, **d. 14 Nov.** in Highland Co. of small pox, age, 47yrs.
    parents, Wm. J. & M. Wilson. born Pendleton Co.
    occ. farmer. consort of Caroline Wilson.
    info, A. H. Armstrong, A. H. Armstrong.

Curry, Melissa, WF, **d. 7 Dec.** in Highland Co. of fever, age, 21yrs.
    parents, E. Curry & A. Curry. born Highland Co. occ. ____.
    consort of ____. info, T. J. Husk, T. J. Husk.

Hook, ____, WM, **d. 17 Jan.** in Highland Co. of eresypelas, age, 16dys.
    parents, J. M. & D. Hook. born Highland Co. occ. ____.
    consort of ____. info, J. M. Hook, father.

McCray, Jos., WM, **d. 8 June** at Port Republic, of died from wounds, age, 25yrs.
    parents, St. Clair & M. McCray. born Pendleton Co. occ. farmer.
    consort of Elizabeth McCray. info, John Leach, father-in-law.

Murphy, Mary, WF, **d. __ Nov.** in Highland Co. of unknown, age, 1yr, 6mos.
    parents, John & S. Murphy. born Highland Co. occ. ____.
    consort of ____. info, Jacob Siron, Jacob Siron.

Siron, Jno., WM, **d. 8 June** at Port Republic, of killed, age, 30yrs.
    parents, Jacob & L. Siron. born Pendleton Co.
    occ. farmer. consort of Julia Siron info, Jacob Siron, father.

Botkin, Isaac N., WM, d. ____ **June** in Highland Co. of fever, age, 33yrs.
    parents, ____ & ____ Botkin. born Pendleton Co. occ. farmer.
    consort of Polly Botkin. info, Elizth. Siron, E. Siron.

Meadows, Thos., J., WM, **d. 22 Feb.** in Highland Co. of fever, age, 40yrs.
    parents, Jacob & N. Meadows. born Bath Co.
    occ. farmer. consort of Phebe Meadows. info, P. Meadows, wife.

Douglass, Robt., WM, d. ____ **July** in Highland Co. of pneumonia, age, 41yrs.
    parents, Jas. & M. Douglass. born Bath Co. occ. farmer.
    consort of Sarah Douglass. info, Thos. Douglass, bro.

Lamb, Wm. H. H., WM, d. ____ **Jan.** in Highland Co. of diptheria, age, 21yrs.
    parents, Jno. & E. J. Lamb. born Pendleton Co.
    occ. farmer. single. info, Peter F. Lamb, bro.

Hiner, Harmon A., WM, d. ____ **Aug.** in Highland Co. of typhoid fever, age, 35yrs.
    parents, Alex. & H. Hiner. born Pendleton Co. occ. farmer.
    consort of Martha Hiner. info, J. Layne, Jos. Layne.

Pullin, Saml., WM, d. ____ **Jan.** in Highland Co. of typhoid fever, age, 44yrs.
    parents, Loftus & F. Pullin. born Pendleton Co. occ. farmer.
    consort of S. E. Pullin. info, S. Ruleman, mother-in-law.

Hull, Geo., W., WM, d. ____ **April** in Augusta Co. of typhoid fever, age, 45yrs.
    parents, Peter & Rachel Hull born Pendleton Co. occ. farmer.
    consort of Sarah A. Hull. info, B. R. Swoope, brother-in-law.

Armstrong, Jared, WM, **d. 5 Nov.** in Highland Co. of small pox, age, 78yrs.
    parents, Wm. & ____ Armstrong. born London. occ. farmer.
    consort of Martha Armstrong. info, Josiah Armstrong, son-in-law.

Armstrong, Martha, WF, **d. 11 Nov.** in Highland Co. of small pox, age, 70yrs.
    parents, Jas. & E. Wilson born Pendleton Co. occ. ____.
    consort of Jared Armstrong. info, Josiah Armstrong, son-in-law.

Kiracofe, Margt. A., WF, **d. 4 Nov.** in Highland Co. of small pox, age, 25yrs.
    parents, Jared & M. Armstrong. born Pendleton Co. occ. ____.
    consort of Geo. M. Kiracofe.
    info, Josiah Armstrong, brother-in-law.

Kiracofe, Geo. M., WM, **d. 10 Nov.** in Highland Co. of small pox, age, 30yrs.
    parents, Geo. & J. Kiracofe. born Augusta Co. occ. mechanic.
    consort of Margt. A. Kiracofe.
    info, Josiah Armstrong, brother-in-law.

Blagg, Saml. H., WM, **d. 10 Nov.** in Highland Co. of small pox, age, 48yrs.
    parents, Jno. & M. Blagg. born Pendleton Co. occ. farmer.
    consort of Mary Blagg. info, Josiah Armstrong, Josiah Armstrong.

Blagg, Jr., Jno., WM, **d. 11 Nov.** in Highland Co. of small pox, age, 38yrs.
    parents, Jno. & M. Blagg. born Pendleton Co. occ. farmer.
    consort of Elizabeth Blagg.
    info, Josiah Armstrong, Josiah Armstrong.

Blagg, Sr., Jno., WM, **d. 20 Nov.** in Highland Co. of small pox, age, 85yrs.
    parents, ____ & ____ Blagg. born Pendleton Co. occ. farmer.
    consort of Mary Blagg. info, Josiah Armstrong, Josiah Armstrong.

Blagg, ____, WF, **d. 21 Nov.** in Highland Co. of small pox, age, 2dys.
    parents, Jno. & E. Blagg. born Highland Co. occ. ____.
    consort of ____. info, Josiah Armstrong, Josiah Armstrong.

Blagg, Jane, WF, **d. 23 Nov.** in Highland Co. of small pox, age, 75yrs.
    parents, ____ & ____ McCoy. born Pendleton Co. occ. ____.
    consort of Abraham Blagg.
    info, Josiah Armstrong, Josiah Armstrong.

Blagg, Henry J., WM, **d. 22 Nov.** in Highland Co. of small pox, age, 52yrs.
    parents, Ab'm. & J. Blagg. born Pendleton Co. occ. farmer.
    consort of Phebe Blagg. info, Josiah Armstrong, Josiah Armstrong.

Blagg, Wm., WM, **d. 22 Nov.** in Highland Co. of small pox, age, 18yrs.
    parents, H. J. & P. Blagg. born Pendleton Co. occ. ____.
    consort of ____. info, Josiah Armstrong, Josiah Armstrong.

Woodle, Wm., WM, **d. 20 Oct.** in Highland Co. of small pox, age, 57yrs.
    parents, ____ & ____ Woodle. born Augusta Co. occ. mechanic.
    consort of M. Woodle. info, Josiah Armstrong, Josiah Armstrong.

Lunsford, Wm., WM, **d. 1 Feb.** in Highland Co. of tifoid fever, age, 48yrs, 9mos, 10dys.
    parents, Jno. & S. Lunsford. born Pocahontas Co.
    occ. shoe maker. consort of Naoma Lunsford.
    info, Joshua Lunsford, son.

Lunsford, Mary, WF, **d. __ Dec.** in Highland Co. of diptheria, age, 13yrs, 7mos.
  parents, Wm. & N. Lunsford. born Highland Co. occ. ____.
  consort of ____. info, Joshua Lunsford, bro.

Seiver, Jas. S., WM, **d. ____ Oct.** in Higland Co. of infl. of bowels, age, 1yr, 21mos.
  parents, J. W. & M. K. Seiver. born Highland Co. occ. ____.
  consort of ____. info, J. W. Seiver, father.

Arbogast, Morgan B., WM, **d. 2 Dec.** in Highland Co. of diptheria,
  age, 18yrs, 9mos, 27dys. **parents, M. & S. Arbogast.**
  born Pocahontas Co. occ. ____. single. info, A. Keller, bro-in-law.

Snyder, Amanda, WF, **d. 24 Aug.** in Highland Co. of diptheria, age, 7yrs, 3mos, 5dys.
  parents, D. & H. Snyder. born Highland Co. occ. ____.
  consort of ____. info, D. Snyder, father.

Snyder, Hannah, WF, **d. 27 Aug.** in Highland Co. of diptheria,
  age, 35yrs, 4mos, 22dys. **parents, Jac. & M. Hevener.**
  born Pendleton Co. occ. ____. consort of D. Snyder.
  info, D. Snyder, husband.

Hoover, Cain, WM, **d. ____ Jan.** in Highland Co. of tifoid fever, age, 44yrs.
  parents, Jac. & S. Hoover. born Pendleton Co. occ. mechanic.
  consort of N. C. Hoover. info, D. Snyder, cousin.

Waybright, Jno., WM, **d. ____ Jan.** in Highland Co. of tifoid fever, age, 45yrs.
  parents, David & ____ Waybright. born Pendleton Co.
  occ. farmer. consort of E. A. Waybright. info, D. Snyder, cousin.

Wimer, Margt. Ann, WF, **d. ___ Dec.** in Highland Co. of tifoid fever, age, 28yrs, 7mos.
  parents, Sol. & Eleanor Rexrode. born Pendleton Co. occ. ____.
  consort of Philip Wimer. info, Sol. Rexrode, father.

Grogg, Jas. T., WM, **d. 4 Sept.** in Highland Co. of diptheria, age, 3yrs, 1dy.
  parents, A. & C. Grogg. born Highland Co. occ. ____.
  consort of ____. info, Catherine Grogg, mother.

Grogg, Rebecca H., WF, **d. 21 Sept.** in Highland Co. of diptheria,
  age, 1yr, 8mos, 21dys. **parents, A. & C. Grogg.**
  born Highland Co. occ. ____. consort of ____.
  info, Catherine Grogg, mother.

Vance Wm. H., WM **d. 5 Nov.** in Highland Co. of diptheria, age, 12yrs, 9mos, 27dys.
  parents, Wm. H. & A. Vance. born Highland Co. occ. ____.
  consort of ____. info, Alcinda Vance, mother.

Peck, Enos, WM, **d. __ Nov.** in Augusta Co. of small pox, age, 29yrs.
        parents, Jno. & S. Peck. born Pendleton Co. occ. farmer.
        consort of Huldah Peck. info, Jno. Peck, father.

Rimer, Elizabeth, WF, **d. 10 Feb.** in Highland Co. of typhd pneumonia, age, 52yrs.
        parents, Jno. & E. Peck. born Pendleton Co. occ. ____.
        consort of Thos. Rimer. info, T. Rymer, son.

Peck, Elizabeth, WF, **d. 3 Feb.** in Highland Co. of typhd pneumonia, age, 84yrs.
        parents, Jno. & ____ Beverage. born Pendleton Co. occ. ____.
        consort of Jno. Peck. info, Thos. Rimer, grand-son.

Wimer, Susan C., WF, **d. ____ Dec.** in Highland Co. of liver complt., age, 11mos.
        parents, Wm. & E. Wimer. born Highlland Co. occ. ____.
        consort of ____. info, Wm. Wimer, father.

Mulinax, John H., WM, **d. 19 Aug.** in Highland Co. of typhd pneumonia,
        age, 48yrs, 4mos. **parents, Jac. & H. Mulinax.**
        born Pendleton Co. occ. farmer.
        consort of Rachl. Mulinax. info, R. Mulinax, wife.

Wilfong, Joseph, WM, **d. ____** in Highland Co. of measles, age, 1yr, 11mos.
        parents, Eli & Sabina Wilfong. born Highland Co. occ. ____.
        consort of ____. info, Eli Wilfong, father.

Mauzy, Whitfield, WM, **d. 28 Dec.** in Highland Co. of diphtheria, age, 9yrs.
        parents, David L. & Polly Mauzy. born Highland Co. occ. ____.
        consort of ____. info, David Mauzy, father.

Stephenson, Virginia, WF, **d. ____ Jan.** in Highland Co. of diphtheria, age, 8yrs.
        parents, Wm. & E. J. Stephenson. born Highland Co. occ. ____.
        consort of ____. info, Wm. Stephenson, father.

Stephenson, Alvaretta, WF, **d. ____ Jan.** in Highland Co. of diphtheria, age, 4yrs.
        parents, Wm. & E. J. Stephenson. born Highland Co. occ. ____.
        consort of ____. info, Wm. Stephenson, father.

Waggy, Wm., WM, **d. 19 Dec.** in Highland Co. of diphtheria, age, 13yrs, 3mos, 5dys.
        parents, Abr. & S. Waggy. born Highland Co. occ. ____.
        consort of ____. info, Susan Waggy, mother.

Folks, Geo. A., WM, **d. 15 Oct.** in Highland Co. of diphtheria, age, 4yrs, 6mos, 22dys.
        parents, Val & M. Folks. born Highland Co. occ. ____.
        consort of ____. info, Valentine Folks, father.

Folks, Chas. D., WM, **d. 10 Oct.** in Highland Co. of diphtheria, age, 1yr, 3mos, 7dys. **parents, Val & M. Folks.** born Highland Co. occ. ____. consort of ____. info, Valentine Folks, father.

Thompson, Flavius, J., WM, **d. 25 Nov.** on Jacksons River of diphtheria, age, 10yrs, 7mos, 7dys. **parents, Wm. S. & M. Thompson.** born Highland Co. occ. ____. consort of ____. info, Wm. S. Thompson, father.

Curry, Hugh, WM, **d. 12 Feb.** on Jacksons River of typhoid pneumonia, age, 21yrs, 6mos, 11dys. **parents, Jas. & A. Curry.** born Bath Co. occ. farmer. single. info, Jas. Curry, father.

McGlaughlin, Jno., WM, **d. 2 Feb.** on Jacksons River of paralysis, age, 61yrs. **parents, Jno. & A. McGlaughlin.** born Bath Co. occ. farmer. consort of Sarah McGlaughlin. info, S. McGlaughlin, wife.

Hamilton, Jas. W., WM, **d. 29 Jan.** on Jacksons River of typhoid pneumonia, age, 26yrs. **parents, Musto & S. Hamilton.** born Bath Co. occ. farmer. single. info, S. McGlaughlin, mother.

Robertson, And. J., WM, **d. __ Aug.** on Jacksons River of killed, age, 28yrs. **parents, Wm. & M. Robertson.** born Bath Co. occ. farmer. consort of Mary A. Robertson. info, S. McGlaughlin, S. McGlaughlin.

Griffin, Jas. E., WM, **d. ____ Nov.** on Dry Branch of diphtheria, age, 2yrs. **parents, Wm. J. & R. Griffin.** born Highland Co. occ. ____. consort of ____. info, S. McGlaughlin, S. McGlaughlin.

Wiley, Robt. C., WM, **d. ____ Oct.** on Jacksons River of diphtheria, age, 13yrs. **parents, R. & S. Wiley.** born Highland Co. occ. ____. consort of ____. info, Jas. M. Terry, J. M. Terry.

Wiley, Eliza J., WF, **d. 11 Feb.** on Jacksons River of nervous disease, age, 10yrs. **parents, Jno. & E. Wiley.** born Highland Co. occ. ____. consort of ____. info, Elizth. Sheridan, mother.

Turner, St. Clair, WM, **d. ____ July** on Jacksons River of from wound, age, 30yrs. **parents, ___ & M. A. Turner.** born Rockingham Co. occ. farmer. consort of Susan Turner. info, Wm. Wilson, Wm. Wilson.

Slave Lucy of S. E. Stephenson, F, **d. ____ Nov.** on Jacksons River of diphtheria, age, 8yrs. **parents, ____ & ____.** born Highland Co. occ. ____. consort of ____. info, S. E. Stephenson, mistress.

Slave Sally of S. E. Stephenson, F, **d. ____ Nov.** in Highland Co. of diphtheria, age, 2yrs. **parents, ____ & ____.** born Highland Co. occ. ____. consort of ____. info, S. E. Stephenson, mistress.

Stephenson, Wash. A., WM, **d. 26 Nov.** on Jacksons River of diphtheria, age, 4yrs, 8mos. **parents, W. & S. E. Stephenson.** born Highland Co. occ. ____. consort of ____. info, S. E. Stephenson, mother.

Carpenter, Wm. W., WM, **d. 22 Nov.** in Big Valley of diphtheria, age, 3yrs. **parents, Jno. M. & R. M. Carpenter.** born Highland Co. occ. ____. consort of ____. info, R. M. Carpenter, mother.

Townsend, Wm., WM, **d. ____ Nov.** in Big Valley of pneumonia, age, 60yrs. **parents, S. & ____ Townsend.** born Bath Co. occ. farmer. consort of R. Townsend. info, R. Carpenter, R. Carpenter.

Seybert, Mary S., WF, **d. 20 Jan.** on South Branch of diphtheria, age, 15yrs. **parents, Jac. & C. Seybert.** born Highland Co. occ. ____. consort of ____. info, Jacob Seybert, father.

Hansel, Matthew W., WM, **d. 16 May** in Green Co. of typhoid pneumo, age, 20yrs, 8mos, 4dys. **parents, B. & Mary Hansel.** born Pendleton Co. occ. farmer. single. info, B. Hansel, father.

1863

(No entries in the original ledger)

1864

Armstrong, Josiah, WM, **d. 14 Sept.** in prison at Elmira, NY of chronic dysentery, age, 34yrs. **parents, Geo. & Sarah Armstrong.** born Bull Pasture Mt. occ. farmer. consort of Matherial Armstrong. info, Henry C. Jones, brother-in-law.

Ball, Wm. B., WM, **d. 21 July** at Monterey of remittent fever, age, 10yrs, 6mos, 14dys. **parents, Amos R. & Frances E. Ball.** born McDowell, Highland Co. occ. student. unmarried. info, Amos R. Ball, father.

Bowers, Solomon, WM, **d. 10 April** on Straight Creek of typhoid fever,
   age, 31yrs, 10mos, 3dys. **parents, Joseph & Barbara Bowers.**
   born S. Branch, Pendn Co. occ. farmer. unmarried.
   info, Barbara Bowers, mother.

Beverage, Robert, WM, **d. 25 June** at Liberty, Bedford Co. of typhoid pneumonia,
   age, 19yrs, 10mos, 25dys. **parents, Wm. & Mary Beverage.**
   born Straight Creek, Highland Co. occ. farmer. unmarried.
   info, Wm. Beverage, father.

Beverage, William, WM, **d. 11 Nov.** near Beverley, Randolph Co. of wound,
   age, 22yrs, 3mos, 9dys. **parents, Wm. & Mary Beverage.**
   born St. Creek, Highland Co. occ. farmer. unmarried.
   info, Wm. Beverage, father.

Beverage, Martin H., WM, **d. 10 April** on Straight Creek of diphtheria,
   age, 3yrs, 25dys. **parents, Jno. & Susan Beverage.**
   born St. Creek, Highland Co. occ. none. unmarried.
   info, John Beverage, father.

Blagg, Frances H., WF, **d. 3 June** at hd of Bull Pasture of diphtheria,
   age, 46yrs, 3mos, 8dys. **parents, John & Mary Blagg.**
   born hd Bull Pasture. occ. house keeper. unmarried.
   info, James H. Blagg, brother.

Botkin Samuel, WM, **d. 6 Dec.** on Bull Pasture Mt. of typhoid fever,
   age, 18yrs, 3mos, 13dys. **parents, Samuel & B. Botkin.**
   born Bull Pasture Mt. occ. farmer. unmarried.
   info, Samuel Botkin, father.

Slave Samuel Brown, M, d. ____ **July** at Monterey of consumption, age, 22yrs.
   parents, Wood Brown & mothers name unknown.
   born Bath Co. occ. farmer. consort of Martha Brown.
   info, John Trimble, former master.

Beathe, Martha F., WF, **d. 6 Sept.** on Dry Branch, Jacksons River, of scarlet fever,
   age, 22 mos. **parents, John & Martha Beathe.** born Bull Pasture.
   occ. none. unmarried. info, John Beathe father.

Bird, James, WM, **d. 4 March** in Upshur Co., W.Va. of consumption, age, 37yrs.
   parents, Wm. & Sarah Bird. born Back Creek. occ. farmer.
   consort of Mary J. Bird. info, Wm. Bird, father.

Bird, Otho M., WM, **d. 10 July** at Liberty, Bedford Co. of wound, age, 27yrs, 7mos.
   parents, Peter H. & Sophia Bird. born Back Creek. occ. farmer.
   unmarried. info, Peter H. Bird, father.

Beverage, Harvey, WM, **d. 5 June** at Spotsylvania C. H. of wound,
age, 34yrs, 7mos, 2dys. **parents, Geo. & Hannah Beverage.**
born Crab Bottom. occ. farmer. consort of Lucinda Beverage.
info, Lucinda Beverage, wife.

Carrol, Harvey H., WM, **d. 6 June** at Spotsylvania C. H. of wound, age, 24yrs, 15dys.
parents, Jesse & L. F. Carroll. born Bull Pasture. occ. farmer.
unmarried. info, John D. Carroll, brother.

Colaw, Clara Elizth., WF, **d. 24 Sept.** at Crab Bottom of diphtheria,
age, 1yr, 9mos, 16dys. parents, **Allen & Roxanna Colaw.**
born Crab Bottom. occ. none. unmarried. info, Allen Colaw, father.

Church, Joseph, WM, **d. 20 May** at Richmond, Va. of wound, age, 26yrs.
parents, Wm. & Elizth. Church. born Shaws Ridge.
occ. farmer. consort of Mary Church.
info, Jonas W. Chew, brother-in-law.

Davis, James S., WM, **d. 8 June** on Bull Pasture of wound, age, 21yrs, 10mos, 6dys.
parents, Lewis & Sarah A. Davis. born Bull Pasture. occ. farmer.
unmarried. info, Lewis Davis, father.

Eagle, Harman H., WM, **d. 14 Dec.** at Camp Chase, O. of typhoid fever,
age, 20yrs, 8mos, 20dys. **parents, Saml. C. & Martha M. Eagle**
born Doe Hill. occ. farmer. unmarried.
info, Samuel C. Eagle, father.

Eagle, Sallie O., WF, **d. 13 June** at Doe Hill of diphtheria, age, 11yrs, 8mos, 28dys.
parents, Saml. C. & Martha M. Eagle. born Doe Hill. occ. none.
unmarried. info, Samuel C. Eagle, father.

Eagle, Martha C., WF, **d. 29 May** at Doe Hill of diphtheria, age, 2yrs, 8mos, 20dys.
parents, Saml. C. & Martha M. Eagle. born Doe Hill. occ. none.
unmarried. info, Samuel C. Eagle, father.

Eagle, Enoch, WM, **d. 23 Aug.** on Bull Pasture of pneumonia, age, 46yrs.
parents, Phillip & Sarah Eagle. born Rockingham Co.
occ. carpenter. consort of Susan Eagle. info, Martha Siron, neice.

Gum, George W., WM, **d. 18 May** at New Market, Va. of wound,
age, 19yrs, 10mos, 4dys. **parents, John & Polly Gum.**
born hd Jacksons River. occ. farmer. unmarried.
info, Polly Gum, mother.

Gibson, Sarah, WF, **d. 5 Dec.** near Woodsboro of paralytic, age, 75yrs, 8dys.
parents, Robt. & Margt. Given.
born hd Jacksons River, Bath Co. occ. house keeper.
consort of Saml. Gibson, decd.
info, Allice Gibson, daughter-in-law.

G--, Leond. W., WM, **d. 14 Nov** at Hilton hd, S.C. of consumption, age, 25yrs.
parents, Wm. & Patsy Gum. born hd Jacksons River.
occ. farmer. consort of Mary Ann Gum.
info, Mary Ann Gum, wife.

---, ----nie, E., WF, **d. 10 Dec.** on Back Creek of diphtheria, age, 2yrs, 11mos, 25dys.
parents, Elliot & Betty E. Gum. born Back Creek. occ. none.
unmarried. info, Jas. W. Wade, grandfather.

Gum, Abisha R., WM, **d. 16 Oct.** at Pt. Lookout, Md. of dysentery, 22yrs, 3mos.
parents, Isaac & Mary Gum. born Back Creek. occ. farmer.
unmarried. info, Nancy Gum, stepmother.

Gum, Agnes S., WF, **d. 16 Aug.** on Back Creek of scarlet fever, age, 2yrs, 6mos, 16dys.
parents, Peter & Nancy Gum. born Back Creek occ. none.
unmarried. info, Nancy Gum, mother.

Gum, Jared W., WM, **d. 15 May** at New Market, Va. of killed in battle,
age, 20yrs, 8mos, 15dys. **parents, Cornelius & Jane Gum.**
born Jacksons River occ. farmer. consort of Sarah Gum.
info, Nancy Gum, grandmother.

Gum, Cornelius, WM, **d. 26 June** in Botetourt Co. of dysentery, age, 49yrs, 1mo.
parents, Roger & Matil Gum. born Jacksons River. occ. farmer.
consort of Jane Gum. info, Nancy Gum, mother-in-law.

Hupman, John, WM, **d. 14 Sept.** in the hosp, Staunton, Va. of wound, age, 29yrs.
parents, Peter & Mary Hupman. born Cow Pasture. occ. farmer.
consort of Louisa Hupman. info, Peter Hupman, father.

Hiner, Harmon A., WM, **d. 19 May** at Spotsylvania C. H. of killed in battle,
age, 24yrs, 9mos, 25dys. **parents, Wm. & Eliza Jane Hiner.**
born Bull Pasture. occ. farmer. unmarried. info, John Hiner, uncle.

Kramer, Henry, WM, **d. 12 Aug.** in Frederick Co., Va. of killed in battle, age, 22yrs.
parents, Conrad & Elizth. R. Kramer. born Crab Bottom.
occ. farmer. unmarried. info, Conrad Kramer, father.

Kinkaid, William, WM, **d. 7 May** at New Hope, Augusta Co. of killed in battle, age, 43yrs, 3mos, 16dys. **parents, Charles & Mary Kinkaid.** born Cow Pasture. occ. farmer. consort of Hetty H. Kinkaid. info, Hetty H. Kinkaid, wife.

Ketterman, Flora A., WF, **d. 23 April** at Crab Bottom of not known, age, 1mo. **parents, Esau & Jane Ketterman.** born Crab Bottom. occ. none. unmarried. info, Esau A. Ketterman, father.

Lantz, Daniel, WM, **d. 5 Oct.** at Elmira, NY of scurvy, age, 40yrs, 9mos, 28dys. **parents, Benj. & Jemimah Lantz** born Crab Bottom. occ. farmer. consort of Elizth M. Lantz. info, Elizth M. Lantz, wife.

Leach, John, WM, **d. 12 May** on Bull Pasture Mt. of typhoid pneumonia, age, 71yrs. **parents, John & Margt. Leach.** born Ireland. occ. farmer. consort of Jane Sommers & Catherine McCray. info, Catherine Leach, wife.

Leach, John T., WM, **d. 4 June** at Spotsylvania C. H. of wound, age, 32yrs. **parents, John & Jane Leach.** born Black Thorn, Pendtn Co. occ. farmer. unmarried. info, John T. Armstrong, neighbor.

McCray, Jr. St. Clair, WM, **d. 30 May** at Gaines Mills of killed in battle, age, 25yrs. **parents, St. Clair & Margt. McCray.** born South Fork. occ. farmer. unmarried. info, Margaret McCray, mother.

McCray, Thomas, WM, **d. __ Nov.** at Beverly, Randolph Co. of killed in battle, age, 20yrs. **parents, St. Clair & Margt. McCray.** born Cow Pasture. occ. farmer. unmarried. info, Margaret McCray, mother.

Pullin, Jesse B. M., WM, **d. 16 Dec.** at Harrisonburg, Va. of wound, age, 19yrs, 4mos, 4dys. **parents, John S. & Nancy Pullin.** born Jacksons River. occ. tanner. unmarried. info, John S. Pullin, father.

Rexrode, Barbara A., WF, **d. 23 July** on South Fork of diphtheria, age, 7yrs, 2mos. **parents, Joseph & Sarah Rexrode.** born South Fork. occ. none. unmarried. info, Joseph Rexrode, father.

Rexrode, George F., WM, **d. 3 Aug.** on South Fork of diphtheria, age, 14yrs, 2mos, 13dys. **parents, Joseph & Sarah Rexrode.** born South Fork occ. none. unmarried. info, Joseph Rexrode, father.

Revercomb, Jacob A., WM, **d. 7 May** at Spotsylvania C. H. of killed in battle, age, 26yrs, 3mos. **parents, Geo. & Rebecca Revercomb.** born Jacksons River, Bath Co. occ. farmer. unmarried. info, George Revercomb, father.

Steward, Ferdinand, WM, **d. ____ Dec.** at Pt. Lookout, Md. of small pox, age, 19yrs. **parents, Wm. R. & Elizth. Steuart.** born Cow Pasture. occ. farmer. unmarried. info, George Steuart, nephew.

Seybert, William, WM, **d. 19 Sept.** at Winchester, Va. of killed in battle, age, 27yrs, 10mos, 14dys. **parents, Henry & Lucinda Seybert.** born St. Creek. occ. farmer. unmarried. info, Henry Seybert, father.

Steuart, Charles W., WM, **d. 24 June** at Spotsylvania C. H. of wound, age, 34yrs. **parents, Chas. & Tericy Stuart.** born Bull Pasture. occ. farmer. consort of Elizth Steuart info, Virginia Stephenson, sister.

Wilson, Saml. L., WM, **d. 10 Oct.** at Doe Hill of diphtheria, age, 13yrs, 4mos, 28dys. **parents, Hamilton & Jos.* Wilson** born Doe Hill. occ. none. unmarried. info, Hamilton Wilson, father.

Wilson, Matilda J., WF, **d. 10 July** at Doe Hill of diphtheria, age, 16yrs, 7mos. **parents, Hamilton & Jos.* Wilson.** born Doe Hill. occ. none. unmarried. info, Hamilton Wilson, father.

Wilson, V. A. Alice, WF, **d. 28 June** at Doe Hill of diphtheria, age, 3yrs, 10mos, 24dys. **parents, Hamilton & Jos.* Wilson.** born Doe Hill. occ. none. unmarried, info, Hamilton Wilson, father.

Wilson, George Anna, WF, **d. 2 July** at Doe Hill of diphtheria, age, 1yr. 8mos, 1dy. **parents, Hamilton & Jos.* Wilson.** born Doe Hill. occ. none. unmarried. info, Hamilton Wilson, father.

Woods, David B., WM, **d. 28 Dec.** at Elmira, NY of small pox, age, 37yrs, 7mos, 3dys. **parents, John & Mary Woods.** born ack Creek. occ. farmer. unmarried. info, Mary Woods, mother.

Waggoner, Henry, WM, **d. 15 June** at Crab Bottom of killed by the swamps, age, 65yrs. **parents, Joseph & Catherine Waggoner.** born Crab Bottom. occ. farmer. consort of Barbara Waggoner. info, Peter Gum, neighbor.

---

* abbreviation for Josephine

Waggoner, Jacob, WM, **d. 1 Sept.** at Crab Bottom of killed by the swamps, age, 43yrs.
    parents, Henry & Barbara Waggoner. born Crab Bottom.
    occ. farmer. consort of Elizth. Kile & Elizth. Sharp.
    info, Peter Gum, neighbor.

Waggoner, Jesse, WM, **d. 15 Aug.** at Crab Bottom of fever, age, 35yrs.
    parents, Henry & Barbara Waggoner. born Crab Bottom.
    occ. farmer. consort of Jane Waggoner. info, Peter Gum, neighbor.

Doyle, Jacob, WM, **d. 14 Sept** at Elmira, NY of mumps, age, 26yrs.
    parents, J. C. & Margt. Doyle. born Jacksons River. occ. farmer.
    consort of Elizth. Doyle. info, Eli Doyle, brother.

1865

Armstrong, Jared, WM, **d. 24 June** at Pt. Lookout, Md. of chronic dysentery,
    age, 24yrs, 9mos. **parents, John T. & Jane Armstrong.**
    born Bull Pasture Mt. occ. farmer. unmarried.
    info, John T. Armstrong, father.

Armstrong, Jared, WM, **d. 16 April** on Bull Pasture River of general debility,
    age, 80yrs. **parents, John Armstrong & Nancy Armstrong.**
    born Leesburg, Loudon Co. occ. miller. consort of Agnes Hiner.
    info, Allen Armstrong, son.

Bishop, John, WM, **d. 15 Aug.** on Bull Pasture River of heart disease, age, 35yrs, 2mos.
    parents, John & Lucy Bishop. born Albemarle Co., Va.
    occ. farmer. consort of Sarah Hicklin.
    info, Peachy Steuart nephew.

Colaw, Howard Milton, WM, **d. 3 Dec.** at Crab Bottom of croup, age, 2yrs, 4mos, 7dys.
    parents, Jonas & America Colaw born Crab Bottom. occ. ____.
    unmarried. info, Jonas Colaw, father.

Campbell, Newton A., WM, **d. 6 Oct.** on Knap's Creek, Poc. Co., W.Va.
    of consumption, age, 21yrs, 4mos.
    parents, Thos. & Elizth. Campbell. born Back Creek occ. farmer.
    consort of Margt. J. Bower. info, Margaret J. Campbell, wife.

Clendenen, Adam S., WM, **d. 4 April** at Petersburg, Va. of wound, age, 25yrs. **parents, John & Catherine Clendenen.** born Pocahontas Co., W.Va. occ. blacksmith. unmarried. info, John Clendenen, father.

Campbell, Etta Jane, WF, **d. 23 Nov.** on Back Creek of (not known to the informant and the physicians differed as to the name of the disease), age, 2yrs, 6mos. **parents, Newton A. & Margt. J. Campbell.** born Back Creek. occ. ____. unmarried. info, Thomas Campbell, grandfather.

Fisher, Charles Harvey, WM, **d. 28 May** in Upshur Co., W.Va. of whooping cough, age, 4yrs, 2mos, 2dys. **parents, Jas. & Louisa Fisher.** born hd of the River, Highland Co. occ. ____. unmarried. info, James Fisher father.

Fisher, Sarah Ann, WF, **d. 8 May** Upshur Co., W.Va. of whooping cough, age, 1mo, 3dys. **parents, Jas. & Louisa Fisher.** born hd of the River, Highland Co. occ. ____. unmarried. info, James Fisher father.

Givens, David, WM, **d. 8 June** on Bull Pasture River of consumption, age, 37yrs. **parents, David & Milly Givens.** born Bull Pasture River. occ. farmer. unmarried. info, Robt. Lockridge, employer.

Griffin, Naomi Frances, WF, **d. 8 June** in Big Valley of not known, age, 8mos. **parents, Robert H. & Sarah M. Griffin.** born Big Valley. occ. ____. unmarried. info, Robt. H. Griffin, father.

Gammon, Jane, WF, **d. 17 April** in Back Creek Valley of disease of stomach, age, 73yrs. **parents, ____ & ____ Bradshaw.** born Huntersville, Poc. Co., W. Va. occ. ____. consort of Thos. Gammon. info, Cyrus Gammon, son.

Hiner, Andrew A., WM, **d. 10 Feb.** on Jacksons River of killed by fall of tree, age, 19yrs. **parents, John & Rachel Hiner.** born Jacksons River. occ. farmer. unmarried. info, John Hiner, father.

Kramer, Adam, WM, **d. 11 May** at Elmira, NY, of not known, age, 22yrs. **parents, Conrad & Elizth. Kramer.** born Cow Pasture. occ. farmer. unmarried. info, Conrad Kramer, father.

Kelly, Wm. D WM, **d. 3 April** at Staunton, Va. of dysentery, age, 35yrs, 3mos, 17dys. **parents, John Sharp & Ann Kelly.** born Dry Branch. occ. farmer. consort of Eliza J. Kelly. info, Ann Kelly, mother.

Lantz, Mary Ann WF, **d. 31 July** at Crab Bottom of consumption, age, 36yrs.
    parents, Wm. H. & Mary Fox. born Pendleton Co., W.Va.
    occ. ____. consort of Cyrus Lantz. info, Cyrus Lantz, husband.

Mulinax, Elizth., WF, **d. 25 Nov.** at Crab Bottom of influenza, age, 66yrs.
    parents, John & Polly Lambert.
    born Dry Run, Pendleton Co., W.Va. occ. ____.
    consort of Geo. Mulinax. info, Phebe White daughter-in-law.

Nicholas, Francis, WM, **d. 13 Dec.** at Crab Bottom of old age, age, 90yrs, 2mos, 14dys.
    parents, Geo. & Mary Nicholas. born Straight Creek.
    occ. farmer. consort of Catherine Nicholas.
    info, Peter Gum, son-in-law.

Oakes, Wm. Rufus, WM, **d. 6 Feb.** on Hatcher's Run of killed in battle, age, 25yrs.
    parents, Thos. & Malinda Oakes. born Rockingham Co.
    occ. farmer. unmarried. info, Malinda Oakes, mother.

Pullin, Henry, WM, **d. 10 Dec.** on Bull Pasture River of gravel,
    age, 68yrs, 11mos, 14dys. **parents, Thos. & Jane Pullin.**
    born Bath Co., Va. occ. farmer. unmarried.
    info, Robt. C. Pullin, nephew.

Rexrode, ____, WM, **d. ____ Oct.** hd of Crab Run of not known, age, 3dys.
    parents, John & Sidney Rexrode. born hd of Crab Run.
    occ. ____. unmarried. info, John Rexrode, father.

Steuart, Henry C., WM, d. 6 Feb. on Hatcher's Run of wound, age, 21yrs, 14dys.
    parents, Edwd. & Caroline Steuart. born Bull Pasture River.
    occ. farmer. unmarried. info, Edwd. Steuart, father.

Stephenson, Washington, WM, **d. 24 April** on Jacksons River of croup, age, 1yr, 1mo.
    parents, Wm. & Eliza J. Stephenson. born Jacksons River.
    occ. ____. unmarried. info, Eliza J. Stephenson, mother.

Tompkins, Sarah A., WF, **d. 1 Aug.** at hd of Jacksons River of flux, age, 2yrs.
    parents, Jane Tompkins. born hd of Jacksons River. occ. ____
    unmarried. info, Wm. M. Sommers, employer of childs mother.

Tompkins, ____, WF, **d. 1 Aug.** at hd of Jacksons River of flux, age, 5mos.
    parents, Jane Tompkins. born hd of Jacksons River. occ. ____
    unmarried. info, Wm. M. Sommers, employer of childs mother.

Wise, Jonathan, WM, **d. 8 April** in Prince Edward Co.., Va. of wound, age, 24yrs, 5mos. **parents, Michl. & Elizabeth Wise.** born Deerfield, Augusta Co., Va. occ. farmer. unmarried. info, Michael Wise, father.

White, Allen, WM, **d. ____ May** in hospital, Richmond, Va. of rheumatism, age, 46yrs. **parents, Thos. & ____ White.** born Randolph Co., W. Va. occ. farmer. consort of Phebe White. info, Phebe White, wife.

Wade, Matilda M., WF, **d. 4 Feb.** in Back Creek Valley of diphtheria, age, 18yrs. **parents, Chas. & Catherine Wade.** born Back Creek, Bath Co. occ. __. unmarried. info, Charles Wade father.

Wade, John Thomas, WM, **d. 18 Dec.** in Back Creek Valley of not known, age, 1dy. **parents, Anson O. & Adella C. Wade.** occ. ____. unmarried. info, Anson O. Wade, father.

1866

Arbogast, Ephraim, WM, **d. 8 March** on South Branch of pneumonia, age, 59yrs, 3mos. **parents, Henry & Elizth. Arbogast.** born Crab Bottom. occ. farmer. consort of Gracy A. Arbogast. info, Gracy A. Arbogast, wife.

Beath, ____, WM, **d. ____ Dec**. on Dry Branch of bold hives, age, 7dys. **parents, Jno. P. & Martha A. Beath.** born Dry Branch. occ. ____. unmarried. info, Jno. P. Beath, father.

Brown, James, WM, **d. 17 June** on Shaws Fork of disease of heart, age, 45yrs. **parents, Thos. & Elizth. Brown.** born Washington City. occ. ____. consort of Margaret Brown. info, Margaret Brown, wife.

Campbell, Clarence, WM, **d. __ Feb.** on Back Creek of not known, age, 1yr, 8mos. **parents, Newton & Margt. J. Campbell.** born Back Creek. occ. ____. unmarried. info, Thos. Campbell, grandfather.

Campbell, Margt. J., WF, **d. 9 May** on Back Creek of disease of bowels, age, 56yrs. **parents, Jas. & Polly Hamilton.** born Back Creek. occ. ____. consort of Thos. Campbell & Addison Boner. info, Thos. Campbell, husband.

Davis, Sarah A., WF, **d. 5 Dec.** on waters Bull Pasture of cancer of the womb,
　　　　　age, 52yrs, 6mos. **parents, Andrew & Mary R. Trumbull.**
　　　　　born Pendleton Co., W. Va. occ. ____. consort of Lewis Davis.
　　　　　info, Lewis Davis, husband.

Daggy, Saml. B., WM, **d. 11 March** at Mt. Zion Church, Augusta Co. of bronchitis,
　　　　　age, 23yrs, 10mos, 11dys. **parents, Noah & Susannah Daggy.**
　　　　　born Augusta Co., Va. occ. farmer. unmarried.
　　　　　info, Susannah Daggy, mother.

Ervin, Elizabeth, WF, **d. 4 Sept.** on Back Creek of consumption, age, 49yrs.
　　　　　parents, Saml. & Mary Ruckman. born Back Creek occ. ____.
　　　　　consort of Jno. P. Ervin. info, David V. Ruckman, brother.

Fleisher, Cora Lee, WF, **d. 12 May** on Bull Pasture Mt. of not known, age, 1yr, 2mos.
　　　　　parents, Henry J. & Barbara A. Flesher
　　　　　born Upshur Co., W.Va. occ. ____ unmarried.
　　　　　info, Henry J. Fleisher, father.

Grogg, John, WM, **d. 10 Feb.** Harrison Co. W. Va. of rheumatism, age, 30yrs.
　　　　　parents, Henry & Christina Grogg. born Crab Bottom.
　　　　　occ. farmer. unmarried. info, Henry Grogg, father.

Gum, Sr., Jno. E., WM, **d. 6 Sept.** in Crab Bottom of apoplexy, age, 69yrs.
　　　　　parents, Isaac & Jane Gum. born Crab Bottom.
　　　　　occ. farmer. consort of Jane Gum. info, Jane Gum, wife.

Hull, Renick M., WM, **d. 24 Oct.** at McDowell of typhoid fever, age, 18yrs, 2mos.
　　　　　parents, Felix & Elizth. M. Hull. born McDowell. occ. student.
　　　　　unmarried. Elizabeth M. Hull, mother.

Harold, Hannah E., WF, **d. 15 Sept.** near Monterey of not known,, age, 1yr, 6mos.
　　　　　parents, Danl. & Sarah Harold. born near Monterey. occ. ____.
　　　　　unmarried. info, Danl. Harold, father.

Newman, ____, WM, **d. 20 Sept.** at Crab Bottom of not known, age, 3dys.
　　　　　parents, Jas. C. & Louisa M. Newman. born Crab Bottom.
　　　　　occ. ____. unmarried. info, Louisa M. Newman, mother.

Newman, ____, WF, **d. 15 Nov.** at Crab Bottom of whooping cough, age, 2mos, 1dy.
　　　　　parents, Jas. C. & Louisa M. Newman. born Crab Bottom.
　　　　　occ. ____. unmarried. info, Louisa M. Newman, mother.

Pullin, Sarah A., WF, **d. 28 Feb.** on St. Creek of J. R. of child birth, age, 25yrs.
　　　　　parents, David & Jane Gwin. born Big Valley, Bath Co.
　　　　　occ.____.consort of Jno. E. C. Pullin. info, Jno. E. C. Pullin, father.

Puffenbarger, Ambrose H., WM, **d. 5 May** on South Fork, Pendleton Co., W.Va. of whooping cough, age, 3mos.
    parents, Elijah & Amanda S. Puffenbarger. born South Fork.
    occ. ____. unmarried. info, Elijah Puffenbarger, father.

Rodgers, Reuben, WM, **d. 5 March** at hd of Jacksons River of consumption, age, 60yrs.
    parents, Gordon & Fany Rodgers. born Rockingham Co., Va.
    occ. merchant. consort of Margt. A. King & Harriet W.
    info, Louisa Campbell, daughter.

Ruckman, Mary C., WF, **d. 10 June** on Back Creek of whooping cough, age, 1yr, 6mos.
    parents, David V. & Anna H. Ruckman. born Back Creek.
    occ. ____. unmarried. info, David V. Ruckman, father.

Sharp, John, WM, **d. 25 July** on Dry Branch of J. River of old age, age, 103yrs.
    parents, Sharp-given names not known. born Pennsylvania.
    occ. farmer. consort of Betsy Sharp.
    info, David McNulty, neighbor.

Varner, Anna, WF, **d. 26 April** on St. Creek of old age, age, 85yrs.
    parents, Jno. & ____ Cook. born South Fork. occ. ____.
    consort of Peter Varner. info, David Varner, son.

White, Judson P., WM, **d. 23 Oct.** on St. Creek of croup, age, 1yr, 5mos, 23dys.
    parents, Harman & Mary M. White. born St. Creek occ. ____.
    unmarried. info, Harman White, father.

1867

Armstrong, Agnes, WF, **d. 16 Oct.** on Bull Pasture of dropsy of chest, age, 76yrs.
    parents, John & ____ Hiner. born Pendleton Co. occ. ____.
    consort of Jared Armstrong. info, Abel H. Armstrong, son.

Armstrong, Sarah, WF, **d. 2 Feb.** on Bull Pasture Mt. of cold, age, 20yrs, 6mos.
    parents, Townsend & Jane Price. born Rockingham Co.
    occ. ____. consort of Wm. Armstrong.
    info, Wm. Armstrong, husband.

Botkin Mary, WF, **d. 15 Dec.** on Bull Pasture Mt. of rheumatism,
    age, 75yrs, 1mo, 16dys. **parents, Jno. & Nancy Armstrong.**
    born Bull Pasture Mt. occ. ____. consort of Jno. Botkin.
    info, Jno. Botkin, son.

Botkin John L., WM, **d. 8 May** on Crab Run of disease of bowels, age, 21yrs, 7mos. **parents, Robt. & Elizth Botkin.** born Crab Run. occ. laborer. unmarried. info, Robt. Botkin, father.

Beverage, Henry, WM, **d. 15 Oct.** on St. Creek of consumption, age, 33yrs. **parents, ____ & Hannah Beverage.** born St. Creek. occ. laborer. unmarried. info, Jno. Beverage, brother.

Cross, Eliza J., WF, **d. 18 July** at Crab Bottom of typhoid fever, age, 27yrs, 6mos, 14dys. **parents, Henry & Christina Grogg.** born Crab Bottom. occ. ____. consort of Jno. E. Cross. info, Jno. E. Cross, husband.

Gwin, Moses, WM, **d. 27 April** on Cow Pasture River of old age, age, 70yrs, 3mos. **parents, Joseph & Mary Gwin.** born Cow Pasture. occ. farmer. consort of Elizabeth Gwin. info, Rachel Gwin, daughter-in-law.

Gwin, James, WM, **d. 6 Jan.** on Jacksons River of fever & pneumonia, age, 50yrs. **parents, James & Rachel Gwin.** born Back Creek occ. farmer. consort of Mahala Gwin. info, Mahala Gwin, wife.

Hammer, Leonard, WM, **d. 28 June** at Crab Bottom of cancer, age, 86yrs. **parents, Balser & Elizth Hammer.** born South Branch. occ. farmer. unmarried. info, David Mauzy, nephew.

Jack, Mary, WF, **d. 1 Dec.** at Crab Bottom of fever, age, 54yrs, 7mos, 17dys. **parents, Jacob & Susan Hoover.** born South Fork. occ. ____. consort of David Jack. info, David Jack, husband.

Kramer, Wm. F., WM, **d. 11 Sept.** at Crab Bottom of croup, age, 3yrs. **parents, Conrad & Barara Kramer.** born Crab Bottom. occ. __. unmarried. info, Conrad Kramer, father.

Michael, John, WM, **d. 12 Nov.** on South Fork of paralysis, age, 79yrs. **parents, Jno. & ____ Michael.** born Augusta Co. occ. farmer. consort of Elizabeth Michael. info, David Michael, son.

Mowry, ____, WM, **d. 17 March** on St. Creek of not known, age, 3dys. **parents, Saml. & Matilda J. Mowry.** born St. Creek. occ. ____. unmarried. info, Saml. Mowry, father.

Miller, Adam G., WM, **d. 10 June** at Crab Bottom of apoplexy, age, 74yrs. **parents, Geo. & Mary Miller.** born Pendleton Co. occ. farmer. consort of Mary M. & Sarah A. Miller. info, Sarah A. Miller, wife.

Pullin, Rachel J., WF, **d. 19 Nov.** on Bull Pasture of fever, age, 21yrs. **parents, Saml. & Sarah Pullin.** born Bull Pasture River. occ. ____. unmarried. info, H. M. Pullin, brother.

Pullin, Sarah E., WF, **d. 4 Feb.** on Bull Pasture of stricture of bowels, age, 10yrs. **parents, Saml. S. & Susan Pullin.** born Bull Pasture River. occ. ____. unmarried. info, Thos. Reed, stepfather.

Ruckman, Margt., WF, **d. 14 June** on Back Creek of old age, age, 76yrs. **parents, John & Elizth. Slaven.** born Pocahontas Co. occ. ____. consort of Saml. Ruckman. info, D. V. Ruckman, son.

Slaven, Mary P., WF, **d. 7 July** on Back Creek of fever, age, 32yrs, 1mo, 22dys. **parents, Jacob & Eleanor Slaven.** born Pocahontas Co. occ. ____. consort of Jesse B. Slaven. info, Jesse B. Slaven, husband.

Shinneberry, Jacob, WM, **d. 19 June** at Crab Bottom of dropsy, age, 57yrs. **parents, Jacob & Margt. Shinneberry.** born Crabbottom. occ. farmer. consort of Sally Shinneberry. info, Naomi Hevener, neighbor.

Snyder, Samuel, WM, **d. 19 July** at Crab Bottom of pneumonia, age, 21yrs, 7mos, 12dys. **parents, Saml. & Mary Snyder.** born Crabbottom. occ. laborer. unmarried. info, Isabella Snyder, sister.

Tharp, Amos, WM, **d. 20 Jan.** on Bull Pasture of dropsy, age, 80yrs. **parents, ____ & ____ Tharp.** born not known. occ. farmer. unmarried. info, Jonathan Siron, neighbor.

Terry, Sarah M., WF, **d. 15 July** on Back Creek of not known, age, 1dy. **parents, Warrick & Cassa Terry.** born Back Creek occ. ____. unmarried. info, Warrick Terry, father.

1868

Armstrong, ____, WM, **d. 23 June** on Bull Pasture Mtn. of hives, age, 1dy. **parents, John E. & Barbara Armstrong.** born Bull Pasture Mt. occ. ____. unmarried. info, John E. Armstrong, father.

Gwin, Edith G., WF, **d. 9 Aug.** at Monterey of not known, age, 1mo, 22dys.
    parents, H. F. & Jane S. Gwin. born Monterey. occ. ____.
    unmarried. info, Houston F. Gwin, father.

Holt, Wm. F., WM, **d. ____ Jan.** on Bull Pasture of pneumonia, age, 25yrs.
    parents, Thos. & Minerva Holt. born Augusta Co.
    occ. tinner. consort of Martha F. Holt.
    info, Townson Price, neighbor.

Hansel, Fanny, WF, **d. 2 June** at Crabottom of disease of brain, age, 2mos, 3dys.
    parents, Jno. H. & Margt. Hansel. born Crabbottom occ. ____.
    unmarried. info, John H. Hansel, father.

Harouff, Harriet, WF, **d. 18 Sept.** on Bull Pasture of general debility, age, 36yrs.
    parents, Joseph & Christina Burns. born Bath Co. occ. ____.
    consort of Christian H. Harouff. info, C. H. Harouff, husband.

Hupman, ____, WM, **d. ____ Nov.** on Cow Pasture of croup, age, 3dys.
    parents, John H. & Synthia Hupman. born Cow Pasture.
    occ. ____. unmarried. info, Elizabeth Kinkead, neighbor.

Huff, Boling, WM, **d. 17 Feb** at McDowell of pneumonia, age, 8mos.
    parents, John T. & Louisa C. Huff. born McDowell.
    occ. ____. unmarried. info, John T. Huff, father.

Hull, Rachel, WF, **d. 19 Oct.** at Crabbottom of pneumonia, age, 73yrs.
    parents, Jas. & Elizth. Tallman. born Pocahontas Co. occ.____.
    consort of Peter Hull, decd. info, Matthew H. Hull, son.

Jordan, Sarah C., WF, **d. 16 Dec.** on St. Creek of J. R. of not known, age, 5yrs.
    parents, Harvey M. & Mary E. Jordan. born St. Creek of J. R.
    occ. ____. unmarried. info, H. M. Jordan, father.

Jack, David, WM, **d. 28 Dec.** at Crabbottom of palsy, age, 53yrs, 5mos, 3dys.
    parents, John & Sarah Jack. born Pendleton Co. occ. laborer.
    consort of Mary Jack. info, Benj. Rexrode, neighbor.

Kinkead, Gracey M., WF, **d. 23 March** at Crabbottom of pneumonia, age, 29yrs.
    parents, David L. & Polly Mauzy. born Pendleton Co.
    occ. ____. consort of Wm. P. Kinkead.
    info, Wm. P. Kinkead, husband.

Kinkead, Matilda, WF, **d. 1 Jan** on Cow Pasture of consumption, age, 56yrs, 9mos.
    parents, Chas. L. & Nancy Kinkead. born Bath Co. occ. ____.
    unmarried. info, Jas. S. Hupman, neighbor.

Leach, Henry S., WM, **d. ____ Feb.** on Bull Pasture Mt. of croup, age, 2yrs.
    parents, ____ & Catherine Leach. born Bull Pasture Mt.
    occ. ____. unmarried. info, Nancy Propst, neighbor.

Nicholas, Solomon, WM, **d. 19 March** at Crabbottom of murdered, age, 46yrs.
    parents, Francis & Catherine Nicholas. born Crabottom.
    occ. farmer. consort of Jane Nicholas.
    info, Henry Nicholas, brother.

Rutherford, ____, WM, **d. 16 Dec.** at Crabbottom of not known, age, 1dy.
    parents, Jno. E. & Elizth Rutherford. born Crabbottom.
    occ. ____. unmarried. info, John E. Rutherford, father.

Rexrode, Susan, WF, **d. 25 April** near Monterey of jaundice & dropsy, age, 67yrs.
    parents, Michael & Cath. Waybright. born St. Creek.
    occ. ____. consort of Saml. Rexrode. info, Saml. Rexrode, husband.

Snyder, Saml. WM, **d. 2 Aug.** at Crabottom of erysipelas, age, 54yrs.
    parents, ____ & ____ Snyder. born Pendleton Co. occ. laborer.
    consort of Mary Snyder. info, Sidney Snyder, daughter.

Smith, James, WM, **d. 5 July** on Bull Pasture Mt. of old age, age, 80yrs.
    parents, ____ & ____ Smith. born Pendleton Co. occ. farmer.
    consort of Rebecca Smith. info, John Wilson, neighbor.

Smith, Hannah, WF, **d. 15 May** on Bull Pasture Mt. of hives, age, 1mo, 9dys.
    parents, ____ & Christina Smith. born Bull Pasture Mt.
    occ. ____. unmarried. info, Sarah A. Simmons, 2nd cousin.

Sitlington, John, WM, **d. 17 March** on Bull Pasture of pneumonia, age, 87yrs.
    parents, Robt. & Margt. Sitlington. born Pennsylvania.
    occ. grazier. consort of Barbara & Elizth. Sitlington.
    info, Robert Sitlington, son.

Vint, Elizabeth, WF, **d. 30 Aug.** on Shaws Fork of paralysis, age, 65yrs.
    parents, ____ & ____ Botkin. born Pendleton Co.
    occ. ____. consort of Wm. Vint. info, Esau Vint, son.

Wimer, Ruhama, WF, **d. 10 Nov.** at Monterey of disease of heart, age, 51yrs.
    parents, Wm. & Christina Mulinax. born Pendleton Co.
    occ. ____. consort of Nathan Wimer.
    info, Nathan Wimer, husband.

1869

Armstrong, Sally, WF, **d. 26 March** in Stonewall Township of disease of bowels, age, 63yrs, 1mo. **parents, Harmon & Jeremiah Hiner.** born Pendleton Co. occ. __. consort of Geo. Armstrong. info, Jno. M. Armstrong, son.

Beverage, Susan, WF, **d. 24 April** in Monterey Twp. of typhoid fever, age, 40yrs. **parents, Martin & Sarah Moyers.** born Stonewall Twp. occ. ____. consort of John Beverage. info, Jno. Beverage, husband.

Carpenter, Robert, WM, **d. ____ Dec.** in Monterey Twp. of disease of brain, age, 44yrs, 8mos. **parents, Robt. & Rebecca Carpenter.** born Monterey Twp. occ. farmer. consort of Eliz. F. Carpenter. info, Jared M. Carpenter, brother.

Carlisle, Margaret, WF, **d. ____ Jan.** in Stonewall Twp. of paralysis, age, 50yrs. **parents, Jno. & Elizth Carlisle.** born Stonewall Twp. occ. ____. unmarried. info, Jas. S. Helms, nephew.

Devericks, Jane, WF, **d. 27 Dec.** in Stonewall Twp. of not known, age, 74yrs, 10mos. **parents, Jno. & Margt. Leach.** born Pendleton Co. occ. ____. consort of Wm. Devericks. info, Margt. Devericks, daughter.

Devericks, Hester Ann, WF, **d. 6 Oct.** in Stonewall Twp. of inflamation bowels, age, 1yr, 12dys. **parents, Allen H. & Lucinda T. Devericks.** born Augusta Co. occ. ____. unmarried. info, Allen H. Devericks, father.

Graham, Thomas, WM, **d. ____ Dec.** in Stonewall Twp. of diarrhea, age, 84yrs. **parents, ____ & ____ Graham.** born Bath Co. occ. farmer. consort of Elizabeth Graham. info, Elizabeth Graham, wife.

Hiner, Catherine C., WF, **d. 14 June** in Stonewall Twp. of scrofula, age, 21yrs. **parents, Peter Swope & Caroline Hiner.** born Stonewall Twp. occ. ____. unmarried. info, Caroline Hiner, mother.

Hodge, Nova, WF, **d. 3 Sept** in Stonewall Twp. of fever, age, 2yrs, 7mos. **parents, Jas. A. & Eliz. A. Hodge.** born Stonewall Twp. occ. __. unmarried. info, Jas. A. Hodge, father.

Helms, Toody, WF, **d. 9 Aug.** in Stonewall Twp. of typhoid fever, age, 6yrs. **parents, ____ & Eliz. A. Helms.** born Stonewall Twp. occ. ____. unmarried. info, Jas. S. Helms, uncle.

Helms, Betsy A., WF, **d. 23 July** in Stonewall Twp. of typhoid fever, age, 38yrs. **parents, John & Jane Helms.** born Stonewall Twp. occ. ____. unmarried. info, Jas. A. Helms, brother.

Michael, John F., WM, **d. 13 May** in Stonewall Twp. of diptheria, age, 4yrs, 8mos. **parents, Peter & Eliz. Michael.** born Stonewall Twp. occ. ____. unmarried. info, Peter Michael, father.

Pray, Elizabeth, WF, **d. 5 Aug.** in Monterey Twp. of dropsy, age, 77yrs. **parents, Lot & Phebe Eustis.** born New York. occ. midwife. consort of John Pray. info, Mahala Gwin, daughter.

Pullin, Loftus, WM, **d. 22 March** in Monterey Twp. of gravel, age, 66yrs. **parents, Thos. & Jane Pullin.** born Stonewall Twp. occ. farmer. consort of Susan Pullin. info, Susan Pullin, wife.

Rodgers, Sarinah, WF, **d. 30 Aug.** in Monterey Twp. of bilious fever, age, 34yrs. **parents, Robt. & Mary Gwin.** born Bath Co., Va. occ. ____. consort of Nelson Rodgers. info, Nelson Rodgers, husband.

Rexrode, Adam, WM, **d. 29 June** in Blue Grass Twp. of hernia, age, 76yrs. **parents, Jno. & Margaret Rexrode.** born Pendleton Co. occ. farmer. consort of Elizabeth Rexrode. info, Jno. M. Rexrode, son.

Rexrode, Sidney, WF, **d. 19 April** in Monterey Twp. of consumption, age, 34yrs. **parents, Frank & Susan McCluster.** born Pendleton Co. occ. ___. consort of Jno. Rexrode. info, Jno. Rexrode, husband.

Rusmisel, Harmon H., WM, **d. 26 Feb.** in Stonewall Twp. of pneumonia, age, 8mos. **parents, Jno. & Eliz. E. Rusmisel.** born Stonewall Twp. occ. ____. unmarried. info, Jno. J. Rusmisel, father.

Snyder, Elizabeth, WF, **d. 1 Oct.** in Blue Grass Twp. of infl of brain, age, 61yrs. **parents, Jno. & Susan Halterman.** born Pendleton Co. occ. ____. consort of Jno. Snyder. info, Jas. R. Snyder, son.

Wilson, Phebe, WF, **d. 14 Oct.** in Blue Grass Twp. of disease of liver, age, 65yrs, 10mos,10dys. **parents, Jno. & Frances Hicks.** born Pendleton Co. occ. ____. consort of Jas. Wilson. info, Osborne Wilson, son.

Waggoner, Eleanor, WF, **d. 27 Dec.** in Monterey Twp. of disease of heart, age, 33yrs. **parents, Thos. & Mary E. Beverage.** born Monterey Twp. occ.____. consort of Jno. B. Waggoner. info, Jno. B. Waggoner, husband.

1870

Blue Grass Twp

Byrd, Lyddia, WF, **d. 17 Oct.** in Highland Co., of cancer, age 53yrs,
    parents, William & Rebecca Byrd. born Botetort Co.
    occ.____.unmarried. info, James H. Byrd, brother & physician.

Not Named, WF, **d. 13 July** in Highland Co., of (not known), age ____.
    parents, David H. & Eliza Campbell, born Highland Co.
    occ. ____, infant, info, David H. Campbell, father.

Not Named, WF, **d. 26 July** in Highland Co.of (not known), age ____.
    parents Jacob F. & Elizabeth Clendinnen, born Highland Co.
    occ. ____. infant. info, Jacob F. Clendinnen, father.

Gum, Susan J., WF, **d. 16 Oct.** in Highland Co., of confinement at childbirth,
    age, 30yrs, 2mos, 13dys. **parents, William & Hannah Kincade,**
    born Highland Co. occ. housekeeper, wife,
    consort of Adam F. Gum, info, William Kincade, father.

Hull, Robert R., WM, **d. 9 Nov.** in Highland Co., of typhoid fever, age, 33yrs.
    parents, John & Margaret Hull, born Highland Co. occ. farmer
    husband of Ellen Hull. info, Sarah A. Hull, sister.

Hull, John E. M., WM, **d. 25 Nov.** in Highland Co. of (not known),
    age, 1yr, 8mos, 8dys, **parents, Joseph & Amanda Hull.**
    born Highland Co. occ. ____. child. info, Joseph Hull, father.

Tomlinson, Zachariah, WM, **d. 5 Jan.** in Highland Co., of consumption, age 63yrs.
    parents, not known. born not known,
    husband of Hulda Tomlinson, info, Henry Tomlinson, son.

Valentine, Bolir, WM, **d. 15 March** in Highland Co. of sore throat, age 3yrs.
    parents, J. C. & Elizabeth Valentine, born Highland Co.
    occ. ____, child, info, Elizabeth Valentine, mother.

Valentine, Jasper, WM, **d. 5 March** in Highland Co., of sore throat, age 1yr, 6mos.
    parents, J. C. & Elizabeth Valentine, born Highland Co.
    occ.____ child. info, Elizabeth Valentine, mother.

Monterey Twp.

Fagan, William, CM, **d. ____April** at Monterey of fever, age, 50yrs.
        parents, ____ & ____ Fagan. born Bath Co. occ. laborer,
        consort of ____ Fagan. info, Wm W. Fleming, employer.

Gibson, ____, WM, **d. 20 May** near Woodsborough of spasms, age,15dys.
        parents, Jno. L. & Alice S. Gibson, born near Woodsborough
        occ. ____. not married. info, Jno. L. Gibson, father.

Hull, Frederick K., WM, **d. 21 Oct.** in Blue Grass District of typhoid pneumonia,
        age, 65yrs. **parents, Adam & Hester Hull.** born Pendleton Co.,
        occ. farmer, consort of ____ & Julia A. Hull.
        info, Julia A. Hull, wife.

Jordan, Harvey M., WM, **d. 24 Oct.** on St. Creek of J. R.* of (not known),
        age, 49yrs. **parents, Jno. & Anne Jordan.** born Rockingham Co.
        occ. farmer. consort of Mary E. Jordan.
        info, Margart. A. Jordan, daughter.

Puffenbarger, ___, WF, **d. 3 March** on St. Creek of S.B.** of (not known),
        age, 3mos,11dys. **parents, Solomon & S.E. Puffenbarger.**
        born St. Creek of S.B. occ. ____. not married.
        info, Solomon Puffenbarger, father.

Wimer, Margt. A., WF, **d. 1 April** at Monterey of paralysis, age, 26yrs.
        parents, Amos & Susan Snyder. born near Monterey. occ.____.
        consort of Joseph Wimer. info, Joseph Wimer, husband.

Stonewall Twp.

Anderson, Mahala Harriet, CF, **d. 5 Dec.** at Shas' Fork of pneumonia, age, 9mos.
        parents, Jno. & Harriet Anderson. born Shas Fork. occ. ____
        unmarried. info, Mahala Anderson, grandmother.

Anderson, Harriet, CF, **d. 12 Dec.** at Shas' Fork of consumption, age, 37yrs.
        parents, Israel & ____ Minor. born Cow Pasture. occ. __.
        consort of Jno. Anderson. info, Mahala Anderson, mother-in-law.

Burk, John, WM, **d. 9 Nov** at Shas' Fork, drauned***, age, 65yrs.
        parents, (unknown). born Ireland. occ. farmer.
        consort of Sarah Burk. info, Robert McCrae, neighbor.

---

*Straight Creek of Jacksons River
** Straight Creek of South Branch
*** drowned

Devericks, Naomi Jane, WF, **d. 22 Aug.** at Shas' Fork of pneumonia, age, 4yrs.
   parents, Allen & Lucinda G. Devericks, born Augusta Co.
  occ.____. unmarried. info, Allen N. Devericks, father.

Douglass, Thomas, WM, **d. 28 Dec.** near McDowell of general debility,
  age, 75yrs. **parents, James & ____ Douglass.** born Pendleton Co.
  occ. farmer. consort of Magdalena Douglas.
  info, John Lamb, neighbor.

Flesher, Henry A., WM, **d. 14 March** near McDowell of typhoid fever, age, 47yrs.
   parents, Henry & Hannah Flesher. born Pendleton Co.
  occ. farmer. consort of Barbara Flesher.
  info, Thomas Flesher, son.

Hicklin, Harvey H., WM, **d. 23 Oct.** near McDowell of dyspepsia, age, 56yrs.
   parents, Geo. & Eliz. Hicklin. born Highland Co. occ. farmer
  unmarried. info, John S. Hicklin, son.

Hicklin, Henry B., WM, **d. 15 April** near McDowell of fever, age, 21yrs.
   parents, Jas. C. & Rebecca Hicklin. born Highland Co.
  occ. farmer, unmarried. info, Geo. W. Hicklin, brother.

Masters, Sarah B., WF, **d. 17 April** near McDowell of consumption, age, 39yrs.
   parents, Joseph & Sarah Jones. born Highland Co. occ.____.
  consort of Andrew M. Masters. info, A.M. Masters, husband.

Lamb, Catherine, WF, **d. 1 May** near McDowell of dropsy, age, 81yrs.
   parents, Nich^s & Mary Keys. born Hardy Co. occ.____.
  consort of John Lamb. info, John Lamb, son.

Michael, John Franklin, WM, **d. 25 April** at Bull Pasture Mt. of dyptheria,
  age, 4yrs. **parents, Peter & Eliz. Michael.** born Highland Co.
  occ. ____. unmarried. info, Peter Michael, father.

Pleasants, Sarah, CF, **d. 4 Jan** at Bull Pasture Mt. of consumption, age, 18yrs.
   parents, Anthony & Mahala Pleasants. born Highland Co.
  occ.____. unmarried. info, Anthony Pleasants, father.

Smith, Sidney, WF, **d. 7 Mar.** at West Va., Gilmer Co. of typhoid fever, age, 19yrs.
   parents, Jos. & Magdalene Smith. born Highland Co.
  occ.____. unmarried. info, Joseph Smith, father.

Reynolds, Alice Gray, WF, **d. 27 Aug** at Shas' Fork of dyptheria, age, 1yr.
   parents, Steph J. & Eliz. Reynolds. born Highland Co. occ.____.
  unmarried. info, Stephen J. Reynolds, father.

1871

Blue Grass Twp.

_____, **Betty**, CF, **d. 20 Feb.** on Back Creek of old age, age, 95yrs.
        parents, (not known). born (not known). occ. a servant, unmarried. info, James Erwin, son of former owner.

Not Named, WM, **d. 18 Nov.** at Crabbottom of (not known), age, 3dys.
        parents, Charles & ____ Folks. born Crabbottom. occ. ____. consort of Malvina*. info, Charles Folks, father.

Terry, Warwick, WM, **d. 20 Nov.** on E. B. Creek** of consumption, age, 45yrs.
        parents, James & Nancy Terry. born Bath Co. occ. a farmer consort of Carrie Terry. info, widow.

Not Named, WM, **d. 25 April** at Cr Bottom of (not known), age, 1yr.
        parents, Samuel & Nancy Grogg. born Crabbottom. occ. mechanic*** consort of ____. info, S. Grogg, father.

Carty, Jemima, WF, **d. 10 April** at Cr Bottom of old age, age, 71yrs.
        parents, (not known). born Crabbottom. occ. housewife. consort of Benjamin Carty. info, Cyrus Carty, son.

Stone, Joel, WM, **d. 25 Aug** at Cr. Bottom of typhoid fever, age, 20yrs.
        parents, Solomon & Mary Stone born Pendleton Co. occ. laborer, single. info, Solomon Stone, father

___, **Elizabeth**, WF, **d. 13 June** at Cr. Bottom of old age, age, 77yrs.
        parents, (unknown). born Augusta Co. occ. housewife. consort of Benjamin Swecker. info, Benjamin Swecker, husband.

Simmons, Margaret, WF, **d. 5 May** at Cr. Bottom of dropsy, age 89yrs, 2mos, 3dys.
        parents, (not known). born Augusta Co. occ. Housewife, consort of ____. info, William Simmons, son.

Flesher, Henry, WM, **d. 30 Nov.** at Cr. Bottom, of diebetes, age, 57yrs,0mos,7dys.
        parents, Benjamin Flesher & ____. born Pendleton Co. occ. farmer, husband of Nancy Flesher. info, Benjamin Varner, friend.

---

* almost certainly the name of deceased's mother.
** East Back Creek
*** almost certainly the occupation of deceased's father

Woods, John, WM, **d. 14 July** on E. B. Creek of flux, age,10mos.
        parents, Peter & Rachel Woods. born E. B. Creek.
        occ. farmer, consort of ____. info, Peter Woods, father.

White, John, WM, **d. 22 April** at Cr. Bottom of old age, age, 91yrs.
        parents, ____,& ____. born Augusta Co. occ. ____.
        husband of Susan White. info, Jacob White, son.

Monterey Twp.

Fleisher, Andrew, WM, **d. 24 June** on South Branch of disease of kidney, age 67yrs.
        parents, Henry & Catherine Fleisher. born Pendleton Co.
        occ. farmer, consort of Elizabeth Fleisher.
        info, Solomon Fleisher, son.

Gwin, Samuel, WM, **d. 24 July** on Jacksons River of consumption, age, 48yrs.
        parents, Jas. & Rachel Gwin. born Bath Co. occ. farmer.
        consort of Ellen Gwin. info, Ellen Gwin, wife.

Halterman, Joseph, WM, **d. ____Dec.** on Straight Creek of scarlet fever,
        age, 9mos,11dys. **parents, Geo. A. & Barbara J. Halterman.**
        born St. Creek. occ. ____, unmarried.
        info, Geo. A. Halterman, father.

Halterman, Jeremiah, WM, **d. ____Dec.** on Straight Creek of scarlet fever,
        age, 3yrs, 14dys. **parents, Geo. A. & Barbara J. Halterman.**
        born St. Creek. occ.____, unmarried.
        info, Geo. A. Halterman, father.

Smily, John W., WM, **d. 15 Sept.** near Monterey of cholera infantum, age, 1yr, 9mos.
        parents, Sarah A. Smily born near Monterey
        occ. ____, unmarried. info, Sarah A. Smily, mother.

Samples, Sarah, WF, **d. 12 July** on St. Creek of dropsy, age, 77yrs,1mo,7dys.
        parents, ____ & ____ Zickafoose. born Crabbottom. occ. ____,
        consort of John Samples. info, Elijah Samples, son.

Turner, Frances, WF, **d. 25 May** on Jacksons River of billious, age, 13yrs.
        parents, Mathias & Ann Turner. born Jacksons River
        occ. ____, unmarried. info, Mary Turner, grandmother.

Whitelaw, Lucy, WF, **d. 30 Oct.** in Monterey, of old age, age, 81yrs.
        parents, Rob't. & ____ Chewning. born Orange Co. occ.____,
        consort of Alexander Whitelaw. info, N. A. Whitelaw, son.

Stonewall Twp.

Armstrong, George, WM, **d. 27 March** on Bull Pasture Mt. of paralysis,
    age, 78yrs. **parents, John & Nancy Armstrong.**
    born Pendleton Co. occ. farmer. consort of Sarah Armstrong,
    info, Geo. W. Armstrong, son.

Armstrong, James A., WM, **d. 28 Oct.** on Bull Pasture Mt. of dyptheria, age 5yrs.
    parents, Allen & Eliz. Armstrong. born Highland Co.
    occ.____. unmarried. info, Allen Armstrong, father.

Armstrong, Sarina, WF, **d. 22 Dec.** on South Fork of consumption, age, 34yrs.
    parents, Phillip & Eliz. Varner. born Pendleton Co. occ. ____.
    consort of Jared M. Armstrong. info, Christine Botkin sister.

Blagg, Alberta F., WF, **d. 2 Sept.** near Doe Hill of acute dysentery, age, 3yrs.
    parents, James H. & Amanda J. Blagg. born Highland Co.
    occ. ____. unmarried. info, H.H. Jones, physician.

Dalton, Rachel, WF, **d. 25 Nov.** near Doe Hill of cancer of lung, age, 48yrs.
    parents, Jacob & Sarah Dalton. born Highland Co. occ.____.
    unmarried. info, H.H. Jones, physician.

Douglass, Martin, CM, **d. 25 Dec.** on Bull Pasture River of consumption,
    age, 30yrs. **parents, ____ & ____ Douglass.** born Botetort Co.
    occ. laborer. consort of Harriet Douglass.
    info, Elick Wilson, brother-in-law.

Gwin, Blackburn, WM, **d. 14 Dec.** on Cow Pasture River of rheumatism,
    age, 44yrs. **parents, Robt. & Eliz Gwin.** born Highland Co.
    occ. laborer. unmarried. info, John Friel, brother-in-law.

Hoover, Susan, WF, **d. 14 March** on South Fork of general debility, age, 82yrs.
    parents, ____ & ____. born Pendleton Co. occ.____.
    consort of ____. info, Eli Hoover, son.

Hiner, Susan Jane, WF, **d. 22 May** near Doe Hill of inflammation of brain,
    age, 7yrs. **parents, William & Eliz Hiner.** born Highland Co.,
    occ.____. unmarried. info, William Hiner, father.

Kirby, Rebecca, WF, **d. 3 July** on Bull Pasture River of (not known), age, 1yr,2mos.
    parents, ____ & Almira Kirby. born West Va. occ.____.
    unmarried. info, Jane Malcom, neighbor.

Malcom, James, WM, **d. 9 Jun.** on Bull Pasture River of chronic dysentery, age, 71yrs. **parents, Elick & ____ Malcom.** born Highland Co., occ. cooper. consort of Frances Malcom.
info, George Malcom, son.

Pullin, Martha, WF, **d. 17 Sept.** on Bull Pasture River of puer peral fever, age, 40yrs. **parents, Francis C. & ____ Dever.** born Rockingham Co. occ.____. consort of Balser H. Pullin
info, Henry B. Pullin, brother-in-law.

Stephenson, Clement, WM, **d. 20 July** on Cow Pasture River of pneumonia, age, 4yrs. **parents, Asgil & Virginia C. Stephenson.** born Highland Co. occ.____. consort of ____.
info, A.C. Stephenson, father.

Rusmisel, Malissa C., WF, **d. 21 Dec.** near Doe Hill of diptheria, age, 2yrs,6mos. **parents, John J. & Estalene Rusmisel.** born Highland Co. occ.____. consort of ____. info, John J. Rusmisel, father.

Rusmisel, Miami Augusta, WF, **d. 27 Dec.** near Doe Hill of diptheria, age, 1yr. **parents, John J. & Estalene Rusmisel.** born Highland Co. occ.____. consort of ____. info, John J. Rusmisel, father.

Reynolds, William H. H., WM, **d. 8 Nov.** on Shaws Fork of consumption, age, 26yrs. **parents, Stephen J. & Eliz. Reynolds.** born Highland Co., occ. farmer. unmarried. info, W. Scott Reynolds, brother.

Ranson, John, CM, **d. 3 Feb.** on Bull Pasture River of scrofula, age, 14yrs. **parents, John & Margaret Ranson.** born Highland Co. occ. laborer. unmarried. info, Henry Wilson, grandfather.

Rymer, Susan, CF, **d. 9 Nov.** on Cow Pasture River of consumption, age, 35yrs. **parents, Isrial & Rachel Minor.** born Highland Co. occ.____. consort of Anthony Rymer.
info, Anthony Rymer, husband.

Williams, Florence May, WF, **d. 4 June** on Bull Pasture River of pneumonia, age, 10mos. **parents, Thomas J. & Sarah J. Williams** born West Va. occ.____. consort of ____. info, Thomas J. Williams, father.

1872

Blue Grass Twp.

Wade, Elizabeth, WF, **d. 22 March** on Back Creek of dropsy, age, 40yrs. **parents, William Bird.** born Back Creek. occ.____. widow of Otho Wade, decd . info, William Bird, father.

Not Named, WF, **d. 10 Feb.** on Back Creek of (not known), age, 1mo,6 days. **parents, Charles & Mary Clendennen.** born Back Creek. occ.____. infant. info, John Clendennen, grandfather.

Gum, Abraham, WM, **d. 1 Oct.** on Back Creek of urinal affection, age, 76yrs. **parents, (not known).** born Back Creek. occ. farmer. husband of Mary Gum. info, Charles W. Gum, son.

Gay, James W., WM, **d. 20 May** on Head of Jacksons River of pneumonia, age, 63yrs. **parents, (not known).** born Bath Co. occ. farmer husband of Susan Gay. info, Susan Gay, widow.

Puffenbarger, Barsillis McNear, WM, **d. 9 Oct** on Allegheny Mt. of diptheria, age, 5yrs,9mos. **parents, Jonas & Sarah E. Puffenbarger.** born Allegheny Mt. occ.____. child. info, Joel Puffenbarger, uncle.

Puffenbarger, Birta Alice, WF, **d. 22 Sept.** on Allegheny Mt. of diptheria, age, 2yrs,10mos. **parents, Jonas & Sarah E. Puffenbarger.** born Allegheny Mt. occ.____. child. info, Joel Puffenbarger, uncle.

Snyder, Olive, WF, **d. 4 Dec.** at Crab Bottom of inflamation stomach, age, 2yrs. **parents, Calvin & Louisa Snyder.** born Crab Bottom. occ.____. child. info, David Snyder, grandfather.

Simmons, Margaret, WF, **d. 5 May** at Crab Bottom of dropsy, age, 89yrs,2mos. **parents, (not known).** born Crab Bottom. occ.____. widow. info, William Simmons, son.

Stonewall Twp.

Alexander, James Steele, WM, **d. 17 Feb.** on Bull Pasture River, of diptheria, age, 3yrs. **parents, J.W. & Nannie Alexander.** born Highland Co. occ.____. consort of ____. info, John W. Alexander, father.

Botkin, Martin V., WM, **d. Oct 27** on South Fork of epilepsy, age 30yrs.
    parents, Joseph & Margaret Botkin. born Highland Co.
    occ. miller. consort of Christina Botkin.
    info, Joseph Botkin, father.

Curry, Edward E., WM, **d. 19 April** on Bull Pasture River of rheumatism,
    age, 78yrs. **parents, James & Molly Curry.**
    born Highland Co. occ. wool carder. consort of ____.
    info, Joseph Alexander, neighbor.

Devericks, Rachel, WF, **d. 16 Feb.** on Shaws Fork of consumption, age, 36yrs.
    parents, James & Nancy Campbell. born Highland Co. occ.____.
    consort of A.P. Devericks. info, A.P. Devericks, husband.

Moyers, Sarah, WF, **d. 18 Oct.** on Bull Pasture River of insanity, age, 61yrs.
    parents, Martin & Sarah Moyers. born Highland Co. occ.____.
    unmarried. info, Saml. Moyers, brother.

Stuart, Charles, WM, **d. 14 May** on Bull Pasture River of general debility,
    age, 84yrs. **parents, Edward & ____ Stuart.** born Highland Co.
    occ. farmer. consort of (not known). info, E.J. Stuart, son.

Wilson, Presley, CM, **d. 13 Nov.** on Bull Pasture River of bronchitis, age, 9yrs.
    parents, Henry & Jane A. Wilson. born Highland Co. occ.____.
    consort of ____. info, Henry Wilson, father.

Wilson, Charles W., WM, **d. 13 June** on Bull Pasture River of consumption,
    age, 46yrs. **parents, William & Mary Wilson.**
    born Highland Co. occ. farmer. consort of Margaret Wilson.
    info, John B. Wilson, son.

Wooddell, John, WM, **d. 29 Jan.** on Bull Pasture River of rheumatism,
    age, 70yrs. **parents, John & Sarah Wooddell**
    born Augusta Co. occ. farmer. consort of Eliza Wooddell.
    info, Martha Wooddell, daughter.

Monterey Twp.

Grogg, Charles, WM, **d. ____Nov.** on St. Creek of dropsy, age, 3yrs,2mos.
    parents, James & Emily Grogg. born Highland Co. occ.____.
    consort of ____. info, Christian Puffenbarger, neighbor.

Jones, Gideon B., WM, **d. 30 Jan.** at Monterey of (unknown), age 2yrs.
    parents, Joseph & Sarah Jones. born Highland Co. occ.____.
    consort of ____. info, Joseph Jones, father.

Helmick, Thos. H., WM, **d. 15 March** on St. Creek of cold, age, 2mos,12dys.
        parents, Philip & Malinda Helmick. born Highland Co.
        occ.____. consort of ____. info, Philip Helmick, father.

1873

Blue Grass Twp.

Colaw, George, WM, **d. 9 Jan.** at Crabbottom of old age, age, 88yrs.
        parents, (not known). born Pennsylvania. occ. farmer.
        consort of Elizabeth. info, son.

Clendennen, Hulda, WF, **d. 15 Aug.** on Back Creek of worms, age, 10mos.
        parents, Charles Clendennen. born B. Creek. occ. farmer*.
        consort of Mary Clendennen. info, father.

Not Named, WF, **d. 15 July** on Back Creek of worms, age, 5mos.
        parents, John Gum. born B. Creek. occ. farmer*. info, father.

Gray, William C., WM, **d. 15 Nov.** at Cr. Bottom of diptheria, age, 4yrs.
        parents, James Gray. born Cr. Bottom. occ.____. info, father.

Hamilton, Charles, WM, **d. 6 Jan.** on B. Creek of old age, age, 85yrs.
        parents, ____. born B. Creek. occ. farmer. consort of ____.
        info, son.

Sutton, John H., WM, **d. 7 April** at Cr. Bottom of scarletina, age, 3yrs.
        parents, George M. Sutton. born Cr. Bottom. occ. farmer.*
        consort of Lucinda J. Sutton.** info, father.

Varner, Mary E., WF, **d. 10 Nov.** on B. Creek of hydrocephalus, age, 2mos.
        parents, Adam L. Varner. born B. Creek. occ.____. infant.
        info, father.

Waggoner, James M., WM, **d. 4 Mar.** at Cr. Bottom of fits, age, 1mo,14dys.
        parents, Iriah* Waggoner.** born C. Bottom. occ.____. infant.
        info, father.

Waggoner, Elener, WF, **d. 14 Jan.** at Cr. Bottom of cancer, age, 66yrs,3mos.
        parents, John & Margaret Beveridge. born C. Bottom. occ.____.
        wife of Sol. Waggoner. info, husband.

---

* almost certainly the occupation of deceased's father.
** consort of deceased's father.
*** Uriah?

Waggoner, Luella, WF, **d. 13 Jan.** at Cr. Bottom of ____. age, 2mos.
        parents, Isaac Waggoner. born C. Bottom. occ.____. infant.
        info, father.

Monterey Twp.

Hiner, Alexander, WM, **d. 10 May** on Jacksons River of typhoid pneumonia,
        age, 87yrs. **parents, John & Francis Hiner.** born Doe Hill,
        Highland Co. occ. farmer. consort of Harriett Hiner.
        info, John Hiner, son.

Helmick, Ida, WF, **d. 15 Aug.** on St. Creek of (not known), age, 3mos.
        parents, Philip & Malinda Helmick. born St. Creek. occ.____.
        consort of ____. info, Phillip Helmick, father.

Rymer, Amanda, WF, **d. 10 Nov.** on St. Creek of disease of throat, age, 27yrs.
        parents, Wm & Margaret Powers. born St. Creek. occ.
        housekeeper. consort of Thos. J. Rymer.
        info, Thos. J. Rymer, husband.

Stephenson, Hester R., WF, **d. 30 June** on Jacksons River of consumption,
        age, 55yrs. **parents, Robt. & Mary Gwin.** born Jacksons River.
        occ. housekeeper. consort of David Stephenson.
        info, David Stephenson, husband.

McClintic, Frank, CM, **d. 2 Nov.** on Jacksons River of (not known), age, 10yrs.
        parents, Leah McClintic. born Bath Co. occ.____. unmarried.
        info, David Stephenson, employer at time of death.

(Not Named), WF, **d. 10 Nov.** on St. Creek of (not known), age,1mo.
        parents, Jno. B. & Una Waggoner. born St. Creek, Highland Co.
        occ.____. unmarried. info, Jno. B.Waggoner, father.

Williams, Minnie F., WF, **d. ____ July** in Stonewall Twp. of pneumonia,
        age, 1yr, 2mos. **parents, Thos. J. & Sarah J. Williams.**
        born Stonewall Twp. occ.____. unmarried.
        info, Thos. J. Williams, father.

Stonewall Twp.

Hook, Robert S., WM, **d. 10 Aug.** on Cow Pasture River of information {sic}bowels,
        age, 80yrs. **parents, (not known).** born Rockingham Co.
        occ. farmer. single. info, J. M. Hook, son.

Harrouff, Susan Catherine, WM, **d. 1 Sept.** on Bull Pasture River of consumption, age, 30yrs. **parents, Noah & Susan Waggy.** born Augusta Co. occ. farmers wife. consort of C.H.Harrouff.
info, C. H. Harrouff, husband.

Godden, Mary, WF, **d. ____ July** at Crabbottom of consumption, age, 28yrs. **parents, Thomas & Sarah Jane Hilderbran.** born Rockingham Co. occ. farmer wife. consort of Isaac Godden.
info, Thomas Hilderbran, father.

_____, Roxanna, CF, **d. ____ Nov.** on Cow Pasture River of consumption, age, 22yrs. **parents, (not known by informant).** born Cow P. River. occ.____. single. info, Wm A.B. Gwin, friend.

Knisely, Arthur Lee, WM, **d. ____ May** at Doe Hill of scrofula, age, 15yrs. **parents, Susan S. & Geo. W. Knisely.** born Augusta Co. occ. farmer. single. info, Geo. W. Knisely, father.

Not Named, WF, **d. ____ Feb.** on Bull Pasture River of still born, age,____. **parents, Susan & Wm Lockridge.** born Bull Pasture River. consort of ____. info, Wm Lee Lockridge, father.

Masters, Wm Andrew, WM, **d. ____ Dec** on Allegheny Co., Jacksons River of accidental shooting, age, 23yrs. **parents, Martha & Frederick Masters** born Allegheny Co. occ. farmer. consort of Alan Masters*[sic]*.
info, Frederick Masters, father.

Propst, Geo. J., WM, **d. ____ Jan.** at Bull Pasture Mt. of croup & diptheria, age, 8yrs. **parents, Henry & Nancy Propst.** born Bull Pasture Mt. occ. farmer. single.
info, Henry Propst, father.

Stuart, David G., WM, **d. 13 Nov.** on Bull Pasture River of consumption, age, 24yrs, **parents, Jacob W. & Sinthia Ann Stuart.** born Bull Pasture River. occ. farmer. single.
info, Estaline Gladwell, sister.

Stuart, Wm. R., WM, **d. ____ Sept.** on Cow Pasture River of paralysis, age, 84yrs. **parents, James Stuart.** born Cow Pasture River. occ. farmer. single. info, Floyd Kincaid, son-in-law.

Stuart, Margaret, WF, **d. ____ Sept.** on Bull Pasture River of paralysis, age, 60yrs. **parents, Robert Malcomb.** born Bull Pasture River. occ. farmer's wife. consort of John B. Stuart.
info, James Stuart, son.

Siron, Jacob, WM, **d. ____ June** on Bull Pasture River of consumption, age, 73yrs.
        parents, John & Hester Siron. born Bull Pasture River.
        occ. farmer. consort of Levina Siron. info, Jacob Siron, son.

_____, Elizabeth Jane, CF, **d. ____ Mar.** on Bull Pasture River of dropsy, age, 11yrs.
        parents, Manda Wilson. born Bull Pasture River. occ.____.
        single. info, Henry Wilson, grandfather.

Wilson, Wm. Henry, WM, **d. ____ April** on Shaws Fork of pneumonia, age, 11mos.
        parents, John G. & Margaret H. Wilson. born Shaws Fork.
        occ. farmer's son. consort of ____.
        info, Margaret H. Wilson, mother.

1874

Blue Grass Twp.

Arbogast, Catherine, WF, **d. 15 Aug** at Crabbottom of diabetus, age, 57yrs.
        parents, (unknown). born Crabbottom. occ.____.
        consort of Levi Arbogast. info, Levi Arbogast, husband.

Campbell, Amos J., WM, **d. 8 Mar.** on Hd. J. River of pneumonia, age, 22yrs.
        parents, John & Sallie Campbell. born Hd Jac. River.
        occ. farmer. unmarried. info, John Campbell, father.

Clendennen, Hulda H., WF, **d. 8 Aug.** near Monterey of flux, age, 1yr.
        parents, Charles & Mary Clendennen. born B. Creek. occ.____.
        unmarried. info, Charles Clendennen, father.

Shrader, Martha, WF, **d. 8 Mar.** on Hd Jac River of consumption, age, 20yrs.
        parents, Jane Shrader. born Pendleton. occ.____.
        consort of ____. info, Jane Lightner, friend.

Not Named, WF, **d. 5 April** on B. Creek of still born, age, ____.
        parents, James K. & Georgia E. Campbell. born B. Creek.
        occ.____. consort of ____. info, James K. Campbell, friend{*sic*}.

Wade, John, WM, **d. 3 Feb.** on B. Creek of old age, age, 85yrs.
        parents, ____ & ____. born Bath Co. occ. farmer.
        consort of ____. info, Anson O. Wade, son.

Monterey Twp.

Botkin, Mary Susan, WF, **d. 15 Oct.** on Crab Run of dropsy, age, 23yrs. **parents, Robt. & Elizabeth Botkin.** born Crab Run. occ. housekeeper. unmarried. info, Robert Botkin father.

Gibson, Charles, WM, **d. 17 Feb.** at Vanderpool Gap of disease of brain, age, 2yrs. **parents, Jno. L. & Alice B. Gibson.** born Vanderpool Gap. occ.____. unmarried. info, John L. Gibson, father.

Helmick, Malinda, WF, **d. 23 Aug.** on St. Creek of childbirth, age, 40yrs. **parents, Henry & Catherine Peck.** born Pendleton Co. occ. housekeeper. consort of Philip Helmick. info, Philip Helmick, husband.

Pray, John, WM, **d. 10 Feb.** near Vanderpool Gap of old age, age, 93yrs. **parents, John & Elizabeth Pray.** born Staten Island, NY. occ. shoemaker. consort of Elizabeth Pray. info, Mahala Gwin, daughter.

Stephenson, ____, WM, **d. 25 Aug.** at Monterey of (not known), age, 21dys. **parents, L.H. & Mary L. Stephenson.** born Monterey. occ. none unmarried. info, L.H. Stephenson, father.

Wilson, Elizabeth, WF, **d. 14 May** at Monterey of hemorage and superindus by pregnancy, age, 33yrs,10mos,6dys. **parents, John & Elizabeth Whitmer.** born Rockbridge Baths. occ. housekeeper. consort of Osborne Wilson. info, Osborne Wilson, husband.

Stonewall Twp.

Armstrong, Rosa, WF, **d. 8 Aug.** on Bull Pasture Mt. of inflammation of brain, age, 1yr. **parents, Jno. E. & Barbara Armstrong.** born Highland Co. occ. ____. single. info, Jno. E. Armstrong, father.

Alexander, Henry E.E., WM, **d. 27 Feb.** on Bull Pasture River of spasms, age, 5yrs. **parents, Jno. W. & Nannie Alexander.** born Highland Co. occ.____. single. info, Jno. W. Alexander, father.

Blagg, Mary, WF, **d. 9 April** on Bull Pasture River of dropsy, age, 82yrs. **parents, Jno. & Mary Hiner.** born Pendleton Co. occ.____ consort of Jno. Blagg, Senr. info, James H. Blagg, son.

Botkin, Margaret, WF, **d. 24 Dec.** at Bull Pasture Mt. of inflamation of brain,
    age, 60yrs. **parents, Silas & Katy Sims.** born Pendleton Co.
    occ.____. consort of Joseph Botkin. info, Joseph Botkin, husband.

Holt, Mary E., WF, **d. 27 Nov.** on Bull Pasture River of burned, age, 8 mos.
    parents, Jno. E. & Martha I. Holt. born Highland Co.
    occ.____. unmarried. info, Jno. E. Holt, father.

Hamilton, Rebecca G., WF, **d. 2 Aug.** on Bull Pasture River of dropsy,
    age, 69yrs. **parents, Christopher & Jane Graham.**
    born Highland Co. occ.____. consort of Alexander Hamilton.
    info, James Wright, nephew.

Not Named, WM, **d. 24 Aug** on Shaws Fork of (not known), age, 1dy.
    parents, Chas. H. & Mary Marshall. born Highland Co.
    occ. ____. unmarried. info, Saml. M. Marshall, grandfather.

Malcom, Leona E., WF, **d. 15 Feb.** on Bull Pasture River of ____.
    age, 13yrs, 3mos, 23dys. **parents, Geo. W. & Jane Malcom.**
    born Highland Co. occ. ____ unmarried.
    info, Jane Malcom, mother.

Pleasants, Emily J., CF, **d. 4 July** on Bull Pasture Mt. of consumption, age, 5yrs.
    parents, Anthony & Venus Pleasants. born Highland Co.
    occ.____. unmarried. info, Anthony Pleasants, father.

Robinson, Magdalina E., WF, **d. 10 Aug.** on Dry Branch of cold, age, 17yrs.
    parents, Jesse & Alcinda Robinson. born Highland Co. occ.____.
    unmarried. info, P.H. Stuart, brother-in-law.

Tewning, Robt. E., WM, **d. 4 Nov.** on Bull Pasture Mt. of pneumonia,
    age, 2yrs, 4mos. **parents, Albert & Mary H. Tewning.**
    born Highland Co. occ. ____. unmarried.
    info, Albert Tewning, father.

Not Named, CM, **d. 14 July** on Bull Pasture River of (not known), age, 17dys.
    parents, Thomas & Lucy Wilson. born Highland. occ. ____.
    unmarried. info, Thomas Wilson, father.

Wilson, Mary Margaret, WF, **d. 7 May** on Bull Pasture River of dysentery,
    age, 2yrs. **parents, ERV & Susan Wilson.** born Highland Co.
    occ.____. unmarried. info, ERV Wilson, father.

Young, Ellen, CF, **d. 14 July** on Bull Pasture Mt. of consumption, age, 58yrs.
    parents, (not known). born (not known). occ. ____. unmarried.
    info, Anthony Pleasants, neighbor.

1875

Bird, Peter H., WM, **d. 4 April** on Back Creek of heart disease, age, 68yrs.
    parents, Jno. & Sarah Bird, born Bath Co., occ. farmer,
consort of Sophia Bird. info, James H. Bird, son-in-law.

Benson, Eddie, WM, **d. 24 Oct.** on St. Creek* of dyptheria, age, 9yrs.
    parents, W.W. & Ada Benson. born Highland Co. occ.____.
single, info, W.W. Benson, father.

Benson, Robert F., WM, **d. 27 Oct.** on St. Creek* of dyptheria, age, 5yrs.
    parents, W.W. & Ada Benson. born Highland Co. occ.____.
single. info, W.W. Benson, father.

Benson, Calvin Y., WM, **d. 8 Nov.** on St. Creek* of dyptheria, age, 7yrs.
    parents, W.W. & Ada Benson. born Highland Co., occ.____,
single, info, W.W. Benson, father.

Hicklin, July A., WF, **d. 6 Sep.** on Bullpasture River of dyspepsia, age 63yrs.
    parents, Nancy Pullin. born Bath Co. occ.____.
consort of Henry Hicklin. info, Stuart Hicklin, son.

Bird, William, Sr., WM, **d. 21 Nov.** on Back Creek of kidney disease, age, 79yrs.
    parents, Adam & Elizabeth Bird. born Bath Co. occ. farmer.
consort of ____ Bird. info, Valentine Bird, brother.

Not Named, WF, **d. ____ July** on Bull Pasture Mt. of inflammation of brain, age, 6 mos.
    parents, Benami & Mary Curry born Highland Co.
occ.____ single. info, Wm. R. Keister, friend.

Hiner, Joseph, WM, **d. 4 Aug.** on Bull Pasture River of cancer, age, 54yrs.
    parents, Jacob & Nancy Hiner born Pendleton Co.
occ. farmer. consort of Margt. Hiner. info, Margt. Hiner, widow.

Hidy, Sally, WF, **d. 30 July** on Bull Pasture River of childbirth, age, 30yrs.
    parents, Jno. & Elizabeth Sitlington born Pendleton Co.
occ. ____ consort of Henry C. Hidy. info, Robt. Sitlington, brother.

Hull, Minnie A., WF, **d. 30 Nov.** on St. Creek* of diphtheria, age, 5yrs.
    parents, Jacob N. & Eliza J. Hull born Highland Co., occ. ____
single. info, Jacob N. Hull, father.

---

* Strait Creek of Jacksons River

Hevener, Barbara, WF, **d. 8 June** at Crab Bottom of pirma,* age, 47yrs.
        parents, John & Elizabeth Snyder. born Pendleton Co.
        occ. ____. consort of William Hevener.
        info, Wm. Hevener, husband.

Gwin, Ann, WF, **d. 24 Nov.** on Jackson's River of dropsy, age, 60yrs.
        parents, James & Rachel Gwin. born Bath Co. occ. ____.
        single. info, Mahala Gwin, sister-in-law.

Malcom, Jane, WF, **d. 15 July** on Bull Pasture River of palpitation of the heart,
        age, 60yrs. **parents, James & Rachel Malcom.**
        born Pocahontas Co. occ. ____. single. info, Jas. A. Steuart, friend.

Metheney, John G., WM, **d. 18 May** on Back Creek of inflammation of the bowels,
        age, 46yrs. **parents, Levi & Mary Metheney.** born Bath Co.
        occ. farmer. consort of Mary J. Metheney.
        info, Mary J. Metheney, wife.

Metheney, James Cecil, WM, **d. 14 Sep.** at Monterey of diptheria, age, 6yrs.
        parents, Jacob C. & Elizabeth J. Metheney.
        born Monterey. occ. ____. single. info, Jacob C. Matheney, father.

Hiner, Elmipa E.V., WF, **d. 28 Aug.** on Dry Branch of accident, age, 9yrs.
        parents, Wm. & Mary Hiner. born Highland Co. occ. ____.
        single. info, Wm. Hiner, father.

Rexrode, Nicholas, WM, **d. 4 Mar.** on St. Creek of catarrh, age, 54yrs.
        parents, Conrad & Catherine Rexrode. born St. Creek.
        occ. farmer. consort of ____ Rexrode. info, ____ Rexrode, widow.

Suddarth, Susan, WF, **d. 3 April** at CrabBottom of heart disease, age, 30yrs.
        parents, James W. & Martha K. Seiver. born CrabBottom.
        occ. ____. consort of B. F. Suddarth. info, James W. Seiver, father.

Sommers, Wm. T., WM, **d. 26 Aug.** on Jackson's River of diptheria,
        age, 5yrs, 10mos. **parents, Wm. M. & Susan A. Sommers.**
        born McDowell. occ. ____. single. info, Wm. M. Sommers, father.

Sommers, Hatti, WF, **d. 29 Aug.** on Jackson's River of diptheria, age, 4yrs, 8mos.
        parents, Wm. M. & Susan A. Sommers. born McDowell.
        occ.____. single. info, Wm. M. Sommers, father.

---

* unknown malady

Slaven, Helen A., WF, **d. 14 Dec.** on St. Creek* of diptheria, age, 6yrs. **parents, J. B. & Mary H. Slaven.** born, Back Creek. occ. ____. single. info, Jesse B. Slaven, father.

Slaven, Lucy J., WF, **d. 25 Dec.** on St. Creek* of diptheria, age, 4yrs, 10mos. **parents, J. B. & Mary H. Slaven.** born, Jackson's River. occ. ____. single. info, Jesse B. Slaven, father.

Simmons, Wm. H., WM, **d. 17 Sep.** on St. Creek of diptheria, age, 1mo. **parents, Wm. G. & ____ Simmons.** born, St. Creek. occ.____. single. info, W. G. Simmons, father.

Whitelaw, Earnest J., WM, **d. 12 Aug.** at Monterey of diptheria, age, 4yrs. **parents, N. A. & Lucy H. Whitelaw.** born, Monterey. occ.____. single. info, N. A. Whitelaw, father.

Not Named, WF, **d. 12 June** on Jackson's River of diptheria, age,1mo,12dys. **parents, James M. & Sarah Woods.** born, Jackson's River. occ. ____. single. info, James M. Woods, father.

Wilson, Samuel, WM, **d. 29 July** on Shaw's Fork of old age, age, 84yrs. **parents, Wm. & Mary Wilson.** born, Shaw's Fork. occ. farmer. consort of ____Wilson. info, Samuel Wilson, son.

Wilson, Mary F., CF, **d. 24 Aug.** on Bull Pasture River of measils, age, 1mo. **parents, Theo & ____ Wilson.** born, Bull Pasture River. occ.____. single. info, ____, mother.

Jack, Barbara A., WF, **d. ____ June** on CrabBottom of sinal affections{sic}, age, 28yrs. **parents, John & Sarah Jack.** born, Pendleton Co. occ.____. single. info, Levi Jack, brother.

1876

Armstrong, Felix G., WM, **d. 27 April** on Bull Pasture Mt. of diarrhea, age, 2yrs,11mos,15dys. **parents, J. H. & Mary M. Armstrong.** born, Bull Pasture Mt. occ. ____. single. info, J. H. Armstrong, father.

---

* Straight Creek of Jacksons River.

Armstrong, Jared, WM, **d. 30 April** on Bull Pasture Mt. of diarrhea,
    age, 1yr,11mos. **parents, J. H. & Mary M. Armstrong**
    born, Bull Pasture Mt. occ. ____.single.
    info, J. H. Armstrong, father.

Bird, Valentine, WM, **d. 13 May** on Back Creek of accident, age, 71yrs,10mos,15dys.
    parents, Adam & Elizth. Bird. born, Bath Co. occ. farmer.
    married. info, S. R. Bird, son.

Botkin, Elizabeth, WF, **d. 20 Oct.** on South Fork of old age,
    age, 98yrs,5mos,4dys. **parents, not known.** born, Pennsylvania.
    occ. ____. married. info, J. A. Botkin, grandson.

Ball, Francis E., WF, **d. 19 Oct.** at Monterey of disease of lungs, age, 47yrs.
    parents, Geo. & Virginia Gordon. born, Staunton.
    occ. ____. married. info, A. R. Ball, husband.

Colaw, Catherine C., WF, **d. 9 Aug.** at CrabBottom of disease of heart,
    age, 37yrs,6mos,9dys. **parents, Geo. & Nancy Hammer.**
    born, Pendleton Co. occ. ____. married.
    info, A. J. Colaw, husband.

Davis, Phoebe, WF, **d. 5 Sep.** on Bull Pasture River of old age, age, 87yrs.
    parents, Paul Sommers. born, Pendleton Co. occ. ____.
    married. info, A. S. T. Davis, grandson.

Dabney, Nancy, CF, **d. ____ June** at CrabBottom of dropsy, age, 22yrs.
    parents, Thos. & Adaline Dabney. born, Rockbridge Co.
    occ. ____. single. info, Tho. Dabney, father.

Fox, John, WM, **d. 30 Dec.** at CrabBottom of old age, age, 88yrs.
    parents, Michael & ____ Fox. born, Pennsylvania. occ. farmer.
    married. info, Geo. W. Fox, grandson.

Gwin, John, WM, **d. 14 April** on Jacksons River of heart disease, age, 48yrs.
    parents, Jas. & Rachel Gwin. born, Bath co. occ. farmer.
    married. info, Nancy Gwin, widow.

Hidy, Catherine, WF, **d. 27 June** at Cr. Bottom of old age, age, 85yrs,10mos,5dys.
    parents, Adam & Ester Hull. born, Pendleton Co. occ.____.
    married. info, Jno. A. Hidy, son.

Not Named, WM, **d. 21 Nov.** at Cr. Bottom of not known, age, 4dys.
    parents, Jac. H. & Martha Hidy. born, Highland Co. occ.____.
    single. info, Jac. H. Hidy, father.

Hinegardner, M. J., WF, **d. 19 June** on Jacksons River of diabetis, age, 42yrs.
        parents, Eliz* & Nancy Wright. born, Bath Co. occ.____.
        married. info, H. B. Hinegardner, husband.

Hevener, Jacob, WM, **d. 3 July** on Jacksons River of diabetis, age, 86yrs.
        parents, Jac. & Catherine Hevener. born, Pendleton Co.
        occ. farmer. married. info, Geo. W. Hevener, son.

Hiner, Chas. D., WM, **d. 20 Oct.** at Big Valley of brain fever, age, 4yrs, 17dys.
        parents, U** & Sarah V. Hiner. born, Highland Co.
        occ. ____. single. info, U. B. Hiner, father.

Howdyshell, Jno. D., WM, **d. 16 June** on Jacksons River of spasms, age, 19yrs.
        parents, Jno. H. & Biddy Howdyshell. born, Highland Co.
        occ. ____. single. info, S. A. Howdyshell, sister.

Judy, Amanda J., WF, **d. 16 Sep.** at CrabBottom of ____, age, 27yrs.
        parents, Jac. & Eliz. White. born, Highland Co. occ. ____.
        married. info, Allen Judy, husband.

Jackson, Lou A., CF, **d. 22 May** on Cow Pasture River of whooping cough, age, 3yrs.
        parents, Albert & Mary Jackson. born, Highland Co. occ. ____.
        single. info, Albert Jackson, father.

Jackson, Whalen, CM, **d. 15 May** on Cow Pasture River of whooping cough, age, 1yr.
        parents, Albert & Mary Jackson. born, Highland Co. occ.____.
        single. info, Albert Jackson, father.

Not Named, CM, **d. 1 Aug.** on Cow Pasture River of fits, age, 9dys.
        parents, Albert & Mary Jackson. born, Highland Co. occ.____.
        single. info, Albert Jackson, father.

Kincaid, Elizabeth H., WF, **d. 15 May** on Cow Pasture River of consumption,
        age, 34yrs. **parents, Jno. & Mary McClung.** born, Bath Co.
        occ.____. married. info, W. C. Kincaid, husband.

Kincaid, Perry L., WF, **d. 6 Dec.** on Cow Pasture River of brain fever, age, 11yrs.
        parents, W. C. & Elizth. H. Kincaid. born, Highland Co.
        occ.____.single. info, W. C. Kincaid, father.

Not Named, WM, **d. 29 Sep.** on Cow Pasture River of heart disease, age, 9dys.
        parents, H. H. & Cynthia H. Kincaid. born, Highland Co.
        occ. ____. single. info, D. N. Kincaid, grandfather.

---

* Elisha Wright, male.
** Uriah

Lockridge, Nancy, WF, **d. 5 June** on Bull Pasture River of pneumonia, age, 42yrs. **parents, Peter & Elizth Burns.** born, Bath Co. occ. ____. married. info, Wm. Lockridge, husband.

Lowry, Wm., WM, **d. 28 Oct.** on Jackson's River of not known, age, 71yrs. **parents, Wm. & Sarah Lowry.** born, Bath Co. occ. mechanic. married. info, Mary Lowry, widow.

Marshall, Wm., WM, **d. 25 Aug.** at CrabBottom of dropsy, age, 79yrs. **parents, ____ & ____ Marshall.** born, Hampshire Co. occ. mechanic. married. info, W. W. Marshall, son.

McClung, Ada W., WF, **d. 20 April** on Bull Pasture River of not known, age, 1yr, 5mos. **parents, L. M. & Sue E. McClung.** born, Highland Co. occ. ____. single. info, Sue E. McClung, mother.

Marshall, Maude, WF, **d. 25 July** at CrabBottom of chicken pox, age, 1yr,9mos. **parents, F. J. & Elizth. H. Marshall.** born, Highland Co. occ.____. single. info, F. J. Marshall, father.

Newman, Sarah E., WF, **d. 10 Dec.** at CrabBottom of consumption, age, 31yrs. **parents, Geo. & Margt. Rymer.** born, Pendleton Co. occ.____. married. info, P. T. Newman, husband.

Robinson, Martha J., WF, **d. 29 May** in Big Valley of brain fever, age, 9yrs,3mos. **parents, Mary A. Robinson.** born, Highland Co. occ.____. consort of ____. info, Mary A. Robinson, mother.

Simmons, William, WM, **d. 10 May** at Cr. Bottom of flux, age, 62yrs. **parents, Mark & Sarah Simmons.** born, Pendleton Co. occ. farmer. married. info, Mark Simmons, son.

Wills, W. W., WM, **d. 9 April** at Cr. Bottom of not known, age, 68yrs. **parents, ____ & ____ Wills.** born, Shenandoah Co. occ. tailor. married. info, ____ Wills, wife.

Wright, L. D. C., WM, **d. 4 April** in Big Valley of not known, age, 8yrs. **parents, A. T. & S. A. Wright.** born, Highland Co. occ. ____. consort of ____. info, A. T. Wright, father.

Wright, L. G., WF, **d. 5 July** in Big Valley of whooping cough, age, 2yrs, 10mos. **parents, A. T. & S. A. Wright.** born, Highland Co. occ. ____. consort of ____. info, A. T. Wright, father.

Wright, J. R. L., CM, **d. 21 Aug.** on Bull Pasture River of pneumonia, age, 4yrs. **parents, Allie Wright.** born, Highland Co. occ. ____. consort of ____. info, James Wright, friend.

Not Named, WM, **d. 17 April** at McDowell of hemorrhage, age, 12dys. **parents, A. L. & M. C. Varner.** born, Highland Co. occ. ____. consort of ____. info, A. L. Varner, father.

Not Named, WM, **d. 1 May** on Bull Pasture River of pneumonia, age, 5mos. **parents, Jno. N. & Virginia Eagle.** born, Highland Co. occ. ____. consort of ____. info, Jno. N. Eagle, father.

Not Named, WM, **d. 25 Mar.** on Bull Pasture Mt. of not known, age, 4mos. **parents, Christ. & Sarah Simmons.** born, Highland Co. occ.____. consort of ____. info, Christian Simmons, father.

Shiplett, Cora B., WF, **d. 25 July** on Bull Pasture River of whooping cough, age, 3mos. **parents, Jno. M. & ____ Shiplett.** born, Highland Co. occ. ____. consort of ____. info, Jno. M. Shiplett, father.

Hull, Amanda E., WF, **d. 2 Mar.** on Jackon's River of unknown, age, 23yrs. **parents, Solomon & Nellie Rexrode.** born, Highland Co. occ. ____.consort of ____. info, W. C. Hull, husband.

1877

Not Named, WM, **d. 18 April** on Bull Pasture Mt. of not known, age, 1dy. **parents, Wm. H. & S. J. Armstrong.** born, Bull Pasture Mt. occ. none. consort of ____. info, S. J. Armstrong, mother.

Briscoe, Jacob, WM, **d. 27 Mar.** on Back Creek of not known, age, 74yrs. **parents, Isaac & Priscilla.** born, Bath Co. occ. farmer. married. info, Priscilla Briscoe, sister.

Byrd, Julia A., WF, **d. 29 Nov.** on Back Creek of consumption, age, 34yrs. **parents, Jas. & Martha Black.** born, Augusta Co. occ. ____. married. info, F. M. Bird, husband.

Beverage, Sallie, WF, **d. 11 Feb.** at Hightown of consumption, age, 34yrs. **parents, Frank & Susan McCluster.** born, Pendleton Co. occ. ____.married. info, Wesley Beverage, husband.

Carver, F. H., WM, **d. 25 Sep.** at Monterey of diabetes, age, 54yrs,1mo.
        parents, Joseph & Martha S. born Goochland Co.
        occ. mechanic. married. info, Nancy F. Carver, widow.

Devericks, William, WM, **d. 30 Mar.** on Shaw's Fork of not known, age, 74yrs.
        parents, not known. born South Fork. occ. farmer. married.
        info, Wm. M. Devericks, grandson.

Not Named, WM, **21 Oct.** on Bull Pasture River of not known, age, 1 dy.
        parents, A. S. T. & E. J. Davis. born Bull Pasture River.
        occ. ____.consort of ____. info, A. S. T. Davis, father.

Harding, James A., WM, **d. 14 Feb.** at Crabbottom of softening of brain, age, 64yrs.
        parents, William & Mary. born Faquier Co. occ. physician.
        married. info, E. J. Harding, widow.

Harrow, Nancy G., WF, **d. 2 Sep.** on Jackson's River of not known, age, 50yrs.
        parents, William & Martha Griffen. born Jackson's River.
        occ.____. married. info, Wm. Griffen, father.

Middleton, Leonidas, WM, **d. 6 Nov.** at Crabbottom of not known, age, 13dys.
        parents, Hezekiah & Ellen. born Crabbottom. occ.____.
        consort of ____. info, Benj. Varner, uncle.

Marshall, Saml. M., WM, **d. 9 Jan.** on Shaw's Fork of pneumonia, age, 65yrs.
        parents, John & Elizabeth. born Augusta Co. occ. farmer.
        married. info, John L. Marshall, son.

Ralston, Urania, WF, **d. 29 Sep.** on Back Creek of not known, age, 26yrs, 2 mos.
        parents, Joseph & Ardenia Vint. born Pendleton Co. occ.____.
        married. info, S. R. M. Ralston, husband.

Rexrode, Elizabeth, WF, **d. 8 Mar.** at Hightown of old age, age, 85yrs.
        parents, Michael & Elizabeth Fox. born Maryland. occ. ____.
        married. info, J. M. Rexrode, son.

Rymer, Anthony, CM, **d. 30 Sep.** on Cow Pas River of not known, age, 56yrs.
        parents, not known. born not known. occ. farmer. married.
        info, Sarah Gwin, no relation.

Seiver, James W., WM, **d. 11 April** at New Hampden of diabetes, age, 59yrs, 11mos.
        parents, Frederick & Margaret. born Shenandoah Co.
        occ. tailor. married. info, Martha R. Seiver, widow.

Sipe, Maggie S., WF, **d. 21 June** at Monterey of inflamed bowels, age, 2 yrs, 6mos.
  parents, William A. & Mary A. born Strait Creek. occ.____.
  consort of ____. info, Wm. A. Sipe, father.

Simmons, Charles J., WM, **d. 1 Mar.** on Bull Pasture Mt. of not known, age, 3 mos.
  parents, Christian & Sally born Bull Pasture Mt. occ. ____.
  consort of ____. info, Christian Simmons, father.

Not Named, CF, **d. 3 May** on Bull Pasture River of not known, age, 3dys.
  parents, John & Mary Scott. born Bull Pasture River. occ.____.
  consort of ____. info, James Wright, no relation.

Wilson, Jane, WF, **d. 19 April** on Shaw's Fork of not known, age, 72yrs.
  parents, Wm. & Jane Malcomb. born Kentucky. occ. ____.
  married. info, Lucinda Devericks, daughter.

Not named, WM, **d. 15 Nov.** on Middle Mt. of not known, age, 15 dys.
  parents, N. & Ellen Waybright. born Middle Mt. occ.____.
  consort of ____. info, Geo. W. Waybright, uncle.

1878

Alexander, Nannie S., WF, **d. 1 Dec.** near McDowell of heart disease, age, 46yrs.
  parents, Robt. & Nancy Sitlington. born Highland Co.
  occ. housekeeping. consort of Jno. W. Alexander.
  info, Jno. W. Alexander, husband.

Armstrong, Samuel E., WM, **d. 30 Aug.** on Shaw's Fork of inflammation of bowels,
  age, 74yrs. **parents, not known,** born Pendleton Co. occ. farmer.
  consort of ____ Armstrong. Info, Wm. H. Armstrong, son.

Bishop, Mary, WF, **d. 1 Oct.** on Bull Pasture River of consumption, age, 15yrs.
  parents, John & Sarah Bishop. born Highland Co. occ. ____.
  single. info, Lewis M. McClung, neighbor.

Fox, Margaret, WF, **d. 12 Nov.** on Back Creek of consumption, age, 34yrs.
  parents, Abraham & Mary Wade. born Highland Co. occ. ____.
  consort of A. H. Fox info, A. H. Fox, husband.

Hull, ____, WF, **d. 21 Sep.** on Jacksons River of not known, age, 1dy.
  parents, Cyrus S. & Ellen Hull. born Highland Co. occ. ____.
  consort of ____. info, C. S. Hull, father.

Hevener, N. B., WF, **d. 14 May** at CrabBottom of not known, age, 37yrs.
parents, George & Sarah Mullenax. born Highland Co. occ. __.
consort of Jacob P. Hevener. info, Jac. P. Hevener, father*{sic}*.

Kinkead, Cora, WF, **d. 15 Mar.** on Bull Pasture Mt. of brain fever, age, 7mos.
parents, Robt. A. & Theresa Kinkead. born Highland Co.
single. info, R. A. Kinkead, father.

Mauzy, James C., WM, **d. 17 July** at CrabBottom of cholera infantum,
age, 10mos,19dys. **parents, Geo. W. & Emma J. Mauzy.**
born Highland Co. occ. ___. single. info, Emma J. Mauzy, mother.

Metheny, Lizzie J., WF, **d. 1 Feb.** at Monterey of not known, age, 35yrs.
parents, Jas. H. & Alice Byrd. born Highland Co. occ.____.
consort of J. C. Metheny. info, J. C. Metheny, husband.

Mackey, Wm. H., WM, **d. 26 Sep.** on Jacksons River of poison adm. by self, age, 39yrs.
parents, Henry & Nancy Mackey. born Rockbridge Co.
occ. physician. consort of Mary M. Mackey.
info, M. M. Mackey, wife.

Nicholas, Sarah, WF, **d. 28 Dec.** at CrabBottom of not known, age, 73yrs.
parents, Catherine & Francis Nicholas. born Pendleton Co.
occ. ____. single. info, Henry Nicholas, brother.

Nicholas, Wally C., WM, **d. 23 Dec.** at CrabBotton of cold, age,15dys.
parents, H. B. & ____ Nicholas. born Highland Co. occ. ____.
single. info, Eliz'th J. Nicholas, grandmother.

Norman, Ella, WF, **d. 15 June** on Bull Pasture River of not known, age, 62yrs.
parents, not known. born North Carolina. occ. ____.
consort of Henry Norman. info, L. M. McClung, neighbor.

Pritt, Charlotte S., WF, **d. 27 Feb.** on Jacksons River of pneumonia,
age, 2yrs, 4 mos. **parents, Jno. C. & Almira Pritt.**
born Highland Co. occ. ____. single. info, Jno. C. Pritt, father.

Rivercomb, George, WM, **d. 31 Nov.***{sic}* on Bull Pasture River of not known,
age, 87yrs. **parents, ____ & ____ Rivercomb.** born Bath Co.
occ. farmer. consort of ____ Rivercomb.
info, Jno. A. Bonner, son-in-law.

Rexrode, Edna, WF, **d. 9 April** on Crab Run of not known, age, 1yr,11mos.
parents, Geo. K. & Sarah J. Rexrode. born Highland Co.
occ.____. single. info, G. K. Rexrode, father.

Slaven, Reuben, WM, **d. 6 Nov.** at Meadowdale of pneumonia, age, 83yrs.
        parents, Steuart & Isabella Slaven. born Pendleton Co.
        occ. farmer. consort of Elizabeth Slaven. info, S. C. Slaven, son.

Stephenson, David, WM, **d. 21 Feb.** on Jacksons River of consumption, age, 71yrs.
        parents, John & Jane Stephenson. born Bath Co. occ. farmer.
        widower. info, A. F. Stephenson, son.

Snyder, Willie G., WM, **d. 4 Oct.** at CrabBottom of diphtheria, age, 8yrs.
        parents, James L. & Jennie Snyder. born Highland Co.
        occ.____. single. info, J. L. Snyder, father.

Varner, Jacob, WM, **d. 26 Dec.** on Bull Pasture Mt. of inflammation of the brain,
        age, 41yrs. **parents, Henry & ____ Varner.** born unknown,
        occ. laborer. consort of Luthenia Varner. info, ____, daughter.

Wilfong, Matilda, WF, **d. 5 April** on Allegheny Mt. of consumption, age, 40yrs.
        parents, Emmanuel & Charlotte Wilfong. born Pendleton Co.
        occ.____. single. info, D. Wilfong, cousin.

1879

Beverage, Amanda, WF, **d. 16 Aug.** on Straight Creek of consumption, age, 33yrs.
        parents, Addison & Frances Ralston. born Highland Co.
        occ. housekeeping. consort of Jno. Beverage, Jr.
        info, Jno. Beverage, husband.

Crummett, Pollie, WF, **d. 15 July** on Fleisher's Draft of dropsy, age, 72yrs.
        parents, unknown. born Pendleton Co. occ. ____.
        consort of Jas. Crummett. info, Geo. O. Fleisher, friend.

Caricoff, R. J., WF, **d. 21 Nov.** near McDowell of acute bronchitis,
        age, 43yrs, 4mos. **parents, unknown.** born Pendleton Co. occ.
        housekeeping. consort of L. A. Caricoff.
        info, L. L. Quidore, physician.

Carter, G. W., CM, **d. 29 Nov.** near McDowell of acute bronchitis, age, ____.
        parents, unknown. born unknown. occ. laborer.
        consort of Maria Carter. info, L. L. Quidore, physician.

Dear, Wellington, Jr., WM, **d. 13 Oct.** at New Hampden of gaestro intestinal, age, 7mos,15dys. **parents, W. W. & Anna Dear.** born New Hampden. occ.____. consort of ____. info, Dr. W. W. Dear, father.

Fleisher, Sarah Rebecca, WF, **d. 6 July** at Monterey of epilepsy, age, 27yrs. **parents, A. H. & Rachel Fleisher.** born Highland Co. occ. ____. unmarried. info, Amanda Campbell, sister.

Johnson, Nancy J., WF, **d. 17 Oct.** on Bull Pasture River of peritonitis, age, 33yrs. **parents, Jno. & Nancy Siron.** born Pendleton Co. occ. housekeeping. consort of James Johnson. info, H. H. Jones, physician.

Kiracoff, Mary E., WF, **d. 7 Dec.** near Doe Hill of consumption, age, 44yrs. **parents, Jno. L. & ____ Blackemore.** born Augusta Co. occ. housekeeping. consort of Benj. I. Kiracoff. info, H. H. Jones, physician.

Layne, Joseph, WM, **d. ____** near McDowell of malignant tumor, age, ____. **parents, ____ & ____.** born ____. occ. farmer. consort of Polly Layne. info, L. L. Quidore, physician.

Not Named, CM, **d. 9 May** on Back Creek of unknown, age, 1 ½ dys. **parents, Henry & Emaline Lewis.** born Back Creek. occ.____. consort of ____. info, Ellen Lewis, grandmother.

Matheny, Margt.,* WF, **d. 26 Feb.** at Monterey of general debility, age, 79yrs. **parents, John Bird.** born Bath Co. occ. ____. widow. info, J. C. Matheny, son.

Michael, Mary Hester, WF, **d. 6 April** on Bull Pasture Mt. of unknown. age, 15yrs. **parents, David & Martha Michael.** born unknown. occ. ____. consort of ____. info, Martha Michael, mother.

Michael, Jared, WM, **d. 20 April** on Bull Pasture Mt. of diphtheria, age, 4yrs. **parents, David & Martha Michael.** born Bull Pasture Mt. occ. ____. consort of ____. info, H. H. Jones, physician.

Not Named, WM, **d. 24 May** on Bull Pasture River of unknown, age, 2dys. **parents, M. V. & Elizabeth Malcom.** born Bull Pasture River. occ. ____. consort of ____. info, M. V. Malcom, father.

---

*entered on original 1881 list.

Pullin, Maggie L., WF, **d. 21 June** on Jacksons River of pneumonia, age, 10yrs. **parents, J. H. & Susan Pullin.** born Jacksons River. occ.____. consort of ____. info, J. H. Pullin, father.

Ralston, Indiana F., WF, **d. 22 Sep.** on Bull Pasture River of diphtheria, age, 8yrs. **parents, Jno. & ____ Ralston.** born B. P. R. occ.____. consort of ____. info, L. L. Quidore, physician.

Somers, Wm. W., WM, **d. 5 Nov.** on Jacksons River of paralysis, age, 47yrs. **parents, Sam'l & Susan Somers.** born Shenandoah Co. occ. farmer. consort of Agnes Somers. info, Aggie Somers, wife.

Slaven, Gracie Dare, WF, **d. 4 Feb.** at Vanderpool of brain fever, age, 6yrs. **parents, Jesse & Mary Slaven.** born Meadow Dale. occ. ____. consort of ____. info, Jesse Slaven, father.

Steuart, Mary S., WF, **d. 16 Aug.** on Bull Pasture River of heart disease, age, 38yrs. **parents, Jesse & Lucinda Robinson.** born Bull Pasture River. occ. housekeeping. consort of P. H. Steuart. info, P. H. Steuart, husband.

Smith, Susan, WF, **d. 20 Oct.** on Bull pasture River of diphtheria, age, 12yrs. **parents, unknown.** born unknown. occ. ____. consort of ____. info, H. H. Jones, physician.

Stephenson, Augustus T., WM, **d. 18 Aug.** on Jacksons River of laudanum, age, 19mos. **parents, A. T. & G.E. Stephenson.** born Jacksons River occ. ____. consort of ____. info, A. T. Stephenson, father.

Stephenson, Georgie E., WF, **d. 26 May** on Jacksons River of unknown, age, 38yrs. **parents, S. C. & E. M. Shelton.** born Albemarle Co. occ. housekeeping. consort of A. T. Stephenson. info, A. T. Stephenson, husband.

Simmons, Martha E., WF, **d. 4 Sep.** on Jacksons River of scrofula, age, 3mos. **parents, Jno. S. & Betty Simmons.** born Jacksons River. occ. ____. consort of ____. info, Jno. S. Simmons, father.

Varner, Mary, WF, **d. 11 April** on Bull Pasture Mt. of diphtheria, age, 15yrs. **parents, Wm. & Sarah Varner.** born unknown. occ.____. unmarried. info, D. Michael, neighbor.

Vance Jennie, WF, **d. 1 Sep.** on Shenandoah Mt. of diphtheria, age, 11yrs. **parents, W. H. & Helen Vance.** born Bull Pasture River. occ. ____. consort of ____. info, Helen Vance, mother.

Waybright, Susan, WF, **d. 12 Sep** at New Hampden of apoplexy, age, 55yrs.
       parents, unknown. born, unknown. occ. housekeeping.
       consort of Peter Waybright. info, W. W. Dear, physician.

Wilfong, Elias Sr., WM, **d. 30 July** on Allegheny Mt. of kidney disease, age, 71yrs.
       parents, Henry & Elizabeth Wilfong. born, Pendleton Co.
       occ. farmer. consort of Sabina Wilfong.
       info, Sabina Wilfong, wife.

Weeks, Jno. H., WM, **d. 27 April** at Monterey of kidney disease, age, 59yrs.
       parents, unknown. born, Rockbridge Co. occ. laborer.
       consort of Nancy Weeks. info, G. W. Snyder, son-in-law.

Wimer, Rumsey Smithson, WM, **d. 22 Oct.** at CrabBottom of unknown,
       age, 4mos. **parents, Susan & C. Wimer.** born, CrabBottom.
       occ.____. consort of ____. info, C. Wimer, father.

Wright, Corda J., WF, **d. 26 Nov.** on Jacksons River of whooping cough, age, 8yrs.
       parents, A. L. & Susan Wright born, Jacksons River.
       occ.____ consort of ____. info, A. L. Wright, father.

Wilson, Sam'l. Boyd, WM, **d. 18 June** on Bull Pasture River of pneumonia,
       age, 7mos. **parents, A. E. & Margaret A. Wilson.**
       born, near Doe Hill. occ. ____. consort of ____.
       info, A. E. Wilson, father.

1880

Armstrong, Caroline, WF, **d. 10 May** on B. P. Mt.** of puerperal convulsions,
       age, 27yrs,10mos. **parents, David & Leah Simmons.**
       born, Pendleton Co. occ. housekeeping.
       consort of A. H. Armstrong. info, H. H. Jones, physician.

Benson, George H., WM, **d. 4 Jan.** on C. P. R.*** of disease of the kidneys,
       age, 65yrs. **parents, Hamilton & Elizabeth Benson.**
       born, Cow Pasture R. occ. farmer. widower.
       info, Geo. H. Steuart, son-in-law.

Botkin, Robert, WM, **d. 1 June** at Monterey of pneumonia, age, 68yrs.
       parents, ____ & ____ Botkin. born, C. Pasture R. occ. farmer.
       consort of Elizabeth Bodkin. info, W. W. Bodkin, son.

** Bull Pasture Mountain
*** Cow Pasture River

Campbell, Mary, WF, **d. 5 April** on Back Creek of heart disease, age, 64yrs. **parents, Jas. & Elizabeth McGuffin.** born, Warm Springs. occ. housekeeper. consort of W. M. Campbell. info, J. N. Campbell, son.

Corrigan, Caroline, WF, **d. 26 Aug.** on Jacksons River of croup, age, 1yr,1mo. **parents, Jas. & Amanda Corrigan.** born, Jacksons River. occ. ____. consort of ____. info, Malinda Houlihan, aunt.

Curry, John, WM, **d. 29 Feb.** on Back Creek of pneumonia, age, 69*yrs. **parents, Adam & Phoebe Curry.** born, Back Creek. occ. farmer. widower. info, F. A. Doyle, grandson.

Clendenen, Mary E., WF, **d. 11 July** at Green Hill of childbirth, age 33yrs. **parents, Geo. & ____ Bird.** born, Back Creek Valley. occ. housekeeper. consort of Jac. F. Clendenen. info, Jac. F. Clendenen, husband.

Chew, Lavina, WF, **d. ____** at CrabBottom of apoplexy, age, 74yrs. **parents, Henry & Elizabeth Arbogast.** born, CrabBottom. occ. housekeeper. widow. info, W.W. Dear, physician.

Doyle, ____, WM, **d. 12 Sep.** on Jacksons River of croup, age, 24dys. **parents, Geo. W. & Sarah J. Doyle.** born, Jacksons R. occ. none. consort of ____. info, Geo. W. Doyle, father.

Eagle, ____, WM, **d. 8 Dec.** at Doe Hill of thrush, age, 15dys. **parents, S. C. & Martha J. Eagle.** born, Doe Hill. occ. none. consort of ____. info, S. C. Eagle, father.

Ervin, Edward, WM, **d. 8 Nov.** on Back Creek of pneumonia, age, 69yrs. **parents, Robt. & Naomi Ervin.** born, Back Creek. occ. farmer. consort of Eliza Ervin. info, Geo. W. Ervin, son.

Ervin, John W., WM, **d. 8 June** on B. P. Mt. of consumption, age, 25yrs. **parents, Wm. & Elizabeth Ervin.** born, B. P. Mt. occ. farmer. consort of Margaret Ervin. info, Robt. N. Ervin, brother.

Folks, Valentine, WM, **d. 10 Oct.** on Dry Branch of hemorragh of the lungs, age, 55yrs,7mos. **parents, Geo. & Margt. Folks.** born, Crab Bottom. occ. farmer. consort of Mary Folks. info, Nancy J. Folks, sister-in-law.

---

* the age, 69 is crossed out in the original.

Fox, W. H., WM, **d. 19 April** at Crab Bottom of __, age, 64yrs, 3mos.
parents, Isaac & ____ Fox. born, Bath Co. occ. farmer.
consort of Margaret Folks. info, Chas. H. Folks, son.

Fleisher, Solomon, WM, **d. 24 Jan.** at Forks of the Water of epilepsy, age, 50yrs.
parents, Andrew & Elizabeth Fleisher. born, Highland Co.
occ. farmer. consort of Eliza J. Fleisher.
info, A. H. Fleisher, cousin.

Gilbert, Huggard, CM, **d. ____ Feb.** on B. P. River of pneumonia, age, 50yrs.
parents, ____ & ____ Gilbert. born, B. P. River. occ. laborer.
consort of Fannie. info, R. Sitlington, neighbor.

Gum, Adam L., WM, **d. 9 Jan.** on Back Creek of typhoid pneumonia, age, 59yrs.
parents, Otho & Eliz. Gum. born, Back Creek. occ. farmer.
consort of Sallie Gum. info, Sallie Gum, wife.

Hamilton, Dan'l. C., WM, **d. 22 April** on B. P. River of inflammation of bowels,
age, 58yrs, 6mos. **parents, Chas. & ____ Hamilton.** born,
Back Creek. occ. farmer. consort of Margt. R. Hamilton.
info, T. A. Hamilton, son.

Hicklin, James C., WM, **d. 18 Mar.** on B. P. River of stricture of the bladder,
age, 74yrs. **parents, Geo. & Eliz. Hicklin.** born, B. P. R.
occ. farmer. consort of Malinda Hicklin.
info, Jesse H. Hicklin, son.

Hicklin, Viola J., WF, **d. 4 July** on B. P. River of flux, age,15mos.
parents, Jno. S. & Martha Hicklin. born, B. P. R. occ. none.
consort of ____. info, Jno. S. Hicklin, father.

Hupman, Pollie, WF, **d. 30 Dec.** on C. P. R. of epilepsy, age, 78yrs.
parents, James & Margt. Steuart. born, C. P. R.
occ. housekeeper. widow. info, P. H. Hupman, son.

Hevener, Luemma V., WF, **d. 5 May** at Crab Bottom of consumption, age, 18yrs.
parents, Jos. & Millie Hevener. born, Crab Bottom.
occ. housekeeper. unmarried. info, Jos. Hevener, father.

Hansel, Benami, WM, **d. 18 Nov.** at Crab Bottom of hemorraghe of the bladder,
age, 71yrs,* **parents, Chas. & Martha Hansel.** born, Bath Co.
occ. farmer. consort of Mary Hansel.
info, Jno. S. Newman, son-in-law.

---

*date is struck through--may have been altered from 75 to 71yrs.

Kinkead, Peter H., WM, **d. 23 Jan.** at Crab Bottom of pneumonia, age 78yrs.
        parents, Thos. & Mary Kinkead. born, Bath Co.,
occ. farmer. consort of Nancy J. Kinkead.
info, F.H.H. Kinkead, son.

Kayser, Henry, CM, **d.** ____ at Crab Bottom of pneumonia, age, 70yrs.
        parents, ____ **&** ____ **Kayser.** born, ____. occ. laborer.
consort of Jane Kayser. info, W.W. Dear, physician.

Minor, Allen, CM, **d. 11 Dec.** at Cow P. R. of dropsy, age, 80yrs.
        parents, unkown. born, C. P. R. occ. laborer. widower.
info, Fred Minor, son.

McClung, ____, CM, **d. 15 July** at Crab Bottom of unknown, age, 5 dys.
        parents, Morrison & Sally McClung. born, Crab Bottom
occ. ____. consort of ____. info, Morrison McClung, father.

Mullenax, Winnie F., WF, **d. 12 July** at Crab Bottom of puerperal convulsions,
        age, 42yrs, 4mos. **parents, Aaron &** ____ **Calhoun.**
born, North Fork. occ. housekeeper.
consort of Edward Mullenax. info, W. W. Dear, physician.

Malcom, Walter, WM, **d. 10 Jan.** on B. P. R. of tonsillitis, age, 10yrs.
        parents, Geo. & Jane Malcom. born, B. P. R. occ. none.
consort of ____. info, L. L. Quidore, physician.

Puffenbarger, ____, WF, **d. 24 May** at Hightown of unknown, age, 3dys.
        parents, ____ **& Naomi Puffenbarger.** born, ____.
occ. ____. consort of ___. info, Jno. E. Gum, neighbor.

Rexrode, Nellie, WF, **d. 20 June** at New Hampden of gastroenteritis, age, 60 yrs.
        parents, Thos. & Anne Rymer. born, North Fork. occ.
housekeeper. consort of Solomon Rexrode. info, W. W. Dear,
physician.

Steuart, Robt. A., WM, **d.** ____ on B. P. River of paralysis, age 75yrs.
        parents, James & Margaret Steuart. born, C. P. River.
occ. Quack Doctor. divorced widower.
info, H. H. Jones, physician.

Stanton, James, CM, **d. 1 June** on C. P. River of unknown, age, 85yrs.
        parents, ____ **&** ____. born, C. P. River. occ. laborer.
consort of Mary Stanton. info, P. H. Hupman, neighbor.

Smith, Rebecca, WF, **d. 1 Mar.** on B. P. Mt. of dyspepsia, age, 70yrs.
    parents, ____ **Woods.** born, B. P. Mt. occ. housekeeper.
    widow. info, Delilah Michael, neighbor.

Smith, Malinda, WF, **d. 2 Feb.** on B. P. Mt. of unknown, age, 40yrs.
    parents, ____ **&** ____ **Smith.** born, B. P. Mt. occ. domestic.
    unmarried. info, H. H. Jones, physician.

Stone, Malinda, WF, **d.** ____ on Back Creek of unknown, age, ____.
    parents, Solomon & Fannie Stone. born, Crab Bottom.
    occ. domestic. unmarried. info, Mrs. H. M. Tomlinson, neighbor.

Sloat, A. H., WM, **d. 27 Mar.** at McDowell of heart clot, age, ____.
    parents, ____ **&** ____ **Sloat.** born, Illinois. occ. professor.
    widower. info, L. L. Quidore, physician.

Terry, Eli Orten, WM, **d. 20 June** in Big Valley of typhoid fever, age, 1yr,2mos.
    parents, Hy M. & Eliz. M. Terry. born Big Valley. occ. none.
    consort of ____. info, Hy M. Terry, father.

Taylor, Wm. H., WM, **d. 25 Nov.** on B. P. River of consumption, age, 29yrs.
    parents, ____ **& Betsy Varner.** born, Pendleton Co. occ. laborer.
    consort of Fannie Taylor. info, Henry Varner, step father.

Trimble, William, WM, **d. 9 Mar.** in Steam Valley of fever, age, 62yrs.
    parents, James & Catherine Trimble. born St. Creek.
    occ. farmer. consort of Mary J. Trimble.
    info, Mary J. Trimble, wife.

Wright, Nancy, WF, **d. 19 July** in Big Valley of flux, age, 101yrs.
    parents, Robt. Wright & ____ **Wiley.** born, Augusta Co.
    occ. domestic. unmarried. info, A. T. Wright, grandson.

Wise, Michael, WM, **d. 25 July** on Jacksons River of paralyzed in throat, age, 80yrs.
    parents, Jehu & ____ **Wise.** born, Staunton. occ. farmer. widower
    info, A. B. McClintic, son-in-law.

Wilson, ____, WM, **d. 1 Aug.** on Shaw's Fork of unknown, age, 1 mo.
    parents, Jonathan & Maggie Wilson. born, Shaw's Fork.
    occ. ____. consort of ____. info, Jonathan Wilson, father.

Wade, ____, WM, **d. 6 July** at Green Hill of croup, age, 2mos, 1 dy.
    parents, Howard & Mary A. Wade. born, Green Hill. occ. ____.
    consort of ____. info, Howard Wade, father.

Wade, Mariah, WF, **d. 16 Dec.** at Green Hill of consumption, age, 29yrs,
   parents, Valentine & Hester Bird. born, Green Hill.
   occ. housekeeper. consort of Wm. Boon Wade.
   info, Abraham Wade, father-in-law.

Waybright, John, WM, **d. 12 Dec.** at Crab Bottom of pneumonia, age, 1yr,2mos.
   parents, D. J. & Molly Waybright. born, Crab Bottom. occ. ____
   consort of ____. info, W. W. Dear, physician.

Waybright, Viola, WF, **d. 10 May** at Crab Bottom of inflammation of the bowels,
   age, 3mos. **parents, S. S. & Jennie Waybright.** born,
   Crab Bottom. occ. ____. consort of ____. info, Sam'l. S.
   Waybright, father.

Wimer, ____, WM, **d. 20 Jan.** at New Hampden, of ____, age, 1 dy.
   parents, Jos. & Sally Wimer. born, Crab Bottom. occ. ____.
   consort of ____. info, Jos. Wimer, father.

Wooddell, Mary, WF, **d. ____.** at B. P. Mt. of disease of the heart, age, ____.
   parents, ____ & ____. born, B. P. Mt. occ. housekeeper.
   consort of Wm. Wooddell. info, H. H. Jones, physician.

1881

Campbell, William M., WM, **d. 4 April** in B. C. Valley of apoplexy, age, ____.
   parents, Alex & Margt. Campbell. born, Back Creek.
   occ. farmer. widower. info, Filmore T. Campbell, son.

Ervine, William B., WM, **d. 10 Oct.** on Back Creek of consumption, age 28yrs.
   parents, Benj. & Nancy Ervine. born Back Creek.
   occ. farmer. single. info, John B. Ervin, brother.

Folks, ____, WF, **d. 27 May** on Dry Branch of ____, age, ____.
   parents, J.L. & Harriett M. Folks. born Dry Branch. occ. ____.
   consort of ____. info, Jasper L. Folks, father.

Fleisher, Sarah, WF, **d. 19 Sep.** on St. Creek of old age, age, 89yrs.
   parents, Adam & ____ Hull. born St. Creek. occ. domestic.
   widow. info, Jacob Seybert, son-in-law.

Gum, Pollie, WF, **d. 25 Dec.** on Back Creek of consumption, age 76yrs.
   parents, Leonard & Anna Gum. born Back Creek. occ. domestic.
   consort of Abraham Gum. info, H. M. Tomlinson, neighbor.

Gwin, Nancy, WF, **d. ____ Oct.** on Jackson's River of abscess on lungs, age, 40yrs.
    parents, James McLaughlin. born Jackson's River. occ. domestic. widow. info, Jno. L. Gibson, neighbor.

Hite, Susan, WF, **d. ____ April** in Big Valley of pneumonia, age 40yrs.
    parents, Peter & Sophia Bird. born, Green Hill. occ. domestic. consort of Allen Hite. info, N. A. Buzzard, neighbor.

Helms, Jane, WF, **d. 26 Feb.** on B. P. River of pneumonia, age, 76yrs.
    parents, Robt. & Eliza Carlisle. born B. P. River. occ. domestic. widow. info, J. W. Helms, son.

Hiner, William, WM, **d. 12 Mar.** on Dry Branch of heart disease, age, 70yrs, 4mos.
    parents, Alex & May Hiner. born ____. occ. farmer. consort of Mary A. Hiner. info, S. Brown Hiner, son.

Hite, George W., WM, **d. 16 Feb.** on Jackson's River of pneumonia, age, 56yrs.
    parents, Isaac & Mary Hite. born, Bath Co. occ. farmer. consort of Cecilia Hite. info, Cecilia Hite, wife.

Kelley, Eliza J., WF, **d. 11 Mar.** in Big Valley of consumption, age, 39yrs.
    parents, John & Elizabeth Waugh. born Big Valley. occ. farmer. widow. info, Chas. E. Kelley, son.

Karicofe, Maria Jane, WF, **d. ____ Sep.** at Doe Hill of consumption, age, 18yrs.
    parents, B. I. & Mary Karicofe. born Doe Hill. occ.____. single. info, Benj. I. Karicofe, father.

Kinkead, F. H. H., WM, **d. 23 July** at Crab Bottom of heart disease, age, 25yrs.
    parents, P. H. & Nancy J. Kinkead. born Crab Bottom. occ. farmer. single. info, S. W. Sterrett, brother-in-law.

Long, Annie, B. B., WF, **d. 20 Nov.** at Monterey of scrofula, age, 3yrs, 7mos, 10dys.
    parents, James C. & Eliza. M. Long. born Monterey. occ.____ single. info, James C. Long, father.

Lewis, Jesse, CM, **d. 22 May** in B. C. Valley of unknown, age, 56yrs.
    parents, ____ & Frankie Lewis. born Back Creek. occ. laborer. consort of Ellen Lewis. Info, Ellen Lewis, wife.

Miller, ____, CF, **d. 4 Oct.** on B. P. River of ____, age, ____.
    parents, Wm. & Agnes Miller. born B. P. River. occ. ___. consort of ____. info, Wm. Miller, father.

Pullin, Jane, WF, **d.** ____ on B. P. River of unknown, age, 70yrs.
      parents, Thos. & ____ Pullin. born B. P. River. occ. ____.
single. info, J. H. Pullin, cousin.

Revercomb, Susan R., WF, **d. 30 Jan.** on B. P. River of unknown, age, 11yrs.
      parents, John R. & Susan Revercomb. born B. P. River.
occ. ____. single. info, John R. Revercomb, father.

Reed, ____, WF, **d.** ____ on Jackson's River of ____ age, ____.
      parents, John W, & Mahala Reed. born Jackson's River.
occ. ____ consort of ____. info, ____.

Simmons, Luella, WF, **d. 13 April** near Monterey of diphtheria, age, 1yr, 1mon.
      parents, John & Eliza. Simmons. born near Monterey.
occ. ____.consort of ____. info, John S. Simmons, father.

Seybert, John W., WM, **d. 31 Dec.** at Crab Bottom of ____, age, 39yrs.
      parents, And. & Eliza. Seybert. born ____. occ. clerk. single.
info, Sam'l Sullenberger, uncle.

Varner, William H., WM, **d.** ____ June on B. P. Mt. of diphtheria age, 12yrs.
      parents, Wm. H. & M. Varner. born B. P. Mt. occ. ____.
single. info, Wm. H. Varner, father.

Varner, Daniel, WM, **d. 12 May** near Monterey of diabetes, age, 74yrs.
      parents, Peter & Annie Varner. born near Monterey. occ. farmer.
consort of Margt. Varner. info, John A. Varner, son.

Varner, Margt., WF, **d. 29 Oct.** near Monterey of ____, age, 70yrs, 8mos, 29dys.
      parents, John & Susan Lunsford. born ____. occ. domestic.
widow. info, John A. Varner, son.

Woods, Sarah, WF, **d. 18 Nov.** on Jackson's River of unknown, age, 39yrs.
      parents, John & Susan Wiley. born Jackson's River.
occ. domestic. consort of James Wood.
info, James M. Woods, husband.

Wade, Joseph G., WM, **d. 15 Aug.** on Back Creek of epilepsy, age, 12yrs, 11mos,15dys.
      parents, Abraham & Nancy Wade. born Back Creek. occ. ____
consort of ____. info, Abraham Wade, father.

1882

Allen, Reese, WM, **d.** ____ Oct. at Monterey of diabetes, age, 27yrs.
      parents, Rob & ____ Allen. born Highland Co. occ. laborer.
unmarried. info, J. M. Rexrode, uncle.

Benson, Chas. H., WM, **d. ____ Feb.** on Cow Pasture R. of pneumonia, age, 25yrs.
    parents, Geo. H. & Margt. Benson. born Highland Co.
    occ. laborer. unmarried. info, W. L. C. Benson, uncle.

Botkin Chas., WM, **d. ____** on Bull P. Mt. of unknown, age, ____.
    parents, Jos. & Margt. Botkin. born Highland. Co. occ. farmer.
    consort of Sarah J. Botkin. info, Jos. Botkin father.

Botkin, ____, WF, **d. ____** on Bull P. Mt. of unknown, age, ____.
    parents, Chas. & Sarah J. Botkin. born Highland Co. occ. ____
    consort of ____. info, Jos. Botkin, grandfather.

Campbell, John, WM, **d. ____** in Steam Valley of ____, age, ____.
    parents, Alex.& Margt. Campbell. born Highland Co.
    occ. farmer, consort of Sally Campbell.
    info, H. M. Patterson, son-in-law.

Campbell, Rachel, WF, **d. 26 Sep.** in Big Valley of cancer of the throat, age, 86yrs.
    parents, Arthur & ____ Grimes. born Pocahontas Co. occ. ____.
    widow. info, J. A. Buzzard, son.

Doyle, Sallie, WF, **d. 25 Oct.** on J. River of cancer of the breast, age, 50yrs.
    parents, Michael & Ann Doyle. born Highland Co. occ. ____.
    widow. info, Jas. Corrigan, neighbor.

Doyle, Ann, WF, **d. ____ May** on J. River of dropsey, age, 70yrs.
    parents, Jno. & Ann Sproul. born Highland Co. occ. ____.
    widow. info, Jas. Corrigan, neighbor.

Eye, Elizabeth, WF, **d. 25 April** on St. Creek of cancer of the liver, age, 59yrs.
    parents, Christian & Leah Rexrode. born Highland Co.
    occ. ____ consort of Henry Eye.
    info, Emmanuel Prospt, son-in-law.

Eye, Curtis Deve, WM, **d. 14 Aug.** at C. Bottom of chronic diarrhea, age, 2mos,7dys.
    parents, S. H. & Caroline Eye. born Highland Co. occ. ____.
    consort of ____. info, S. H. Eye, father.

Eye, Cora Susan, WF, **d. 7 Aug.** at C. Bottom of chronic diarrhea, age, 1yr, 2mos.
    parents, S. H. & Caroline Eye. born Highland Co. occ. ____.
    consort of ____. info, S. H. Eye, father.

---

* Jackson's River

Fleisher, Elizabeth, WF, **d. 12 Nov.** on South Branch of apoplexy. age, 78yrs.
   parents, ____ & ____ **Vandevender.** born Highland Co.
   occ. ____. widow. info, Orion Fleisher, grandson.

Gardner, Catherine, WF, **d.** ____ **Oct.** on J. River of consumption age, 55yrs.
   parents, Rudolph & Mary Fry. born Highland Co.
   occ.____ widow. info, Frank Gardner, son.

Gibson, Lillie W., WF, **d. 10 Jan.** at Vanderpool of scarlet fever age, 2yrs, 7mos.
   parents, John L. & Alice M. Gibson. born Highland Co.
   occ. ____. consort of ____. info, John L. Gibson, father.

Gwin, W. A. B., WM, **d. 17 May** on Cow Pasture R. of bronchitis age, 61yrs.
   parents, Moses & Elizabeth Gwin. born Highland Co.
   occ. farmer. consort of Rachel Gwin. info, F. N. Gwin, son.

Graham, Geo. W., WM, **d. 25 July** on Head of J. River of consumption age, 70yrs.
   parents, ____ & ____ **Graham.** born, Highland co. occ. farmer.
   widower. info, N. B. Woods, nephew.

Galford, James, WM, **d. 21 Mar.** on E. B. Creek* of consumption age, 29yrs.
   parents, Wm. & Jane Galford. born Pocahontas Co. occ. farmer.
   single. info, Nancy Kirkpatrick, aunt.

Gum, Alice, WF, **d. 22 Sep.** at Hightown of pneumonia age, 69yrs.
   parents, Roger & Alice Gum. born Highland Co. occ. ____.
   consort of McBride Gum. info, O. H. Gum, son.

Hiner, Bernie Gay, WF, **d. 18 Dec.** on J. River of scarlet fever age, 1yr, 9mos.
   parents, Benj. F. & Mary E. Hiner. born Highland Co.
   occ. ____. consort of ____. info, Mary E. Hiner, mother.

Hevener, Catherine, WF, **d. 27 Nov.** at C. Bottom of unknown age, 32yrs.
   parents, Adam & Mary Folks. born Highland Co. occ.____.
   consort of J. G. Hevener. info, J. G. Hevener, husband.

Hevener, Ellen, WF, **d. 20 Feb.** at C. Bottom of of unknown age, 92yrs.
   parents, ____ & ____ **Hiner.** born Pendleton Co. occ. ____.
   widow. info, J. G. Hevener, grandson.

Hevener, ____, WF, **d.** ____ **June** at C. Bottom of inflammation of the head age, 2mos.
   parents, J. P. & Phoebe Hevener. born Highland Co. occ. ____.
   consort of ____. info, J. P. Hevener, father.

---

*East Back Creek

Hidy, ____, WF, **d. ____ July** at New Hampden of inflammation of the bowels age, 10mos. **parents, J. H. & Martha Hidy.** born Highland Co. occ. ____.consort of ____. info, J. H. Hidy, father.

Hiner, ____, WM, **d. 20 Sep.** at Crab Bottom of unknown age, ____. **parents, B. & Mary Hiner.** born Highland Co. occ. ____. consort of ____. info, B. Hiner, father.

Hiner, U. B., WM, **d. ____ June** at Monterey of cerebro spinal meningitis age, 45yrs. **parents, Wm. & ____ Hiner.** born Highland Co. occ. farmer. consort of Virginia Hiner. info, Virginia Hiner, wife.

Helmick, ____, WM, **d. 31 Mar.** on St. Creek of unknown age, ____. **parents, ____ & ____ Helmick.** born Highland Co. occ. farmer. consort of unknown. info, Sam Varner, grandson.

Jones, Henry C., WM, **d. 15 Oct.** on Cow Pasture R. of apoplexy age, 57yrs. **parents, Thos. & Mary Jones.** born Highland Co. occ. farmer. consort of Victoria Jones. info, Jno. M. Jones, son.

Jones, Martha O., WF, **d. 25 Dec.** at Doe Hill of inflamm' of the bowels age, 4yrs. **parents, Dr. H. H. & Jemima Jones.** born Highland Co. occ.____ consort of ____. info, Dr. Jones, father.

Kelly, Eliza, WF, **d. 11 Mar.** in Big Valley of consumption age, ____. **parents, Jno. & Eliz. Ratcliff.** born Highland Co. occ. ____. widow. info, Jno. A. Kelley, son.

Karicofe, Marietta, WF, **d. 30 Nov.** at Doe Hill of membranous croup age, 9yrs. **parents, B.I. & Elvira Karicofe.** born Highland Co. occ. ____. consort of ____. info, B. I. Karicofe, father.

Lamb, ____, WF, **d. ____** on St. Creek of unknown age, 1 dy. **parents, Nathaniel & Malinda Lamb.** born Highland Co. occ.____. consort of ____. info, Nathaniel Lamb, father.

Lamb, ____, WF, **d. ____** on St. Creek of unknown age, 2 dys. **parents, Nathaniel & Malinda Lamb.** born Highland Co. occ. ____. consort of ____. info, Nathaniel Lamb, father.

Lamb, John, WM, **d. 5 Jan.** on B. P. River of apoplexy age, 73yrs. **parents, Jno. & Catherine Lamb.** born Highland Co. occ. farmer. consort of Eliza J. Lamb. info, B. H. Pullin, neighbor.

Lightner, Adam, WM, **d. 7 July** in B.C. Valley of consumption age, 74yrs, 3 mos. **parents, Adam & Susan Lightner.** born Highland Co. occ. farmer. consort of Ellen Lightner. info, Anthony Lightner, son.

Mauzy, Willis Whitfield, WM, **d. 30 Nov.** at New Hampden of diphtheria age, 3yrs, 3mos, 18dys. **parents, Geo. W. & Emma J. Mauzy.** born Highland Co. occ. ____. consort of ____. info, Geo. W. Mauzy, father.

Malcom, Georgie, WF, **d. ____ June** on Bull Pasture R. of bronchitis age, 16yrs. **parents, Geo. W. & Jane Malcom.** born, Highland Co. occ.____. consort of ____. info, Geo. W. Malcom, father.

Mauzy, ____, WF, **d. ____ July** at Crab Bottom of unknown age, ____. **parents, M. C. & Georgie Mauzy.** born Highland Co. occ. ____. consort of ____. info, M. C. Mauzy, father.

Malcom, Lewis H., WM, **d. ____ Feb.** at Crab Bottom of diabetes age, 17yrs. **parents, Walter & Sarah Malcom.** born Highland Co. occ. ____. consort of ____. info, Geo. W. Malcom, father.

Nicholas, Robt., WM, **d. 8 April** at Crab Bottom of diabetes age, 15yrs, 2mos. **parents, Sol & Eliza J. Nicholas.** born, Highland Co. occ.____. consort of ____. info, Geo. A. Nicholas, brother.

Newman, ____, WM, **d. __ Dec.** at Crab Bottom of unknown age, ____. **parents, Salisbury & Phoebe Newman.** born Crab Bottom. occ.____. consort of ____. info, S. Newman, father.

Pleasants, Anthony, CM, **d. 28 Feb.** at McDowell of general debility age, 72yrs. **parents, ____ & ____ Pleasants.** born ____. occ. laborer. widower. info, Charlie Pleasants, neighbor.

Pruitt, Bishop Marvin, WM, **d. 27 Dec.** on J. River of scarlet fever age, 4yrs, 5mos, 4dys. **parents, Jas. C. & Almira Pruitt.** born Jackson's River. occ. carpenter.*[sic]* consort of ____. info, Jas. C. Pruitt, father.

Patterson, Edna, WF, **d. 12 Aug.** at Monterey of ____ age, ____. **parents, Hy M. & E. J. Patterson.** born Monterey. occ. ____. consort of ____ info, H. M. Patterson, father.

---

* almost certainly the occupation of the father.

Reed, James P., WM, **d. 14 Nov.** on Jackson's River of pneumonia age, 66yrs. **parents, Alex. & ____ Reed.** born Bath Co. occ. none. consort of Margt. Reed. info, Susan Turner, neighbor.

Rexrode, Catherine, WF, **d. 18 Feb.** at Hightown of pneumonia age, 55yrs. **parents, Jno. & Catherine Cook.** born Bath Co. occ.____. consort of Jno. M. Rexrode. info, Jno. M. Rexrode, husband.

Seybert, Zeb., WM, **d. ____** at Crab Bottom of cancer age, 70yrs. **parents, ____ & ____ Seybert.** born Bath Co. occ. none. single. info, Jno. Waybright, neighbor.

Swecker, Ambrose, WM, **d. ____ Nov.** at Crab Bottom of cerebro spinal meningitis age, 61 yrs. **parents, Benj. & Betsy Swecker.** born Bath Co. occ. farmer. consort of Polly Swecker. info, Polly Swecker, wife.

Steuart, Coleman, CM, **d. 27 June** at McDowell of unknown age, ____. **parents, Sam'l & Nancy Steuart.** born McDowell. occ. ____. consort of ____. info, Sam'l. Steuart, father.

Steuart, Catherine, WF, **d. 20 June** on B. P. River of unknown age, 7 dys. **parents, Robt. E. & Almira Steuart.** born B. P. River. occ. ____ consort of ____. info, Robt. E. Steuart, father.

Snyder, William D. WM, **d. 27 Aug.** at Crab Bottom of worms age, 2 yrs. 6 mos. **parents, C. C. & Louisa Snyder.** born Crab Bottom. occ. ____. consort of ____. info, C. C. Snyder, father.

Splaun, Marg't, WF, **d. 20 Nov.** on Shaw's Fork of diphtheria age, 17yrs. **parents, Dan'l & M. J. Splaun.** born Augusta Co. occ. ____. consort of ____. info, Daniel Splaun, father.

Varner, John A., WM, **d. ____ Nov.** at Monterey of diabetis age, 48yrs. **parents, Dan'l & Marg't Varner.** born Highland Co. occ. farmer. consort of ____. info, Sam'l Varner, cousin.

Varner, Mary R., WF, **d. ____ Dec.** at Crab Bottom of scrofula age, 11 mos, 16 dys. **parents, Benj. & C. Varner.** born Crab Bottom. occ. ____ consort of ____. info, Benj. Varner, father.

Waybright, Ben, WM, **d ____ April** at Crab Bottom of epilepsy age, 45yrs. **parents, Wm. & Pollie Waybright.** born Crab Bottom. occ. ____. single. info, Jno. Waybright, brother.

Woods, Mary, WF, **d. 17 April** at Hightown of pneumonia age, 72yrs.
   parents, ____ **&** ____ **Graham.** born, unknown. occ. ____.
   widow. info, N. B. Woods, son.

Wilfong, Willie P., WM, **d. 17 Dec.** at Hightown of diphtheria age, 5yrs.
   parents, Jonas & Caroline Wilfong. born Hightown. occ. ____.
   consort of ____. info, Jonas Wilfong, father.

Wilfong, Robt. L., WM, **d. 19 Dec** at Hightown of diphtheria age, 11yrs.
   parents, Jonas & Caroline Wilfong. born Hightown. occ. ____.
   consort of ____. info, Jonas Wilfong, father.

Wilfong, Walter A., WM, **d. 21 Dec.** at Hightown of diphtheria age, 8yrs.
   parents, Jonas & Caroline Wilfong. born Hightown. occ. ____.
   consort of ____. info, Jonas Wilfong, father.

Wooden, Jonathan, WM, **d. 22 April** on St. Creek of unknown age, 80yrs.
   parents, ____ **&** ____ **Wooden.** born unknown. occ. none.
   widower. info, J. B. Waggoner, neighbor.

Waggy, Michie B., WF, **d. 21 Dec.** at Doe Hill of unknown age, 19yrs.
   parents, ____ **&** ____ **Waggy.** born St. Creek. occ. ____.
   single. info, Dr. H. H. Jones, physician.

1883

Armstrong, Abel H., WM, **d. 19 Oct.** on Bull Past. Mt. of cancer of the neck age, ____.
   parents, Jared & Agnes Armstrong. born Pendleton Co.
   occ. farmer. consort of Mary Armstrong.
   info, Jas. C. Armstrong, son.

Armstrong, ____, WM, **d. 7 Mar.** on Bull Past. Mt. of ____ age, ____.
   parents, W. H. & Susan Armstrong. born Highland Co.
   occ. ____. consort of ____. info, W. H. Armstrong, father.

Beverage, Annie M., WF, **d. 12 Mar.** on St. Creek of infl. of stomach, age, 3yrs 6mos.
   parents, Jas. C. & Frances Beverage. born Highland Co.
   occ. ____. consort of ____. info, Jas. C. Beverage, father.

Beathe, Jos. A., WM, **d. 18 Aug.** on Crab Run of dyspepsia age, 64yrs.
   parents, Jas. & Mary Beathe. born Highland Co. occ. shoemaker.
   bachelor. info, S. P. Beathe, brother.

Bryant, Clarence R., WM, **d. 22 Oct.** at McDowell of quenzy, age, 5yrs.
parents, H. E. & Mary F. Bryant. born Highland Co.
occ. ____.consort of ____. info, H. E. Bryant, father.

Bucher, David O., WM, **d. 21 Nov.** at Doe Hill of bronchial pneumonia
age, 1yr, 3mos. **parents, J. D. & E. A. Bucher.** born Highland Co.
occ. ____. consort of ____. info, J. D. Bucher, father.

Campbell, ____, WF, **d. 7 Mar.** at Monterey of ____ age, 2mos, 14dys.
parents, W. P. & R. Gertrude Campbell. born Highland Co.
occ.____. consort of ____. info, W. P. Campbell, father.

Campbell, Sam'l B., WM, **d. 26 Nov.** at Head of J. River of kidney disease age, 74yrs.
parents, Alex & Margt Campbell. born Pendleton Co.
occ. farmer. consort of Isabel. info, Rollin Campbell, son.

Crummett, Mary H., WF, **d. 20 Mar.** on Spring Run of dropsy age, 45yrs.
parents, Sampson Jordan & Nancy Michael. born Highland Co.
occ. domestic. consort of Wm. L. Crummett. info, W. L. Crummett, husband.

Devericks, Allen P., WM, **d. 4 Dec.** on Cow Pasture R. of dropsy age, ____.
parents, Jno. & Margt. Devericks. born Highland Co. occ. teacher. consort of Louisa. info, W. M. Douglas, brother.

Eye, Cora S., WF, **d. 11 Aug.** at New Hampden of infantum age, 6mos.
parents, S. H. & C. V. Eye. born Highland Co. occ. ____.
consort of ____. info, S. H. Eye, father.

Eye, Custie D., WF, **d. 15 Aug.** at New Hampden of infantum age, 6mos. 3dys.
parents, S. H. & C. V. Eye. born Highland Co. occ. ____.
consort of ____. info, S. H. Eye, father.

Ervine, Azinia V., WF, **d. 28 June** at McDowell of inflammation of the B.* age, ____.
parents, Aug. & Louisa Ervine. born Highland Co. occ. ____.
consort of ____. info, Aug. Ervine, father.

Evick, Sallie C., WF, **d. 21 Dec** at McDowell of typhoid pneumonia age, 24yrs.
parents, Stephen J. & Sarah C. Few. born Augusta Co.
occ. ____. consort of Dice Evick. info, Dice Evick, husband.

---

*probably brain or bowels.

Eagle, Samuel C., WM, **d. 29 Mar.** at Doe Hill of congestion of the lungs age 74yrs.
        parents, Chris. & ____ Eagle. born Pendleton Co.
        occ. merchant. consort of Martha. info, S. C. Eagle, Jr., son

Freeman, J. C., WM, **d. 29 Mar.** at Monterey of consumption age, 30yrs.
        parents, Sam'l & Mary Freeman. born Highland Co.
        occ. laborer. single. info, Mary Freeman, mother.

Gilmer, Alex., WM, **d. 11 April** on Back Creek of ____ age, ____.
        parents, ____ & ____ Gilmer. Born Rockingham Co.
        occ. farmer. widower. info, S. A. Gilmer, son.

Hise, Kenney, WM, **d. 9 Jan.** on Head of J. River of diphtheria age, 5yrs.
        parents, Sam'l & Ellen Hise. born Rockingham Co.
        occ. ____. consort of ____. info, Sam'l Hise, father.

Hevener, Naomi, WF, **d. 9 June** at Crab Bottom of cancer age, 73yrs.
        parents, Henry & ____ Swadley. born Rockingham Co.
        occ. ____.widow. info, W. W. Hevener, son.

Hoover, Mary E., WF, **d. 8 Mar.** on Back Creek of ____ age, 41yrs.
        parents, W. C. & Sarah Bird. born Highland Co. occ. ____.
        consort of S. W. Hoover. info, S. W. Hoover, husband.

Hoover, ____, WF, **d. 8 March** on Back Creek of ____ age, ____.
        parents, S. W. & Mary Hoover. born Highland Co. occ. ____.
        consort of ____. info, S. W. Hoover, father.

Hansel, Mary, WF, **d. 23 March** at Crab Bottom of spinal affiction age, 75yrs.
        parents, ____ & ____ Wallace. born Bath Co. occ. ____.
        widow. info, Jno. S. Newman, son-in-law.

Helmic, Jascah, WM, **d. ____ Sep.** at St. Creek of gravl, age, ____.
        parents, ____ & ____ born, Pendleton Co. occ. laborer.
        consort of ____. info, And. Rexrode, neighbor.

Jack, Mary E., WF, **d. 7 June** at Monterey of cancer of the bowels,
        age, 4yrs, 2mos, 4dys. **parents, Jno. G. & Eliza J. Kuglar.**
        born, Rockingham Co. occ.____ consort of L. S. Jack.
        info, L. S. Jack, husband.

Jack, Sarah, WF, **d. ____ Aug.** at CrabBottom of general debility, age, 93yrs.
        parents, Jno. & ____ Beverage. born, Pendleton Co. occ.____.
        widow. info, L.S. Jack, son.

---

* probably gravel.

Ker, Sarah A., WF, **d. 26 Dec.** on St. Creek of unknown, age,____.
    parents, Oliver & ____ McCoy. Born, Pendleton Co. occ.____.
    widow. info, Jas. W. Ker, son.

Layne, Mary, WF, **d. 8 April** on Bull Pasture R. of kidney afflictions,
    age, 76yrs, 2mos, 1dy. **parents, Martin & ____ Moyers.**
    born, Bath Co. occ.____. widow. info, P. Maloy, son-in-law.

Lunsford, Wm M., WM, **d. 28 Nov.** on Cow Pasture R. of consumption,
    age, 32yrs, 9mos, **parents, Wm & Naomi Lunsford.**
    born, Highland Co. occ. farmer. consort of Sarah A. Lunsford.
    info, S. A. Lunsford, wife.

Mausy, Peter, CM, **d. ____ Sep.** at McDowell of pneumonia, age, 70yrs.
    parents,____ & ____ born, Pendleton Co. occ. laborer.
    consort of ____. info, W. Smith, neighbor.

McClung, Frank W., WM, **d. 10 Oct.** on Bull Pasture R. of croup, age, 4yrs, 2mos.
    parents, L. M. & S. C. McClung. born, Highland Co. occ.____.
    consort of ____. info, L. M. McClung, father.

McClung, Willie B., WM, **d. 17 Oct.** on Bull Pasture R. of croup, age, 6yrs, 4mos,
    parents, L. M. & S. C. McClung. born Highland Co. occ.____.
    consort of ____. info, L. M. McClung, father.

Jones, ____, WF, **d. 28 Nov.** at Hightown of ____, age, 2dys.
    parents, J. A. & Bell C. Jones. born, Highland Co.
    occ.____. consort of ____. info, J. A. Jones, father.

Newman, Sarah E., WF, **d. 12 June** at CrabBottom of suicide, age, 38yrs.
    parents, B. & Mary Hansel. born, Pendleton Co. occ.____.
    consort of Jno. S. Newman. info, Jno. S. Newman, husband.

Pullin, Maggie B., WF, **d. ____ April** on Crab Run of burned to death, age, 1yr, 6mos.
    parents, H. B. & Lydia Pullin born Highland Co. occ.____
    consort of ____ info, H. B. Pullin, father.

Pullin, Sallie, WF, **d. 10 March** on Little Crab Run of cancer, age, 81yrs.
    parents, Leonard & Eliz. Propst. born Pendleton Co. occ. ____
    widow. info, H. M. Pullin, son.

Quidore, Ella, WF, **d. ____March** at McDowell of ____ age, ____.
    parents, L. L. & H. Quidore. born, Highland Co. occ.____
    consort of ____ info, L. L. Quidore, father.

Steuart, St. C., WM, **d. 19 July** on Cow P. R. of genl debility, age, 83yrs, 1mo, 1dy.
    parents, Jas. & Jane Steuart. born, Bath Co. occ. farmer.
    widower. info, Jno. E. Steuart, son.

Steuart, Edw., WM, **d. 11 Aug.** on Bull P. R. of cancer, age, 80yrs.
    parents, Jno. & Hannah Steuart. born, Bath Co. occ. farmer.
    consort of Caroline Steuart. info, Car. Steuart, wife.

Sheffer, Maggie G., WF, **d.** ____ on Bull P. R. of erysipilous, age, 1yr, 3mos.
    parents, D. A. & Sarah Sheffer. born Highland Co. occ.____
    consort of ____. info, Sarah Sheffer, mother.

Trimble, Lucy J., WF, **d. 1 Jan.** on St. Creek of blood poison, age, 42yrs.
    parents, Addison & Mary McCoy. born, Pendleton Co.
    occ. domestic. consort of H. I. Trimble.
    info, H. I. Trimble, husband.

Terry, N. M., WM, **d. 2 Sep.** on Dry Branch of pneumonia, age, 48yrs.
    parents, Jas. & Sarah Terry. born, Bath Co. occ. farmer.
    consort of Eliz. Terry. info, Eliz. Terry, wife.

Varner, Samuel, WM, **d.** ____ Staunton of ____, age, 30yrs.
    parents, David & ____ Varner. born, Highland Co., occ. farmer
    consort of Lucy Varner. info, Lucy Varner, wife.

Williams, Christian, WF, **d. 17 July** in Big Valley of unknown, age, ____.
    parents, ____ & ____ Gibbs. born, ____ occ.____
    consort of Jno. S. Williams. info, A. T. Wright, neighbor.

Williams, Narsy, CF, **d.** ____ **Sep.** on B. P. Mt. of ____, age, 84yrs.
    parents, ____ & ____ Williams. born, ____ occ.____
    consort of ____. info, Jno. W. Sheffer, neighbor.

Williams, Otho G., WM, **d. 8 Jan.** on B. Creek of ____, age, 7dys.
    parents, Chas. J. & Ida Williams. born, Highland Co. occ.____
    consort of ____ info, C. J. Williams, father.

Wade, Sophia N., WF, **d. 9 July** on B. Creek of rheumatism, age, 73yrs.
    parents, Isaac & Priscilla Briscoe. born, Bath Co. occ.____
    consort of J. W. Wade. info, J. W. Wade, husband.

Wiley, Priscilla, WF, **d. 28 June** on Dry Branch of ____, age, 36yrs.
    parents, Jas. W. & Sophia Wade. born Highland Co. occ.____
    consort of A. T. Wiley, info, A. T. Wiley, husband.

Wilfong, Samuel, WM, **d. 18 Feb.** on Allegheny Mt. of by accident, age, ____.
parents, Elias & Barbara Wilfong. born, Highland Co.
occ. farmer. unmarried. info, Mary Wilfong, sister-in-law.

Wilson, Naomi, WF, **d.** ____ **Sep.** at Doe Hill of general debility, age, 74yrs.
parents, Jno. & Mary Blagg. born, Highland Co. occ.____
widow. info, A. E. Wilson, son.

Waybright, Isaac S., WM, **d. 27 Sep.** on St. Fork of epilepsy, age, 21yrs.
parents, Morgan & Lucinda Waybright. born, Highland Co.
occ. laborer. unmarried. info, Lucinda Chew, mother.

Waybright, Peter, WM, **d.** ____ **May** near Staunton of accidentally, age, ____.
parents, Wm. & Mary Waybright. born, Highland Co.
occ. laborer. widower, info, N. C. Rexrode, son-in-law.

Wimer, Lelia May, WF, **d. 13 Nov.** at CrabBottom of diphtheriatic croup,
age, 4yrs, 10mos, 7dys. **parents, Ephraim & Martha Wimer.**
born, Highland Co. occ.____ consort of ____.
info, E. Wimer, father.

1884

Armstrong, Samuel A., WM, **d. 8 Nov.** on Bull Pasture Mt. of diphtheria, age, 4yrs.
parents, Hudson & ____ Armstrong. born, Bull Pasture Mt.
occ.____ consort of ____ info, H. Armstrong, father.

Atchinson, E. D., WM, **d. 4 Jan.** near Monterey of lynched & shot, age 35yrs.
parents, ____ & ____ Atchinson. born New York, occ. clerk,
consort of May Atchinson. info, O. Wilson, corner.

Bright, John, WM, **d. 16 Nov.** on Allegheny Mt. of pneumonia, age, 68yrs.
parents, Jacob & Mary Bright. born, Pendleton Co. occ. farmer.
consort of Marg't Bright. info, Mary Wilfong, daughter.

Bucher, __, WM, **d. 24 Nov.** at Doe Hill of spasms, age, 4dys.
parents, J. D. & Emily A. Bucher. born Doe Hill. occ.____
consort of ____. info, J. D. Bucher, father.

Colaw, Rob't. E. L., WM, **d. 19 Sep.** at Crab Bottom of unknown, age, 13yrs.
parents, D. & Sarah J. Colaw. born, Crab Bottom. occ. ____.
consort of ____ info, D. Colaw, father.

Carroll, Julia A., WF, **d. __ Mar.** on Bull P. R. of diseased liver, age, 45yrs.
    parents, B. & Nancy Wilson. born, Highland Co.
    occ. housekeeping. consort of Wm. J. Carroll.
    info, J. Siron, neighbor.

Campbell, B. B., WM, **d. 13 March,** at head J. River of Bright's disease, age 71yrs.
    parents, Alex. & Marg't Campbell. born Pendleton Co. occ.
    farmer. consort of L. R. Campbell. info, L. E. Campbell, son.

Campbell, Jas. B., WM, **d. 27 April** at head of J. River of heart disease, age, 48yrs.
    parents, B. B. & Marg't Campbell. born Highland Co. occ.
    farmer & miller. Consort of Amanda Campbell.
    info, L. E. Campbell, brother.

Carpenter, Preston R., WM, **d. 29 April** in big Valley of croup, age, ____.
    parents, D. W. & Sarah J. Carpenter. born, Highland Co.
    occ. ____ consort of ____. info, D. W. Carpenter, father.

Dever, Annie, WF, **d. 10 Jan.** on Back Creek of consumption, age, 33yrs.
    parents, Chas. & Katie Wade. born, Highland Co.
    occ. housekeeping. consort of Samuel G. Dever.
    info, Sam'l. G. Dever, husband.

Ervine, John, WM, **d. 22 Sep.** on Cow P. R. of meningitis, age, 68yrs.
    parents, Wm. & Frances Ervine. born, Pendleton Co.
    occ. farmer. unmarried. info, E. V. Ervine, brother.

Eye, Estille, WF, **d. ____ May** near Monterey of unknown, age, 1 mo.
    parents, Jas. P. & Mary Eye. born Highland Co.
    occ.____ unmarried. info, Jas. P. Eye, father.

Fleming, W. C., WM, **d. ____** at Charleston, S.C. of consumption, age, 31yrs.
    parents, W. W. & Marg't Fleming. born Highland Co.
    occ. minister. unmarried. info, ____.

Gaines, Lossing, WM, **d. ____ June*** on Bull P. Mt. of general debility, age, 80yrs.
    parents, ____ & ____ Gaines. born Bath Co. occ. laborer.
    widower. info, Fannie Smith, neighbor.

Gum, Sally, WF, **d. 28 June** at Meadow Dale of Bright's Disease, age, __.
    parents, Wm. J. & ____ Ryder. born Bath Co. occ.
    housekeeping. widow. info, Susan Campbell, sister-in-law.

---

* entered on original 1885 list.

Hull, Edw. H., WM, **d. 31 Dec.** at head of J. River of ____, age, 13dys. **parents, C. S. & Ellen Hull.** born Highland Co. occ.____. consort of ____. info, C. S. Hull. father.

Hiner, Helen E., WF, **d. 24 March** at Crabbottom of diphtheria, age, 16yrs. **parents, B. & Marg A. Hiner.** born, Pendleton Co. occ. ____ unmarried. info, B. Hiner, father.

Hiner, Arch Mc., WM, **d.** ____ **Aug.** in Monterey of enlargement of the brain, age, 10dys. **parents, G. J. & Fanny Hiner.** born Highland Co. occ.____. unmarried. info, G. J. Hiner, father.

Hiner, ____, WM, **d. 13 Aug.** in Monterey of ____, age, 3 dys. **parents, Jos. A. & Lucy C. Hiner.** born Highland Co. occ. ____. unmarried. info, Jos. A. Hiner, father.

Helmic, Isaac T., WM, **d.** ____ **March,** on St. Creek of ____, age, 1 yr,1mo. **parents, P. & Mahulda Helmic.** born, Highland Co. occ.____. unmarried. info, P. Helmic, father.

Hupman, Lillie F., WF, **d.** ____ **Oct.** on Cow P. R. of diphtheria, age, 15yrs. **parents, P. H. & Annie B. Hupman.** born, Highland Co. occ.____ unmarried. info, P. H. Hupman, father.

Hupman, Lizzie C., WF, **d.** ____ **Oct.** on Cow P. R. of diphtheria, age, 10yrs. **parents, P. H. & Annie B. Hupman.** born, Highland co. occ.____ unmarried. info, P. H. Hupman, father.

Hively, Nancy, WF, **d. 1 Oct.** at Doe Hill of inflam. of the bowels, age, 67yrs. **parents, Jos. & Jane Hiner.** born, Pendleton Co. occ. housekeeping. widow. info, Wm. Hiner, brother.

Jordan, Nancy, WF, **d. 18 Feb.** on Spring Run of apoplexy, age, 78yrs. **parents, Jno. & Eliz. Michael.** born, Pendleton Co. occ. housekeeping. unmarried. info, A. J. Jordan, son.

Jones, Effie, WF, **d. 11 May** in Monterey of bronchitis, age, 2 yrs. **parents, Jos. & Sarah Jones.** born, Monterey. occ.____ unmarried. info, Jos. Jones, father.

Kiracofe, Turner J., WM, **d. 14 June** at Stribling Springs, Va., of consumption, age, 21yrs, 2mos, 12dys. **parents, B. I. & Mary E. Kiracofe.** born, Doe Hill. occ.____. unmarried. info, B. I. Kiracofe, father.

Kincaid, Theresa G., WF, **d.** ____ July on Bull P. R. of childbirth, age, 35yrs. **parents, Edw. & Caroline Steuart.** born, Highland Co. occ. housekeeping. consort of Robert A. Kincaid. info, Thos. G. Steuart, brother.

Lee, ____, CF, **d.** ____ Jan. on Jackson's River of unknown, age,____ **parents, Jno. & Eliz. Lee.** born, Rockbridge Co. occ. ____ consort of ____. info, A. McClintic, friend.

Lewis, Emeline, CF, **d. 19 July** near Monterey of spinal affliction, age, 26yrs. **parents, Jos. Brown,** born, Pocahontas Co. occ. housekeeping. consort of Henry Lewis. info, Henry Lewis, husband.

Lightner, Eleanor, WF, **d.** ____ July in Back Creek Valley of general debility, age, 76yrs. 6mos, 4dys. **parents, Stuart & Isabel Slaven.** born, Bath Co. occ. housekeeping. widow. info, Wm. S. Lightner, son.

Lowman, Jacob, WM, **d.** ____ March in Monterey of consumption, age, 73yrs. **parents, ____ & ____ Lowman.** born, Rockingham Co. occ. stone mason. widower. info, G. J. Hiner, son-in-law.

Lockridge, ____, WM, **d.** ____ Nov. on Bull P. R. of ____, age, 2dys. **parents, W. P. B. & Jane H. Lockridge.** Born, Bull P. R. occ. ____ consort of ____ info, Reese Lockridge, uncle.

Michael, Jemima S., WF, **d.** ____ on Bull P. Mt. of thrown from a buggy, age, 19yrs, 10mos, 2dys. **parents, Jno. & Nancy Ralston.** born, Bull P. River. occ. housekeeping. consort of Dan'l. T. Michael. info, Dan'l. T. Michael, husband.

Mauzy, Jos., WM, **d.** ____ Feb. on South Branch, W.Va. of suicide by drowning, age, 65yrs. **parents, Michael & Gracie Mauzy.** born, Rockingham Co. occ. farmer. consort of Susan Mauzy. info, David Mauzy, brother.

Miller, Geo. B., WM, d. 15 Feb. on Cow P. River of unknown, age, 16yrs. **parents, Robt. S. & Amanda S. Miller.** born, Highland Co. occ.____. unmarried. info, Robt. S. Miller, father.

McGlaughlin, ____, WM, d. 9 Aug. on Jackson R. of ____, age, 1dy. **parents, E. A. & Lizzie McGlaughlin.** born, Highland Co. occ.____. unmarried. info, E. A. McGlaughlin, father.

Nicholas, Solomon, WM, **d.** ____ Dec. at Crabbottom of unknown, age, 9mos.

parents, H. B. & Mattie B. Nicholas. born, Highland Co. occ.____. consort of ____. info, H. B. Nicholas, father.

Peterson, Maggie, WF, **d. 5 Sep.** at McDowell of meningitis, age, 19yrs.
parents, Chas. W. & Mary Peterson. born, Augusta Co., occ. ____. unmarried. info, Chas. W. Peterson, father.

Price, Lillie E., WF, **d. ____ Nov.** on B. P. River of diptheria, age, 19yrs, 6mos, 6dys.
parents, T. & Caroline Price. born, Highland Co. occ. ____. unmarried. info, Townsend Price, father.

Rexrode, Samuel, WM, **d. 23 Dec.** at Monterey of paralysis, age, 89yrs.
parents, Daniel & ____ Rexrode. born, Pendleton Co. occ. farmer. consort of Sarah A. Rexrode. info, Sarah A. Rexrode, wife.

Rexrode, Gertie, WF, **d. 3 Oct.** on Crab Run of unknown, age, 2yrs, 6mos.
parents, Geo. K. & Sarah J. Rexrode. born, Highland Co. occ. ____. consort of ____. info, Geo. K. Rexrode, father.

Ratcliff, Andrew, WM, **d. 26 Aug.** on Jackson's River of suicide by hanging, age, 65yrs.
parents, ____ & ____ Ratcliff. born, Bath Co. occ. farmer. widower. info, O. Wilson, coroner.

Ruff, A. W., WM, **d. 26 Aug.** on Back Creek of congestion of the bowels, age, 37yrs.
parents, ____ & ____ Ruff. born, Rockbridge Co. occ. minister. consort of Lelia Ruff. info, Laura Campbell, friend.

Simmons, Magdalen, WF, **d. 18 Mar.** on Bull P. Mt. of bronchitis, age, 78yrs.
parents, ____ & Hally Hoover. born, Pendleton Co. occ. housekeeping. widow. info, Jno. Botkin, Admr.

Steuart, P. K., WM, **d. 1 Aug.** on Bull P. R. of cancer of the bowels, age, 50yrs.
parents, Wm. & Jane Steuart. born, Bath Co. occ. farmer. widower. info, Jno. S. Hicklin, cousin.

Smith, Jemima J., WF, **d. 3 Dec.** at Doe Hill of pneumonia, age, 1mo, 6dys.
parents, D. & Martha Smith. born, Highland Co. occ. ____. consort of ____. info, D. Smith, father.

Smith, ____, WF, **d. 17 April** at Doe Hill of ____, age, 1dy.
parents, D. & Martha Smith. born, Highland Co. occ. ____ consort of ____ info, D. Smith, father.

Sitlington, Henrietta, WF, **d. 10 Feb.** at McDowell of consumption, age, 71yrs.
parents, Wm. & ____ Ewing. born, Rockingham Co. occ. housekeeping. consort of Robt. Sitlington. info, R. Sitlington, husband.

Siron, Tilden, WM, **d. 8 Nov.** on Bull P. R. of diphtheria, age, 9yrs.
      parents, Jno. M. & Mary J. Siron. born, Highland Co. occ. ____.
  consort of ____. info, J. Siron, grandfather.

Seybert, Lucinda, WF, **d. 17 Dec.** on St. Creek of dyspepsia, age, 74yrs, 1mo, 7dys.
      parents, Harmon & Jemima Hiner. born, Pendleton Co. occ.
  housekeeping. consort of Henry Seybert. info, H. H. Seybert, son.

Simmons, Luther E., WM, **d. 28 Dec.** on St. Creek of croup, age, 1mo.
      parents, Lafe & Susie Simmons. born, Highland Co. occ. ____.
  consort of ____. info, Lafe Simmons, father.

Sutton, Allie, WF, **d. 7 May** on Back Creek of strichonea of the bowels,
      age, 16yrs, 8mos.**parents, Geo. M. & Lucinda Sutton.**
  born, Highland Co. occ. housekeeping. unmarried.
  info, Geo. M. Sutton, father.

Varner, Henry, WM, **d.** ____ **May** on B. P. River of consumption, age, ____.
      parents, ____ **&** ____ **Varner.** born, ____. occ. farmer.
  consort of Eliz. Varner. info, Jas. M. Malcomb.

Woods, Mary S., WF, **d. 30 April** on Jackson's River of typhoid fever, age, 23yrs.
      parents, Jas. M. & ____ **Woods.** born, Highland Co.
  occ. house-keeping. unmarried. info, Jas M. Woods, father.

Woods, ____, WM, **d. 1 May** on Jackson's River of ____, age, 1yr.
      parents, ____ **& Mary S. Woods.** born Highland Co.
  occ.____ consort of ____. info, Jas. M. Woods, grandfather.

Wilson, Lucy S., WF, **d. 23 Feb.** at Monterey of pneumonia, age, 42yrs, 7mos. 22dys.
      parents, Geo. W. & Sally Armstrong. born, Highland Co. occ.
  housekeeping. consort of O. Wilson. info, O. Wilson, husband.

Williams, ____, WM, **d.** ____ in B. C. Valley of croup, age, ____.
      parents, Erasmus & ____ **Williams.** born, Highland Co.
  occ. ____. consort of ____. info, Susan Campbell, neighbor.

1885

Armstrong, Sally, WF, **d. 27 Jan.** in Big Valley of consumption,
      age, 23yrs, 0mos, 26dys. **parents, Jno. M. & Esther Armstrong.**
  born Highland Co. occ. domestic. unmarried.
  info, Jno. M. Armstrong, father.

Armstrong, Jane E., WF, **d. 26 Jan.** on Bull P. Mt. of meningitis, age, 19yrs, 1mo.
   parents, B. & M. C. Armstrong. born, Highland Co. occ. domestic. unmarried. info, B. Armstrong, father.

Brock, Lizzie C., WF, **d. 8 July** at Hightown of child birth, age, 24yrs.
   parents, Geo. W. & M. C. Hevener. born, Highland Co. occ. domestic. consort of Chas. A. Brock. info, Chas. A. Brock, husband.

Bird, Jesse H., WM, **d. 6 June** on Back Creek of consumption, age, 2yrs, 2dys.
   parents, ____ & Eva J. Bird. born, Highland Co. occ.____ consort of ____. info, Jas. S. Wade, uncle.

Burns, Hattie V., WF, **d. 1 June** in Augusta Co. of accidental, age, 5yrs,11mos,11dys.
   parents, Peter S. & Ruhama Burns. born, Highland Co. occ. ____ consort of ____. Info, P.S. Burns, father.

Bowen, Barbara, WF, **d. 17 Jan.** on St. Creek of dysentery, age, 95yrs,
   parents, ____ & ____ Vandevender. born, Pendleton Co. occ. domestic. widow. info, W. Strathy, grandson.

Bowen, James E., WM, **d. 27 Feb.** on St. Creek of meningitis, age, 16yrs.
   parents, Wm. & Barbara Bowen. born Highland Co. occ. ____. consort of ____. info, Wm. Bowen, father.

Bowen, Dora Ellen, WF, **d. 27 Feb.** on St. Creek of meningitis, age, 11yrs.
   parents, Wm. & Barbara Bowen. born, Highland Co. occ. ____ consort of ____. info, Wm. Bowen, father.

Bird, Sophia, WF, **d. 4 June** on Back Creek of pneumonia, age, 78yrs.
   parents, Otho & ____ Wade. born, Bath Co. occ. domestic. widow. info, J. W. Bird, cousin.

Campbell, Lou, WF, **d. ____Feb.** at Hightown of consumption, age, ____.
   parents, Reuben & Harriet Rodgers. born, Bath Co. occ. domestic. consort of Rollin Campbell. info, W. G. Rodgers, brother.

Campbell, Ed J., WM, **d. ____March** in Augusta Co. of consumption, age, 19yrs.
   parents, R. & Lou Campbell. born, Highland Co. occ. ____. consort of ____. info, W. G. Rodgers, uncle.

Calhoun, Louisa, WF, **d. 7 July** on Buzzard's Run of apoplexy, age, 26yrs.
   parents, Henry & ___ Hoover. born, Highland Co. occ. domestic. consort of Eph. Calhoun. info, Eph. Calhoun, husband.

Carson, ___, Mrs., WF, **d. ___** at New Hampden of pneumonia, age, 50yrs. **parents, ___ & ___.** born, ___. occ. domestic. widow. info, W. W. Marshall, neighbor.

Carpenter, Martha S., WF, **d. 30 Dec.** in Big Valley of dropsy, age, 72yrs. **parents, Robt. & Rebecca Carpenter.** born, Bath Co. occ. domestic. single. info, J. M. Carpenter, brother.

Chew, Jos., WM, **d. 7 Sep.** at St. Fork of inflam. of bowels, age, 6mos. **parents, D. S. & Susan Chew.** born, Highland Co. occ. ___. consort of ___. info, D. S. Chew, father.

Carver, Mary M., WF, **d. 1 May** at Monterey of pneumonia, age, 34yrs. **parents, F. H. & N. S. Carver.** born, Highland Co. occ. ___. single. info, H. D. Carver, brother.

Cobb, Emily C., WF, **d. 14 April** on St. Creek of meningitis, age, 28yrs. **parents, Abra. & Susan Peck.** born, Highland Co. occ. ___. consort of Jno. H. Cobb. info, Jno. H. Cobb, husband.

Carr, Geo., CM, **d. ___ May** on B. P. River of ___, age, 2yrs. **parents, Jas. & Harriett Carr.** born, Highland Co. occ. ___ consort of ___. info, Jas. Carr, father.

Crummett, Sarah, WF, **d. ___ June** on B. P. Mt. of heart disease, age, 23yrs. **parents, H. W. & Amanda Crummett.** born, Highland Co. occ. domestic. consort of ___. info, H. W. Crummett, father.

Ervine, ___, WF, **d. ___** on B. P. R. of unknown, age, 8yrs. **parents, Aug. & ___ Ervine.** born, Highland Co. occ. domestic. consort of ___. info, ___.

Gum, John, WM, **d. 24 April** at Hightown of rheumatism, age, 72yrs. **parents, McB. & Alice Gum.** born, Pendleton. occ. farmer. consort of ___. info, A. F. Gum, son.

Gwin, Eliza J., WF, **d. 25 Jan.** on Jackson's R. of pneumonia, age, 69yrs. **parents, Jno. & ___ Stephenson,** born, Bath Co. occ. domestic. consort of D. Gwin. info, A. E. Bonner, daughter.

Gwin, David, WM, **d. 28 Feb.** on Jackson's R. of fever, age, 66yrs. **parents, ___ & ___ Gwin.** born, Bath Co. occ. farmer, widower. info, A. E. Bonner, daughter.

Griffen, Ascola, WF, **d. 21 July** on Jackson's R. of ____, age, 5yrs.
        parents, ____ **&** ____ **Griffen.** born, Highland Co.
        occ. ____ consort of ____. info, ____.

Groves, Sally,* WF, **d.** ____ on Jackson's R. of cancer, age, 40yrs.
        parents, Mich. & Ann Doyle. born, ____. occ. housekeeping.
        consort of ____ Groves. info, W. H. McNett, neighbor.

Gillespie, James, WM, **d. 8 April** on Jackson's R. of paralysis, age, 92yrs,2mos.
        parents, Ashby & Rosie Gillespie. born, Bath Co. occ. farmer.
        widower. info, M. F. Wiley, grandson.

Gum, James, P., WM, **d.** ____ **March** on St. Creek of suicide.
        parents, Amos & Sally Gum. born, Pendleton Co. occ. farmer.
        consort of Louisa Gum. info, Louisa Gum, wife.

Gwin, Jane, WF, **d. 18 Feb.** on C. P. River of paralysis, age, 78yrs.
        parents, David & Sarah Gwin. born Bath Co. occ. housekeeping.
        widow. info, Rachel Gwin, daughter.

Hevener, ____, WM, **d. 16 Aug.** at Crabbottom of unknown, age, 4mos,1dy.
        parents, Ed. H. & P. Hevener. born, Highland Co. occ. ____.
        consort of ____. info, Ed. H. Hevener.

Hoover, Rufus, WM, **d.** ____ **Nov.** at Staunton of insanity, age, 69yrs.
        parents, ____ **&** ____ **Hoover.** born, Bath Co. occ. ____,
        consort of Mary Hoover. info, Geo. Hoover, son.

Hoover, Mary, WF, **d. 5 March** at New Hampden of consumption, age, 40yrs.
        parents, Leah & Nannie Hoover. born, Pendleton Co.
        occ. housekeeping. single. info, Clara Hoover, sister.

Hiner, Bessie, WF, **d.** ____ **Dec.** in Monterey of unknown, age, 7dys.
        parents, Jos. A. & Lucy Hiner. born, Highland Co. occ.____
        consort of ____. info, Jos. A. Hiner, father.

Hoffman, Henry, WM, **d. 24 Sep.** on Brushy Fork of diphtheria, age, 10yrs.
        parents, ____ **& Mary S. Hoffman.** born, Highland Co.
        occ.____. consort of ____. info, Andy Hoffman, grandfather.

Hook, Ella V., WF, **d. 8 July** on Cowpasture R. of consumption, age, 12yrs.
        parents, R. N. & Susan Hook. born, Highland Co. occ. ____
        consort of ____. info, Robt. N. Hook, father.

---

* entered on original 1886 list.

Hull, ____, WF, **d. ____ Dec.** at Hightown of unknown, age, 3yrs.
    parents, C. S. & Ellen E. Hull. born, Highland Co. occ. ____.
    consort of ____. info, W. C. Rexrode, uncle.

Joyce, Fanny G., WF, **d. ____ Nov.** at McDowell of diphtheria, age, 5yrs.
    parents, C. A. & Fanny Joyce. born, Maryland. occ. none.
    consort of ____. info, Emma Slaven, friend.

Keister, Marcilla, WF, **d. 5 Feb.** on Bull P. Mt. of diphtheria, age, 15yrs.
    parents, W. R. & Martha Keister. born, Highland Co. occ. none.
    consort of ____. info, Martha Keister, mother.

Keister, K. C., WM, **d. 21 March** on Bull P. Mt. of diphtheria, age, 11yrs.
    parents, W. R. & Martha Keister. born, Highland Co. occ. none.
    consort of ____. info, Martha Keister, mother.

Keister, Cammie V., WF, **d. 15 Feb.** on Bull P. Mt. of diphtheria, age, 13yrs.
    parents, W. R. & Martha Keister. born, Highland Co. occ. none.
    consort of ____. info, Martha Keister, mother.

Keister, Gracie, WF, **d. 23 Feb.** on Bull P. Mt. of diphtheria, age, 9yrs.
    parents, W. R. & Martha Keister. born, Highland Co. occ. none
    consort of ____. info, Martha Keister, mother.

Keister, W. R., WM, **d. 29 Oct.** on Bull P. Mt. of pneumonia, age, 48yrs.
    parents, ____ & Ann Keister. born, Pendleton Co. occ. farmer.
    consort of Martha Keister. info, Martha Keister, wife.

Kelly, Samelle, WF, **d. 29 Feb.** at McDowell of meningitis, age, 40yrs.
    parents, ____ & ____. born, Augusta Co. occ. housekeeper.
    consort of J. W. Kelly. info, Dice Evick, friend.

Lunsford, Tim, WM, **d. 29 Feb.** at CrabBottom of unknown, age, 1yr, 6mos.
    parents, Noah & Vallena Lunsford. born, Pocahontas Co.
    occ. ____. consort of ____. info, Ed H. Hevener, friend.

Lightner, Paul, WM, **d. 18 Jan.** at Hightown of pneumonia, age, 50yrs.
    parents, Jno. & Virginia Lightner. born, Bath Co. occ. farmer.
    single. info, Paul Gay, nephew.

Lockridge, W. H., WM, **d. 28 June** on Bull P. R. of heart disease, age, 39yrs, 7mos.
    parents, Robt. & Emma Lockridge. born Bath Co. occ. farmer.
    single. info, Robt. Lockridge, father.

Losh, Jos., WM, **d. 23 May** on Brushy Fork of pistol shot, age 9yrs.
parents, ____ & Hulda Losh. born Highland Co. occ.____.
consort of ____. info, Andy Hoffman, stepfather.

McClung, Sudie, WF, **d. 8 Aug.** on Bull P. River of consumption, age, 36yrs.
parents, D. P. & Rachel Reamer. born, Augusta Co.
occ. housekeeping. consort of L. M. McClung.
info, L. M. McClung, husand.

McClung, Reamer, WM, **d. 4 Feb.** on Bull P. River of ____, age, 3yrs.
parents, L. M. & Sudie McClung. born Highland Co.
occ. ____. consort of ____. info, L. M. McClung, father.

Mullenax, Susan, WF, **d. 6 March** at Crab Bottom of meningitis, age, 49yrs.
parents, Jonus & Lina Bland. born Pendleton Co.
occ. housekeeping. consort of J. K. Mullenax.
info, H. Mullenax, brother-in-law.

Mullenax, Jas. K., WM, **d. ____ March,** at Crab Bottom of meningitis, age, 37yrs.
parents, Wm. & Nancy Mullenax. born Pendleton Co.
occ. farmer. widower. info, H. Mullenax, brother.

McAllister, ____, WF, **d. ____ Dec.** on Dry Branch of unknown, age, 7dys.
parents, Chas. H. & Eliza McAllister. born, Highland Co.
occ. ____. consort of ____. info, C. H. McAllister, father.

Malcom, John, WM, **d. ____ Jan.** on Bull P. R. of general debility, age, 85yrs.
parents, Thos. & Jane P. Malcom. born Pendleton Co.
occ. farmer. widower. info, J. M. Malcom, son.

McCray, Rodie R., WF, **d. 17 Sep** on Bull P. Mt. of diphtheria, age, 18yrs,*12dys.
parents, Alex & Mary McCray. born Highland Co.
occ. ____. single. info, Alex McCray, father.

McCray, Cami Erdine, WF, **d. 4 Oct.** on Bull P. Mt. of diphtheria, age, 5yrs.
parents, Alex & Mary McCray. born Highland Co.
occ. ____. single. info, Alex McCray, father.

McCray, Jas. H., WM, **d. 29 Aug.** on Bull P. Mt. of diphtheria, age, 14yrs.
parents, Alex & Mary McCray. born Highland Co.
occ. ____ single. info, Alex McCray, father.

---

* year number overwritten in the original and is unclear.

Newlin, Fan, WF, **d. ____ March** at Monterey of heart disease, age, 40yrs.
   parents, Aug. & Bettie Shumate. born Rockingham Co.
   occ. seamstress. widow. info, A. A. Shumate, brother.

Pullin, Jerry, CM, **d. ____ Nov.** on Dry Branch of pneumonia, age, 65yrs.
   parents, ____ & ____ Pullin. born Bath Co. occ. laborer.
   consort of Annie Pullin. info, Jno. Pullin, son.

Propst, Daniel, WM, **d. 29 Aug.** on St. Creek of unknown, age, 8yrs.
   parents, Emanuel & M. Propst. born Highland Co.
   occ. ____ consort of ____. info, E. Propst, father.

Peterson, Willie May, WF, **d. 29 Feb.** at McDowell of meningitis, age, 16yrs.
   parents, Chas. W. & Mary Peterson. born Rockingham Co.
   occ. ____. single. info, C. W. Peterson, father.

Price, Lillie, WF, **d. 1 Dec.** on Bull P. R. of diphtheria, age, 18yrs.
   parents, T. & Caroline Price. born Highland Co. occ. ____.
   single. info, T. Price, father.

Propst, Bella Morgan, WF, **d. 2 Dec.** on Shaw's Fork of unknown,
   age, 4yrs, 1mos, 1dy. **parents, Jas. K. & Mary Propst.**
   born Highland Co. occ. ____. single. info, Jas. K. Propst, father.

Quidore, L. L., WM, **d. 19 Feb.** at McDowell of meningitis, age, 34yrs.
   parents, ____ & ____ Quidore. born Augusta Co. occ. physician.
   consort of H. R. Quidore. info, H. E. Bryant, brother-in-law.

Ralston, Malinda, WF, **d. ____ June** on Jack Mt. of dyspepsia, age, 40yrs.
   parents, Ab. & ____ Waggy. born Bath Co. occ. housekeeping.
   consort of Josiah Ralston. info, J. Siron, neighbor.

Rexrode, John WM, **d. 30 Dec.** on Crab Run of dyspepsia, age, 59yrs. Susan Rexrode
   parents, Sam'l & Susan Rexrode. born Pendleton Co.
   occ. farmer. widower. info, O. F. Rexrode, son.

Robertson, Wm., WM, **d. 4 Feb.** on Jackson's River of paralysis, age, 100yrs.
   parents, Jas. & Martha Robertson. born Bath Co. occ. farmer.
   widower. info, Jesse Robertson, son.

Rexrode, Mary S., WF, **d. ____ Oct.** on Crab Run of consumption, age, 30yrs.
   parents, Jno. & Sidney Rexrode. born Highland Co. occ. ____.
   single. info, O. F. Rexrode, brother.

Seig, Bolling L.,* WM, **d. 13 Dec.** at Waynesboro of suicide, age, 22yrs. **parents, Jas. M. & F. V. Seig.** born Highland Co. occ. ____. unmarried. info, S. B. Seig, brother.

Seiver, Martha, WF, **d. 18 Feb.** at New Hampden of pneumonia, age, 63yrs. **parents, ____ & ____ Sullenberger.** born Pendleton Co. occ. housekeeping. widow. info, Geoff Mauzy, son-in-law.

Snyder, Alice, WF, **d. 13 June** at Crab Bottom of childbirth, age, 23yrs, 9mos, 11dys. **parents, Adam & Sarah Arbogast.** born Pocahontas Co. occ. housekeeping. consort of W. E. Snyder. info, W. E. Snyder, husband.

Wilson, Kenney B., WM, **d. ____ June** at Doe Hill of diphtheria, age, 11yrs. **parents, E. R. V. & Susan A. Wilson.** born Highland Co. occ. ____. consort of ____. info, E. R. V. Wilson, father.

Slaven, Rebecca, WF, **d. ____** on Back Creek of pneumonia, age, 70yrs. **parents, Ben & ____ Tallman,** born Pocahontas Co. occ. housekeeping. widow. info, Emma Slaven, granddaughter.

Wade, Sarah A., WF, **d. 6 April** on Back Creek of consumption, age, 26yrs. **parents, W. C. & Sarah Bird.** born Back Creek. occ. housekeeping. consort of Jas. S. Wade. info, Jas. S. Wade, husband.

Simmons, Rodie, WF, **d. 16 Jan.** on Bull P. R. of diphtheria, age, 11yrs. **parents, W. H. & Tacy Simmons.** born Highland Co. occ. ____. consort of ____. info, W. H. Simmons, father.

Smith, ____, WF, **d. 16 April** at Doe Hill of unknown, age, 1dy. **parents, D. & Martha Smith.** born Highland Co. occ. ____. consort of ____. info, D. Smith, father.

Williams, Mary WF, **d. 4 Sep.** in Big Valley of cholera infantum, age, 1yr. **parents, Ashley & Rosie Williams.** born Highland Co. occ. ____. consort of ____. info, Ashley Williams, father.

Whistleman, Betty, WF, **d. 27 Sep.** on Bull P. Mt. of diphtheria, age, 5yrs. **parents, Jno. & Susan Whistleman.** born Pendleton Co. occ. ____. consort of ____. info, Susan Whistleman, mother.

---

*entered on the original 1886 list.

Whistleman, Artella, WF **d. 28 Sep.** on Bull P. Mt. of diphtheria, age, 7yrs. **parents, Jno. & Susan Whistleman.** born, Pendleton Co. occ. ____. consort of ____. info, Susan Whistleman, mother.

Whistleman, Geo. A., WM, **d. 14 Sep.** on Bull P. Mt. of diphtheria, age, 17yrs. **parents, Jno. & Susan Whistleman.** born Pendleton Co. occ. ____. consort of ____. info, Susan Whistleman, mother.

Whistleman, Lavina, WF, **d. 12 Sep.** on Bull P. Mt. of diphtheria, age, 15yrs. **parents, Jno. & Susan Whistleman.** born Pendleton Co. occ. ____. consort of ____. info, Susan Whistleman, mother.

Whistleman, Jas. H., WM, **d. 29 Sep.** on Bull P. Mt. of diphtheria, age, 4yrs. **parents, Jno. & Susan Whistleman.** born Pendleton Co. occ. ____. consort of ____. info, Susan Whistleman, mother.

Wilson, Olin Dice, WM, **d. 15 June** at Doe Hill of diphtheria, age, 2yrs. **parents, A. E. & Mary Wilson.** born Highland Co. occ. ____. consort of ____. info, A. E. Wilson, father.

Wilson, W. J. J., WM, **d. 20 Dec.** at Doe Hill of enlargement of heart, age, 36yrs. **parents, Alex & Mary Wilson.** born Highland Co. occ. teacher. unmarried. info, A. E. Wilson, father.

Wilson, Clara B., WF, **d. 10 June** at Doe Hill of diphtheria, age, 26yrs. **parents, A. E. & Mary Wilson.** born Highland Co. occ. ____. consort of ____. info, A. E. Wilson, father.

Wilson, Clara J., WF, **d. 10 June** at Doe Hill of diphtheria, age, 19yrs. **parents, E. R. V. & Susan Wilson.** born Highland Co. occ. ____. consort of ____. info, E. R. V. Wilson, father.

Wilson, Mary, WF, **d. 25 Sep.** at Doe Hill of inf. of bowels, age, 1mo, 8dys. **parents, Jno. . & Martha Wilson.** born Highland Co. occ. ____. consort of ____. info, Jno. Wilson, father.

Pullin, Mary, WF, **d. 26 June** on B. P. R. of general debility, age 85yrs. **parents, Thos. & Jane Pullin.** born Bath Co. occ. housekeeping. unmarried. info, Mrs. R. C. Pullin, aunt.*

---

*niece?

1886

Armstrong, Mary, WF, d. ____ April on Shaw's Fork of dropsy, age, ____.
        parents, ____ & ____. born Pendleton Co. occ. housekeeper.
        widow. info, Dr. J. R. Cook, physician.

Beverage, Hannah, WF, d. ____ at Hightown of apoplexy, age, 69yrs.
        parents, Jacob & Cath. Hevener. born ____. occ. housekeeper.
        widow. info, Wesley Beverage, son.

Bird, Nettie, WF, d. ____ Feb. on Back Creek of diphtheria, age, 4yrs.
        parents, M. R. & ____ **Bird.** born Highland Co. occ. ____.
        consort of ____. info, Jno. M. Wade, neighbor.

Botkin Henry H., WM, d. ____ March on Jack Mt. of pneumonia, age, 11yrs.
        parents, A. J. & Sarah Botkin. born Highland Co. occ. ____.
        consort of ____. info, Charles W. Botkin, brother.

Botkin, A. J., WM, d. 5 April on Jack Mt. of pneumonia, age, 61yrs.
        parents, ____ & ____ **Botkin.** born Pendleton Co. occ. laborer.
        consort of Sarah Botkin. info, Chas. W. Botkin, son.

Botkin, A. J., Jr., WM, d. ____ March on Jack Mt. of pneumonia, age, 17yrs.
        parents, A. J. & Sarah Botkin. born Highland Co. occ. laborer.
        consort of ____. info, Chas. W. Botkin, brother.

Beard, Lillie, CF, d. ____ June in Monterey of diphtheria, age, 15yrs.
        parents, Chas. & Letitia Beard. born Highland Co. occ. ____.
        consort of ____. info, Chas. Beard, father.

Brown, Thos. T., WM, d. 10 Aug. in Big Valley of pneumonia, age, 80yrs.
        parents, Sam'l & Martha Brown. born North Carolina.
        occ. farmer. consort of Cynthia Brown. info, Cynthia Brown, wife.

Brown, W. E., CM, d. 31 Dec. on Bull P. R. of consumption, age, 30yrs.
        parents, Elijah & Ann Brown. born Highland Co. occ. laborer.
        single. info, J. L. Shumate, executor.

Botkin, Joseph, WM, d. ____ March on Bull P. Mt. of typhoid fever, age, 83yrs.
        parents, Jno. & Eliz. Botkin. born Pendleton Co. occ. farmer.
        widower. info, Sam'l Botkin, brother.

Colaw, W. E. Cameron, WM, d. 16 March at Crab Bottom of whooping cough,
        age, 1yr. 1mo, 3dys. **parents, Dan'l & Sarah Colaw.**
        born Crab Bottom occ. ___ consort of ___ info, D. Colaw, father.

Carrol, Jesse, WM, **d. 24 March** on Jackson's River of paralysis, age, 86yrs.
  parents, David & Margaret Carroll. born ____. occ. laborer.
  widower. info, Margt. Shafier, daughter.

Cobb, John H., WM, **d. 8 Sep.** on St. Creek of cancer, age, 60yrs.
  parents, ____ & ____ Cobb. born Georgia. opcc. farmer.
  widower. info, J. C. Beverage, neighbor.

Carpenter, Ivy W., WM, **d. 7 Feb.** at Bolar Springs of spinal affection, age, 7yrs.
  parents, Chas. R. & M. S. Carpenter. born Bath Co. occ. ____.
  consort of ____. info, C. R. Carpenter, father.

Campbell, Susan, WF, **d. 27 Oct.** on Back Creek of consumption, age, 60yrs.
  parents, Otho & Eliza Gum. born Bath Co. occ. housekeeper.
  widow. info, Peter Gum, brother.

Crummett, Jacob, WM, **d. 31 March** on South Fork of dropsy, age, 77yrs, 2mos.
  parents, ___ & ___ Crummett. born Pendleton Co. occ. farmer.
  consort of Susan Crummett. info, G. S. Crummett, son.

Daugherty, Mary E., CF, **d. ____ June** at Monterey of diphtheria, age, 11yrs.
  parents, Wm. & Fan Daugherty. born Monterey. occ. ____.
  consort of ____. info, Wm. Daugherty, father.

Daugherty, Lucretia Bell, CF, **d. 26 March** at Monterey of burned, age, 4yrs.
  parents, Wm. & Fan Daugherty. born Monterey. occ. ____.
  consort of ____. info, Wm. Daugherty, father.

Daugherty, Maggie, CF, **d. ____ June** at Monterey of laryngitis, age 2yrs,8mos.
  parents, Wm. & Fan Daugherty. born Monterey. occ. ____.
  consort of ____. info, Wm. Daugherty, father.

Doyle, ____, WF, **d. ____ March** on Jackson's R. of unknown, age, 2mos.
  parents, Amanda Doyle. born Jackson's River. occ. ____.
  consort of ____. info, Jas. Corrigan, neighbor.

Doyle, Willis, WM, **d. ____ July** on Jackson's R. of epilepsy, age, 17yrs.
  parents, Asa Doyle. born Jackson's River. occ. ____.
  consort of ____. info, Jas. Corrigan, neighbor.

Ervin, Mary, WF, **d. 29 Jan.** on Back Creek of consumption, age, 81yrs.
  parents, Jas. & Jennie Curry. born, ____. occ. ____. widow.
  info, Geo. W. Ervine, nephew.

Ervin, Eliza H., WF, **d. 4 Oct.** on Back Creek of diarrhea, age 75yrs.
parents, Francis & Tersy Gardner. born ____. occ. ____.
widow. info, Geo. W. Ervin, son.

Gum, Lucinda, WF, **d. 26 Dec.** at Crab Bottom of consumption, age 54yrs.
parents, Wm. & ____ Mullenax. born ____. occ. housekeeping.
widow. info, Chas. Arbogast, son-in-law.

Gum, Nellie, WF, **d. 18 Jan.** at Hightown of diabetes, age, 63yrs.
parents, Adam & Sarah Gum. born ____. occ. housekeeping.
unmarried. info, Frank Gum, nephew.

Hoffman, Geo., WM, **d. ____ March** on Brushy Fork of diphtheria, age, 17yrs.
parents, And. & Mary Hoffman. born Highland Co. occ. ____.
consort of ____. info, And. Hoffman, father.

Hevener, ____, WF, **d. ____ Oct.** at Crab Bottom of inf. of bowels, age, 6mos, 2dys.
parents, J. P. & Phoebe Hevener. born Highland Co. occ. ____.
consort of ____. info, J. P. Hevener, father.

Hoover, Mary, WF, **d. 5 March** at Crab Bottom of consumption, age, 40yrs.
parents, Cain & M. Hoover. born Crab Bottom. occ. ____.
unmarried. info, Clara Hoover, sister.

Helmick, Nancy, WF, **d. __ Nov.** at county farm of apoplexy, age, 70yrs.
parents, ____ & ____ Helmick. born Crab Bottom. occ.____.
consort of ____. info, Henry Mullenax, Supt. of farm.

Hodge, Wm., WM, **d. ____ April** on Shaw's Fork of congestion of lungs, age, 79yrs.
parents, Jno. & Mary Hodge. born ____. occ. farmer. widower.
info, Jas. Hodge, son.

Joyce, Lulu J., WF, **d. 9 Jan.** at McDowell of typhoid fever, age, 18yrs.
parents, C. A. & Fannie Joyce. born ____. occ. ____.
unmarried. info, Edmonia Slaven, friend.

Jackson, Mary J., CF, **d. 10 May** on Cow P. River of consumption, age, 53yrs.
parents, ____ & Sally Gibson. born ____. occ. housekeeping.
consort of Albert Jackson. info, Albert Jackson, husband.

Johns, Mary B., WF, **d. 24 April** on Cow P. River of cancer, age, 91yrs.
parents, Jno. & Mary Devericks. born ____. occ. housekeeping
widow. info, Jno. Wilson, son.

Kramer, Conrad, WM, **d. 3 March** at Crab Bottom of hem. of bowels, age, 73yrs.
    parents, __ & __ Kramer. born Germany. occ. farmer. consort of Barbara Kramer. info, S. N. Kramer, son.

Kelley, Mary, WF, **d. ____ June** on Back Creek of general debility, age, 76yrs.
    parents, ____ & ____ Kelley. born ____. occ. ____. unmarried. info, Jno. M. Wade, neighbor.

Kincaid, Mary, WF, **d. ____ Dec.** on Jackson's River of pneumonia, age, 26yrs.
    parents, D. G. & Mary A. Kincaid. born Jackson's River. occ. ____. unmarried. info, D. G. Kincaid, father.

Lightner, Jane, WF, **d. ____ May** on head of J. River of dropsy, age, 75yrs.
    parents, Jno. & ____ Moore. born Pocahontas Co. occ. housekeeping. widow. info, S. A. Porter, grandson-in-law.

Lockridge, Hattie E., WF, **d. 15 Aug.** on Bull P. River of cold, age, 17yrs.
    parents, S. A. & L. A. Lockridge. born Highland Co. occ. ____. unmarried. info, S. A. Lockridge, father.

Matheny, Daniel, WM, **d. 20 April** on Back Creek of dyspepsia, age, 60yrs.
    parents, Abijah & Marg't Matheny. born Bath Co. occ. farmer. consort of Sarah Matheny. info, J. C. Matheny, brother.

Matheny, Edith, WF, **d. 18 Feb.** at Monterey of laryngitis, age, 4yrs, 6mos.
    parents, J. C. & Lizzie Matheny. born Highland Co. occ. ____. consort of ____. info, J. C. Matheny, father.

McAllister, Rob't Cecil, WM, **d. 2 Oct.** on Dry Branch of burned, age, 3yrs, 6mos.
    parents, C. H. & Mary McAllister. born Dry Branch. occ. ____. consort of ____. info, C. H. McAllister, father.

McAllister, John, WM, **d. 7 Oct.** in Big Valley of apoplexy, age, 84yrs.
    parents, Benj. & ____ McAllister. born __. occ. laborer. consort of Sarah McAllister. info, C. H. McAllister, son.

Matheny, ____, WF, **d. 17 Aug.** at Monterey of ____, age, ____.
    parents, J. C. & Lizzie Matheny. born Monterey. occ. ____. consort of ____. info, J. C. Matheny, father.

McClung, Nannie V., CF **d. 8 Aug.** at Monterey of pneumonia, age, 1yr, 5mos,
    parents, Mor. & Sally McClung. born Monterey. occ. ____. consort of ____. info, Mor. McClung, father.

Murphy, John, WM, **d.** ____ **May** at county farm of bronchitis, age, 65yrs.
   parents, ____ **&** ____ **Murphy.** born Ireland. occ. ____.
   consort of Sarah Murphy. info, Henry Mullenax, Supt. of farm.

Montgomery, ____, CM, **d.** ____ at Crab Bottom of ____, age, 1dy.
   parents Henry & A. Montgomery. born Crab Bottom. occ. ____.
   consort of ____. info, Mor. McClung, friend.

Montgomery, ____, CF, **d.** ____ at Crab Bottom of ____, age, 1dy.
   parents, Henry & A. Montgomery. born Crab Bottom occ. ____.
   consort of ____. info, Mor. McClung, friend.

Northern, Sarah, WF, **d. 26 March** at Monterey of cancer & paralysis, age, 70yrs.
   parents, ____ **&** ____. born ____. occ. ____ widow.
   info, Don Sullenberger, grandson.

Neil, Della Gertrude, WF, **d. 3 May** on Cow P. R. of diphtheria, age, 1yr, 0mos, 3dys.
   parents, S. M. & Jemima Neil. born Cow P. River. occ. ____
   consort of ____. info, S. M. Neil, father.

Parmer, Christian, WM, **d. 3 Sep.** at Crab Bottom of diabetis, age, 66yrs.
   parents, David & Jane Parmer. born ____. occ. farmer.
   consort of Mary K. Parmer. info, J. H. Parmer, son.

Pullin, Georgie, CF, **d.** ____ in Big Valley of consumption, age, 12yrs.
   parents, Jerry & Annis Pullin. born Highland Co. occ. ____.
   consort of ____. info, John Pullin, brother.

Pullin, Mollie, CF, **d.** ____ in Big Valley of consumption, age, 15yrs.
   parents, Jerry & Annis Pullin. born Highland Co. occ. ____.
   consort of ____. info, John Pullin, brother.

Peck, Mortie, WM, **d.** ____ **Oct.** on St. Creek of ____, age, 1yr.
   parents, Bine & Caroline Peck. born St. Creek. occ. ____.
   consort of ____. info, Bine Peck, father.

Rexrode, Sol, WM, **d.** ____ **Feb.** at Crab Bottom of general debility, age, 84yrs.
   parents, Jno. & ____ **Rexrode.** born ____. occ. farmer.
   widower. info, S. H. Eye, son-in-law.

Rexrode, Rebecca J., WF, **d. 25 March** at McDowell of fever, age, 31yrs.
   parents, D. C. & M. R. Hamilton. born Bath Co.
   occ. housekeeping. consort of John R. Rexrode.
   info, Jno. R. Rexrode, husband.

Ralston, Nancy, WF, d. ____ **May** on Bull P. River of fever, age, ____.
parents, ____ **&** ____ **Botkin.** born Highland Co.
occ. housekeeping. consort of Jno. Ralston.
info, Jas. R. Beathe, son-in-law.

Ralston, Jesse LeRoy, WM, **d. 5 April** on Bull P. River of billous fever,
age, 1yr, 11mos. **parents, Conrad & Nannie Ralston.**
born Highland Co. occ. ____. consort of ____.
info, Conrad Ralston, father.

Reid, ____, WM, d. ____ **Feb.** in Little Valley of ____, age, ____.
parents, Lloyd & ____ **Reid.** born Highland Co. occ. ____.
consort of ____. info, ____ neighbor.

Simmons, Cora E., WF, **d. 10 Oct.** on St. Creek of diphtheria, age, 3yrs.
parents, Sam'l & Hannah Simmons. born Pendleton Co.
occ. ____. consort of ____. info, Hannah Simmons, mother.

Simmons, John A., WM, **d. 23 Aug.** on St. Creek of diphtheria, age, 7yrs, 7mos.
parents, Sam'l & Hannah Simmons. born Pendleton Co.
occ. ____. consort of ____. info, Hannah Simmons, mother.

Simmons, Carrie Etta, WF, **d. 13 Sep.** on St. Creek of diphtheria, gae, 2yrs.
parents, Sam'l & Hannah Simmons. born Pendleton Co.
occ. ____. consort of ____. info, Hannah Simmons, mother.

Simmons, Sally, WF, **d. 4 Jan.** at Crab Bottom of old age, age, 90yrs.
parents, Mark & ____ **Simmons.** born Pendleton Co.
occ. ____. widow. info, M. A. Simmons, grandson.

Simmons, ____, WM, **d. 12 July** in Big Valley of ____, age, 2dys.
parents, Wesley & M. J. Simmons. born Highland Co.
occ. ____. consort of ____. info, Jno. Simmons, grandfather.

Sirams, Sally, WF, d. ____ **Dec.** on South Fork of general debility, age, 88yrs.
parents, ____ **&** ____ **Hiner.** born ____. occ. ____. widow.
info, Geo. P. Crummett, grandson.

Stephenson, Wm., WM, **d. 1 April** on Jackson's River of pneumonia, age, 83yrs.
parents, Jno. & Nancy Stephenson. born Bath Co. occ. laborer.
consort of Eliza Stephenson. info, C. L. Stephenson, son.

Scott, ____, CF, d. ____ **March** on County Farm of whooping cough, age, 1mo.
parents, ____ **& Lizzie Scott.** born Highland Co. occ. ____.
consort of ____. info, H. Mullenax, Supt. of Farm.

Scott, ____, CM, **d. ____ March** on County Farm of whooping cough, age, 1mo.
    parents, ____ & Lizzie Scott. born Highland Co. occ. ____.
    consort of ____. info, H. Mullenax, Supt. of Farm.

Simmons, Charley, WM, **d. ____ March** on St. Creek of hem. of brain, age, 1yr, 1mo.
    parents, W. G. & Hannah Simmons. born Highland Co.
    occ. ____. consort of ____. info, W. G. Simmons, father.

Stephenson, ____, WM, **d. 27 Dec.** on J. River of unknown, age, 2dys.
    parents, A. F. & Lina V. Stephenson. born Highland Co.
    occ. ____. consort of ____. info, A. F. Stephenson, father.

Splawn, Daniel, WM, **d. 31 Jan.** on Shaw's Fork of apoplexy, age, 71yrs.
    parents, ____ & ____ Splawn. born Ireland. occ. laborer.
    consort of Mary J. Splawn. info, Mary J. Splawn, wife.

Turner, Rachel, CF, **d. ____ April** on Bull P. Mt. of pneumonia, age, 23yrs.
    parents, Nelson & Sophia Carter. born Highland Co.
    occ. domestic. consort of Frank Turner. info, F. Turner, husband.

Taylor, Geo. P., WM, **d. 4 March** at Hightown of unknown, age, 8mos.
    parents, Geo. W. & Mary J. Taylor. born Highland Co.
    occ. ____. consort of ____. info, Geo. W. Taylor, father.

Townsend, Jas. B., WM, **d. 18 Sep.** on Back Creek of meningitis, age, 32yrs.
    parents, Jno. & Mary Townsend. born Highland Co.
    occ. teacher. consort of Ruhama Townsend.
    info, Jno. Townsend, father.

Varner, Eliz., WF, **d. 6 Feb.** at Crab Bottom of unknown, age, 4dys.
    parents, Benj. & S. C. Varner. born Highland Co. occ. ____.
    consort of ____. info, B. Varner, father.

Waybright, ____, WM, **d. 6 Oct.** at Crab Bottom of unknown, age, 4dys.
    parents, Nick & Ella Waybright. born Highland Co.
    occ. ____. consort of ____. info, N. Waybright, father.

Wilfong, Daniel, WM, **d. 30 April** on Allegheny Mt. of diabetis, age, 81yrs.
    parents, ____ & Eliz. Wilfong. born Pendleton Co. occ. farmer.
    widower. info, D. Wilfong, son.

Wilfong, Charlotte, WF, **d. 7 March** on Allegheny Mt. of paralysis, age, 71yrs.
    parents, Lewis & ____ Wise. born Pendleton Co. occ.
    housekeeping. consort of D. Wilfong. info, D. Wilfong, son.

Wimer, ____, WM, **d. 1 July** at Crab Bottom of brain fever, age, 2mos.
        parents, Cor. & Susan Wimer. born Highland Co. occ. ____.
        consort of ____. info, Cor. Wimer, father.

Whistleman, Geo., WM, **d. ____ May** on Brushy Fork of dropsy, age, 80yrs.
        parents, ____ & ____ Whistleman. born Pendleton Co.
        occ. farmer. widower. info, Jno. Todd, son-in-law.

Wiseman, Minnie, WF, **d. 20 Sep.** on Cow P. R. of diphtheria, age, 15yrs.
        parents, ____ & ____ Wiseman. born Highland Co.
        occ. ____. unmarried. info, ____, neighbor.

1887

Arbogast, Benj., WM, **d. ____ Feb.** at Crab Bottom of stricture of bowels, age, 68yrs.
        parents, Henry & Eliz. Arbogast. born Pendleton Co.
        occ. farmer. consort of Amelia A. Arogast.
        info, A. P. Arogast, nephew.

Arbogast, Levi, WM, **d. 18 May** at Crab Bottom of paralysis, age, 78yrs.
        parents, Henry & Eliz. Arbogast. born Pendleton Co.
        occ. farmer. widower. info, A. P. Arbogast, nephew.

Arbogast, Benj. S., WM, **d. 25 Jan.** at Crab Bottom of rupture, age, 27yrs.
        parents, Henry & Mary Arbogast. born Highland Co.
        occ. carpenter. single. info, A. P. Arbogast, brother.

Anderson, David W., WM, **d. 18 March** at Crab Bottom of brain fever, age, 8mos.
        parents, J. A. & Delia Anderson. born Nebraska. occ. ____.
        consort of ____. info, J. A. Anderson, father.

Beard, Patsy, WF, **d. ____ Feb.** at head of J. River of general debility, age, 70yrs.
        parents, ____ & ____. born ____. occ. domestic. widow.
        info, Chas. Beard, son.

Brennaman, ____, WM, **d. 1 Sep.** at Monterey of ____, age, 1dy.
        parents, W. W. & L. G. Brennaman. born ____. occ. ____.
        consort of ____. info, W. W. Brennaman, father.

Bowers, James F., WM, **d. 5 Sep.** on St. Creek of scrufla, age, 7yrs.
        parents, Wm. & Barbara Bowers. born St. Creek. occ. ____.
        consort of ____. info, Wm. Bowers, father.

Baker, Howard, WM, **d. ____ Jan.** on St. Creek of ____, age, 5mos.
        parents, Jonas & Susan Baker. born St. Creek. occ. ____.
        consort of ____. info, Jonas Baker, father.

Bryant, Chas. B., WM, **d. 4 Sep.** at McDowell of cholera infantum, age, 4mos.
        parents, H. E. & Frances Bryant. born McDowell. occ. ____.
        consort of ____. info, H. E. Bryant, father.

Bird, Martha E., WF, **d. 4 Feb.** on Back Creek of blood poison, age, 30yrs.
        parents, J. & M. Bird. born Back Creek. occ. housekeeping.
        consort of M. R. Bird. info, M. R. Bird, husband.

Bird, Sarah Ann, WF, **d. 9 May** on Back Creek of dropsy, age, 70yrs.
        parents, M. & Eliz. A. Curry. born Back Creek.
        occ. housekeeping. consort of W. C. Bird.
        info, M. R. Bird, son.

Colaw, ____, WM, **d. 12 Oct.** at Crab Bottom of ____, age, 2dys.
        parents, D. E. & Mary Colaw. born Crab Bottom. occ. ____.
        consort of ____. info, D. E. Colaw, father.

Daugherty, Ida E., CF, **d. 17 June** at Monterey of dropsy, age, 8yrs.
        parents, Wm. & Fanny Daugherty. born Monterey. occ. ____.
        consort of ____. info, Wm. Daugherty, father.

Doyle, Arthur F., WM, **d. 16 May** on Jackson's R. of worms, age, 2yrs.
        parents, ____ & Leona Doyle. born J. River. occ. ____.
        consort of ____. info, Jas. Corrigan, neighbor.

Eagle, Lizzie, WF, **d. 22 Aug.** on St. Creek of inflam of bowels, age, 5mos, 8dys.
        parents, P. R. & H. Eagle. born St. Creek. occ. ____.
        consort of ____. info, P. R. Eagle, father.

Eckard, Preston, WM, **d. 23 July** on J. River of flux, age, 2yrs.
        parents, Job & Ruhama Eckard. born J. River. occ. ____.
        consort of ____. info, Job Eckard, father.

Elyard, Jacob, WM, **d. ____ Nov.** on Bull P. Mt. of diabetes, age, 70yrs.
        parents, Jacob & ____ Elyard. born Pendleton Co. occ. laborer.
        consort of ____. info, Eli Botkin, neighbor.

Ervin, Robt. B., WM, **d. 20 Nov.** on Allegheny Mt. of scrofula, age, 2yrs, 1mo.
        parents, R. F. & Sarah Ervin. born Bath Co. occ. ____.
        consort of ____. info, R. F. Ervin, father.

Fleisher, Jno. W., WM, **d. 22 Aug.** on South Branch of cholera infantum,
        age, 3mos, 2dys. **parents, H. C. & Mary Fleisher.**
        born South Branch. occ. ____. consort of ____.
        info, H. C. Fleisher, father.

Fagan, Bundy, CM, **d. ____ April** on Jackson's R. of general debility, age, 80yrs.
        parents, ____ & ____ Fagan. born ____. occ. ____.
        consort of ____ info, Beverly Trent, son-in-law.

Fox, ____, WM, **d. 27 May** at Crab Bottom of ____, age, 1dy.
        parents, C. H. & M. Fox. born Crab Bottom. occ. ____.
        consort of ____. info, C. H. Fox, father.

Gillespie, James E., WM, **d. 4 Dec.** on Jackson's R. of hives, age, 6mos.
        parents, Jas. A. & Gay Gillespie. born Jackson's R. occ. ____.
        consort of ____. info, J. A. Gillespie, father.

Gwin, Rachel, WF, **d. 16 Jan.** on Cow P. R. of veneral, age, 60yrs.
        parents, W. K. & Jane Gwin. born Cow P. R. occ. housekeeping.
        widow. info, J. W. Arbogast, admr.

Gwin, Fannie, B., WF, **d. ____ July** in Big Valley of scarlet fever, age, 11yrs.
        parents, Moses & Eliz. A. Gwin. born Big Valley. occ. ____.
        consort of ____. info, Moses Gwin, father.

Gum, Otho, WM, **d. ____ Sep.** on Back Creek of consumption, age, 70yrs.
        parents, Leonard & ____ Gum. born Back Creek. occ. farmer.
        widower. info, Chas. W. Gum, son.

Helmick, Nancy, WF, **d. 9 May** at poor farm of apoplexy, age, 70yrs.
        parents, ____ & ____ Helmick. born ____. occ. ____.
        consort of ____. info, Henry Mullenax, overseer.

Hildebrand, Rev. Thos., WM, **d. ____ Oct.** at McDowell of soft of the rain, age, 76yrs.
        parents, ____ & ____ Hildebrand. born ____. occ. minister.
        consort of Mag. A. Hildebrand. info, J. C. Matheny, friend.

Hiner, ____, WF, **d. 4 Aug.** at Monterey of ____, age, 1dy.
        parents, Jos. A. & Lucy E. Hiner. born Monterey. occ. ____.
        consort of ____. info, Jos. A. Hiner, father.

Helms, J. S., WM, **d. 18 May** on B. P. R. of heart disease, age, 47yrs, 6mos.
        parents, ____ & ____ Helms. born Bath Co. occ. farmer.
        consort of Mary Helms. info, J. W. Helms, brother.

Hicklin, Ida E., WF, **d. 29 Aug.** on B. P. R. of brain fever, age, 8yrs.
    parents, Geo. H. & H. S. Hicklin. born Bull P. R. occ. ____.
    consort of ____. info, Geo. H. Hicklin, father.

Hidy, John A., WM, **d. 8 Nov.** at Crab Bottom of catarrh, age, 77yrs.
    parents, Jacob & Cath. Hidy. born Pendleton Co. occ. farmer.
    consort of Matilda Hidy. info, Jas. B. Hidy, son.

Homan, Henry, WM, **d. 6 Oct.** in B. C. Valley of dropsy, age, 3yrs.
    parents, Geo. & Laura Homan. born ____. occ. ____.
    consort of ____. info, Mrs. Matheny, friend.

Gum, Lucinda*, WF, **d. 8 Dec.** at Crab Bottom of consumption, age, 54yrs.
    parents, Wm. & A. Mullenax. born Crab Bottom.
    occ. housekeeping. widow. info, Chas. Arbogast, son-in-law.

Jackson, James, CM, **d. 30 May** on Cow P. River of consumption, age, 20yrs.
    parents, Albert & Mary Jackson. born Cow P. R. occ. laborer.
    single. info, A. Jackson, father.

Jackson, Albert, M., CM, **d. 14 June** on Cow P. River of consumption, age, 24yrs.
    parents, Albert & Mary Jackson. born Cow P. R. occ. laborer.
    single. info, A. Jackson, father.

Jack, Jacob, WM, **d. 14 July** at Crab Bottom of unknown, age, 63yrs.
    parents, John & Sarah Jack. born Crab Bottom. occ. farmer.
    unmarried. info, M. M. Jack, brother.

Kincaid, Sarah A., WF, **d. 24 Jan.** on Cow Pasture R. of consumption, age, 69yrs.
    parents, David & Sally Kincaid. born Cow Past. R. occ.
    housekeeping. unmarried. info, D. N. Kincaid, brother.

Lockridge, Laura A., WF, **d. 24 Sep.** on Bull Pasture R. of consumption,
    age, 44yrs, 10mos. **parents, Addison & Betty Ervin.**
    born Pocahontas Co. occ. housekeeping.
    consort of S. A. Lockridge. info, S. A. Lockridge, husband.

Lockridge, ____, WF, **d. 22 Sep.** on Bull Pasture R. of pneumonia, age, 2dys.
    parents, S. A. & L. A. Lockridge. born Bull P. R. occ. ____.
    consort of ____. info, S. A. Lockridge, father.

---

*This name lined out, but remainder of entry is clear. Same name and data appears on original 1886 list with death date of 26 Dec. See p. 137.

McClintic, A. B., WM, **d. 23 June** on Jackson's River of paralysis, age, 47yrs.
    parents, Wm. & Nancy McClintic. born Jackson's R.
    occ. farmer. consort of M. E. McClintic.
    info, Jno. W. McClintic, son.

Madison, Thomas, WM, **d.** ____ **Oct.** at McDowell of pneumonia, age, 32yrs.
    parents, ____ **&** ____ **Madison.** born Rockingham Co.
    occ. teamster. single. info, Robt. N. Ervin, neighbor.

McCray, Carrie, WF, **d. 10 Sep.** on Shaw's Fork of not known, age, 1yr, 6mos.
    parents, H. H. & Rebecca McCray. born Shaw's Fork.
    occ. ____. consort of ____. info, H. H. McCray, father.

Oaks, Malinda, WF, **d.** ____ **March** on Bull P. R. of diarrhea, age, 60yrs.
    parents, ____ **&** ____ **Blaine.** born ____. occ. housekeeping.
    widow. info, W. R. Pullin, grandson.

Pullin, Isy, CF, **d.** ____ **Aug.** on J. River of diptheria, age, ____.
    parents, Jerry & Annis Pullin. born J. River. occ. ____.
    consort of ____. info, Jno. Pullin, brother.

Pullin, Cora, CF, **d.** ____ on J. River of diphtheria, age, ____.
    parents, ____ **& Louisa Pullin.** born J. River occ. ____.
    consort of ____. info, Jno. Pullin, uncle.

Pullin, Sallie, CF, **d.** ____ **June** on J. River of diphtheria, age, ____.
    parents, Jerry & Annis Pullin. born J. River. occ. ____.
    consort of ____. info, Jno. Pullin, brother.

Pleasants, John, CM, **d. 6 March** on Bull P. R. of pneumonia, age, 6mos.
    parents, Wm. & Jane Pleasants. born Bull Pasture occ. ____.
    consort of ____. info, Wm. Pleasants, father.

Ralston, Josiah, WM, **d.** ____ **Nov.** in Augusta Co. of accident, age, 67yrs.
    parents, Saml & Ann Ralston. born Bull Pasture. occ. farmer.
    consort of Jemima Ralston. info, Saml Ralston, brother.

Ralston, James A., WM, **d.** ____ **Aug.** on Bull P. R. of unknown, age, 75yrs.
    parents, Saml & Ann Ralston. born Bull Pasture. occ. farmer.
    consort of Fanny Ralston. info, Saml Ralston, brother.

Ralston, ____, WF, **d. 28 Nov.** on Davis Run of whooping cough, age, 2mos, 2dys.
    parents, D. C. & S. Ralston. born Bull Pasture. occ. ____.
    consort of ____. info, D. C. Ralson, father.

Ralston, Luke, E., WM, **d. 15 Sep.** on Back Creek of ____, age, 3mos. **parents, R. M. & Dollie B. Ralston.** born Back Creek. occ. ____. consort of ____. info, R. M. Ralston, father.

Rexrode, Benj., WM, **d. 16 Oct.** at Crab Bottom of gen. debility, age, 85yrs, 5mos, 16dys. **parents, Jno. & Mary Rexrode.** born Crab Bottom. occ. farmer. consort of Eleanor Rexrode. info, Geo. A. Rexrode, son.

Stanton, Amanda, CF, **d.** ____ on poor farm of consumption, age, 20yrs. **parents, ____ & ____ Stanton.** born Bull P. River. occ. domestic. single. info, Henry Mullenax, overseer.

Seybert, Jacob, WM, **d. 1 Dec.** on South Branch of neuralgia of stom., age, 74yrs, 10mos, 15dys. **parents, Jacob & Mary Seybert.** born Pendleton Co. occ. farmer. consort of Cath. Seybert. info, Cath. Seybert, wife.

Stephenson, John W., WM, **d. 6 Nov.** on J. River of heart disease, age, 78yrs, 6mos. **parents, Jno. & Jane Stephenson.** born ath Co. occ. farmer. unmarried. info, A. Stephenson, brother.

Stone, Sol., WM, **d. 29 Aug.** on Cra Run of diabetis, age, 68yrs. **parents, Dan'l & ____ Stone,** born Pendleton Co. occ. laborer. consort of Mary Stone. info, Sol Stone, son.

Smith, Joseph, WM, **d.** ____ **Nov.** on Bull P. Mt. of unknown, age, 70yrs. **parents, ____ & ____ Smith.** born B. P. R. occ. laborer. consort of ____. info, Eli C. Botkin, neighbor.

Stinespring, Mrs., WF, **d.** ____ at McDowell of alsthemia*, age, 78yrs. **parents, ____ & ____ .** born ____. occ. ____. consort of ____. info, Jno. D. Cook, physician.

Snyder, ____, WM, **d.** ____ **July** at Crab Bottom of ____, age, 1dy. **parents, T. J. & Mollie Snyder.** born Crab Bottom. occ. ____. consort of ____. info, A. N. Colaw, neighbor.

Snyder, Chas. P., WM, **d. 18 Jan.** at Crab Bottom of diphtheria, age, 2yrs, 5mos. **parents, C. C. & Louisa Snyder.** born Crab Bottom. occ. ____. consort of ____. info, C. C. Snyder, father.

---

*probably a misspelling of asthenia.

Trimble, John Z., WM, **d. 5 Aug.** at Monterey of ____, age, 1mo, 2dys.
  parents, I. H. & Mat. Trimble. born Monterey. occ. ____.
  consort of ____. info, I. H. Trimble, father.

Turner, Sam'l., CM, **d.** ____ **June** on Bull P. R. of pneumonia, age, 1mo.
  parents, Geo. & Hetty J. Turner. born Bull P. occ. ____.
  consort of ____. info, Geo. Turner, father.

Turner, Alex., CM, **d.** ____ **Dec.** on Bull P. R. of hives, age, 3mos.
  parents, Frank & Fanny Turner. orn Bull P. R. occ. ____.
  consort of ____. info, Frank Turner, father.

Townsend, ____, WM, **d.** ____ **Dec.** on Back Creek of ____, age, 6mos.
  parents, G. W. & Louisa Townsend. born Back Creek.
  occ. ____. consort of ____. info, G. W. Townsend, father.

Trainer, Rachel, WF, **d. 16 Jan.** on Back Creek of not known, age, 72yrs, 8mos, 5dys.
  parents, L. & A. Gum. born Bath Co. occ. housekeeping. consort of Mich. Trainer. info, Mich. Trainer, husband.

Whistleman, Geo., WM, **d. 8 Aug.** on Brushy Run of dropsy, age, 79yrs.
  parents, ____ & ____ Whistleman. born Pendleton Co.
  occ. farmer. widower. info, John Todd, son-in-law.

Wilson, ____, CF, **d. 25 Dec.** on B. P. R. of ____, age, 14dys.
  parents, ____ & Leze Wilson. born . B. P. R. occ. ____.
  consort of ____. info, Jas. Stanton, friend.

Woods, Robbie B., WM, **d. 12 May** at Meadow Dale of diphtheria,
  age, 17yrs, 2mos, 5dys. **parents, T. J. & Elvira A. Woods.**
  born Meadow Dale. occ. ____. consort of ____.
  info, T. J. Woods, father.

Woods, Chas. P., WM, **d. 12 Aug.** at Meadow Dale of diphtheria, age, 16yrs.
  parents, T. J. & Elvira A. Woods. born Meadow Dale.
  occ. ____. consort of ____. info, T. J. Woods, father.

Woods, Jno. Willie, WM, **d. 26 Aug.** at Meadow Dale of diphtheria, age, 8yrs.
  parents, T. J. & Elvira A. Woods. born Meadow Dale.
  occ. ____. consort of ____. info, T. J. Woods, father.

Woods, Maude B., WF, **d. 30 July** at Meadow Dale of diphtheria,
  age, 5yrs, 5mos, 18dys. **parents, N. B. & Lucy Woods.**
  born Meadow Dale. occ. ____. consort of ____.
  info, N. B. Woods, father.

1888

Arbogast, W. G., WM, **d.** ____ **Dec.** at Crab Bottom of neuralgia, age, 27yrs.
    parents, J. E. & Jane Arbogast. born ____. occ. farmer.
consort of Mary Arbogast. info, ____.

Arbogast, Jno. D., WM, **d.** ____ at Crab Bottom of measles, age, 28yrs.
    parents, H. & Mary Arbogast. born ____. occ. farmer.
consort of Sue Arbogast. info, ____.

Armstrong, Emma C., WF, **d. 3 April** on Bull Pasture R. of eresypelas, age, 12dys.
    parents, M. M. & S. E. Armstrong. born Bull Pasture R.
occ.____. consort of ____. info, S. E. Armstrong, father.

Bird, Allen, CM, **d.** ____ at poor farm of rheumatism, age, 70yrs.
    parents, ____ **&** ____. born ____. occ. ____.
consort of ____. info, ____, Supt. of Poor.

Beverage, Virgil, WM, **d. 22 Jan.** at Monterey of convulsions, ag, 3yrs.
    parents, W. A. & Jennie Beverage. born Monterey. occ. ____.
consort of ____. info, ____, father.

Beverage, Mary M., WF, **d. 30 July** on St. Creek of catarrh of stomach, age, 71yrs.
    parents, John & N. Hevener. born ____. occ. ____
consort of John Beverage. info, W. A. Beverage, son.

Beverage, Thomas, WM, **d. 24 July** on St. Creek of general debility, age, 79yrs, 17dys.
    parents, John & M. Beverage. born St. Creek. occ. ____.
consort of Eliz. Beverage. info, ____.

Byrd, Elizabeth, WF, **d. 12 Feb.** on Cow Pasture of old age, age, 91yrs, 1mo, 1dy.
    parents, ____ **&** ____ **Capetoe.** born ____. occ. ____ widow.
info, J. T. Byrd, son.

Botkin, ____, WF, **d.** ____ on B. P. Mt. of measles, age, 40yrs.
    parents, J. & ____ **Botkin.** born B. P. Mt. occ. ____. single.
info, ____.

Clendenen, John, WM, **d.** ____ **Oct.** at Mill Gap of paralysis, age, 89yrs.
    parents, ____ **&** ____ **Clendenen.** born ____. occ. lacksmith.
widower. info, J. Clendenen, son.

Crummett, Minnie, WF, **d. 31 Aug.** on Shaw's Fork of diphtheria, age, 6yrs.
        parents, Eli & L. E. Crummett. born South Fork. occ. ____.
consort of ____. info, Eli Crummett, father.

Davis, Lizzie, P., WF, **d. 12 Jan.** on Crab Run of consumption, age, 18yrs, 9mos, 19dys.
        parents, A. S. T. & E. J. Davis. born Davis Run.
occ. ____. single. info, A. S. T. Davis, father.

Dever, ____, WF, **d.** ____ **May** on Jackson's River of ____, age, 3mos.
        parents, ____ & Mary Dever. born Highland Co. occ. ____.
consort of ____. info, ____.

Ervine, Nancy, WF, **d. 2 Oct.** on Back Creek of complication of D., age, 76yrs.
        parents, ____ & ____. born Highland Co. occ. ____. widow.
info, E. A. Wade, N. P.

Ervine, Sarah A., WF, **d. 4 Nov.** on Back Creek of typhoid fever, age, 24yrs.
        parents, ____ & ____. born Highland Co. occ. ____.
consort of Francis Ervine. info, E. A. Wade, N. P.

Eye, ____, WM, **d.** ____ **May** on St. Creek of unknown, age, 24dys.
        parents, J. Pope & Mary Eye. born Highland Co. occ. ____.
consort of ____. info, J. P. Eye, father.

Ervine, Thomas, WM, **d. 28 Jan.** on Bull Pasture Mt. of consumption, age, 22yrs.
        parents, Wm. & E. Ervine. born Highland Co. occ. farmer.
consort of ____. info, ____, father.

Evick, Mary A., WF, **d. 15 Oct.** at McDowell of consumption, age, 38yrs.
        parents, ____ & ____ Few. born Virginia. occ. ____.
consort of Dice Evick. info, D. Evick, husband.

Fisher, ____, CF, **d.** ____ at McDowell of ____, age, 3mos.
        parents, ____ & ____ Fisher. born Virginia. occ. ____.
consort of ____. info, J. L. Fisher, undertaker.

Fleisher, Wm. Olin, WM, **d.** ____ **Aug.** on St. Creek of cholera infantum, age, 1mo.
        parents, H. C. & Mary M. Fleisher. born Virginia. occ. ____.
consort of ____. info, H. C. Fleisher, father.

Grogg, Julia, WF, **d.** ____ **Aug.** at Crab Bottom of ____, age, ____.
        parents, ____ & ____ Grogg. born Virginia. occ. ____.
consort of ____. info, H. Mullenax, overseer poor.

Griffin, Mattie, WF, **d.** ____ on Jackson's River of ____, age, ____.
   parents, ____ **&** ____ **Gum.** born Virginia. occ. ____.
   consort of William Griffen. info, W. Griffen, husband.

Hiner, Ruth, WF, **d. 28 July** near Montery of rheumatism, age, 66yrs.
   parents, Joseph & Sarah Jones. born Virginia. occ. ____.
   consort of Joseph B. Hiner. info, J. Hiner, husband.

Hite, Harley, W., WM, **d. 16 Feb.** on Jackson's River of pneumonia, age, 14mos.
   parents, Lee & Maggie Hite. born Virginia. occ. ____.
   consort of ____. info, L. Hite, father.

Kinkead, William, WM, **d.** ____ at poor farm of ____, age, ____.
   parents, ____ **&** ____ **Kinkead.** born ____. occ. ____.
   consort of ____. info, A. T. Stephenson, Supt. of Poor.

Keister, Ann, WF, **d.** ____ **Sep.** on Bull Pasture River of old age, age, 85yrs.
   parents, ____ **&** ____. born ____. occ. ____. widow.
   info, ____.

Lewis, ____, CF, **d.** ____ at McDowell of __, age, 2mos.
   parents, ____ **&** ____ **Lewis.** born ____. occ. ____.
   consort of ____. info, J. T. Edins, undertaker.

Lamb, Mary L., WF, **d. 13 Oct.** at Palo Alto of diptheria, age, 16yrs, 11mos, 1dy.
   parents, E. & ____ **Lamb.** born Virginia. occ. ____.
   consort of ____. info, E. Lamb, father.

Lightner, Clevie R., WF, **d. 15 Oct.** at Mill Gap of pneumonia, age, 4yrs, 19mos.
   parents, R. & G. Lightner. born Virginia. occ. ____.
   consort of ____. info, R. Lightner, father.

Miller, Jno. A., CM, **d. 17 July** on Bull Pasture R. of pneumonia, age, 22yrs.
   parents, Wm. & ____ **Miller.** born Virginia. occ. laborer.
   consort of Amy Miller. info, ____, father.

Miller, William B., CM, **d. 1 Sep.** on Jackson's River of ____, age, ½ dy.*
   parents, Geo. & Blanche Miller. born Virginia. occ. ____.
   consort of ____. info, ____.

Miller, Blanche, CF, **d. 26 July** on Jackson's River of consumption, age, 18yrs.
   parents, ____ **& Mary Fagan.** born Virginia. occ. ____.
   consort of Geo. Miller. info, G. Miller, husband.

---

* age almost certainly inaccurate—see following entry.

Porter, Helen N. C., WF, **d.** ____ **Jan.** on head of Jackson's River of laryngitis, age, 5mos. **parents, S. A. & Lillie Porter.** born Virginia. occ. ____. consort of ____. info, S. A. Porter, father.

Pullin, Willis, CM, **d.** ____ **March** on Jackson's River of consumption, age, 19yrs. **parents, Jerry & Annis Pullin.** born Virginia. occ. ____. consort of ____. info, ____.

Pullin, Icy*, CF, **d.** ____ **March** on Jackson's River of consumption, age, 6yrs. **parents, Jerry & Annis Pullin.** born Virginia. occ. ____. consort of ____. info, ____.

Pullin, S. H., WM, **d. 16 May** on Bull Pasture of cancer, age, 52yrs. **parents, S. & S. Pullin.** born Virginia. occ. farmer. consort of Henrietta Pullin. info, H. Pullin, wife.

Propst, Nancy E., WF, **d. 1 March** on Bull Pasture Mt. of pneumonia, age, 68yrs. **parents,** ____ **&** ____ **McQuain.** born Virginia. occ. ____. consort of Henry Propst. info, H. Propst, husband.

Prit, Bell, WF, **d.** ____ **Jan.** on Bull Pasture Mt. of ____, age, 26yrs. **parents,** ____ **& Sally Prit.** born Virginia. occ. ____. consort of ____. info, ____.

Rexrode, Sarah E., WF, **d. 26 March** on St. Creek of consumption, age, 21yrs. **parents, Leonard & Lavinia Rexrode.** born Virginia. occ. ____. unmarried. info, ____, brother.

Rider, Geo. W., WM, **d. 20 May** at Valley Center of liver disease, age, 36yrs. **parents, Jas. K. & Nancy Rider.** born Virginia. occ. farmer. consort of Mary Rider. info, ____, physician.

Ratcliff, Arch, WM, **d. 20 Sep.** on Jackson's River of consumption, age, 30yrs. **parents, Jno. & E. Ratcliff.** born Virginia. occ. farmer. consort of E. A. Ratcliff. info, ____, physician.

Reynolds, Ida, WF, **d.** __ **Aug.** on Shaw's Fork of typhoid fever, age, 22yrs. **parents, Wm. & Louisa Reynolds.** born Orange Co. occ. ____. consort of ____. info, S. J. Reynolds, uncle.

Robertson, ____, WF, **d. 9 Dec** on J. River of ____, age, ____. **parents,** ____ **&** ____ **Douglas.** born Highland Co. occ. ____. consort of Jesse Robertson. info, J. Robertson, husband.

---

* similar entry on original 1887 list.

Rexrode, Leonard, WM, **d. 17 Dec.** on St. Creek of kidney disease, age, 83yrs.
   parents, L. & M. Rexrode. born Pendleton Co. occ. farmer.
   consort of Lavinia Rexrode. info, L. Rexrode, wife.

Siron, Jonathan, WM, **d. 7 Feb.** on B. P. Mt. of heart disease, age, 75yrs.
   parents, ____ & ____. born ____. occ. farmer.
   consort of E. Siron. info, J. M. Siron, son.

Snyder, Abe, CM, **d. ____** at New Hampden of old age, age 75yrs.
   parents, ____ & ____. born Virginia. occ. blacksmith.
   consort of Mary Snyder. info, ____.

Simmons, Mrs. W. H., WF, **d. 6 May** on Bull Pasture Mt. of pneumonia, age, 50yrs.
   parents, S. E. & . Armstrong. born Virginia. occ. ____.
   consort of ____. info, ____.

Steuart, Henrietta, WF, **d. 6 May** on Bull Pasture River of ____, age, 41yrs, 10mos.
   parents, J. & Cornelia Gentry. born Albemarle Co. occ. ____.
   consort of M. V. Steuart. info, M. V. Steuart, husband.

Steuart, Sally, WF, **d. ____** on Cow Pasture River of old age, age, 78yrs.
   parents, Wm. & ____ Steuart. born ____. occ. ____.
   consort of ____. info, W. B. Steuart, son.

Steuart, ____, WF, **d. ____** at McDowell of ____, age, ____.
   parents, John & ____ Steuart. born Virginia. occ. ____.
   consort of ____. info, ____, father.

Steuart, ____, WF, **d. ____** at McDowell of ____, age, ____.
   parents, Sam'l. & ____ Steuart. born ____. occ. ____.
   consort of ____. info, L. A. Carichoff, undertaker.

Snyder, Mary, CF, **d. ____** at New Hampden of overdose of morphia, age, ____.
   parents, ____ & ____. born ____. occ. ____.
   consort of ____. info, R. Trimble, physician.

Simmons, Geo. W., WM, **d. 11 Dec.** at poor farm of scrofula, age, 3mos.
   parents, Jno. & E. Simmons. born Virginia. occ. ____.
   consort of ____. info, ____, Supt.

Simmons, Granville, WM, **d. 1 July** on St. Creek of consumption, age, 54yrs.
   parents, Eli & Margt Simmons. born Virginia. occ. laborer.
   consort of Rebecca Simmons. info, L. Simmons.

Taylor, ____, WF, **d. ____ May** at Hightown of ____. age, 1yr.
        parents, G. W. & Mary Taylor born Virginia. occ. ____.
        consort of ____. info, G. W. Taylor, father.

Taylor, Mary Jane, WF, **d. ____ Feb.** at Hightown of consumption, age, 35yrs.
        parents, Wesley & M. Wilson. born Virginia. occ. ____.
        consort of Geo. W. Taylor. info, G. W. Taylor, husband.

Townsend, Darius, WM, **d. ____ Dec.** on Bull Pasture of ____, age, 6mos.
        parents, G. W. & Alice Townsend. born Bull Pasture. occ. ____.
        consort of ____. info, ____, father.

Turner, ____. WM, **d. ____** in Highland Co. of consumption, age, 9yrs.
        parents, F. & Fanny Turner. born Virginia. occ. ____.
        consort of ____. info, ____, father.

Trimble, ____, WM, **d. ____ Aug.** on Crab Run of ____, age, 1dy.
        parents, James & M. Trimble. born Virginia. occ. ____.
        consort of ____. info, J. Trimble, father.

Trimble, Alley, WM, **d. __ Jan.** at Monterey of hydrocephalis, age, 5mos.
        parents, Kenton & Mollie Trimble. born Virginia. occ. ____.
        consort of ____. info, K. Trimble, father.

Waybright, John, WM, **d. ____ Nov.** at Crab Bottom of Bright's disease, age, 75yrs.
        parents, ____ & ____ Waybright. born Virginia. occ. miller.
        consort of Mary Wayright. info, ____, son.

Waybright, Jennie, WF, **d. ____** at Crab Bottom of consumption, age, 29yrs.
        parents, David & ____ Snyder. born Virginia. occ. ____.
        consort of S. S. Waybright. info, S. S. W., husband.

Waggoner, Solomon,* WM, **d. 18 March** at Crab Bottom of paralysis, age, 82yrs.
        parents, ____ & ____ Waggoner. born ____. occ. farmer.
        widower. info, J. S. Waggoner, son.

Wilfong, Sabina,* WF, **d. 31 July** on Allegheny Mt. of dropsy, age, 70yrs.
        parents, J & M. Simmons. born ____. occ. housekeeping.
        widow. info, Jonas Wilfong, son.

Weeks, A. J., WM, **d. 2 May** at Hightown of mean whiskey, age, 24yrs.
        parents, Jno. & Nancy Weeks. born Virginia. occ. laborer.
        consort of Susan Weeks. info, L. Simmons, brother-in-law.

---

* these two entered on the original 1887 list.

Varner, David, WM, **d. 28 Nov.** on St. Creek of diabetis, age, 76yrs.
parents, Peter & Ann Varner. born Virginia. occ. farmer.
consort of Sarah Varner. info, J. K. Varner, son.

1889

Arbogast, Charles C., WM, **d. 9 Aug.** at Crab Bottom of St. Vitus dance, age, 19yrs.
parents, Henry & Mary Arbogast. born Highland Co. occ. farmer. unmarried. info, Henry Arbogast, father.

Arbogast, Robbie W., WM, **d. 28 Nov.** at Monterey of diphtheria, age, 15yrs.
parents, J. W. & Amanda Arbogast. born Highland Co. occ. ____. unmarried. info, A. W. Arbogast, brother.

Arbogast, Jno. W., WM, **d. ____ Jan.** at Monterey of liver disease, age, ____.
parents, ____ & ____ Arbogast. born Highland Co. occ. sheriff. consort of Amanda Arbogast. info, A. W. Arbogast, son.

Benson, Annie, WF, **d. 12 Jan.** at Vanderpool of diphtheria, age, 12yrs.
parents, W. W. & Adelaide Benson. born Highland Co. occ. ____. consort of ____. info, W. W. Benson, father.

Byrd, J. H., WM, **d. 1 Oct.** in Highland Co. of general debility, age, 72yrs.
parents, ____ & ____ Byrd. born Botetourt Co. occ. physician. consort of Mary Byrd. info, W. W. Benson, son-in-law.

Campbell, A. Hanson, WM, **d. ____ Jan.** at Monterey of diabetes, age, 76yrs.
parents, Alexander & Mar. Campbell. born Pendleton Co. occ. farmer. consort of Isabelle Campbell.
info, L. H. Stephenson, son-in-law.

Chew, Jesse, WM, **d. ____** in Highland Co. of old age, age, 80yrs.
parents, ____ & ____ Chew. born Pendleton Co. occ. farmer. widower. info, Geo. Chew, son.

Crummett, Catherine, WF, **d. ____** in Highland Co. of unknown, age, ____.
parents, ____ & ____. born ____. occ. ____. widow.
info, Jno. W. Brown, neighbor.

Cobb, ____, WM, **d. 12 May** in Highland Co. of ____, age, 1dy.
parents, Sam'l. & M. Cobb. born Highland Co. occ. ____. consort of ____. info, M. Cobb, mother.

Dettimore, Esther A., WM, *[sic]* **d. 9 Nov.** in Highland Co. of ____, age, 11mos.
        parents, D. F. & ____ Dettimore. born Highland Co. occ. ____.
consort of ____. info, D. F. Dettimore, father.

Doyle, James, WM, **d. 9 Nov.** in Highland Co. of accidently shot, age, 30yrs.
        parents, ____ & ____ Doyle. born Highland Co. occ. laborer.
consort of Melissa Doyle. info, M. Doyle, wife.

Erwin, Geo. W., WM, **d. 8 June** in Highland Co. of internal acess, age, 38yrs.
        parents, Edw. & Eliza Erwin. born Highland Co. occ. farmer.
unmarried. info, ____.

Eye, Henry, WM, **d. 11 April** in Highland Co. of consumption, age, 71yrs.
        parents, Jno. & ____ Eye. born Highland Co. occ. laborer.
widower. info, P. Eye, son.

Fleisher, Carrie S. WF, **d. 26 Nov.** at Monterey of heart disease, age, 17yrs.
        parents, A. H. & Hannah Fleisher. born Highland Co. occ. ____.
unmarried. info, B. E. Fleisher, brother.

Fleisher, Adam H., WM, **d. 22 March** at Monterey of diabetes, age, 70yrs.
        parents, Benj. & ____ Fleisher. born Highland Co. occ. farmer.
consort of Hannah P. Fleisher. info, B. E. Fleisher, son.

Gibson, Wm. D., WM, **d. 15 Sep.** at Monterey of dropsy, age, 65yrs.
        parents, S. A. & Sally Gibson. born Bath Co. occ. farmer.
consort of E. A. Gibson. info, E. A. Gibson, wife.

Gum, Omega, WF, **d. 11 Nov.** in Highland Co. of unknown, age, 16yrs.
        parents, Amos & N. Gum. born Highland Co. occ. ____.
consort of ____. info, A. Gum, father.

Griffen, Ashby, WM, **d. ____ Feb.** in Highland Co. of unknown, age, 5yrs.
        parents, Jesse & ____ Griffen. born Highland Co. occ. ____.
consort of ____. info, Jesse Griffen, father.

Gwin, Mrs. Morgan, WF, **d. ____** in Highland Co. of unknown, age, ____.
        parents, T. & M. Sorrel. born Highland Co. occ. ____.
consort of Morgan Gwin, info, M. Gwin, husband.

Gwin, Sally, WF, **d. ____** in Highland Co. of unknown, age, ____.
        parents, ___ & ____. born ___. occ. ____. unmarried. info, ____.

Hevener, Emma, WF, **d. 27 July** in Highland Co. of pupuerpual fever, age, 19yrs.
        parents, John & Marg't Hughs. born Pocahontas Co. occ. ____.
consort of Jonas Hevener. info, J. Hevener, husband.

Helmic, John A.,* WM, **d.** ____ **March** in Highland Co. of unknown, age, 2mos.
        parents, Cora Helmic. born Highland Co. occ. ____.
        consort of ____. info, ____.

Hevener, Phebe, WF, **d.** ____ **Aug.** in Highland Co. of heart disease, age, 40yrs.
        parents, Wm. & Naomi Hevener. born Highland Co.
        occ. ____. consort of J. P. Hevener.
        info, Jos. H. Hevener, brother-in-law.

Hevener, Wm. D., WM, **d. 15 Feb.** in Highland Co. of gangrene, age, 64yrs.
        parents, Jno. & Eleanor Hevener. born Pendleton Co.
        occ. farmer. consort of Jane Hevener. info, Jonas Hevener, son.

Hevener, ____, WM, **d.** ____ in Highland Co. of ____, age, 16dys.
        parents, Jonas & Emma Hevener. born Highland Co. occ. ____.
        consort of ____. info, Jonas Hevener, father.

Hodge, Chas. G., WM, **d. 4 Feb.** in Highland Co. of diphtheria, age, 6yrs.
        parents, Geo. H. & H. J. Hodge. born Highland Co. occ. ____.
        consort of of ____. info, Geo. H. Hodge, father.

Hook, ____, WM, **d. 5 March** in Highland Co. of ____, age, ____.
        parents, G. W. & P. A. Hook. born Highland Co. occ.____.
        consort of ____. info, G. W. Hook, father.

Hunklefoot, Henry,* CM, **d.** ____ in Highland Co. of old age, age, 80yrs.
        parents, ____ & ____. born Highland Co. occ. ____.
        consort of ____. info, ____, overseer of poor.

Jenkins, Henry, WM, **d. 25 March** in Highland Co. of accidental, age, 8yrs.
        parents, Oz & Nancy Jenkins. born Highland Co. occ. ____.
        consort of ____. info, Geo. Vance, neighbor.

Jackson, Henry, CM, **d. 10 April** in Highland Co. of consumption, age, 30yrs.
        parents, Albert & ____. Jackson. born Highland Co. occ. laborer.
        consort of Frances Jackson. info, Albert Jackson, father.

Jackson, Henry Clay, CM, **d. 15 May** in Highland Co. of ____, age, ____.
        parents, H. & F. Jackson. born Highland Co. occ. ____.
        consort of ____. info, Albert Jackson, grandfather.

---

* a similar entry is on the 1890 list

Jackson, William, CM, d. ____ Sep. in Highland Co. of ____, age, ____.
   parents, H. & F. Jackson. born Highland Co. occ. ____.
   consort of ____. info, Albert Jackson, grandfather.

Malcom, Albert E., WM, **d. 24 Dec.** in Highland Co. of fever, age, 30yrs.
   parents, M. V. & ____ Malcom. born Highland Co. occ. laborer.
   unmarried. info, M. V. Malcom, father.

Minor, Allen, CM, d. ____ Nov. in Highland Co. of hives, age, 2mos.
   parents, Fred & Rachel Minor. born Highland Co. occ. laborer.
   consort of ____. info, ____.

Mullenax, James K., WM, **d. 24 Aug.** in Highland Co. of pneumonia, age, 18yrs.
   parents, W. & Sarah Mullenax. born Highland Co. occ. laborer.
   unmarried. info, W. Mullenax, father.

Newman, Jacob, WM, **d. 31 Dec.** in Highland Co. of paralysis, age, 90yrs.
   parents, L. & M. Newman. born Highland Co. occ. farmer.
   consort of ____ Newman. info, S. Newman, son.

Noel, Mollie L., WF, **d. 30 March** at Hightown of consumption, age, 34yrs.
   parents, ____ & Mary Noel. born Highland Co. occ. ____.
   unmarried. info, R. Noel, brother.

Puffenbarger, Elmer C., WM, **d. 1 Aug.** in Highland Co. of cholera infantum,
   age, 1yr, 7mos, 9dys. **parents, C. L. Puffenarger.**
   born Highland Co. occ. ____. consort of ____.
   info, C. L. Puffenbarger, father.

Pullin, James, CM, d. ____ July in Highland Co. of consumption, age, 19yrs.
   parents, Jerry & Annis Pullin. born Highland Co. occ. ____.
   unmarried. info, A. Pullin, mother.

Pullin, Cameron, WM, **d. 19 Oct.** in Highland Co. of killed by falling tree, age, 21yrs.
   parents, Jno. & Louisa Pullin. born Highland Co. occ. ____.
   consort of ____. info, Jno. Pullin, father.

Ruckman, Samuel H., WM, **d. 23 Oct.** in Highland Co. of diphtheria, age, 18yrs.
   parents, D. V. & Anna Ruckman. born Highland Co. occ. ____.
   consort of ____. info, D. V. Ruckman, father.

Rexrode, Michael, WM, **d.** ____ **March** in Highland Co. of dropsy, age, 73yrs.
   parents, ____ & ____ Rexrode. born Highland Co. occ. farmer.
   consort of ____ Rexrode. info, H. Rexrode, ____.

Rexrode, Wm. A., WM, **d. 7 March** in Highland Co. of consumption, age, 24yrs. **parents, L. & L. Rexrode.** born Highland Co. occ. farmer. unmarried. info, L. Rexrode, mother.

Rodgers, Milburn, CM, **d. ____ March** in Highland Co. of consumption, age, 5yrs. **parents, Jno. & Mary Rodgers.** born Highland Co. occ. ____. consort of ____. info, Albert Jackson, grandfather.

Straughan, Jno. J., WM, **d. 5 July** at Monterey of unknown, age, ____. **parents, ____ & ____.** born ____. occ. editor. consort of ____. info, W. A. Cunningham, A.

Sheffer, Geo. W., WM, **d. 10 March** in Highland Co. gunshot, age, 43yrs. **parents, ____ & ____.** born Highland Co. occ. farmer. consort of Eliz. Sheffer. info, E. Sheffer, wife.

Siron, Sarah J., WF, **d. 4 Feb.** in Highland Co. of La Grippe, age, 17yrs. **parents, A. C. & ____ Siron.** born Highland Co. occ. ____. unmarried. info, ____, father.

Stephenson, Adam, WM, **d. 2 Oct.** in Highland Co. of abcess of stomach, age, 78yrs, 6mos, 17dys. **parents, Jno. & Jane Stephenson.** born Bath Co. occ. farmer. consort of Susan Stephenson. info, L. H. Stephenson, son.

Samples, Thomas J., WM, **d. 19 Oct** in Highland Co. of neuralgia of heart, age, 27yrs. **parents, Elijah & H. Samples.** born Highland Co. occ. farmer. unmarried. info, E. Samples, father.

Scott, James, CM, **d. 9 Aug.** in Highland Co. of ____, age, 71yrs. **parents, ____ & ____.** born ____. occ. farmer. consort of ____. info, ____.

Turner, Hattie, CF, **d. 10 Aug.** in Highland Co. of ____, age, 1dy. **parents, G. R. & H. Turner.** born Highland Co. occ. ____. consort of ____. info, J. M. Siron, neighbor.

Todd, Maggie I., WF, **d. 21 Jan.** in Highland Co. of diphtheria, age, 13yrs. **parents, Jno. & C. Todd.** born Highland Co. occ. ____. consort of ____. info, Jno. Todd, father.

Tracy, Mrs., WF, **d. 23 Feb.** in Highland Co. of dropsy, age, 74yrs. **parents, ____ & ____.** born Highland Co. occ.____. consort of Jno. Tracy. info, J. Tracy, husband.

Turner, Pollie, WF, **d.** ____ in Highland Co. of ____, age, ____
    parents, ____ & ____. born Highland Co. occ. ____.
    consort of ____. info, ____.

Turner, __, WF, **d.** ____ **May** in Highland Co. of ____, age, ____.
    parents, Geo. W. Turner. born Highland Co. occ. farmer.
    consort of ____. info, G. W. Turner, father.

Turner, Emma, CF, **d. 10 Aug.** in Highland Co. of consumption, age, 35yrs.
    parents, ____ & ____. born Highland Co. occ. ____.
    consort of Geo. Turner. info, G. Turner, husband.

Turner, Sam'l G., CM, **d. 10 May** in Highland Co. of unknown, age, 4yrs.
    parents, ____ & ____. born Highland Co. occ. ____.
    consort of ____. info, ____

Wimer, Catherine, WF, **d. 5 May** in Highland Co. of cancer, age, 43yrs.
    parents, ____ & ____. born Highland Co. occ. ____.
    consort of Philip Wimer. info, P. Wimer, husband.

Hiner, ____, WM, **d.** ____ **Oct.** in Monterey of spasms, age, 1dy.
    parents, J. O. & Janie Hiner. born Monterey. occ. ____.
    consort of ____. info, J. O. Hiner, father.

1890

Bird, Hester, WF, **d. 12 June** on Back Creek of old age, age, 73yrs.
    parents, John & Sarah McCarty. born Bath Co. occ. ____.
    widow. info, Louisa Pullin, daughter.

Bird, Lanty, WM, **d.** ____ **Aug.** at Doe Hill of stricture of urinary canal, age, 18yrs.
    parents, Mary Bird. born ____. occ. ____. single.
    info, O. A. Bird, brother.

Beard, Lewis, CM, **d. 21 June** on Jackson's River of inflame of stomach, age, 41yrs.
    parents, Patsy Beard. born Highland Co. occ. laborer.
    consort of Amanda Beard. info, C. Beard, brother.

Beathe, Crawford, WM, **d.** ____ **Feb.** on Crab Run of ____, age, 40yrs.
    parents, James & Marg't Beathe. born Crab Run. occ. laborer.
    single. info, C. Ralston, brother-in-law.

Colaw, Dora Etta, WF, **d. 6 July** at Crab Bottom of scrofula, age, 3yrs.
    parents, Daniel & S. J. Colaw. born Crab Bottom. occ. ____.
    consort of ____. info, D. Colaw, father.

Collins, Mc., WM, **d. 19 May** on Allegheny Mt. of worms, age, 6yrs.
    parents, W. H. & Mary Collins. born ____. occ. ____.
    consort of ____. info, W. H. Collins, father.

Chew, Polly, WF, **d. 19 Sep.** on St. Creek of neuralgia, age, 80yrs.
    parents, Geo. & ____ Arbogast. born ____. occ. ____.
    widow. info, G. E. M. Chew, son.

Cobb, ____, WF, **d. 30 July** on Jack Mt. of ____, age, 1dy.
    parents, S. A. & Martha Cobb. born ____. occ. ____.
    info, Sam Cobb, father.

Chew, Jesse, WM, **d. 15 Sep.** on Bull Pasture River of catarrah, age, 75yrs.
    parents, ____ & ____ Chew. born ____. occ. laborer.
    widower. info, J. D. Carrol, son-in-law.

Cook, Lucinda, WF, **d. 11June** on Bull Pasture River of general debility, age, 70yrs.
    parents, ____ & ____ Tucker. born ____. occ. ____.
    consort of ____. info, ____.

Davis, Elizabeth J., WF, **d. 3 May** on Bull Pasture River of consumption, age, 51yrs.
    parents, J. D. & E. Hamilton. born ____. occ. ____.
    consort of A. S. T. Davis. info, A. S. T. Davis, husband.

Devericks, Mary E., WF, **d. 9 April** on Shaw's Fork of spinal disease, age, 46yrs.
    parents, W. L. & M. Rodgers. born ____. occ. ____.
    consort of T. M. Devericks. info, T. M. Devericks, husband.

Dickson, William, WM, **d. 1 July** at Monterey of dysentery, age, 33yrs.
    parents, Collingwood & H. Dickson. born England. occ. ____.
    unmarried. info, C. A. Dickson, brother.

Dickenson, Lida, WF, **d. 28 Nov.** in Monterey of pyaeria, age, 17yrs, 8mos, 28dys.
    parents, W. A. & E. M. Cunningham. born Monterey. occ. ____.
    consort of L. A. Dickenson. info, W. A. Cunningham, father.

Dawson, Austin, CM, **d. 3 June** on B. P. R. of consumption, age, 29yrs.
    parents, ____ & ____. born ____. occ. laborer.
    consort of Frances Dawson. info, F. Dawson, wife.

Folks, Rachel, WF, **d. 8 Nov.** at Crab Bottom of pyaeria, age, 24yrs.
    parents, Wm. & Lavinia Hevener. born Crabbottom. occ. ____.
    consort of Ruby D. Folks. info, R. D. Folks, husband.

Gwin, Hamilton, WM, **d.** ____ **Aug.** on Cow Pasture River of pneumonia, age, 75yrs.
    parents, Jno. & ____ Gwin. born ____. occ. farmer.
    consort of ____. info, ____.

Hiner, John, WM, **d. 18 June** on Jackson's River of kidney disease,
    age, 81yrs, 2mos, 23dys. **parents, Alex & Harriet Hiner.**
    born J. R. occ. farmer. consort of Jane Hiner. info, ____ Hiner, son.

Helmic, John O., WM, **d.** ____ **Sep.** on Sang Mt. of ____, age, 2mos.
    parents, Cora Helmic. born Sang Mt. occ. ____.
    consort of ____. info, S. Whitecotton, neighbor.

Hevener, J. P., WM, **d. 15 July** at Crabbottom of cancer, age, 50yrs.
    parents, Henry & Naomi Hevener. born Crabbottom.
    occ. farmer. widower. info, J. G. Hevener, neighbor.

Herold, D., WM, **d. 26 June** on St. Creek of dropsy, age, 83yrs.
    parents, ____ & ____ Herold. born ____. occ. ____.
    consort of E. M. Herold. info, Dice Lantz, step-son.

Hunklefoot, Henry, CM, **d.** ____ **June** at poor farm of old age, age 80yrs.
    parents, ____ & ____. born ____. occ. ____. consort of ____.
    info, H. Mullenax, overseer poor.

Helmic, Elizabeth, WF, **d.** ____ **Aug.** on Sang Mt. of dropsy of heart, age, 70yrs.
    parents, ____ & ____ Simmons. born ____. occ. ____.
    consort of ____. info, S. Whitecotton, neighbor.

Jordan, Zula C., WF, **d. 13 March** at Crabbottom of worms, age, 1yr, 6mos, 14dys.
    parents, S. B. & S. E. Jordan. born Crabbottom. occ. ____.
    consort of ____. info, S. B. Jordan, father.

Kirkpatrick, Nancy, WF, **d. 24 Nov.** on Back Creek of pneumonia,
    age, 71yrs, 8mos, 2dys. **parents, John & Jane Galford.**
    born ____. occ. ____. consort of John Kirkpatrick.
    info, J. Kirkpatrick, husband.

Kincaid, C. R., WM, **d. 26 May** on Cow Pature R. of consumption,
    age, 20yrs, 11mos, 20dys. **parents, D. N. & M. E. Kincaid.**
    born C. P. R. occ. ____. consort of ____. info, D. N. Kincaid, father.

Kiracofe, Lenora L., WF, **d. 17 Nov.** at Doe Hill of typhoid fever, age, 19yrs. **parents, B. I. & M. E. Kiracofe.** born ____. occ. ____. unmarried. info, B. I. Kiracofe, father.

Kelley, Gertie V., WF, **d. 19 July** in Big Valley of flux, age, 7yrs. **parents, A. J. & Jennetta Kelly.** born Big Valley. occ. ____. consort of ____. info, A. J. Kelley, father

Kyer, Bessemer, CM, **d. 18 July** on Jackson's River of spinal disease, age, ____. **parents, Elijah & Mary Kyer.** born J. R. occ. ____. consort of ____. info, E. Kyer, father.

Lightner, Clevie Rachel, WF, **d. 5 March** on Back Creek of pneumonia, age, 4yrs, 20dys. **parents, Ro. W. & Augusta Lightner.** born Back Creek. occ. ____. consort of ____. info, R. W. Lightner, father.

Lunsford, Naomi, WF, **d. 20 June** at Hightown of paralysis, age, 78yrs. **parents, Mark & Sally Simmons.** born ____. occ. ____. widow. info, Josh Lunsford, son.

Lockridge, Clara, WF, **d. 12 June** on Bull Pasture of unknown, age, 10dys. **parents, J. J. & Fanny Lockridge.** born B. P. R. occ. ____. consort of ____. info, J. J. Lockridge, father.

McNulty, Jno. S., WM, **d. 6 Jan.** at Meadow Dale of meningitis, age, 27yrs. **parents, Frank & Fanny McNulty.** born Meadow Dale. occ. school teacher. unmarried. info, F. McNulty.

Michael, John H., WM, **d. 28 Nov.** on Cow Pasture of typhoid fever, age, 27yrs, 8mos. **parents, Jos. & Susan Michael.** born Cow Pasture. occ. ____. unmarried. info, Jos. Michael, father.

Moyers, Lucinda, WF, **d. 21 Dec.** on Bull Pasture of bronchitis, age, 70yrs. **parents, Math. & Sally Wallace.** born ____. occ. ____. consort of Samuel Moyers. info, S. Moyers, husband.

Moats, Henry C., WM, **d. 16 Dec** on St. Creek of inflammation, age, 4yrs, 3mos. **parents, J. & A. Moats.** born St. Creek. occ. ____. consort of ____. info, J. Moats, father.

McGuffin, James, WM, **d. 15 April** in Big Valley of cancer, age, 51yrs. **parents, A. G. & Eliza McGuffin.** born Bath Co. occ. farmer. consort of Nannie McGuffin. info, A. G. McGuffin, Jr., son.

Newman, Jacob, WM, **d. 1 Jan.** at Crabbottom of paralysis, age, 89yrs, 10mos. **parents, Leonard & M. Newman.** born ____. occ. farmer. consort of ____ Newman. info, ____ Newman, son.

Nicholas, Floyd, WM, **d. 8 Oct.** at Crabbottom of croup, age, 3yrs, 21mos. **parents, Geo. A. & Phebe J. Nicholas.** born Crabbottom. occ. ____. consort of ____. info, Geo. A. Nicholas, father.

Propst, James K., WM, **d. 6 June** on Shaw's Fork of white swelling, age, 45yrs. **parents, Henry & Nancy Propst.** born Shaw's Fork. occ. ____. consort of Sarah J. Propst. info, S. J. Propst, wife.

Pullin, Samuel J., WM, **d. 5 June** on B. P. River of chronic diarrhea, age, 6mos, 18dys. **parents, H. M. & Mary A. Pullin.** born B. P. R. occ. ____. consort of ____. info, H. M. Pullin, father.

Puffenberger, Chas. Emory, WM, **d. 4 May** on St. Creek of ____, age, 1dy. **parents, A. J. & E. Puffenberger.** born St. Creek. occ. ____. consort of ____. info, A. J. Puffenberger, father.

Propst, ____, WM, **d. ____ Nov.** on St. Creek of ____., age, 1dy. **parents, J. M. & L. D. Propst.** born St. Creek. occ. ____. consort of ____. info, J. M. Propst, father.

Pullin, James, CM, **d. ____** on J. River of consumption, age, 18yrs. **parents, Jerry & Annie Pullin.** born J. River. occ. ____. consort of ____. info, J. M. Propst, father.

Rexrode, Jno. M., WM, **d. 15 April** at Hightown of complication of d., age, 70yrs. **parents, Adam & E. A. Rexrode.** born Virginia. occ. farmer. widower. info, W. Rexrode, son.

Ryder, Carl, WM, **d. ____ Oct.** near Monterey of inflame of bowels, age, 4mos. **parents, Jas. & Sarah Rider.** born near Monterey. occ. ____. consort of ____. info, J. Ryder, father.

Rexrode, Annie V., WF, **d. 20 June** on St. Creek of flux, age, 3yrs, 8mos, 26dys. **parents, W. P. & Mary J. Rexrode.** born St. Creek. occ. ____. consort of ____. info, W. P. Rexrode, father.

Reynolds, Bettie, WF, **d. 8 July** on Shaw's Fork of paralysis, age, 78yrs. **parents, John & Dosia Reynolds.** born Louisa Co. occ. ____. unmarried. info, S. J. Reynolds, brother.

Samples, Harriett, WF, **d. 19 Nov.** on St. Creek of knot of bowels, age, 62yrs, 5mos, 24dys. **parents, S. & Sarah Pullin.** born ____. occ. ____. consort of Elijah Samples. info, E. Samples, husband.

Simmons, Robt. Lee, WF, **d. 11 Aug.** B. Creek of diphtheria, age, 5yrs. **parents, Lewis & M. Simmons.** born B. Creek. occ. ____. consort of ____. info, L. Simmons, father.

Stone, ____, WM, **d. 9 Dec.** at Crabbottom of ____, age, 5dys. **parents, A. & E. Stone** born Crabbottom. occ. ____. consort of ____. info, A. Stone, father.

Spriggs, Mollie B., CF, **d. 1 July** on B. Creek of ____. age, 5mos. **parents, Allen & Mollie Spriggs.** born B. Creek. occ. ____. consort of ____. info, A. Spriggs, father.

Spriggs, Howard, CM, **d. 13 Jan.** in Big ____ of consumption, age, 18yrs. **parents, Allen & Mollie Spriggs.** born B. Creek. occ. ____. consort of ____. info, A. Spriggs, father.

Sipe, Catherine, WF, **d. 24 Jan.** in Big Valley of old age, age, 80yrs. **parents, Edw. & ____ Hatfield.** born ____. occ. ____. widow. info, J. Sipe, son.

Sitlington, Robert, WM, **d. 25 Oct.** at McDowell of cancer of rectum, age, 82yrs. **parents, Jno. & ____ Sitlington.** born ____. occ. farmer. widower. info, W. T. Alexander, grandson.

Swope, Peter, WM, **d. 5 March** on B. P. R. of Bright's disease, age, 82yrs, 10mos. **parents, Henry & Esther Swope.** born B. P. R. occ. farmer. consort of M. M. Swope. info, ____ Swope, son.

Stuart, Caroline, WF, **d. ____ July** on B. P. R. of dropsy, age, 75yrs. **parents, Wm. & Nancy Douglas.** born B. P. R. occ. ____. widow. info, T. G. Stuart, son.

Simmons, Jno. W., WM, **d. 17 Feb.** at Doe Hill of heart disease, age, 25yrs, 11mos. **parents, Polly Simmons.** born ____. occ. laborer. unmarried. info, ____.

Simmons, Harvey, WM, **d. 12 Jan.** at Monterey of cancer, age, 60yrs, 9dys. **parents, T. & Cath. Simmons.** born ____. occ. laborer. consort of Eliz. A. Simmons. info, E. A. Simmons, wife.

Smith, Sarah A., WF, **d. 7 March** at Monterey of inflame of bowels, age, 30yrs.
        parents, G. A. & Cath. Smith. born ____. occ. ____.
        unmarried. info, G. A. Smith, father.

Scott, ____, CM, **d. ____ May** at poor farm of whooping cough, age, 4mos.
        parents, Agg Scott. born Bull Pasture. occ. ____.
        consort of ____. info, H. Mullenax, overseer poor.

Todd, Maggie, WF, **d. 26 June** on Brushy Fork of diphtheria, age, 13yrs.
        parents, Jno. & Cath. Todd. born Brushy Fork. occ. ____.
        consort of ____. info, J. Todd, father.

Varner, Mary C., WF, **d. 24 Feb.** near Monterey of bronchitis, age, 13yrs, 7mos.
        parents, Samuel & Louisa Varner. born near Monterey.
        occ. ____. consort of ____. info, S. Varner, father.

Wilfong, Naomi, WF, **d. ____ Nov.** on Little B. C. of pneumonia, age, 51yrs.
        parents, Jacob & M. Wilfong. born ____. occ. ____.
        consort of Daniel Wilfong. info, M. E. Matheny, neighbor.

Wilfong, Mary C., WF, **d. 12 Nov.** on Allegheny of convulsions, age, 47yrs.
        parents, Jno. & Marg't Bright. born ____. occ. ____.
        consort of Elias Wilfong. info, E. Wilfong, husband.

Wimer, Catherine, WF, **d. 4 April** on Allegheny Mt. of cancer, age, 43yrs.
        parents, Philip & ____ Wimer. born ____. occ. ____.
        consort of ____. info, G. W. Helmic, ____.

Wade, Jas. S., WM, **d. 19 July** on B. Creek of consumption, age, 36yrs.
        parents, Alex. & Mary E, Wade. born ____.
        occ. mechanic. unmarried. info, ____.

Wilson, Laura, WF, **d. ____ Jan.** on Bull Pasture of consumption, age, 16yrs.
        parents, Abr. & Mary E. Wilson. born B. P. occ. ____.
        unmarried. info, Abr. Wilson, father.

Wilson, Henry, CM, **d. 18 Jan.** on Bull Pasture of old age, age, 84yrs.
        parents, ____ & ____ Wilson. born B. P. occ. laborer.
        consort of ____. info, J. Wilson, son.

Wilson, Barbara, WF, **d. 7 July** on Cow Pasture of dysentery, age, 67yrs, 6mos.
        parents, Geo. & Debora Ervine. born B. P. occ. ____.
        consort of John Wilson. info, John Wilson, husband.

Weeks, Nancy, WF, **d. 20 April** at Monterey of inf. Rheumatism, age, 60yrs.
parents, ____ **&** ____. born ____. occ. ____. widow.
info, L. Simmons, son-in-law.

Wilson, Hamilton, WM, **d.** ____ **July** at Doe Hill of dropsy, age, 70 yrs.
parents, ____ **&** ____ **Wilson.** born ____. occ. tanner.
consort of Josephine Wilson. info, J. H. Hiner, son-in-law.

Beard, Rose Ella, CF, **d.** ____ **Nov.** at Monterey of consumption, age, 16yrs.
parents, Chas. & Letitia Beard. born Monterey. occ. ____.
unmarried. info, ____.

Campbell, ____,* WM, **d. 6 Feb.** near Monterey of ____, age, 15dys.
parents, A. J. & Annie L. Campell. born Highland Co.
occ. ____. consort of ____. info, A. J. Campbell, father.

Hiner, Henry,* WM, **d. 16 Jan.** at Monterey of hemor. of brain, age, 42yrs.
parents, J. B. & Ruth Hiner. born Highland Co. occ. farmer.
unmarried. info, J. B. Hiner, father.

Rodgers, Lizzie,* CF, **d.** ____ on Cow P. R. of unknown, age, ____.
parents, ____ **&** ____. born ____. occ. ____. consort of ____.
info, ____.

1891

Allen, D. C., CM, **d.** __ **Feb.** on Bull Past. River. of consumption, age, 25yrs.
parents, Jos. & Sarah Howard. born Highland Co. occ. laborer.
single. info, John Scott, neighbor.

Bird, Peter, WM, **d. 26 Dec.** on Back Creek of pneumonia, age, 62yrs.
parents, Wm. & Sarah Bird. born Bath Co. occ. farmer.
consort of Charlotte Bird. info, F. M. Bird, brother.

Beverage, Mary J., WF, **d. 12 May** on St. Creek of consumption, age, 48 yrs.
parents, Geo. W. & M. Rymer. born Pendleton Co. occ. ____.
consort of S. C. Beverage. info, S. C. Beverage, husband.

Beverage, Gertie May, WF, **d.** ____ on St. Creek of flux, age, 1yr, 5mos.
parents, J. R. & M. M. Beverage. born Highland Co.
born Highland Co. occ. ____. consort of ____.
info, J. R. Beverage, father.

---

* entered on original 1891 list.

Botkin, Eliz. L., WF, **d. 25 Nov.** near Monterey of pneumonia, age, 75yrs.
        parents, Matthew & S. Benson. born Pendleton Co. occ. ____.
widow. info, Jas. H. Botkin, son.

Botkin, Lillie D., WF, **d. 29 March** on Bull Past. of consumption, age, 16yrs.
        parents, Geo. & Matilda Botkin. born Highland Co. occ.____.
single. info, Geo. W. Botkin, father.

Beard, Willie, CM, **d. 1 Sep.** on J. River of whooping cough, age, 9yrs.
        parents, Lewis & Amanda Beard. born Highland Co. occ. ____.
single. info, Amanda Beard, mother.

Chew, Jonas, WM, **d. 27 Jan.** at Crabbottom of Bright's disease, age, 80yrs.
        parents, Eze & Christina Chew. born Highland Co. occ. farmer.
consort of Cassandra Chew. info, O. P. Chew, son.

Cross, John E., WM, **d. ____ March** on St. Fork of abcess, age, 40yrs.
        parents, ____ & ____ Cross. born Highland Co. occ. laborer.
consort of Patsy Cross. info, J. C. Swecker, neighbor.

Carter, Minnie V., CF, **d. ____** on Bull Past. Of unknown, age, ____.
        parents, ____ & ____. born ____. occ. ___. consort of ____.
info, L. A. Caricoff, undertaker.

Carpenter, Harmon B., WM, **d. 10 Aug.** in Big Valley of whooping cough, age, 2yrs.
        parents, D. W. & S. J. Carpenter. born Highland Co. occ. ____.
consort of ____. info, D. W. Carpenter, father.

Curry, Mary, WF, **d. 3 Sep.** on J. River of jaundice, age, 68yrs.
        parents, Isaac & ____ Briscoe. born Highland Co. occ. ____.
consort of John Curry. info, J. Curry, husband.

Curry, W. H., WM, **d. 22 Feb.** on B. P. Mt. of consumption, age, 22yrs.
        parents, Ben & Mary Ann Curry. born Highland Co.
occ. laborer. single. info, Ben Curry, father.

Cobb, Eliz. A., WF, **d. 5 April** on B. P. River of paralysis, age, 60yrs.
        parents, Sam'l & Sally Pullin. born Bath Co. occ. laborer.
widow. info, Susie Cobb, daughter.

Cobb, ____, WM, **d. 17 Aug.** on Jack Mt. of cong. of lungs, age, 1 dy.
        parents, S. A. & Martha J. Cobb. born Highland Co. occ. ____.
consort of ____. info, S. A. Cobb, father.

Davenport, James, CM, **d. 14 April** on Cow Past. River of La Grippe, age, 75. **parents, ___ & ___ Davenport.** born ___. occ. laborer. consort of Mary Davenport. info, Adam Davenport, son.

Eagle, ___, WF, **d. ___ March** on St. Creek of unknown, age, 4mos. **parents, P. R. & Hen. Eagle.** born ___. occ. ___. consort of ___. info, J. B. Waggoner, neighbor.

Griffen, Wm., WM, **d. 20 Nov.** on J. River of pneumonia, age, 88yrs, 3mos, 3dys. **parents, Robt. & S. Griffen.** born New York City. occ. cooper. widower. info, Sus. Turner, daughter.

Gutshall, Samilda Ann, WF, **d. 22 April** on J. River of pneumonia, age, 31yrs, 8mos, 16dys. **parents, A. W. & Sarah Buzzard.** born Highland Co. occ. housekeeping. consort of Geo. G. Gutshall. info, G. G. Gutshall, husband.

Gladwell, Gracie, WM, **d. 22 April** at McDowell of ___, age, 10mos. **parents, Warren L. & Ellie Gladwell.** born Highland Co. occ. ___. consort of ___. info, W. L. Gladwell, father.

Gillespie, Theodore B., WM, **d. 28 May** at Millboro, Va. of abcess of spine, age, 36yrs. **parents, ___ & ___ Gillespie.** born Bath Co. occ. distiller. consort of Jennie G. Gillespie. info, Jennie Gillespie, wife.

Gum, Polly, WF, **d. 31 July** at Hightown of dropsy, age, 75yrs. **parents, Adam & Susan Gum.** born Pendleton Co. occ. ___. widow. info, A. F. Gum, son.

Hull, John W., WM, **d. ___ Nov.** on South Branch of pneumonia, age, 49yrs. **parents, F. K. & Amelia Hull.** born Pendleton Co. occ. farmer. consort of Sarah M. Hull. info, H. C. Fleisher, adm.

Hiner, Bennett, WM, **d. ___ Sep.** on Jackson's River of heart disease, age, 78yrs. **parents, Alex & Harriett Hiner.** born Pendleton Co. occ. ___. consort of Lydia Hiner. info, J. Hiner, brother.

Houlihan, Margaret, WF, **d. 26 Dec.** on Jackson's River of dropsy, age, 7yrs, 10mos, 11dys. **parents, Mich. & M. Houlihan.** born Highland Co. occ. ___. consort of ___. info, M. F. Houlihan, mother.

Harold, Eliz., WF, **d. 3 April** on St. Creek of pneumonia, age, 62yrs. **parents, Eze & Christina Houlihan.** born Pendleton Co. occ. ___. widow. info, R. D. Lantz, son.

Hupman, Wm. Arthur, WM, **d.** ____ **July** on Cow Past. R. of dropsy, age, 17yrs.
   parents, P. H. & Annie B. Hupman. born Highland Co.
   occ. ____. consort of ____. info, P. H. Hupman, father.

Judy, Burke, WM, **d.** ____ **March** at Crabbottom of consumption, age, 18yrs.
   parents, Adam & Mollie Judy. born Ohio. occ. ____.
   consort of ____. info, S S. Wayright, neighbor.

Jones, Jos. Mondell, WM, **d. 8 Jan.** at Monterey of measles, age, 7yrs.
   parents, Jos. & Sarah Jones. born Monterey. occ. ____.
   consort of ____. info, Jos. Jones, father.

Jordan, Mary E., WF, **d. 20 April** in Steam Valley of enlarge of heart, age, 68yrs.
   parents, Luke & Martha Dever. born Rockingham Co.
   occ. ____. widow. info, Margt Jordan, daughter.

Jackson, Clay, CM, **d.** ____ on Bull P. River of ____, age, ____. **parents,** ____ **&** ____.
   born ____. occ. ____ consort of ____. info, ____.

Jordan, Annie, WF, **d. 13 Sep.** on Jackson's River of unknown, age, 2yrs.
   parents, H. A. & E. M. Jordan. born Highland Co. occ. ____.
   consort of ____. info, H. A. Jordan, father.

Johns, Eliz. A., WF, **d. 3 April** on Shaw's Fork of paralysis, age, 57yrs.
   parents, ____ **&** ____ **Smith.** born Highland Co. occ. ____.
   consort of J. W. Johns. info, J. W. Johns, husband.

Killingsworth, ____, WM, **d.** ____ on Cow Past. of ____, age, 1dy.
   parents, ____ **& Mag Killingsworth.** born Highland Co.
   occ. ____. consort of ____. info, E. J. Stuart, neighbor.

Lee, John H., CM, **d.** ____ **Sep.** on J. River of whooping cough, age, 2yrs.
   parents, J. & Eliz. Lee. born Highland Co. occ. ____.
   consort of ____. info, Jack Lee, father.

Lockridge, Robt., WM, **d. 28 March** on Bull Past. of pneumonia, age, 82yrs.
   parents, Robt. & Polly Lockridge. born Bath Co. occ. farmer.
   consort of Emily Lockridge. info, Miss F. Lockridge, daughter.

Lewis, Ben, CM, **d. 1 Dec.** on Bull Past. of pneumonia, age, 50yrs.
   parents, ____ **&** ____ **Lewis.** born Bath Co. occ. laborer.
   consort of Amanda Lewis. info, A. Lewis, wife.

Matheny, Brown S., WM, **d. 4 Dec.** in Little Valley, B. Co. of capillary bronchitis,
   age, 1 yr. **parents, R. L. & Lulu Matheny.** born Little Valley.
   occ. ____. consort of ____. info, R. L. Matheny, father.

Malcom, ____, WF, **d. ____** on Bull Past. of ____, age, ____. **parents, ____ & ____.**
  born ____. occ. ____. consort of ____. info, ____.

Mullenax, Walter W., WM, **d. 21 Oct.** on St. Creek of pneumonia, age, 18yrs, 4mos.
  parents, G. W. & S. E. Mullenax. born St. Creek. occ. ____.
  consort of ____. info, G. W. Mullenax, father.

Moats, Jno. W., WM, **d. ____ Jan.** at Doe Hill of pneumonia, age, ____.
  parents, ____ & ____ Moats. born Pendleton Co. occ. laborer.
  consort of ____. info, Jacob Botkin, undertaker.

McCray, Wm., WM, **d. 27 Aug.** on Shaw's Fork of lightning, age, 18yrs.
  parents, Robt. & Mary McCray. born Shaw's Fork. occ. laborer.
  consort of ____. info, Robt. McCray, father.

Maxey, Sarah, CF, **d. 22 Dec.** at McDowell of heart disease, age, 66yrs.
  parents, ____ & ____. born ____. occ. domestic.
  consort of ____. info, Sam Smith, grandson.

Newman, Malinda, WF, **d. 11 Feb.** at Crabbottom of paralysis, age, 86yrs.
  parents, And. & Mary Trumbo. born Bath Co. occ. ____.
  widow. info, A. T. Newman, son.

Pullin, J. E. C., WM, **d. 12 March** on Back Creek of apoplexy, age, 52yrs.
  parents, John & Nancy Pullin. born Back Creek. occ. ____.
  consort of ____. info, L. C. Pullin, wife.

Parmer, ____, WF, **d. 20 April** on Back Creek of ____, age, 1dy.
  parents, C. K. & Julia Parmer. born Rockingham Co.
  occ. farmer*. consort of Mary Peterson*.
  info, C. K. Parmer, father.

Peterson, Chas. W., WM, **d. ____ Oct.** at McDowell of cancer, age, 68yrs.
  parents, W. & ____ Peterson. born Cow Past. occ. ____.
  consort of ____. info, Mary Peterson, wife.

Rexrode, Rebecca, WF, **d. 23 Sep.** on Allegheny Mt. of hemor. of bowels, age, 68yrs.
  parents, Henry & Polly Penniger. born Pendleton Co.
  occ. housekeeper. consort of Jess Rexrode.
  info, Jess Rexrode, husband.

---

* The occupation and consort information belong to the Peterson entry immediately following.

Ralston, S. R. M., WM, **d. 2 Aug.** on B. Creek of heart disease, age, 43yrs.
        parents, Sam'l & Eliza Ralston. born Highland Co.
    occ. blacksmith. consort of Dolly B. Ralston.
    info, Dolly B. Ralston, wife.

Rodgers, Laura M., WF, **d. ____** on Shaw's Ridge of heart disease, age, 17yrs.
        parents, ____ & Henr. Rodgers. born Shaw's Fork occ. none.
    single. info, T. M. Devericks, neighbor.

Robertson, ____, WF, **d. ____ March** on J. River of ____, age, 1dy.
        parents, Geo. & __ Robertson. born J. River. occ. ____.
    consort of ____. info, Geo. A. Robertson, father.

Spriggs, ____, CF, **d. ____ May** on Back Creek of pneumonia, age, 6yrs.
        parents, Allen & Millie Spriggs. born Back Creek. occ. ____.
    consort of ____. info, Allen Spriggs, father.

Spriggs, ____, CF, **d. ____** on Back Creek of epilepsy, age, 6dys.
        parents, Allen & Millie Spriggs. born Back Creek. occ. ____.
    consort of ____. info, Allen Spriggs, father.

Spriggs, Gertie, CF, **d. ____** on Back Creek of pneumonia, age, 13yrs.
        parents, Allen & Millie Spriggs. born Back Creek. occ. ____.
    consort of ____. info, Allen Spriggs, father.

Sponaugle, ____, WF, **d. ____** on Middle Mt. of ____, age, 1dy.
        parents, Pat & Mary Sponaugle. born Middle Mt. occ. ____.
    consort of ____. info, Amos Sponaugle, grandfather.

Sponaugle, W. J., WM, **d. 5 June** on South Branch of La Grippe, age, 60yrs.
        parents, ____ & Polly Sponaugle. born Pendleton Co.
    occ. farmer. consort of Rachel Sponaugle.
    info, Rachel Sponaugle, wife.

Snyder, Ratie, WF, **d. 27 Dec.** at Crabbottom of unknown, age, 7dys.
        parents, Jos. T. & Judi Snyder. born Crabbottom. occ. ____.
    consort of ____. info, B. Varner, grandfather.

Stewart, Maggie, CF, **d. ____ June** at Monterey of measles, age, 3mos.
        parents, Geo. E. & Annie Stewart. born Monterey. occ. ____.
    consort of ____. info, Geo. E. Stewart, father.

Seybert, Henry, WM, d. 10 Dec. on St. Creek of La Grippe, age, 86yrs, 5mos.
        parents, Jacob & Mary Seybert. born Pendleton Co. occ. farmer.
    widower. info, H. H. Seybert, son.

Samples, A. M., WM, **d. ____ May** on St. Creek of measles, age, 26yrs.
parents, Elijah & Harriett Samples. born St. Creek. occ. farmer.
consort of ____. info, Jno. H. Samples, brother.

Simmons, Betty, WF, **d. ____ Aug.** on St. Creek olf spinal affection, age, 27yrs.
parents, Granville & ____ Simmons. born St. Creek. occ. ____.
consort of J. E. Simmons. info, J. E. Simmons, husband.

Stephenson, L. W., WM, **d. 19 Dec.** on J. River of abcess, age, 21yrs, 6mos.
parents, A. T. & Georgie E. Stephenson. born J. River.
occ. farmer. consort of ____. info, A. T. Stephenson, father.

Stone, Jemima, WF, **d. 1 Jan.** on Crab Run of pneumonia, age, 49yrs.
parents, D. & C. McLuain. born Pendleton Co. occ. ____.
consort of John A. Stone. info, Jno. A. Stone, husband.

Scott, ____, CF, **d. ____** at poor farm of ____, age, ____.
parents, ____ & Mag Scott. born poor farm. occ. ____.
consort of ____. info, A. T. Stephenson, Supt. of poor.

Townsend, Alice H., WF, **d. 11 Jan.** on B. Creek of childbirth, age, 34yrs.
parents, David & Phebe Foster. born B. Creek. occ. ____.
consort of Wash Townsend. info, Wash Townsend, husband.

Townsend, Wash, WM, **d. ____ July** on B. Creek of consumption, age, 34yrs.
parents, Jno. & Mary Townsend. born B. Creek. occ. ____.
widower. info, W. T. Townsend, brother.

Tracy, Betty, WF, **d. ____ June** at county farm of epilepsy, age, 40yrs.
parents, John & Mary Tracy. born Highland Co. occ. none.
consort of ____. info, Jno. Tracy, father.

Terry, Alex, WM, **d. 13 Oct.** on Dry Branch of heart disease, age, 65yrs.
parents, Jas. & ____ Terry. born Bath Co. occ. farmer.
consort of Mary Terry. info, D. G. Terry, son.

Tidd, Amanda, WF, **d. 18 Sep.** on St. Creek of consumption, age, 32yrs.
parents, Jno. & Alcinda Rexrode. born St. Creek.
occ. housekeeping. consort of Geo. W. Tidd.
info, Geo. W. Tidd, husband.

Wayright, Annette M., WF, **d. 22 Oct.** at Crabbottom of whooping cough, age, 3mos.
parents, Geo. W. & Florence Waybright. born Crabbottom.
occ. ____. consort of ____. info, Geo. W. Waybright, father.

Wimer, ____, WF, **d. ____ Aug.** at Crabbottom of whooping cough, age, 2mos.
    parents, Cor. & Susan Wimer. born Crabbottom. occ. ____.
    consort of ____. info, Cor Wimer, father.

Wilson, Maggie, WF, **d. 27 Oct.** at Waynesboro, Va. of consumption, age, 48yrs, 1mo.
    parents, Marion & E. Finlay. born Augusta Co.
    occ. housekeeping. consort of O. Wilson.
    info, O. Wilson, husband.

Wimer, Fannie G., WF, **d. ____ Jan.** on Crab Run of ____, age, 4mos.
    parents, S. W. & Amanda Wimer. born Crab Run. occ. ____.
    consort of ____. info, S. W. Wimer, father.

1892

Arbogast, Geo., WM, **d. 20 Feb**. at Crabbottom of neuralgia of heart, age, 80yrs.
    parents, Henry & E. J. Arbogast. born ____. occ. farmer.
    consort of Eunice Arbogast. info, W. H. A., son.

Barkley, Calvin, WM, **d. 10 Dec.** at Crabbottom of killed by falling tree, age, 35yrs.
    parents, Geo. & ____ Barkley. born ____. occ. laborer.
    consort of Mary Barkley. info, E. B. Wimer, neighbor.

Beathe, Samuel P., WM, **d. 9 Jan.** on Crab Run of La Grippe, age, 74yrs.
    parents, Jas. & Marg't Beathe. born Highland Co. occ. farmer.
    consort of Anna Beathe. info, A. M. Pullin, neighbor.

Byers, Samuel, WM, **d. 14 March** at Monterey of delirium T., age, 60yrs.
    parents, ____ & ____ Byers. born England. occ. jeweler.
    single. info, W. A. C., Admr.

Colaw, Allie, WF, **d. 14 ____** at Crabbottom of childbirth, age, 35yrs.
    parents, Jas. & Mary Gilkeson. born Virginia. occ. ____.
    consort of A. N. Colaw. info, A. N. C., husband.

Chew, Annie Lou, WF, **d. ____ Nov.** at Crabbottom of La Grippe, age, 2mos, 15dys.
    parents, G. Lee & Lou Chew. born C. Bottom occ. ____.
    consort of ____. info, G. L. Chew, father.

Cunningham, R. Stuart, WM, **d. 20 Dec.** at Montery of pneumonia, age, 38yrs.
    parents, ____ & ____ Cunningham. born Virginia. occ. minister.
    consort of May M. Cunningham. info, Capt. M., friend.

Carpenter, Rebecca, WF, **d. 14 Sep.** in Big Valley of rheumatism, age, 70yrs.
    parents, Jno. & Reb. Carpenter. born Virginia. occ. ____.
consort of J. Carpenter. info, H. Gutshall, son-in-law.

Claxton, William, WM, **d. 26 Jan.** on Bull Pasture R. of Grippe, age, 69yrs.
    parents, ____ & ____. born ____. occ. ____.
consort of Mary J. Claxton. info, Ann Brown, friend.

Davis, James H., WM, **d. 1 May** on Bull Pasture R. of consumption, age, 20yrs, 25dys.
    parents, A. S. T. & E. J. Davis. born ____.
occ. farmer. unmarried. info, A. S. T. Davis, father.

Ervine, Willie, WM, **d. 9 Feb.** on Bull Pasture R. of measles, age, 1yr, 9dys.
    parents, H. H. & Della Ervine. born Virginia. occ. ____.
consort of ____. info, H. H. Ervine, father.

Eagle, Bessie T., WF, **d. 23 March** on St. Creek of ____, age, 7mos.
    parents, P. R. Eagle. born St. Creek. occ. ____.
consort of ____. info, P. R. Eagle, father.

Fleisher, Irene E., WF, **d. 5 May** in Highland Co. of paralysis, age, 48yrs.
    parents, Jno. & Mgt. Hull. born Highland Co. occ. ____.
consort of Jas. A. Fleisher. info, J. A. F., husband.

Gilmore, ____, WF, **d. ____ April** on Back Creek of ____, age, 1dy.
    parents, S. L. & C. M. Gilmore. born Highland Co.
consort of ____. info, ____.

Gum, Isaac W., WM, **d. 12 Jan.** in Highland Co. of La Grippe, age, 74yrs, 11mos.
    parents, McB. & Alice Gum. born Highland Co. occ. farmer.
consort of Jane Gum. info, J. Gum, wife.

Gum, Addie E., WF, **d. 13 Aug.** in Highland Co. of paralysis, age, 20yrs.
    parents, A. T. & Priscilla Wiley. born Highland Co. occ. farmer.
consort of H. A. Gum. info, H. A. Gum, husband.

Gum, McBride, WM, d. 29 Feb. at Hightown of La Grippe, age, 81yrs, 6mos.
    parents, McB. & A. Gum. born Pendleton Co. occ. farmer.
widower. info, O. H. Gum, son.

Grogg, Henry, Sr., WM, **d. 29 June** on St. Creek of general debility, age, 80yrs.
    parents, Jno. & ____ Grogg. born St. Creek. occ. farmer.
consort of ____ Grogg. info, H. Grogg, son.

Griffen, ____, WM, **d. 29 June** on Jackson River of ____, age, 1mo.
        parents, W. C. & Eliza Griffen. born Jackson River. occ. ____.
consort of ____. info, W. C. Griffen, father.

Gwin, Mamie, WF, **d. 21 Dec.** on Cow Pasture of ____, age, 5yrs.
        parents, J. & Martha Gwin. born Cow Pasture. occ. ____.
consort of ____. info, J. Gwin, father.

Gwin, Alcinda, WF, **d. ____ Jan.** on Bull Pasture of consumption, age, 70yrs.
        parents, ____ & ____ Gwin. born Highland Co. occ. ____.
divorced. info, G. H. Lockridge, neighbor.

Gregory, J. F., WM, **d. 10 May** on Back Creek of dropsy, age, 54yrs.
        parents, Jas. & Mary A. Gregory. born Pocahontas Co.
occ. laborer. consort of Demy Cath. Gregory.
info, W. J. Gregory, son.

Hevener, Jos. H., WM, **d. 1 Oct.** at Crabbottom of erisypelas, age, 61yrs.
        parents, Henry & Naomi Hevener. born Highland Co.
occ. farmer. consort of Malinda Hevener. info, ____.

Hevener, William, WM, **d. 20 Jan.** at Crabbottom of ____, age, 72yrs.
        parents, Jacob & ____ Hevener. born Highland Co. occ. farmer.
consort of Lavinia Hevener. info, R. D. Fox, son-in-law.

Hott, Jos. B., WM, **d. 7 April** at Crabbottom of consumption, age, 28yrs.
        parents, Rev. J. M. & E. C. Hott. born ____. occ. ____.
unmarried. info, Jos. Hott, father.

Hevener, James Pinckney, WM, **d. 10 April** at Crabbottom of colera morbus, age, 2yrs.
        parents, Ed. H. & Phebe Hevener. born Crabbottom. occ. ____.
consort of ____. info, Ed Hevener, father.

Hicks, Margaret, WF, d. 13 Sep. on Jackson River of asthma, age, 81yrs.
        parents, Mathias & Susan Benson. born Pendleton Co.
occ. ____. consort of Wm. Hicks. info, Wm. Hicks, husband.

Halterman, Margaret, WF, **d. 13 Feb.** on St. Creek of paralysis, age, 60yrs.
        parents, Jno. & Susan White. born ____. occ.____.
consort of P. H. Halterman. info, P. H. Halterman, husband.

Hansel, Margaret, WF, **d. 29 July** at Lexington, Va. of heart failure, age, 54yrs.
        parents, Benj. & Mary Hiner. born Pendleton Co. occ. ____.
consort of Jno. H. Hansel. info, J. H. Hansel, husband.

Hupman, ____, WF, **d. 1 ____** on Cow Pasture of ____, age, ____.
        parents, Bob Hupman. born Cow Pasture. occ. ____.
        consort of ____. info, ____, neighbor.

Jones, Andrew J., WM, **d. 20 Aug.** at Doe Hill of obstruction of bowels,
        age, 77yrs, 8mos, 19dys. **parents, Thos. & Mary Jones.**
        born Pendleton Co. occ. farmer. consort of Jane Jones.
        info, Dr. H. H. Jones.

Jackson, George, CM, **d. 1 May** on Bull Pasture R. of consumption, age, 25yrs.
        parents, Alb. & Mary Jackson. born ____. occ. ____.
        consort of Sarah Jackson. info, Alb. Jackson, father.

Kelley, Jennetta, WF, **d. 18 Feb.** on Dry ranch of consumption, age, 51yrs.
        parents, Jno. & Betsy Ratcliff. born ____. occ. ____.
        consort of A. J. Kelley. info, A. J. Kelley, husband.

Kincaid, Radie, WF, **d. 12 May** on C. P. R. of dropsy, age, 6yrs.
        parents, H. H. & Harriett Kincaid. born Highland Co. occ. ____.
        consort of ____. info, H. H. Kincaid, father.

Losh, Sarah, WF, **d. 8 Jan.** on B. P. Mt. of post partum hemorrhage, age, 40yrs.
        parents, Jno. & ____ Bowers. born Highland Co. occ. ____.
        consort of Urias Losh. info, J. Botkin, neighbor.

Lockridge, William, WM, **d. 4 Jan.** on B. P. Mt. of ____, age, 80yrs.
        parents, Robt. & Polly Lockridge. born Highland Co.
        occ. farmer. consort of Eliza Lockridge. info, ____, son.

Lough, Mrs., WF, **d. ____** on Back Creek of ____, age, ____.
        parents, Jesse & M. Gregory. born B. C. occ. ____.
        consort of ____ Lough. info, ____, neighbor.

McCray, May, WF, **d. ____ April** on Cow Pasture of ____, age, ____.
        parents, R. J. McCray. born Cow Pastur. occ. ____.
        consort of ____. info, ____, neighbor.

McGlaughlin, Kenton G., WM, **d. 29 June** on Jackson River of colera morbus,
        age, 2yrs. **parents, E. A. & Sarah C. McGlaughlin.** born ____.
        occ. ____. consort of ____. info, E. A. McGlaughlin, father.

May, Annie, WF, **d. 20 March** at McDowell of consumption, age, 21yrs.
        parents, M. V. & Etta Stuart. born Highland Co. occ. ____.
        consort of Jas. F. May. info, J. F. May, husband.

Minor, ____, CM, **d.** ____ on Cow Pasture of ____, age, ____.
    parents, Fred & Rachel Minor. born Cow Pasture.
    occ. ____. consort of ____. info, ____.

Minor, ____, CM, **d. 20 Feb.** at McDowell of ____, age, ____.
    parents, Jno. & ____ Minor. born McDowell. occ.____.
    consort of ____. info, ____.

Nicholas, Susie, WF, **d. 8 Nov.** at Crabbottom of piles, age, 70yrs.
    parents, F. & R. Nicholas. born Crabbottom. occ. ____.
    consort of ____. info, H. Nicholas, brother.

Peterson, Ella V., WF, **d. 20 April** at McDowell of pneumonia, age, 23yrs, 10mos.
    parents, J. B. & Mary Bradshaw. born Highland Co. occ.____.
    consort of C. S. Peterson. info, C. S. Peterson, husband.

Pleasants, ____, CM, **d.** ____ April at McDowell of ____, age, ____.
    parents, Chas. Pleasants. born Highland Co. occ. ____.
    consort of ____. info, ____.

Rexrode, Pearley C., WM, **d. 18 April** at Crabbottom of dropsy, age, 15yrs, 14dys.
    parents, Geo. M. & J. Rexrode. born Highland Co. occ. ____.
    consort of ____. info, G. M. Rexrode, father.

Rexrode, ____, WF, **d. 18 Dec.** on St. Fork of ____, age, 5dys.
    parents, J. L. & Barbara Rexrode. born Highland Co. occ. ____.
    consort of ____. info, ____, father.

Robertson, ____, WM, **d.** ____ on Jackson River of ____, age, 1mo.
    parents, Geo. & Clara Robertson. born Highland Co. occ.____.
    consort of ____. info, G. A. Robertson, father.

Robertson, Clara, WF, **d. 18** ____ on Jackson's River of childbirth, age, 22yrs.
    parents, Jesse & Malinda Gregory. born Highland Co. occ. ____.
    consort of Geo. A. Robertson. info, G. A. Robertson, husband.

Ralston, ____, WF, **d. 28** ____ on Bull Pasture of ____, age, 3mos.
    parents, W. & Janie Ralston. born Highland Co. occ. ____.
    consort of ____. info, W.Ralston, father.

Revercomb, Jno. R., WM, **d. 24 March** on Bull pasture R. of Bright's disease, age, 56yrs, 10mos, 9dys. **parents, G. & Reb. Revercomb.** born Bath Co. occ. farmer. consort of Susan Revercomb. info, Mrs. S. R., wife.

Snyder, ____, WF, **d. 23 Dec.** at Crabbottom of ____, age, 8dys.
    parents, Jos. T. & Zudie Snyder. born Crabbottom. occ. ____.
    consort of ____. info, ____.

Snyder, Edgar N., WM, **d. 24 June** at Crabbottom of strangled, age, 2yrs, 3mos.
    parents, W. E. & Ludie Snyder. born Crabbottom. occ. ____.
    consort of ____. info, W. E. S., father.

Sennite, ____, WM, **d. 5 June** at Crabbottom of ____, age, 1dy.
    parents, Abel & Sarah Sennite. born Pendleton Co. occ. ____.
    consort of ____. info, A. Sennite, father.

Simmons, ____, WF, **d. 9 May** at Crabbottom of ____, age, 1dy.
    parents, Jasper & A. Simmons. born CrabB. occ. ____.
    consort of ____. info, J. Simmons, father.

Simmons, Susan, WF, **d. 8 Jan.** at Crabbottom of paralysis, age, 60yrs.
    parents, ____ & ____ Harper. born CrabB. occ. ____.
    consort of Ad. Simmons. info, M. Simmons, son.

Shumate, Jane, WF, **d. 9 March** at Monterey of consumption, age, 61yrs.
    parents, Aug. & Elizabeth Shumate. born ____. occ. ____.
    unmarried. info, Chas. Shumate, brother.

Shumate, Augustus, WM, **d. 19 Feb.** at Monterey of paralysis, age, 88yrs.
    parents, ____ & ____ Shumate. born Augusta Co. occ. taylor.
    consort of Elizabeth Shumate. info, Chas. Shumate.

Swadley, A. F., WM, **d. 5 Oct.** near Monterey of lock of bowels, age, 56yrs.
    parents, Wm. & Marg't Swadley. born Highland Co.
    occ. farmer. consort of Phebe Swadley. info, Will Swadley, son.

Slaven, Lizzie M., WF, **d. 14 May** at Monterey of inf. of bowels, age, 7mos.
    parents, H. & Maud Slaven. born Highland Co. occ. ____.
    consort of ____. info, H. S., father.

Sheffer, ____, WM, **d. ____ Sep.** on Shaws Fork of __, age, 3mos.
    parents, Jos. & Bertie Sheffer. born Highland Co. occ. ____.
    consort of ____. info, Jos. Sheffer, father.

Simmons, Mordecai, WM, **d. 27 May** on Shaw's Fork of dropsy, age, 34yrs, 7mos.
    parents, And. & Eliz. Simmons. born Highland Co. occ. farmer.
    consort of Harriet Simmons. info, ____, brother.

Stuart, ____, WF, **d.** ____ on Bull Pasture of ____, age, ____.
        parents, T. G. & ____ **Stuart.** born Highland Co. occ. ____.
        consort of ____. info, ____.

Townsend, Pinckney, WM, **d. 18 May** on Back Creek of apoplexy, age, 9yrs.
        parents, Wash. & Alice Townsend. born Highland Co. occ. ____.
        consort of ____. info, W. Townsend, father.

Tracy, John, WM, **d.** ____ April at poor farm of dyspepsia, age, 91yrs.
        parents, ____ **&** ____. born ____. occ. ____. consort of ____.
        info, H. Mullenax, overseer poor.

Todd, Nathan F., WM, **d. 3 Jan.** at Palo Alto of typhoid fever, age, 22yrs.
        parents, Jno. & ____ **Todd.** born ____. occ. ____. single.
        info, Jno. Todd, brother.

Trimble, Martha, WF, **d. 16 Jan.** at Vanderpool of ____, age, ____.
        parents, Wm. & ____ **Trimble.** born Highland Co. occ. ____.
        single. info, ____.

Varner, ____, WM, **d. 22 Sep.** on St. Creek of ____, age, 7dys.
        parents, J. K. & Reb. Varner. born St. Creek. occ. ____.
        consort of ____. info, J. K. Varner, father.

Vandevender, Catherine, WF, **d. 19 Aug.** on St. Creek of dropsy, age, 72yrs.
        parents, J. & H. Mullenax. born St. Creek. occ. ____.
        consort of Geo. Vandevender. info, G. Vandevender, husband.

Vance William, WM, **d. 7 Oct.** on BullPasture of old age, age, 85yrs.
        parents, Benj. & H. Vance. born ____. occ. farmer. single.
        info, W. H. Vance nephew.

Wade, Abraham, WM, **d. 27 Jan.** on Back Creek of general debility, age, 82yrs.
        parents, Abr. & ____ **Wade.** born Bath Co. occ. farmer.
        consort of Mary C. Wade. info, E. E. Wade, son.

Wimer, ____, WM, **d.** ____ **Jan.** on Allegheny Mt. of ____, age, 1mo.
        parents, E. B. & C. E. Wimer. born ____. occ. ____.
        consort of ____. info, E. B. Wimer, father.

Waybright, Miles, WM, **d. 18 Dec.** at Crabbottom of apoplexy, age, 60yrs.
        parents, ____ **&** ____. born Highland Co. occ. ____.
        consort of Sarah J. Waybright. info, ____.

Wilson, Matilda, WF, **d. ____ Aug.** at Doe Hill of organic heart disease, age, 65yrs.
    parents, Eli & Naomi Wilson. born Highland Co. occ. farmer. unmarried. info, H. H. Jones, physician.

Wolf, Lewis Franklin, WM, **d. 14 Oct.** on Jackson River of killed by rolling log, age, 5yrs, 2mos, 9dys. **parents, Dan'l & Mary Wolf.** born Highland Co. occ. ____. consort of __. info, D. Wolf, father.

Wimer, Sidney, WF, **d. 21 Dec.** on St. Creek of consumption, age, 64yrs.
    parents, M. & R. Waybright. born Highland Co. occ. ____. consort of Eman. Wimer. info, Em. Wimer, husb.

Williams, Nellie, WF, **d. ____ Oct.** on B. P. R. of ____, age, 15mos.
    parents, W. H. & Price Williams. born Highland Co. occ. ____. consort of ____. info, W. H. Williams, father.

Wolf, Evelyn, CF, **d. 6 Nov.** on Jackson R. of hemorrhage, age, 76yrs.
    parents, Jno. & Margt. Wolf. born Highland Co. occ. ____. consort of ____. info, Susan Wolf, neice.

Wimer, ____, WM, **d. ____ Jan.** on Allegheny Mt. of ____, age, 1mo.
    parents, E. B. & C. E. Wimer. born Allegheny Mt. occ. ____. consort of ____. info, E. B. Wimer, father.

Wimer, ____,* WM, **d. ____ Jan.** on Allegheny Mt. of ____ age, 21dys.
    parents, E. B. & ____ Wimer. born Allegheny Mt. occ. ____. consort of ____. info, H. Mullenax, neighbor.

Wade, D. B., WM, **d. ____ Dec.** on Back Creek of pneumonia, age, 58yrs.
    parents, Abra. & Rachel Wade. born Bath Co. occ. farmer. consort of Mahala C. Wade. info, M. C. Wade, wife.

Wade, Abr.,** WM, **d. 26 June** on Back Creek of general debility, age, 82yrs.
    parents, John & ____ Wade. born Bath Co. occ. farmer. consort of Mary C. Wade. info, M. C. Wade, wife.

Hawley, Louis W.,*** WM, **d. ____ Nov.** at McDowell of pneumonia, age, 1yr.
    parents, J. M. & Kate Hawley. born McDowell. occ. minister. consort of ____. info, J. J. Hiner, neighbor.

Rexrode, Wm.,***WM, **d. ____ May** on Middle Mt. of kidney disease, age, 84yrs.
    parents, Conrad & Cath. Rexrode. born Pendleton Co. occ. farmer. widower. info, Wash Rexrode, son.

---

* duplicate of one immediately above. ** similar to an entry on page above.
*** entered on original 1893 list.

1893

Armstrong, ____, WF, **d. ____** on Cow Pasture River of unknown, age, ____.
parents, Gilbert & ____ Armstrong. born Cow Past. occ. ____.
consort of ____. info, Mrs. S. J. Steuart, neighbor.

Armstrong, Ella Florence, WF, **d. 25 Oct.** on Bull Past. Mt. of Bright's disease,
age, 9yrs. **parents, A. H. & Nancy Armstrong.** born Bull P. Mt.
occ. ____. consort of ____. info, A. H. Armstrong, father.

Armstrong, John T., WM, **d. 20 Oct.** on Cow Past. of heart failure, age, 76yrs.
parents, Jared & Agnes Armstrong. born Bull Past. Mt.
occ. farmer. widower. info, W. H. Armstrong, son.

Bird, Mollie E., WF, **d. 29 April** on Back Creek of pneumonia, age, 53yrs, 3dys.
parents, Robt. & Delila Gilmore. born Rockingham Co.
occ. housekeeping. consort of Jno. W. Bird.
info, Jno. W. Bird, husband.

Bussard, Jesse A., WM, **d. 14 May** on head of Jackson's R. of paralysis, age, 55yrs.
parents, Sol. & Rachel Bussard. born Pocahontas Co.
occ. surveyor. consort of Ann Bussard. info, Wm. A. Bussrad, son.

Brock, Mary L., WF, **d. 28 Dec.** at New Market, Va. of meningitis, age, 12yrs.
parents, C. A. & Lizzie Brock. born Hd. J. River. occ. ____.
consort of ____. info, Geo. D. Dudley, uncle.

Briscoe, Priscilla, WF, **d. 4 May** on B. Creek of pneumonia, age, 70yrs.
parents, Isaac & Priscilla Briscoe. born Back Creek.
occ. domestic. unmarried. info, A. D. Gum, neighbor.

Barkley, Catherine, WF, **d. __ Feb.** on Middle Mt. of stomach trouble, age, 40yrs.
parents, Wm. & ____ Rexrode. born Pendleton Co.
occ. housekeeping. consort of Henry Barkley.
info, H. Barkley, husband.

Brown, Cynthia, WF, **d. 8 Feb.** in Big Valley of ____, age, ____.
parents, ____ & ____ Gwin. born Bath Co. occ. housekeeping.
widow. info, D. N. Buzzard, neighbor.

Buzzard, ____, WM, **d. 17 April** on Jackson's River of unknown, age, ____.
parents, L. A. & ____ Buzzard. born Jackson's River. occ. ____.
consort of ____. info, D. N. Buzzard, cousin.

Botkin ____, WF, **d. 7 April** near Doe Hill of pneumonia, age, ____.
        parents, James & ____ Botkin. born near Doe Hill.
        occ. housekeeping. consort of G. L. Botkin.
        info, Dr. H. H. Jones, physician.

Chew, Cassandra, WF, **d. ____ Nov.** at Crabbottom of consumption, age, 59yrs.
        parents, Geo. & Eliz. Mullenax. born Pendleton Co.
        occ. housekeeping. widow. info, O. P. Chew, son.

Carroll, Lillie F., WF, **d. 14 Oct.** on Dry Branch of childbirth, age, 28yrs.
        parents, Jno. & Rosie Gutshall. born Big Valley.
        occ. housekeeping. consort of Geo. W. Carroll.
        info, G. W. Carroll, husband.

Colaw, Josie M., WF, **d. 28 Nov.** at Monterey of typhoid fever, age, 29yrs, 2mos, 16dys.
        parents, M. & Sarah A. Judy. born Pendleton Co.
        occ. housekeeping. consort of Jno. M. Colaw.
        info, J. M. Colaw, husband.

Dickenson, Lucy B., WF, **d. 18 March** at Monterey of unknown, age, 2mos.
        parents, L. S. & Matie Dickenson. born Monterey. occ. ____.
        consort of ____. info, L. S. Dickenson, father.

Devericks, Henry C., WM, **d. 18 Nov.** on Shaw's Fork of rheumatism, age, 14yrs.
        parents, T. M. & Mary A. Devericks. born Shaw's Fork.
        occ. ____. consort of ____. info, T. M. Devericks, father.

Dever, John Jr., WM, **d. 15 April** on Jackson's River of ____, age, 70yrs.
        parents, ____ & ____ Dever. born Rockingham Co. occ. laborer.
        consort of Cath. Dever. info, Cath. Dever, wife.

Davis, John L., WM, **d. 3 Nov.** on Bull Past R. of consumption,
        age, 20yrs, 3mos, 20dys. **parents, A. S. T. & Eliz. J. Davis.**
        born Bull Past. R. occ. ____. consort of ____.
        info, A. S. T. Davis, father.

Ervin, Benj., WM, **d. ____ March** on Back Creek of pneumonia, age, 80yrs.
        parents, ____ & ____ Ervin. born Back Creek. occ. farmer.
        widower. info, Geo. B. Ryder, neighbor.

Eagle, Harvey, WM, **d. ____ Dec.** on Cow Past. R. of abcess on hip, age, 32yrs.
        parents, Enoch & Susan Eagle. born ____. occ. merchant.
        consort of Ora B. Eagle. info, O. B. Eagle, wife.

Gilmor, Sallie A., WF, **d. 31 March** on Back Creek of consumption, age, 18yrs.
   parents, S. A. & Jennie Gilmor. born Back Creek. occ. ____.
   unmarried. info, S. A. Gilmor, father.

Gregory, Clara E., WF, **d. 6 June** on Back Creek of childbirth, age, 21yrs.
   parents, J. F. & Demy Gregory. born Back Creek. occ. domestic.
   unmarried. info, Joe Gregory, brother.

Gregory, Emma E., WF, **d. 1 June** on Back Creek of ____, age, ____.
   parents, ____ & Clara Gregory. born Back Creek. occ. ____.
   consort of ____. info, Joe Gregory, uncle.

Gum, Nancy, WF, **d. 29 April** on Back Creek of pneumonia, age, 73yrs.
   parents, Isaac & Priscilla Briscoe. born Back Creek
   occ. housekeeping. widow. info, A. D. Gum, step-son.

Gum, Chas. L.M., WM, **d. 14 Feb.** on Back Creek of pneumonia, age, 46yrs.
   parents, Otho & Drusilla Gum. born Back Creek. occ. farmer.
   unmarried. info, Jenny Gum, sister.

Gillespie, ____, WM, **d. 20 Dec.** on Jackson's River of ____, age, 2mos, 17dys.
   parents, Jas. A. & Gay Gillespie. born Big Valley. occ. ____.
   consort of ____. info, J. A. Gillespie, father.

Gillespie, Gay, WF, **d. 24 Dec.** on Jackson's River of La Grippe, age, 29yrs.
   parents, Rob't. & Frances Carpenter. born Big Valley.
   occ. housekeeping. consort of J. A. Gillespie.
   info, J. A. Gillespie, husband.

Griffin, ____, WM, **d. ____ March** on Jackson's River of ____, age, 21dys.
   parents, Clark & Eliza Griffin. born Jackson's River. occ. ____.
   consort of ____. info, Clark Griffin, father.

Gutshall, H. C., WM, **d. 8 Sep.** on Jackson's River of unknown, age, 9mos.
   parents, J. L. & Maggie E. Gutshall. born Jackson"s River.
   occ. ____. consort of ____. info, J. L. Gutshall, father.

Gutshall, John, WM, **d. ____ Aug.** on Dry Branch of dropsy, age, 66yrs, 6mos, 20dys.
   parents, ____ & ____ Gutshall. born Rockingham Co.
   occ. farmer. consort of Rosie Gutshall. info, Wm. Gutshall, son.

Gutshall, Virgil, WM, **d. 18 Sep.** on Jackson's River of meningitis,
   age, 1yr, 6mos, 25dys. **parents, Wm. & Rachel Gutshall.**
   born Jackson's River. occ. ____. consort of ____.
   info, Wm. Gutshall, father.

Gwin, Mamie, WF, **d. 25 Dec.** on Cow Past. of pneumonia, age, 5yrs.
   parents, Jim & Martha Gwin. born Cow Past. occ. ____.
   consort of ____. info, Jim Gwin, father.

Gwin, Harrison, WM, **d. 25 May** on B. P. River of abscess, age, 55yrs.
   parents, ____ & ____. born Cow Past. occ. laborer.
   unmarried info, W. H. Simmons, overseer of poor.

Hidy, Clifton, WM, **d. 1 Jan.** at Crabbottom of unknown, age, 1mo.
   parents, J. B. & Laura V. Hidy. born Crabbottom. occ. ____.
   consort of ____. info, Jas. B. Hidy, father.

Hiner, Ressie B., WF, **d. 3 Feb.** on Back Creek of paralysis, age, 2yrs.
   parents, W. H. & Julia A. Hiner. born Back Creek. occ. ____.
   consort of ____. info, Jas.*{sic}* Hiner, father.

Hiner, Rosie, WF, **d. 28 Oct.** on Jackson's River of inf. of stomach,
   age, 21yrs, 0mos, 5dys. **parents, Jas. P. & Verdalia Hiner.**
   born Jackson's River. occ. farmer. single.
   info, Jas. P. Hiner, father.

Hiner, ____, WF, **d. 3 Nov.** at Monterey of ____, age, 1dy.
   parents, Jos. A. & Lucy Hiner. born Monterey. occ. ____.
   consort of ____. info, Jos. A. Hiner, father.

Hiner, Caroline, WF, **d. 4 Nov.** at Doe Hill of paralysis, age, 74yrs.
   parents, ____ & Jane Hiner. born Pendleton Co.
   occ. housekeeping. unmarried. info, Rob't. K. Hiner, son.

Hull, Sarah M., WF, **d. 5 Dec.** on South Branch of diphtheria, age, 58yrs.
   parents, Jac. & Cath. Seybert. born Pendleton Co.
   occ. housekeeping. widow. info, H. C. Fleisher, son-in-law.

Halterman, Sarah J., WF, **d. 17 Dec.** on St. Creek of meningitis, age, 1yr, 6mos, 25dys*
   parents, Jos. & Mary Church. born Pendleton Co.
   occ. housekeeping. consort of J. F. Halterman.
   info, J. F. Halterman, husband.

Hite, Lee F., WM, **d. 26 Dec.** on J. River of pneumonia, age, 36yrs, 26dys.
   parents, Geo. W. & Cecelia Hite. born Back Creek. occ. farmer.
   consort of Maggie Hite. info, A. T. Carpenter, brother-in-law.

---

* age probably is in error.

Hawley, ____, WM, **d. ____ Oct.** at McDowell of pneumonia, age, 1dy. **parents, J. M. & Kate Hawley.** born McDowell. occ. minister*. consort of ____. info, J. J. Hiner, neighbor.

Hook, Sallie V., WF, **d. 4 Nov.** on Cow Past. of consumption, age, 32yrs, 11mos. **parents, B. T. & Nancy Hook.** born Cow Past. occ. housekeeping. unmarried. info, B. T. Hook, father.

Loche, Ellen, WF, **d. 13 Sep.** on Back Creek of childbirth, age, 21yrs. **parents, J. F. & Demy Gregory.** born Back Creek. occ. housekeeping. consort of ____ Lough. *[sic]* info, Joe Gregory, brother.

Matheny, Mary J., WF, **d. 16 Feb.** on Back Creek of heart failure, age, 61yrs. **parents, Mathias & ____ Cleek.** born Bath Co. occ. housekeeping. widow. info, Edw. L. Matheny, son.

McLaughlin, Isabel, WF, **d. 25 Jan.** in Back Creek Valley of consumption, age, 52yrs. **parents, Adam & Elenor Lightner.** born Bath Co. occ. housekeeping. widow. info, Adam McLaughlin, son.

Mackey, J. Wood, WM, **d. 22 Aug.** at Raphine, Va. Of meningitis, age, 30yrs. **parents, W. H. & M. V. Mackey.** born Bolar. occ. merchant. unmarried. info, John H. Mackey, brother.

Moats, Harry D., WM, **d. ____ Oct.** on St. Creek of ____, age, 2dys. **parents, Jas. & Amanda Moats.** born St. Creek. occ. ____. consort of ____. info, Jas. Moats, father.

Maloy, Patrick, WM, **d. 29 Aug.** on B. P. River of dropsy of the heart, age, 77yrs. **parents, ____ & ____ Maloy.** born Ireland. occ. farmer. consort of Susan J. Maloy. info, E. J. Maloy, son.

Marshall, Nancy G., WF, **d. ____ March** on Shaw's Fork of paralysis, age, 76yrs. **parents, Chas. L. & Nancy Kincaid.** born Cow P. River. occ. housekeeping. widow. info, Jno. L. Marshall, son.

McNulty, F., WM, **d. 25 Dec.** on Hd of J. River of cancer, age, 68yrs. **parents, Jno. & Marg't McNulty.** born Pocahontas Co. occ. farmer. consort of Fannie McNulty. info, Chas. McNulty, son.

Nicholas, Geo. A., WM, **d. 1 April** at Crabbottom of pneumonia, age, 25yrs, 9mos. **parents, Sol & Eliz. J. Nicholas.** born Crabbottom. occ. farmer. consort of Phebe J. Nicholas. info, Jas. M. Nicholas, brother.

---

* probably occupation of the father.

Johnston, Sam'l, CM, **d.** ____ **Feb.** on Bull P. River of gen. debility, age, 89yrs. **parents,** ____ & ____. born __. occ. laborer. unmarried. info, W. H. Simmons, overseer of poor.

Jackson, Mary, CF, **d.** ____ on Cow P. River of ____, age, ____. **parents,** ____ & ____. born ____ occ. ____. consort of ____. info, ____.

Kramer, Barbara, WF, **d.** ____ **Dec.** at Crabbottom of cancer, age, 64yrs. **parents, Sam'l & Marg't Hoover.** born Crabbottom. occ. housekeeping. widow. info, J. H. Kramer, son.

Kirkpatrick, John, WM, **d.** ____ **June** on Back Creek of dropsy, age, 76yrs. **parents,** ____ & ____. born ____. occ. laborer. widower. info, Thos. K. Terry, son-in-law.

Kelly, Polly, WF, **d.** ____ in Big Valley of ____, age, ____. **parents,** ____ & ____. born Big Valley. occ. domestic. widow. info, ____, neighbor.

Pullin, Henry H., WM, **d. 30 Aug.** on Crab Run of heart disease, age, 4yrs. **parents, H. B. & Lydia V. Pullin.** born Crab Run. occ. ____. consort of ____. info, H. B. Pullin, father.

Pullin, Sam'l. B., WM, **d. 5 May** on Crab Run of pneumonia, age, 16yrs. **parents, H. B. & Lydia V. Pullin.** born Crab Run. occ. ____. consort of ____. info, H. B. Pullin, father.

Rexrode, Josephine, WF, **d. 8 Nov.** at Crabbottom of consumption, age, 48yrs, 6mos, 23dys. **parents, D. C. & ____ Stone** born Pendleton Co. occ. housekeeping. consort of G. M. Rexrode. info, G. M. Rexrode, husband.

Rexrode, ____, WF, **d.** ____ on St. Creek of ____, age, ____. **parents, Jno. L. & Barbara Rexrode.** born St. Creek. occ. ____. consort of ____. info, ____, neighbor.

Rexrode, Caroline M., WF, **d.** ____ **Jan.** on St. Creek of pneumonia, age, 60yrs. **parents, M. & ____ Marshall.** born St. Creek. occ. housekeeping. consort of Hez Rexrode. info, Hez Rexrode, husband.

Rexrode, Sam'l C., WM, **d.** ____ **June** on St. Creek of pneumonia, age, 42yrs. **parents,** ____ & ____. born Pendleton Co. occ. farmer. consort of Martha J. Rexrode. info, Minor Rexrode, son.

Robertson, Jess, WM, **d.** ____ **Jan.** on Jackson's River of ____, age, 80yrs.
    parents, Wm. & ____ Robertson. born Bath Co. occ. farmer.
consort of Julia Robertson. info, Julia Robertson, wife.

Rodgers, Nelson, WM, **d.** ____ **April** on Bull Past. of heart disease, age, 84yrs.
    parents, ____ & ____. born ____. occ. ____. widower.
info, H. M. Pullin, son-in-law.

Rodgers, ____, WF, **d.** ____ **Feb.** on Bull Past. of ____, age, 1dy.
    parents, Rob't M. & Harriet Rodgers. born Bull Past. occ. ____.
consort of ____. info, Robt M. Rodgers, father.

Ralston, Fanny, WF, **d.** ____ **May** on Bull Past. of kidney disease, age, 77yrs.
    parents, ____ & ____ Curry. born Bull Past. occ. housekeeping.
widow. info, S. A. Ralston, son.

Snyder, Polly, WF, **d. 5 June** at Crabbottom of paralysis, age, 73yrs.
    parents, Abr. & ____ Eckard. born Pendleton Co.
occ. housekeeping. widow. info, Geo. W. Snyder, son.

Snyder, Mattie, WF, **d. 11 Nov.** at Doe Hill of typhoid fever, age, 28yrs.
    parents, ____ & ____ McCray. born Pendleton Co.
occ. housekeeping. consort of Geo. H. Snyder.
info, Geo. H. Snyder, husband.

Shumate, Eliz., WF, **d. 22 Dec.** at Monterey of paralysis, age, 83yrs, 11mos.
    parents, ____ & ____ Pence. born Rockingham Co.
occ. housekeeping. widow. info, Chas. T. Shumate, son.

Siples, Mary M., WF, **d. 4 April** on Bull Past. River of consumption, age, 27yrs.
    parents, Jos. & Amanda Siples. born Bull P. R.
occ. housekeeper. unmarried. info, Jos. Siples, father.

Smith, Sarah, CF, **d. 31 Sep.** on Bull P. River of consumption, age, 41yrs.
    parents, ____ & Hannah Gordon. born Bull Past. R.
occ. housekeeping. consort of Chas. Smith.
info, Chas. Smith, husband.

Smith, Bessie, CF, **d.** ____ **July** on Bull P. River of consumption, age, 5mos.
    parents, Chas. & Sarah Smith. born Bull Past. R. occ. ____.
consort of ____. info, Chas. Smith, father.

Seybert, Catherine, WF, **d. 6 April** on South Branch of Bright's disease, age, 77yrs.
    parents, Benj. & Sarah Fleisher. born Pendleton Co.
occ. housekeeper. widow. info, H. C. Fleisher, grandson.

Steuart, ____, CF, **d. 6 June** at Monterey of ____, age, 1dy.
    parents, Geo. E. & Annie E. Steuart. born Monterey.
    occ. ____. consort of ____. info, Geo. E. Steuart, father.

Terry, Wm. C., WM, **d. ____ Aug.** in Big Valley of unknown, age, 4mos.
    parents, A. J. & Irene Terry. born Big Valley. occ. ____.
    consort of ____. info, A. J. Terry, father.

Trimble, Lucy H., WF, **d. 11 June** on St. Creek of unknown, age, 10dys.
    parents, Jas. A. & M. M. Trimble. born St. Creek. occ. ____.
    consort of ____. info, Jas. A. Trimble, father.

Vint, M. J., WF, **d. 19 March** near Doe Hill of La Grippe, age, 38yrs.
    parents, Wm. & Cath. Hiner. born Pendleton Co.
    occ. housekeeper. consort of Wm. Vint. Info, Wm. Vint, husband.

Williams, Nellie, WF, **d. 1 Oct.** on Bull Past. R. of ____, age, 1yr, 4mos.
    parents, W. H. & Pricie Williams. born Bull Past. occ. ____.
    consort of ____. info, W. H. Williams, father.

Williams, ____, WF, **d. ____ Sep** on Back Creek of ____, age, 2dys.
    parents, C. J. & Ida Williams. born Back Creek. occ. ____.
    consort of ____. info, Chas. J. Williams, father.

Weeks, ____, WF, **d. ____** at Monterey of ____, age, 7dys.
    parents, W. H. & Mattie E. Weeks. born Monterey. occ. ____.
    consort of ____. info, W. H. Weeks, father.

Wolf, ____, CF, **d. ____** at Meadow Dale of ____, age, ____.
    parents, ____ & Susan Wolf. born Meadow Dale. occ. ____.
    consort of ____. info, ____, neighbor.

1894

Arbogast, Arlie, WM, **d. 26 Sep.** at Crabottom of spasms, age, 1mo, 12dys.
    parents, A. P. & Amanda Arbogast. born Crabbottom. occ. none.
    consort of ____. info, A. P. Arbogast, father.

Arbogast, Amelia, WF, **d. 4 April** at Crabbottom of pneumonia, age, 66yrs.
    parents, ____ & ____ Gray. born Pocahontas Co. occ. ____.
    widow. info, A. P. Arbogast, nephew.

Armstrong, Mary Ann, WF, **d. 1 May** on Bull Past. Mt. of dropsy, age, 75yrs.
parents, S. & ____ Wilson. born Pendleton Co. occ. none. widow. info, A. H. Armstrong, son.

Armstrong, Nancy J., WF, **d. 20 Feb.** on Bull Past. Mt. of epilepsy, age, 32yrs.
parents, J. & Leah Shough. born Pendleton Co. occ. none. consort of A. H. Armstrong. info, A. H. Armstrong, husband.

Bishop, Marguerite, WF, **d. ____ Jan.** at Monterey of pneumonia, age, 3yrs, imo.
parents, V. B. & Minnie M. Bishop. born Monterey. occ. none. consort of ____. info, V. B. Bishop, father.

Bishop, Sarah E., WF, **d. 18 April** on Bull Past. River of Las Grippe, age, 69yrs.
parents, Geo. & Eliz. Hicklin. born Bull Past. R. occ. none. widow. info, Jas. L. Bishop, son.

Boude, Hattie, WF, **d. 9 Nov.** at Crabbottom of pneumonia, age, 26yrs.
parents, Jos. T. & Sarah J. Boude. born Crabbottom. occ. none. single. info, Jos. T. Boude, father.

Benson, Adelaide, WF, **d. ____ Nov.** in Staunton of paralysis, age, 56yrs.
parents, Jas. H. & Alice Byrd. born Bath Co. occ. none. consort of W. W. Benson. info, W. W. Benson, husband.

Benson, Carrie G., WF, **d. 7 April** at Vanderpool of heart disease, age, 20yrs.
parents, W. W. & Adelaide Benson. born Vanderpool. occ. none. single. info, W. W. Benson, father.

Beard, ____, CF, **d. 2 May** at Monterey of ____, age, 2dys.
parents, Chas. D. & Lou Beard. born Monterey. occ. none. consort of ____. info, Chas. D. Beard, father.

Botkin Ruhama, WF, **d. 13 Nov.** on South Fork of childbirth, age, 32yrs.
parents, Jno. & Polly Bowers. born Pendleton Co. occ. none. consort of Jas. M. Botkin. info, Jas. M. Botkin husband.

Botkin Willie, WM, **d. 9 July** on Bull Past. Mt. of diarrhea, age, 1yr, 6mos, 2dys.
parents, Jno. E. & M. Botkin. born Bull Past. Mt. occ. none. consort of ____. info, Jno. E. Botkin father.

Clendenen, C. R., WM, **d. 9 Nov.** in Staunton of scalded, age, 52yrs.
parents, Jno. & Cath Clendenen. born Bath Co. occ. none. divorced. info, J. F. Clendenen, brother.

Crummett, ____, WM, **d. ____ Oct.** on Shaw's Fork of ____, age, 1mo.
    parents, Geo. R. & Sally Crummett. born Shaw's Fork.
    occ. none. consort of ____. info, Geo. F. Crummett, father.

Campbell, Sally, WF, **d. ____ Feb.** near Monterey of pneumonia, age, 72yrs.
    parents, Jesse & ____ Johnston. born ____. occ. ____.
    widow. info, O. J. Campbell, son.

Dever, Sam'l Kent, WM, **d. 11 Dec.** on Back Creek of rheumatism, age, 10yrs.
    parents, Jasper & Julia Dever. born Back Creek. occ. ____.
    consort of ____. info, Julia Dever, mother.

Diehl, Amos, WM, **d. 16 Sep.** on Cow Past. of pneumonia, age, 85yrs, 9mos.
    parents, Jno. & Hannah Diehl. born ____. occ. ____.
    consort of Hannah Diehl. info, Hannah Diehl, wife.

Evick, ____, CM, **d. 13 Dec.** on St. Creek of ____, age, ____.
    parents, ____ & Hannah Evick. born St. Creek. occ. ____.
    consort of ____. info, ____, neighbor.

Eddins, ____, WF, **d. 19 Nov.** at McDowell of ____, age, 2dys.
    parents, Jas. T. & Florence Eddins. born McDowell. occ. ____.
    consort of ____. info, J. T. Eddins, father.

Friel, Amanda, WF, **d. ____ Oct.** at Crabottom of paralysis, age, 79yrs.
    parents, ____ & ____ Friel. born Pocahontas Co.
    occ. ____. widow. info, H. Mullenax, overseer poor.

Fleisher, Finney F., WM, **d. 24 Jan.** on South Branch of heart failure, age, 21yrs.
    parents, Sol & Eliza Fleisher. born South Branch. occ. ____.
    single.info, Chas. T. Fleisher, brother.

Fox, J. W., WM, **d. 20 Nov.** in Big Valley of consumption, age, 26yrs, 8mos.
    parents, J. M. & Harriet Fox. born Big Valley. occ. ____.
    single. info, J. M. Fox, father.

Gillett, Maggie I., WF, **d. ____** on Bull Pasture of cancer, age, ____.
    parents Jno. & Eliz. J. Bradshaw. born Bull Past. R. occ. ____.
    consort of A. W. Gillett. info, A. W. Gillett, husband.

Hupman, Jas. S., WM, **d. 5 Feb.** on Cow Past. of pneumonia, age, 68yrs.
    parents, Peter & Mary Hupman. born Cow P. R. occ. farmer.
    consort of Hettie Hupman. info, P. V. Hupman, son.

Hicks, Wm., WM, **d. 2 Jan.** on Jackson's River of dropsy, age, 85yrs.
   parents, Jno. & ____ Hicks. born Jackson's River. occ. farmer.
   widower. info, Lou Hicks, daughter.

Hiner, Ruth, WF, **d. 11 Dec.** at Monterey of aenemia, age, 4yrs, 6mos.
   parents, Jno. L. & Janie Hiner. born Monterey. occ. ____.
   consort of ____. info, Jno. L. Hiner, father.

Harrison, George, WM, **d. ____** on Jackson River of ____, age, ____.
   parents, ____ & ____ Harrison. born ____. occ. laborer.
   consort of ____. info, ____, neighbor.

Harris, Ben, CM, **d. ____** on Cow Pasture of ____, age, ____.
   parents ____ & ____ Harris. born Bath Co. occ. laborer.
   consort of ____. info, ____, neighbor.

Hite, ____, WF, **d. ____ June** on Jackson's River of worms, age, 3yrs.
   parents, Lee F. & Maggie Hite. born Jackson's River. occ. ____.
   consort of ____. info, A. T. Carpenter, uncle.

Hull, Camilla O., WF, **d. ____ July** near Vanderpool of childbirth, age, 21yrs.
   parents, ____ & ____ Orville. born Tucker Co. W. Va. occ. ____.
   consort of Jno. H. Hull. info, J. N. Hull, father-in-law.

Hammer, Wm. Ashby, WM, **d. 25 Dec.** on B. P. River of pneumonia, age, 7yrs.
   parents, E. A. & Ella Hammer. born Bull Past. occ. ____.
   consort of ____. info, E. A. Hammer, father.

Jones, Jno. A., WM, **d. 24 Feb.** at Monterey of pneumonia, age, 26yrs.
   parents, Jos. & Sarah Jones. born Monterey. occ. mechanic.
   consort of Emma Jones. info, Joseph Jones, father.

Jones, W. H., WM, **d. 17 April** on Cow Past. River of murdered, age, 43yrs.
   parents, D. H. & Jane Jones. born Cow Pasture. occ. farmer.
   consort of ____ Jones. info, T. C. Jones, brother.

Kincaid, Mrs., WF, **d. ____** on Cow Past. of pneumonia, age, 70yrs.
   parents, Harvey & __ Benson. born Cow Pasture. occ. ____.
   widow. info, ____, neighbor.

Lantz, Virginia, WF, **d. 30 March** at Crabbottom of spinal meningitis, age, 60yrs.
   parents, ____ & ____ Grey. born Pendleton Co. occ. ____.
   consort of Cyrus Lantz. info, Cyrus Lantz, husband.

Lantz, Joseph, WM, **d.** ____ at Crabbottom of ____, age, 65yrs.
   parents, ____ **&** ____ **Lantz.** born Pendleton Co. occ. none.
   single. info, Joseph ____*, neighbor.

Lautenschlager, ____, WM, **d.** ____ **July** at Crabbottom of ____, age, ____.
   parents, J. W. F. & Mariha Lautenschlager. born Crabbottom.
   occ. ____. consort of ____. info, ____, neighbor.

Lockridge, Grover C., WM, **d. 5 Aug.** on Bull Pasture of colera infantum,
   age, 1yr, 10mos. **parents, A. R. & Amanda Lockridge.**
   born Bull Past. occ. ____. consort of ____.
   info, A. R. Lockridge, father.

Moats, Nelia,** WF, **d.** ____ **Sep.** near Doe Hill of dropsy, age, 28yrs.
   parents, Wm. & Susan Miller. born Bullpasture R.
   occ. housekeeper. consort of Wm. Moats.
   info, Wm. Moats, husband.

Mullenax, Christina, WF, **d.** ____ **April** on Middle Mt. of bronchitis, age, 60yrs.
   parents, E. & Christine Chew. born Crabbottom. occ. ____.
   consort of Oliver Mullenax. info, Edw. C. Mulenax, son.

Minor, ____, CF, **d.** ____ **Aug.** on Cow Past. of ____, age, 1mo.
   parents, Fred & Rachel Minor. born Cow Past. occ. ____.
   consort of ____. info, Fred Minor, father.

Pritt, Taylor, WM, **d.** ____ on Jackson's River of dropsy, age, 63 yrs.
   parents, ____ **&** ____ **Pritt.** born J. River. occ. laborer.
   consort of ____ Pritt. info, ____, neighbor.

Parmer, Saml., WM, **d.** ____ **May** at Crabbottom of dropsy, age, 75yrs.
   parents, ____ **&** ____ **Parmer.** born ____. occ. laborer.
   consort of Ann Parmer. info, ____, neighbor.

Puffenbarger, Gracie A., WF, **d. 16 Nov.** on St. Creek of congestion of brain,
   age, 36yrs. **parents, Amos & Mary Gum.** born St. Creek.
   occ.____. consort of And. Puffenbarger.
   info, And. Puffenbarger, husband.

Pullin, Isaac H, WM, **d. 20 July** on Bull Past. of diabetis, age, 18yrs.
   parents, H. M. & M. A. Pullin. born Bull Past. occ. ____.
   consort of ____. info, H. M. Pullin, father.

---

* identity oscured by an erasure of original entry.
** entered on original 1895 list.

Rexrode, Eldridge, WM, **d. 7 Sep.** at Crabbottom of fever, age, 2yrs, 5mos, 17dys. **parents, W. A. & S. F. Rexrode.** born Crabottom. occ. ____. consort of ____. info, W. A. Rexrode, father.

Robertson, Lavenia, WF, **d.** ____ on Crab Run of flux, age, 8yrs. **parents, C. R. & Lavenia Robertson.** born Crab Run. occ. ____. consort of ____. info, C. R. Robertson, father.

Ryder, Thomas, WM, **d.** ____ **Sep.** in Big Valley of pneumonia, age, 50yrs. **parents, Jas. K. & Sarah J. Ryder.** born Back Creek. occ. farmer. consort of ____ Ryder. info, ____, neighbor.

Ralston, Mrs. John, WF, **d.** ____ **May** on Bull Past. R. of ____, age, 52yrs. **parents, ____ & ____.** born Pendleton Co. occ. ____. consort of John Ralston. info, ____, neighbor.

Stephenson, Sarah C., WF, **d. 6 April** at Meadow Dale of general debility, age, 80yrs. **parents, Wm. & Sally Wilson.** born Jackson's River. occ. ____. widow. info, O. A. Stephenson, son.

Stephenson, John, WM, **d. 19 Jan.** at Meadow Dale of heart disease, age, 67yrs. **parents, Adam & ____ Stephenson.** born Jackson's River. occ. farmer. consort of Laura Stephenson. info, Brad Stephenson, son.

Swecker, D. W., WM, **d. 9 March** at Crabbottom of pneumonia, age, 69yrs. **parents, Benj. & E. Swecker.** born Crabbottom. occ. farmer. consort of Celia F. Swecker. info, Geo. E. Swecker, son.

Smith, ____, WM, **d. 16 May** at Crabbottom of ____, age, 2dys. **parents, ____ & ____ Smith.** born Crabbottom. occ. ____. consort of ____. info, ____, neighbor.

Stone, Jno. A., WM, **d. 24 June** on Crab Run of La Grippe, age, 52yrs. **parents, Sol & Polly Stone** born Crabottom. occ. farmer. consort of Annie Stone info, Annie Stone, wife.

Townsend, John, WM, **d. 23 July** on Back Creek of dropsy, age, 71yrs. **parents, John & Mary Townsend.** born Back Creek. occ. shoe maker. consort of Mary Townsend. info, Robert Townsend, son.

Turner, Wm., WM, **d. 6 Feb.** on Jackson's River of pneumonia, age, 38yrs. **parents, ____ & Mary Turner.** born Jackson's River. occ. laborer. consort of Suse Turner. info, Suse Turner, wife.

Turner, ____, WF, **d. ____** on Jackson's River of pneumonia, age, 23yrs.
        parents, Mathias & ____ Turner. born Jackson's River.
        occ. ____. consort of ____. info, Suse Turner, cousin.

Tolly, ____, WF, **d. ____** at McDowell of ____, age, ____.
        parents, W. H. & ____ Tolly. born McDowell. occ. ____.
        consort of ____. info, ____, neighbor.

Tolly, Ada E.,* WF, **d. 3 March** at McDowell of rain fever, age, 5mos, 20dys.
        parents, W. H. & Mary Tolly. born McDowell. occ. ____.
        consort of ____. info, F. M. Totten, pastor.

Vint, Martha Ann, WF, **d. 5 April** on Bull Past. Mt. of spinal affection, age, 50yrs.
        parents, J. P. & Lucy M. Bishop. born Bull Pasture. occ. ____.
        consort of John Vint. info, John Vint, husband.

Waybright, Cordelia, WF, **d. ____ July** on Middle Mt. of consumption, age, 23yrs.
        parents, Wm. & __ Nelson. born Pendleton Co. occ. ____.
        consort of Ad. Waybright. info, Ad. Waybright, husband.

Waybright, Mary, WF, **d. 20 Feb.** at Crabbottom of consumption, age, age, 63yrs.
        parents, ____ & ____. born Pendleton Co. occ. ____. widow.
        info, S. S. Waybright, son.

Waggoner, John B., WM, **d. ____ Feb.** on St. Creek of pneumonia, age, 60yrs.
        parents, Sol & ____ Waggoner. born Pendleton Co. occ. farmer.
        consort of Una Waggoner. info, Una Waggoner, wife.

Wright, L. E., WM, **d. 22 Sep.** on Jackson's River of thrown from a horse, age, 28yrs.
        parents, Jas. & Frances Wright. born Harrison Co., W.Va.
        occ. farmer. consort of Annie E. Wright.
        info, Annie E. Wright, wife.

Wilson, Mary J., WF, **d. 13 July** at Monterey of paralysis, age, 75yrs.
        parents, Henry & M. Hille. born W. Va. occ. ____. widow.
        info, W. E. Wilson, son.

Wilson, Wm. Shelton, WM, **d. ____ June** on Shaw's Fork of diarrhea, age, 1yr, 5mos.
        parents, Geo. N. & S. L. Wilson. born Shaw's Fork. occ. ____.
        consort of ____. info, Geo. N. Wilson, father.

Wilson, Geo. Rosser, WM, **d. ____ June** on Shaw's Fork of diarrhea, age, 1yr, 5mos.
        parents, Geo. N. & S. L. Wilson. born Shaw's Fork. occ. ____.
        consort of ____. info, Geo. N. Wilson, father.

---

* entered on original 1895 list.

Wright, Allie, CF, **d. 20 Jan.** on Bull Pasture of paralysis, age, 64yrs, 5mos, 11dys.
  parents, ____ & ____. born Bull Pasture. occ. ____. single.
  info, Jas. Wright, neighbor.

1895

Arbogast, Lulu, WF, **d.** ____ Nov. at Crabbottom of diphtheria, age, 3yrs.
  parents, A. B. & A. F. Arogast. born Crabbottom. occ. ____.
  consort of ____. info, A. B. Arbogast, father.

Arbogast, Jennie, WF, **d. 2 Oct.** at Crabbottom of diphtheria, age, 10yrs.
  parents, Jno. & Susan Arbogast. born Crabbottom. occ. ____.
  consort of ____. info, Jno. D. Arbogast, father.

Arbogast, Ollie, WF, **d.** ____ Dec. at Crabbottom of diphtheria, age, 4yrs.
  parents, A. P. & Susan Arbogast. born Crabbottom. occ. ____.
  consort of ____. info, A. P. Arbogast, father.

Arbogast, J. E., WM, **d. 2 Oct.** at Crabbottom of pneumonia, age, 61yrs.
  parents, Emanuel & ____ Arbogast. born Crabbottom.
  occ. doctor. consort of Mary J. info, Chas. Slaven, son-in-law.

Botkin Annie D., WF, **d. 9 Nov.** on Bullpasture Mt. of consumption, age, 19yrs.
  parents, Wm. & Jemma Taylor. born Bull P. Mt.
  occ. housekeeper. consort of A. S. Botkin.
  info, A. S. Botkin husband.

Botkin Lolo, WF, **d.** ____ on Bullpasture Mt. of diphtheria, age, 9yrs.
  parents, Esther Botkin. born Bull P. Mt. occ. ____.
  consort of ____. info, ____, neighbor.

Campbell, Laura E., WF, **d. 27 Sep.** on Back Creek of dyspepsia, age, 46yrs.
  parents, W. M. & Mary Campbell. born Back Creek.
  occ. housekeeper. consort of ____. info, W. M. Campbell, brother.

Campbell, Isabel W., WF, **d. 17 Aug.** at Meadow Dale of Bright's Disease, age, 63yrs.
  parents, Jas. & Mary Woods. born Meadow Dale.
  occ. housekeeper. widow. info, W. B. Woods, brother.

Colaw, Mary E., WF, **d. 12 June** at Crabbottom of ____, age, 70yrs.
  parents, Jacob & Malinda Newman. born Crabbottom.
  occ. housekeeper. consort of Cornelius Colaw.
  info, Cornelius Colaw, husband.

Colaw, Mary Ruth, WF, **d. 21 Dec.** at Crabbottom of diphtheria, age, 4yrs.
parents, D. E. & Mary M. Colaw. born Crabbottom. occ. ____.
consort of ____. info, D. E. Colaw, father.

Crickenberger, ____, WF, **d. 27 March** on Jackson River of childbirth, age, 23yrs.
parents, Jno. M. & Parthenia Ross. born Jackson R.
occ. housekeeper. consort of J. F. Crickenberger.
info, J. F. Crickenerger, husband.

Corbett, Sallie J., WF, **d. 1 May** on Jackson River of spinal meningitis, age, 6yrs.
parents, W. H. & Victoria Corbett. born Jackson R. occ. ____.
consort of ____. info, W. H. Corbett, father.

Cobb, ____, WM, **d. ____ Sep.** on Jack Mt. of ____, age, 1dy.
parents, S. A. & Martha Cobb. born Jack Mt. occ. ____.
consort of ____. info, S. A. Cobb, father.

Dawson, Millie, CF, **d. ____ Dec.** on Bullpasture of La Grippe, age 66yrs.
parents, Lewis & Millie Dawson. born Bullpasture. occ. servant.
consort of ____. info, Morgan Dawson, son.

Ervine, Wm., WM, **d. 9 March** on March on Bullpasture Mt. of consumption,
age, 68yrs. **parents, Wm. & Nancy Ervine.** born Bullpasture Mt.
occ. farmer. consort of Elizabeth Ervine.
info, Rebecca Ervine, daughter.

Fox, Margaret, WF, **d. 7 March** at Crabbottom of pneumonia, age, 76yrs.
parents, Wm. & ____ Hodge. born Crabbottom.
occ. housekeeper. widow. info, Chas. Fox, son.

Fleisher, Harry, WM, **d. ____ Sep.** on South ranch of croup, age, 3yrs.
parents, Austin & Mary Fleisher. born South Branch. occ. ____.
consort of ____. info, Jno. S. Fleisher, son.*[sic]*

Gum, Harry, WM, **d. 8 Aug.** at Hightown of paralysis, age, 81yrs.
parents, Wm. & Nancy Gum. born Back Creek.
occ. housekeeper. widow. info, Ad. Gum, husband. *[sic]*

Griffen, Sarah M., WF, **d. 6 Sep.** on Jackson River of pneumonia, age, 63yrs.
parents, Wm. & Polly Robertson. born Jackson River.
occ. housekeeper. consort of ____. info, J. R. Griffen, son.

Griffen, Sarah C., WF, **d. 25 Nov.** on St. Creek of ____, age, 1yr.
parents, Calvin & Mollie Griffen. born St. Creek. occ. ____.
consort of ____. info, Calvin Griffen, father.

Hevener, Mima, WF, **d. 7 March** at Crabbottom of childbirth, age, 24yrs.
parents, J. R. & Rebecca Hevener. born Crabbottom.
occ. housekeeper. consort of J. B. Hevener.
info, J. B. Hevener, husband.

Hevener, Jane, WF, **d. 24 March** at Hightown of dropsy, age, 70yrs.
parents, ____ & Ellen Sutton. born Hightown.
occ. housekeeper. widow. info, J. F. Hevener, son.

Harison, Geo. WM, **d. 31 May** on Jackson River of paralysis, age, 75yrs.
parents, ____ & ____. born Jackson R. occ. farmer.
consort of Martha Harison. info, Jas. N. Wood, neighbor.

Hinegardner, Godlove, WM, **d. 12 March** on Jackson River of Bright's d., age, 100yrs.
parents, ____ & ____ Hinegardner. born Jackson R.
occ. farmer. consort of ____. info, Chas. Carrol, neighbor.

Hull, Jno. H., WM, **d. 15 Jan.** at Davis, W. Va. of killed on mill, age, 21yrs.
parents, J. N. & E. J. Hull. born Vanderpool. occ. farmer.
consort of ____. info, J. N. Hull, father.

Hicklin, Malinda, WF, **d. ____ April** on Bullpasture R. of paralyized, age, 80 yrs.
parents, James & Mary Beathe. born Crab Run.
occ. housekeeper. widow. info, Fannie Beathe, sister.

Hamilton, Margaret, WF, **d. 2 Dec.** on Bullpasture R. of rheumatism, age, 75yrs.
parents, Robt. & Susan Wright born Bullpasture R.
occ. housekeeper. widow. info, W. T. Hamilton, son.

Hamilton, Hamey, WF, **d. 15 Aug.** on Bullpasture R. of consumption, age, 40yrs.
parents, Robt. & Emily Lockridge. born Bullpasture.
occ. housekeeper. consort of Jno. Hamilton. info, ____, neighbor.

Hiner, ____, WF, **d. ____ July** at Doe Hill of ____, age, ____.
parents, J. A. & R. L. Hiner. born Doe Hill. occ. ____.
consort of ____. info, J. A. Hiner, father.

Jack, Margaret, WF, **d. 15 Aug.** at Crabbottom of dropsy, age, 73yrs.
parents, Jno. & Sarah Jack. born Crabbottom. occ. housekeeper.
consort of ____. info, M. M. Jack, brother.

Jordan, Zola Estelle, WF, **d. ____ July** at Crabbottom of diptheria, age, 2yrs, 1mo.
parents, S. B. & Sarah E. Jordan. born Crabbottom. occ. ____.
consort of ____. info, S. B. Jordan, father.

Kincaid, Nancy, WF, **d.** ____ **June** on Jackson River of ____, age, 85yrs.
 parents, David & ____ **Kincaid.** born Jackson River.
 occ. housekeeper. consort of ____.
 info, A. T. Stephenson, neighbor.

Kincaid, Martha, WF, **d. 4 Dec.** on Cowpasture R. of dropsy, age, 65yrs.
 parents, ____ **&** ____ **Stanton.** born Cowpasture. occ. ____.
 consort of D. W. Kincaid. info, D. W. Kincaid, husband.

Lockridge, ____, WM, **d. 27 Oct.** on Bullpasture of inflame of bowels, age, 7yrs.
 parents, D. E. & Susie Lockridge. born Bullpasture R. occ. ____.
 consort of ____. info, D. E. Lockridge, father.

Leach, J. S., WM, **d. 24 Jan.** on Bullpasture Mt. of pneumonia, age, __.
 parents, ____ **&** ____ **Leach.** born Bullpasture Mt. occ. farmer.
 consort of Susanna Leach. info, ____.

Marshall, Charlie, WM, **d.** ____ **Aug.** at Crabbottom of diphtheria, age, 2yrs.
 parents, W. & M. Marshall. born Crabbottom. occ. ____.
 consort of ____. info, W. N. Marshall, father.

McCray, ____, WF, **d.** ____ on Bullpasture Mt. of ____, age, ____.
 parents, Robt. & ____ **McCray.** born Bullpasture Mt. occ. ____.
 consort of ____. info, Robert McCray, father.

Malcomb, ____, WF, **d.** ____ on Bullpasture Mt. of diphtheria, age, 1yr.
 parents, Ada Malcomb. born ____. occ. ____. consort of ____.
 info, ____, neighbor.

Nicholis, Henry, WM, **d. 23 Dec.** at Crabbottom of ____, age, 91yrs.
 parents, Francis & Kate Nicholis. born Crabbottom.
 occ. housekeeper. consort of ____. info, ____, neighbor.

Potter, Vergie Bell, WF, **d.** ____ **July** at Crabbottom of diphtheria, age, 2yrs, 5mos.
 parents, Mathew & ____ **Potter.** born Crabbottom. occ. ____.
 consort of ____. info, Mathew Potter, father.

Pritt, Mary Alice, WF, **d.** ____ **Nov.** at Hightown of diphtheria, age, 2yrs.
 parents, J. H. & N. M. Pritt. born Hightown. occ. ____.
 consort of ____. info, J. H. Pritt, father.

Rider, Susan, WF, **d. 9 Nov.** on Allegheny of ____, age, ____.
 parents, Sam'l & B. Rexrode. born near Monterey.
 occ. housekeeper. consort of Jacob M. Rider. info, ____.

Rider, Mary Gracie, WF, **d. 2 June** on Back Creek of pleuracy, age, 7yrs.
    parents, Jno. L. & Estie Rider. born Back Creek. occ. ____.
consort of ____. info, Jno. Rider, father.

Rexrode, Louisa, WF, **d. ____ Oct.** at Baltimore of ulcer, age, 60yrs.
    parents, Sam'l. & ____ Rexrode. born Monterey.
occ. housekeeper. consort of ____. info, James Rexrode, neighbor.

Rexrode, Bertie L., WM, **d. ____ Nov.** at Crabbottom of croup, age, 9yrs, 7mos.
    parents, Geo. & ____ Rexrode. born Crabbottom. occ. ____.
consort of ____. info, Geo. Rexrode, father.

Rexrode, Andrew, WM, **d. 25 Nov.** at McDowell of dirarhia, age, 74yrs.
    parents, Jno. & ____ Rexrode. born McDowell. occ. farmer.
consort of Mary A. Rexrode info, Jno. Rexrode, son.

Ruckman, Thomas, WM, **d. ____** at Crabbottom of paralysis, age, 70yrs.
    parents, Wm. & ____ Ruckman. born Crabbottom. occ. farmer.
consort of Nancy Ruckman. info, S. T. Ruckman, son.

Ralston, Samuel, WM, **d. 22 Nov.** at McDowell of exposure, age, 75yrs.
    parents, Saml & Annie Ralston. born McDowell. occ. farmer.
consort of ____. info, Mrs. Cook, daughter.

Snyder, David, WM, **d. 17 Aug.** at Crabbottom of Bright's d., age, 71yrs.
    parents, Jno. & ____ Snyder. born Crabbottom. occ. farmer.
consort of Caroline Snyder. info, Calvin Snyder, son.

Swecker, Robert W., WM, **d. 7 Oct** at Crabbottom of diphtheria, age, 28dys.
    parents, Geo. E. & Estelle Swecker. born Crabbottom. occ. ____.
consort of ____. info, Geo. Swecker, father.

Swecker, Clara D., WF, **d. 13 Oct.** at Crabottom of diphtheria, age, 2yrs, 1mo.
    parents, Geo. E. & Estelle Swecker. born Crabbottom. occ. ____.
consort of ____. info, Geo. Swecker, father.

Siron, Elizabeth, WF, **d. 21 Nov.** on Bullpasture Mt. of heart disease, age, ____.
    parents, Jas. & Nancy Propst. born Bullpasture Mt.
occ. housekeeper. widow. info, Sarahn Malcom, daughter.

Simmons, Anne Grace, WF, **d. ____ Oct.** on Bullpasture Mt. of croup, age, 4yrs.
    parents, Chris & Sally Simmons. born Bullpasture Mt. occ. ____.
consort of ____. info, Chris Simmons, father.

Simmons, ____, WF, **d. ____ Feb.** on Bullpasture Mt. of ____, age, 1hr.
   parents, J. S. & Minie Simmons. born Bullpasture Mt. occ. ____.
   consort of ____. info, J. S. Simmons, father.

Simmons, ____, WF, **d. ____** on Bullpasture R. of ____, age, ____.
   parents, W. H. & ____ Simmons. born Bullpasture R. occ. ____.
   consort of ____. info, ____, neighbor.

Steuart, ____, WF, **d. 19 Nov.** on Cowpasture of ____, age, 2dys.
   parents, Jno. & Maggie Steuart. born Cowpasture. occ. ____.
   consort of ____. info, Jno. M. Steuart, father.

Turner, Mary J., WF, **d. 22 Nov.** on Bullpasture R. of ____, age, 57yrs.
   parents, Wm. & Martha Griffen. born Jackson River.
   occ. housekeeper. consort of M. B. Turner.
   info, A. T. Stephenson, neighbor.

Terrell, O. H. P., WM, **d. 12 Nov.** on Bullpasture R. of consumption, age, 27yrs.
   parents, J. H. P. & M. Terrell. born ____. occ. teacher.
   consort of ____. info, G. B. Revercomb, neighbor.

Vance George, WM, **d. 14 Sep.** on Bullpasture R. of paralysis, age, 84yrs.
   parents, Benj. & Hannah Vance. born Bullpasture. occ. farmer.
   consort of Dorcas Vance. info, D. E. Lockridge, son-in-law.

Varner, Jno. H., WM, **d. 8 Dec.** on Spring Run of diphtheria, age, 17yrs, 1mo.
   parents, Wm. & Catherine Varner. born Spring Run. occ. ____.
   consort of ____. info, Catherine Varner, mother.

Wills, Madge, WF, **d. 20 July** at Crabbottom of diphtheria, age, 17mos.
   parents, W. P. & Lula Wills. born Crabbottom. occ. ____.
   consort of ____. info, W. P. Wills, father.

Wills, Mary Eliza, WF, **d. 15 July** at Crabbottom of diphtheria, age, 14dys.
   parents, W. P. & Lula Wills. born Crabbottom. occ. ____.
   consort of ____. info, W. P. Wills, father.

White, Jacob, WM, **d. 25 Oct.** at Crabbottom of neuralgia, age, 65yrs.
   parents. Jno. & Matilda White. born Crabbottom. occ. farmer.
   consort of Eliza White. info, Geo. Swecker, neighbor.

Wade, A. O., WM, **d. 2 Feb.** on Back Creek of dyspepsia, age, 73yrs.
   parents, Jno. & ____ Wade. born Back Creek. occ. farmer.
   consort of Adella Wade. info, W. A. Wade, son.

Wimer, Charlie C., WM, **d. 17 Oct.** at Crabbottom of thyphoid fever, age, 20yrs, 8mos. **parents, Ambe & Susan Wimer.** born Crabottom. occ. ____. consort of ____. info, Ambe Wimer, father.

Weese, Arthur, WM, **d. 14 July** on Middle Mt. of diphtheria, age, 2dys. **parents, Harmon & Christina Weese.** born Middle Mt. occ. ____. consort of ____. info, Harmon Weese, father.

Woods, Lillie G., WF, **d. 14 May** at Meadow Dale of peritonitis, age, 15yrs, 7mos. **parents, N. B. & Lucy Woods.** born Meadow Dale. occ. ____. consort of ____. info, N. B. Woods, father.

1896

Bird, Geo. H., WM, **d. 5 Sep.** on Back Creek of pneumonia, age, 77yrs. **parents, David & Eliz. Bird.** born Bath Co. occ. farmer. consort of Matilda M. Bird. info, Geo. A. Bird, son.

Bird, Chas. W., WM, **d. 11 Oct.** on Back Creek of pneumonia, age, 6mos. **parents, Chas. T. & Melissa Bird.** born Back Creek. occ. ____. consort of ____. info, Chas. T. Bird, father.

Blagg, Wm. H., WM, **d. 16 Feb.** on Crab Run Mt. of croup, age, 2yrs, 11mos. **parents, B. H. & S. E. Blagg.** born Crab Run Mt. occ. ____. consort of ____. info, B. H. Blagg, father.

Bowers, Zetie F., WF, **d. 19 May** on St. Creek of rheumatism, age, 6yrs. **parents, W. H. & Eliza Bowers.** born St. Creek. occ. ____. consort of ____. info, W. H. Bowers, father.

Benson, W. W., WM, **d. 26 Jan.** at Monterey of cancer, age, 62yrs. **parents, Matthias & Susan Benson.** born Bath Co. occ. farmer. consort of ____. info, Jas. Benson, son.

Coursey, D. L., WM, **d. ____ Feb.** at Crabbottom of dropsy, age, 62yrs. **parents, ____ & ____ Coursey.** born __. occ. painter. consort of ____. info, S. S. Wayright, Admr.

Crummett, Martha, WF, **d. 19 Oct.** on Shaw's Fork of quinsy, age, 31yrs. **parents, Jas. & Cath Varner.** born Pendleton Co. occ. ____. consort of S. B. Crummett. info, S. B. Crummett, husband.

Crummett, Arlie, WM, **d. 21 April** on Shaw's Fork of inf. of bowels, age, 14dys. **parents, S. B. & Martha Crummett.** born Shaw's Fork. occ. ____. consort of ____. info, S. B. Crummett, father.

Dickenson, Robt. I., WM, **d. 3 Oct.** at Monterey of ____, age, 5mos. **parents, L. S. & Matie Dickenson.** born Monterey. occ. ____. consort of ____. info, L. S. Dickenson, father.

Doyle, Eliza, WF, **d. ____ July** on Jackson's R. of epilepsy, age, 52yrs. **parents, Michael & Ann Doyle.** born Jackson's R. occ. ____. consort of ____. info, Jas. Corrigan, brother-in-law.

Ervin, Marian K., WF, **d. 3 Feb.** at McDowell of cholera infantum, age, 7mos, 11dys. **parents, R. N. & Emma Ervine.** born McDowell. occ. ____. consort of ____. info, R. N. Ervine.

Fleisher, Sadie, WF, **d. 31 Dec.** on St. Creek of croup, age, 6mos. **parents, Austin & Mary Fleisher.** born St. Creek. occ. ____. consort of ____. info, Mary Fleisher, mother.

Fleisher, Sallie, WF, **d. ____ April** on South Branch of croup, age, 3yrs. **parents, Chas. T. & Sarah Fleisher.** born South Branch. occ. ____. consort of ____. info, Chas. T. Fleisher, father.

Fox, Harriet, WF, **d. 20 March** in Big Valley of quinsy, age, 63yrs. **parents, Jas. & ____ Gillespie.** born Bath Co. occ. ____. consort of J. M. Fox. info, J. M. Fox, husband.

Grogg, Margt., WF, **d. 1 Oct.** at Crabottom of pneumonia, age, 49yrs. **parents, Levi Lantz.** born Pendleton Co. occ. ____. consort of Saml Grogg. info, Saml Grogg, husand.

Gay, Susan H., WF, **d. 15 July** on Head of J. River of consumption, age, 72yrs. **parents, John & Jane Lightner.** born Pendleton Co. occ. ____. consort of ____. info, S. A. Porter, son-in-law.

Gwin, Ellen, WF, **d. ____ Oct.** on Jackson's River of pneumonia, age, 66yrs. **parents, Jno. & Eliza Dever.** born Back Creek. occ. ____. consort of ____. info, Job Eckard, son-in-law.

Gwin, Edna, WF, **d. 15 March** on Cowpasture River of ____, age, 2yrs. **parents, Jas. H. & Martha Gwin.** born Cow Past. occ. ____. consort of ____. info, Martha Gwin, mother.

Gibson, Jno. L., WM, **d. 6 Nov.** at Vanderpool of Bright's disease, age, 65yrs, 5mos, 23dys. **parents, Saml & Sally Gibson.** born Pendleton Co. occ. farmer. consort of Alice S. Gibson. info, Willis Gibson, son.

Gutshall Emma V., WF, **d. 10 Nov.** on Jackson's River of burned, age, 6yrs. **parents, J. L. & Maggie Gutshall.** born Jackson's R. occ. ____. consort of ____. info, J. L. Gutshall, father.

Hidy, Matilda, WF, **d.** ____ at Crabbottom of pneumonia, age, 85yrs. **parents, ____ & ____ Peninger.** born Pendleton Co. occ. ____. consort of ____. info, Jas. B. Hidy, son.

Hise, Eva, WF, **d.** ____ **Oct.** at Meadow Dale of diphtheria, age, 8yrs. **parents, Sam & Ellen Hise.** born Meadow Dale. occ. ____. consort of ____. info, Sam Hise, father.

Hise, Fred, WM, **d. 2 Oct.** at Meadow Dale of diphtheria, age, 5yrs. **parents, Sam & Ellen Hise.** born Meadow Dale. occ. ____. consort of ____. info, Sam Hise, father.

Hise, Annie B., WF, **d. 16 Oct.** at Meadow Dale of diphtheria, age, 2yrs. **parents, Sam & Ellen Hise.** born Meadow Dale. occ. ____. consort of ____. info, Sam Hise, father.

Hull, ____, WM, **d.** ____ **Dec.** at Crabbottom of diphtheria, age, 7dys. **parents, Luther & Art. Hull.** born Crabbottom. occ. ____. consort of ____. info, Jos. Hull, grandfather.

Hiner, Mary A., WF, **d. 21 Jan.** at McDowell of consumption, age, 57yrs. **parents, B. & Polly Hansel.** born Crabbottom. occ. ____. consort of B. Hiner. info, J. J. Hiner, stepson.

Jones, Jemima J., WF, **d. 5 Feb.** at Doe Hill of apoplexy, age, 48yrs. **parents, S. C. & M. M. Eagle.** born Doe Hill. occ. ____. consort of Dr. H. H. Jones. info, H. H. Jones, husband.

Kincaid, David G., WM, **d. 7 Nov.** on Jackson's R. of La Grippe, age, 82yrs. **parents, Thomas & Sally Kincaid.** born Jackson's R. occ. farmer. consort of Lucinda Kincaid. info, Edw. S. Kincaid, son.

Kincaid, Martha, WF, **d.** ____ **Feb.** on Cow Past. of cancer, age, 65yrs. **parents, ____ & ____ Rodgers.** born ____. occ. ____. consort of D. H. Kincaid. info, Geo. L. Hupman, neighbor.

Kincaid, Martha, WF, **d. ____ May** on Shaw's Fork of ____, age, 4dys.
      parents, J. M. & Mary Kincaid. born Shaw's Fork. occ. ____.
consort of ____. info, A. H. Devericks, grandfather.

Lockridge, S. A., WM, **d. 21 July** on Bull Past. of consumption, age, 53yrs.
      parents, Robt. & Emma Lockridge. born Bull Past. occ. farmer.
consort of Julia Lockridge. info, Julia E. Lockridge, wife.

Lindsay, Lillie, WF, **d. ____ Oct.** on Bull Past. of pneumonia, age, 14dys.
      parents, Jos. & Ella M. Lindsay. born Bull Past. occ. ____.
consort of ____. info, Joseph Lindsay, father.

Malcom, ____, WM, **d. ____ March** near Monterey of pneumonia, age, 5dys.
      parents, Crawf. & Mary E. Malcom. born near Monterey.
occ. ____. consort of ____. info, Crawf. Malcom, father.

Malcom, Virginia, WF, **d. ____ March** on Jack Mt. of diphtheria, age, 1mo.
      parents, Ada Malcomb. born Jack Mt. occ. ____. consort of ____.
info, Jas. A. Ralston, neighbor.

McCray, Rebecca, WF, **d. ____ Dec.** on Cow Past. of ____, age, 30yrs.
      parents, Thos. & ____ Killingsworth. born Cow Past. occ. ____.
consort of H. H. McCray. info, H. H. McCray, husband.

Minor, Jennie F., CF, **d. ____ May** on Cow Past. of rheumatism, age, 1--yrs.*
      parents, Fred & Rachel Minor. born Cow Past. occ. ____.
consort of ____. info, Fred Minor, father.

Nicholas, Nela C., WF, **d. 19 June** at Crabottom of diphtheria, age, 9yrs, 6mos.
      parents, Jas. N. & Laura Nicholas. born Crabottom. occ. ____.
consort of ____. info, Jas. N. Nicholas, father.

Parmer, Ernest, WM, **d. ____ Jan.** on Back Creek of croup, age, 3yrs.
      parents, W. S. & Ida Parmer. born Back Creek. occ. ____.
consort of ____. info, ____, neighbor.

Patterson, Jessie, WM, **d. 3 Oct.** in Pocahontas Co. of consumption, age, ____.
      parents, Frank & Rachel. born Pocahontas Co. occ. farmer.
consort of Mollie Arbogast. info, Abe Arbogast, brother-in-law.

Pullin, A. M., WM, **d. ____ Nov.** on Bull Past. of pneumonia, age, ____.
      parents, Loftus Pullin. born B. P. River. occ. ____.
consort of M. M. Pullin. info, M. M. Pullin, wife.

---

*page torn in the original—age is 10-19yrs.

Pullin, ____, WM, **d. 24 July** on Bull Past. of ____, age, 4dys.
        parents, A. M. & M. M. Pullin. born B. P. River. occ. ____.
consort of ____. info, M. M. Pullin, mother.

Peterson, Hattie M., WF, **d. 24 April** at Monterey of blood poison, age, 32yrs.
        parents, Sol & Harriet Burtner. born Rockingham Co. occ. ____.
consort of D. H. Peterson. info, D. H. Peterson, husband.

Peck, Jacob, WM, **d. 28 Oct.** on St. Creek of paralysis, age, 87yrs, 7mos.
        parents, Jacob & Annie Peck. born St. Creek. occ. ____.
consort of Mary M. Peck. info, M. M. Peck, wife.

Puffenbarger, Adam, WM, **d. 21 Dec.** on Sang Mt. of dropsy, age, 77yrs.
        parents, Peter & ____ Puffenbarger. born ____. occ. ____.
consort of Eliza Puffenbarger. info, A. J. Puffenbarger, son.

Rexrode, Geo. A., WM, **d. 29 Dec.** on Crab Run of pneumonia, age, 45yrs.
        parents, Jno. M. & Cath. Rexrode. born Hightown. occ. farmer.
consort of Sarah J. Rexrode. info, W. T. Rexrode, brother.

Rexrode, Virginia C., WF, **d. 5 April** on St. Creek of ____, age, 26yrs.
        parents, Eman. & Mary M. Propst. born St. Creek. occ. ____.
consort of O. F. Rexrode. info, O. F. Rexrode, husband.

Rexrode, Ruth, WF, **d. 17 March** at New Hampden of consumption, age, 7mos.
        parents, W. C. & Mary Rexrode. born New Hampden.
occ. ____. consort of ____. info, W. C. Rexrode, father.

Rexrode, Joseph, WM, **d. 30 Sep.** on South Fork of cancer, age, 76yrs.
        parents, Geo. & Eliza Rexrode. born South Fork. occ. farmer.
consort of Sarah Rexrode. info, Ambrose Rexrode, son.

Swadley, Wm., WM, **d. 4 Sep.** at Hightown of ____, age, 84yrs, 3mos, 24dys.
        parents, ____ & ____ Swadley. born Rockingham Co.
occ. farmer. consort of Margt. Swadley.
info, Eliz. Kincaid, daughter.

Smith, ____, WF, **d. ____** on St. Creek of ____, age, ____.
        parents, ____ & Orfie Smith. born St. Creek. occ. farmer.
consort of ____. info, Geo. W. Mullenax, grandfather.

Simmons, Almeda, WF, **d. 24 Nov.** at Crabbottom of quinsy, age, 24yrs.
        parents, ____ & Mary Mullenax. born Crabottom. occ. farmer.
consort of Jasper Simmons. info, Jas. Simmons, husband.

Simmons, Sarah M., WF, **d. 4 June** on Jackson's River of flux, age, 1yr, 7mos, 6dys. **parents, Floyd & M. E. Simmons.** born Jackson's R. occ. ____. consort of ____. info, Floyd Simmons, father.

Simmons, Malinda, WF, **d. 16 Feb.** near Monterey of ____, age, 72yrs. **parents, ____ & ____ Puffenbarger.** born Pendleton Co. occ. ____. consort of Lewis Simmons. info, Sol D. Simmons, son-in-law.

Simmons, Grover C., WF, **d. ____ March** on Bull Past. Mt. of croup, age, 8yrs. **parents, C. & Sally M. Simmons.** born Bull Past. Mt. occ. ____. consort of ____. info, Chris Simmons, father.

Simmons, Wash, WM, **d. 11 Dec.** on St. Creek of diphtheria, age, ____. **parents, Wm. G. & Rebecca Simmons.** born St. Creek. occ. ____. consort of ____. info, Edw. Simmons, brother.

Snyder, Mary A., WF, **d. 7 July** at Crabottom of spinal affection, age, 61yrs. **parents, D. C. & ____ Stone** born Pendleton Co. occ. ____. consort of ____. info, W. E. Snyder, son.

Snyder, Geo. W., WM, **d. 6 Sep.** on St. Creek of pneumonia, age, 41yrs. **parents, Sam'l & Polly Snyder.** born Highland Co. occ. laborer. consort of Sally M. Snyder. info, Sally M. Snyder, wife.

Sponaugle, Rachel, WF, **d. ____ Jan.** on South Branch of ____, age, 70yrs. **parents, Chris & ____ Rexrode.** born Pendleton Co. occ. ____. consort of ____. info, Wm. M. Arbogast, neighbor.

Stephenson, V. C., WF, **d. 3 Feb.** on Cow P. River of heart disease, age, 70yrs. **parents, Chas. & Theresa Steuart.** born Bull Past. occ. ____. consort of A. C. Stephenson. info, A. C. Stephenson husband.

Smith, Laura, CF, **d. 17 Feb.** at McDowell of ____, age, 32yrs. **parents, ____ & ____.** born ____. occ. ____. consort of Saml Smith. info, Saml Smith, husband.

Siron, Joel W., WM, **d. 14 Nov.** on Bull Past. of pneumonia, age, ____. **parents, Jonathan & ____ Siron.** born Bull Past. occ. farmer. consort of ____. info, Sarah M. Malcom, sister.

Trainer, Michael, WM, **d. 2 Sep.** at Meadow Dale of cholera mortus, age, 80yrs. **parents, ____ & Margt. Trainer.** born ____. occ. farmer. consort of Mary A. Trainer. info, Mary A. Trainer, wife.

Terry, ____, WF, **d. ____** in Bath Co. of ____, age, 2mos.
    parents, W. W. & Mollie B. Terry. born Dry Branch. occ. ____.
consort of ____. info, W. W. Terry, father.

Tolly, W. H., WM, **d. 5 June** at McDowell of consumption, age, ____.
    parents, ____ & ____ Tolly. born ____. occ. shoemaker.
consort of Mary Tolly. info, ____, neighbor.

Vandevender, Geo., WM, **d. 6 Oct.** on St. Creek of diabetes, age, 80yrs.
    parents, Geo. & ____ Vandevender. born Pendleton Co.
occ. farmer. consort of ____. info, J. E. Vandevender.

Wamsley, C. A., WM, **d. 31 May** at McDowell of flux, age, 65yrs.
    parents, Jacob & Christian Wamsley. born Randolph Co.
occ. ____. consort of ____. info, M. M. Bradshaw, daughter.

Woods, Mary Jewell, WF, **d. 11 Dec.** at Meadow Dale of diptheria,
age, 3yrs, 6mos, 11dys. **parents, N. B. & Lucy E. Woods.**
born Meadow Dale. occ. ____. consort of ____.
info, N. B. Woods, father.

Wade, Annie P., WF, **d. ____ Jan.** on Back Creek of brain fever, age, 1yr, 1mo, 2dys.
    parents, Sidney & Emma Wade. born Back Creek. occ. ____.
consort of ____. info, Sidney Wade, father.

Wimer, ____, WM, **d. 21 ____.** at New Hampden of ____, age, ____.
    parents, Ambi & Susan Wimer. born New Hampden.
occ. ____. consort of ____. info, Ambi Wimer, father.

Wimer, Virginia F., WF, **d. 7 Nov.** at Crabbottom of unknown, age, 39yrs.
    parents, Mathew & ____ Wimer. born ____. occ. ____.
consort of Lee J. Wimer. info, L. J. Wimer, husand.

Waggoner, ____, WF, **d. ____** at Crabbottom of ____, age, ____.
    parents, Jno. A. & Lena Waggoner. born Crabbottom. occ. ____.
consort of ____. info, Jno. A. Waggoner, father.

1897*

Armstrong, Jno. W. A., WM, **d. 26 Jan** in Big Valley of ____, age, 1dy.

Ashby, Eyster Pence, WM, **d. 8 June** at Crabbottom of ____, age, 11mos, 25dys.

Beverage, ____, WM, **d. 18 Sep.** near Monterey of ____, age, ____.

Bishop, Ella, WF, **d. ____ Dec.** on Bull Pasture of croup, age, 3yrs, 10mos.

Beathe, Mary M., WF, **d. 22 Dec.** on Bull Pasture of La Grippe, age, 48yrs.

Bryant, Robt. C., WM, **d. ____** at McDowell of croup, age, 2yrs.

Carpenter, Georgie E., WF, **d. ____** in Big Valley of ____, age, 2yrs.

Carpenter, Stanley, W., WM, **d. 3 May** in Big Valley, of ____, age, ____.

Carpenter, Clifton C., WM, **d. 4 June** in Big Valley of ____, age, ____.

Carr, Blaine, CM, **d. ____** on Bull Pasture Mt. of ____, age, ____.

Colaw, Sarah, WF, **d. 6 April** on St. Creek of pneumonia, age, 76yrs, 3mos, 6dys.

Chew, ____, WM, **d. ____** at Crabbottom of ____, age, ____.

Carichoff, Stuart, WM, **d. 27 Nov.** on Crab Run of ____, age, 11yrs.

Clinedenst, Waldo, WM, **d. ____** at Doe Hill of ____, age, ____.

Dickson, ____, WF, **d. 8 Nov.** at Monterey of ____, age, 1dy.

Devericks, Allen H., WM, **d. 12 July** on Shaw's Fork of ____, age, ____.

Ervine, E. V., WM, **d. 2 March** on Cow Pasture of brain fever, age, 58yrs

---

* The upper right quarter of the first page of the original 1897 death list is missing. This obliterates information on the first 17 entries for parents, birth location, occupation, consort, and informant. Likewise, the upper left quarter on the reverse, for entries 37-53 are missing. This obliterates information for the decedent, color, gender, date of death, location of death, cause of death, age at death, and part of the parents' name.

Ervine, Sally A., WF, **d. 29 April** on Cow Pasture of catarrh, age, ____.
        parents, James & Sally Leach. born Pendleton Co.
        occ. housekeeper. widow. info, ____, brother-in-law.

Eagle, Patsy, WF, **d.** ____ at Doe Hill of dropsy, age, ____.
        parents, Christian & Jane Eagle. born Pendleton Co.
        occ. housekeeper. consort of ____. info, S. C. Eagle, nephew.

Floyd, Susan Izetta, WF, **d. 28 Oct.** on Bull Past. of ____, age, 82yrs.
        parents, Wm. & Margt. Meeks. born Italy. occ. housekeeper.
        widow. info, Mrs. Masters, daughter.

Gutshall, ____, WM, **d. 5 May** on Back Creek of ____, age, 23 dys.
        parents, Peter & Nannie Gutshall. born Back Creek. occ. ____.
        consort of ____. info, ____, father.

Gutshall, Elsie, WF, **d. 8 June** on Back Creek of ____, age, 4yrs.
        parents, Peter & Nannie Gutshall. born Back Creek. occ. ____.
        consort of ____. info, ____, father.

Gutshall, Charlie, WM, **d. 14 June** on Jackson's River of flux, age, 2yrs, 9mos.
        parents, Jno. L. & Maggie Gutshall. born Jackson's River.
        occ. ____. consort of ____. info, ____, father.

Gum, Barbara,* WF, **d.** ____ at Crabbottom of ____, age, ____.
        parents, ____ & ____ **Nicholas.** born Crabbottom. occ. ____.
        consort of ____. info, H. B. Rexrode, neighbor.

Gum, Peter, WM, **d. 19 June** at Crabbottom of bronchitis, age, 78yrs.
        parents, Adam & Susan Gum. born Crabbottom. occ. ____.
        consort of Barbara Gum. info, Isaac Gum, son.

Graham, Lyman H., WM, **d. 7 June** on Bull Past. of ____, age, 10mos.
        parents, D. C. & Emma V. Graham. born Bull Past. occ. ____.
        consort of ____. info, ____, father.

Girard, Nellie Mina, WF, **d. 23 March** at McDowell of ____, age, 18dys.
        parents, A. M. & Cornelia Girard. born McDowell. occ. ____.
        consort of ____. info, ____, father.

Hise, Clarence, WM, **d. 23 Nov.** on J. River of ____, age, 10mos.
        parents, Saml. & Ella V. Hise. born J. River. occ. ____.
        consort of ____. info, ____, father.

---

*entered on original 1898 list.

Hiner, Saml.,* WF, **d. 15 Dec.** at Doe Hill of pneumonia, age, 83yrs.
        parents, Jacob & ____ Hiner. born Pendleton Co. occ. ____.
        consort of ____. info, Jno. W. Smith, son-in-law.

Harold, Miles, WM, **d. 1 Feb.** at Crabbottom of heart disease, age, 67yrs.
        parents, Dan'l. & ____ Harold. born Pendleton Co.
        occ. merchant. consort of Cath. Harold. info, L. A. Harold.

Harouff, Cleminza, WF, **d. 28 Jan.** on Back Creek of apoplexy,
        age, 51yrs, 11mos, 23dys. **parents, ____ & Jane Helms.**
        born Bull Past. occ. housekeeper. consort of V. F. Harouff.
        info, ____, husband.

Hull, Nora May, WF, **d. 22 Dec.** on J. River of diphtheria, age, 13yrs.
        parents, W. C. & Sally Hull. born Grant Co. occ. ____.
        consort of ____. info, ____, father.

Halterman, Perry C., WM, **d. 14 Dec.** on St. Creek of burned, age, 2yrs, 5mos.
        parents, N. W. & Cora A. Halterman. born Pendleton Co.
        occ. ____. consort of ____. info, ____, father.

Hammer, Saml., WM, **d. 28 June** on Bull Past. of ____, age, 67yrs.
        parents, ____ & ____ Hammer. born Pendleton Co. occ. farmer.
        consort of ____. info, E. A. Hammer, father. *[sic]*

Jones, Jno. Marvin, WM, d. 10 March at Monterey of Bright's disease, age, 6yrs.
        parents, Chas. P. & Mattie W. Jones. born Monterey. occ. ____.
        consort of ____. info, C. P. Jones, father.

Johnston, Lulu, CF, **d. 18 April** on Crab Run of appendicitis, age, 8yrs.
        parents, And. & Ella Johnston. born Crab Run. occ. ____.
        consort of ____. info, ____, father.

Koogler, Eliza J., WF, **d. 25 Aug.** at Monterey of consumption, age, 83yrs, 10mos.
        parents, James & Mary Ervine. born Rockingham. occ. ____.
        consort of ____. info, ------,* daughter.

-----------, **parents, Thos. & Sarah Kincaid.** born Bath Co. occ. none. consort of ____.
        info, Edw. S. Kincaid, nephew.

-----------, **[Ella],** **parents, Saml. & Rachel -----.** born Bath Co. occ. housekeeper.
        consort of Jos. W. Lindsay. info, ____, husband.

---

* name obscured on original page.

** this and all other information in brackets on this and the succeeding page is inferred from other information in the death records or from other sources.

----------, **parents, Jos. W. & Ella [Linds]ay.** born Bull Past. occ. ____.
consort of ____. info, ____, husband.

---------, **parents, Norval & Lucy -----s.** born Bull Past. occ. ____.
consort of ____. info, ____, husband.

[Moats], **parents, Jonas & Sophia [---]ts.** born Pendleton Co. occ. laborer.
consort of Martha Moats. info, Jas. Simmons, neighbor.

[Malcom, Ferguson], **parents, ____ & ____ [Mal]com.** born Bull Past. occ. farmer.
consort of ____. info, E. B. Malcom, son.

[Malcom], -----, **parents, Crawford & Etta [Malcom].** born near Monterey.
occ. ____. consort of ____. info, ____, father.

--------, **parents, James & Nancy ------.** born Jackson's R. occ. housekeeper.
consort of ____. info, E. A. McLaughlin, son.

[Mackey] --------, **parents, W. H. & Mary V. [Mack]ey.** born Bolar. occ. farmer.
consort of ____. info, Jno. H. Mackey, brother.

--------, **parents, Martin & Sarah ------.** born Bull Past. occ. farmer. consort of ____.
info, T. J. Wiseman, neighbor.

[Malcom], ------, **parents, Josiah & Malinda ------.** born Bull Past. occ. housekeeper.
consort of Jas. P. Malcom. info, Jas. P. Malcom, husband.

[Miller], ------, **parents, ____ & ____ [Mil]ler.** born Bath Co. occ. farmer.
consort of Amanda Miller. info, Amanda Miller, wife.

[Newman], ------, **parents, Jacob & Malinda [New]man.** born Pendleton Co.
occ. farmer. widower. info, S. Newman, brother.

[Newman], -------, **parents, Claude D. & Myrtie [New]man.** born Crabbottom.
occ. ____. consort of ____. info, S. Newman, grandfather.

---------, **parents, Matthew & Mary ------.** born ____. occ. ____.
consort of ____. info, ____, father.

[Puffenberger], ------, **parents, C. L. & Sarah S. [Puffe]nberger.** born St. Creek.
occ. ____. consort of ____. info, ____, father.

[Puffenberger], -------, **parents, ____ & ____ [Puffe]nberger.** born St. Creek.
occ. farmer. consort of Eliz. B. Puffenberger.
info, And. Puffenberger, son.

Puffenberger, Eliz. B., WF, **d. 6 Nov.** at ____ of dropsy, age, 74yrs.
    parents, Adam & ____ Halterman. born St. Creek.
    occ. housekeeper. widow. info, And. Puffenberger, son.

Rexrode, Dan'l. H., WM, **d. 12 Aug.** at Crabbottom of dropsy, age, 63yrs, 1mo, 7dys.
    parents, Benj. Rexrode. born Crabbottom. occ. farmer.
    consort of Barbara Rexrode. info, Willie A. Rexrode, son-in-law.

Rexrode, V. J., WF, **d. 10 Dec.** at Crabbottom of ____, age, 5dys.
    parents, E. K. & Martha J. Rexrode. born Crabbottom.
    occ. ____. consort of ____. info, ____, father.

Ryder, ____, WF, **d. 25 Dec.** on Back Creek of ____, age, 1dy.
    parents, Jno. L. & Estie L. Ryder. born Back Creek. occ. ____.
    consort of ____. info, ____, father.

Ruckman, Ora F., WF, **d. 14 Feb.** at Crabbottom of typhoid fever, age, 17yrs.
    parents, Sam'l T. & Ursula Ruckman. born Crabbottom.
    occ. ____. consort of ____. info, ____, father.

Ruckman, Glenn, WM, **d. 20 Feb.** at Crabbottom of typhoid fever, age, ____.
    parents, Sam'l T. & Ursula Ruckman. born Crabbottom.
    occ. ____. consort of ____. info, ____, father.

Simmons, ____, WF, **d. ____** at Crabbottom of ____, age, ____.
    parents, Addison & __ Simmons. born Crabottom.
    occ. ____. consort of ____. info, ____, neighbor.

Samples, Ruhama, WF, **d. 7 Nov.** on Crab Run Mt. of paralysis, age, 45yrs.
    parents, Wm. & Christina Lough. born Pendleton Co. occ.
    housekeeper. consort of John H. Samples. info, ____, husband.

Shumate, Mary E., WF, **d. 9 July** at Franklin, W.Va. of convulsions, age, 1yr, 1mo, 9dys. **parents, A. A. & Mollie C. Shumate.** born near Monterey.
    occ. ____. consort of ____. info, ____, father.

Simmons, Lottie, WF, **d. ____ Aug.** on Back Creek of ____, age, 18yrs.
    parents, Lewis & Nellie P. Simmons. born near Monterey.
    occ. ____. consort of ____. info, ____, father.

Simmons, W. H., WM, **d. 30 Nov.** on Bull Past. of abcess, age, 69yrs.
    parents, Chris & ____ Simmons. born Bull Past. occ. farmer.
    consort of Ruhama Simmons. info, ____, mother.

Stone, Mary E., WF, **d. 16 June** at Crabbottom of consumption, age, 36yrs.
    parents, Esau & Eliza Rexrode. born Crabbottom.
    occ. housekeeping. consort of Sam'l Stone. info, ____, husband.

Slaven, Sarah, WF, **d. 8 Aug.** at Meadow Dale of ____, age, ____.
    parents, Benj. & Sally Fleisher. born St. Creek. occ. housekeeping.
    consort of S. C. Slaven. info, H. H. Slaven, son.

Terry, Wm. H., WM, **d.** ____ **Oct.** on Dry Branch of kicked by a horse, age, 3yrs.
    parents, A. J. & Irene Terry. born Dry Branch. occ. ____.
    consort of ____. info, ____, father.

Varner, Mary, WF, **d. 20 Jan.** on St. Creek of ____, age, 78yrs.
    parents, ____ **&** ____ **Snyder.** born Pendleton Co.
    occ. housekeeping. widow. info, Lafe Simmons, grandson.

Vance Willie M., WM, **d. 21 May** on Bull Past. R. of appendicitis, age, 9yrs, 5mos.
    parents, W. H. & Helen Vance. born Bull Past. occ. ____.
    consort of ____. info, ____, father.

Woodell, Eliza A., WF, **d. 7 Nov.** on Bull Past. R. of ____, age, 84yrs.
    parents, Jno. & Eliza Woodell born Bull Past. occ. housekeeper.
    widow. info, H. I. Woodell, son.

Wilson, John, WM, **d. 25 July** on Cow Past. R. of heart disease, age, 78yrs, 3mos.
    parents, Wm. & Mary Wilson. born Cow Past. R. occ. farmer.
    widower. info, H. H. Wilson, son.

Wade, Jas. W., WM, **d. 11 Feb.** on Back Creek of general debility, age, 82yrs.
    parents, Otho & Catherine Wade. born Back Creek. occ. farmer.
    widower. info, How. Wade, son.

Waybright, ____, WM, **d.** ____ **Nov.** at Crabbottom of ____, age, ____.
    parents, Chas. S. & Maude ---. born Crab---. occ. ----.
    consort of ---. info, ____, father.

Wimer, ____, WM, **d.** ____ on St. Creek of ____, age, ---.
    parents, --- & Rachel A. [Wimer]. born St. Creek. occ.---.
    consort of ---. info, ---,---.

1898

Anderson, John, CM, **d.** ____ on B. Past. Mt. of ____, age, ____.
        parents, ____ & ____ **Anderson.** born ____. occ. laborer.
        consort of ____. info, ____, neighbor.

Blagg, Chas. H., WM, **d. 21 Nov.** at Doe Hill of malaria fever, age, 23 yrs.
        parents, S. J. & Mary Blagg. born Highland Co. occ. laborer.
        consort of ____. info, S. J. Blagg, father.

Biby, Catherine, WF, **d.** ____ **Dec.** at Doe Hill of ____, age, 75yrs.
        parents, ____ & ____ **Chanler.** born Augusta Co. occ. ____.
        consort of J. P. Biby. info, Chris Simmons, son-in-law.

Bird, Eliz. WF, **d. 23 Nov.** on Back Creek of ____, age, 69yrs.
        parents, And. & ____ **Curry.** born Bath Co. occ. ____.
        consort of ____. info, A. W. Bird, son.

Botkin Sarah, WF, **d.** ____ **June** on Bull Past. of ____, age, 65yrs.
        parents, ____ & ____ **Smith.** born Pendleton Co. occ. ____.
        consort of ____. info, J. M. Botkin son.

Beverage, John, WM, **d. 3 March** on St. Creek of old age, age, 84yrs.
        parents, John & ____ **Beverage.** born Pendleton Co. occ. farmer.
        consort of ____. info, W. A. Beverage, son.

Chew, Geo. E. M., WM, **d.** ____ **April** on St. Creek of meningitis, age, 50yrs.
        parents, ____ **& Polly Chew.** born Pendleton Co. occ. farmer.
        consort of Lucinda Chew. info, Jas. A. Bland, neighbor.

Curry, James, WM, **d. 20 Sep.** on Jackson's River of ____, age, 82yrs, 4mos.
        parents, Rich & ____ **Curry.** born Bath Co. occ. farmer.
        consort of Phoebe Curry. info, ____, wife.

Ervin, Margaret A., WF, **d. 17 Aug.** on Back Creek of ____, age, 52yrs.
        parents, Mich. & Rachel Trainer. born Bath Co. occ. ____.
        consort of John S. Ervin. info, ____, husband.

Eagle, Henrietta, WF, **d.** ____ **July** on St. Creek of ____, age, 41yrs.
        parents, Thos. & Polly Beverage. born St. Creek. occ. ____.
        consort of P. R. Eagle. info, ____, husband.

Gum, Isaac, WM, **d. 30 Nov.** at Crabbottom of fever, age, 45yrs.
        parents, Peter & Barbara Gum. born C.Bottom. occ. ____.
        consort of ____. info, H. B. Rexrode, neighbor

Grogg, Allie, WF, **d.** ____ at Crabbottom of ____, age, ____.
        parents, Sam'l. & Margt Grogg born C.Bottom. occ. ____.
    consort of ____. info, ____, neighbor.

Griffen, Lucretia, WF, **d. 31 Dec.** on Dry Branch of childbirth, age, 15yrs.
        parents, P. M. & Nannie Gutshall. born Jackson's R.
    occ. ____. consort of John R. Griffen. info, ____, husband.

Graham, ____, WM, **d. 26 June** on Bull Past. River of ____, age, 2yrs, 1mo.
        parents, George T. & Susie Graham. born Bull P. R.
    occ. ____. consort of ____. info, ____, father.

Hevener, Glendy, WM, **d.** ____ Dec. at New Hampden of erisipilus, age, 10mos.
        parents, Jno. H. & Nora Hevener. born New Hampden.
    occ. ____. consort of ____. info, ____, father.

Harrow, Morgan, WM, **d.** ____ Feb. on Back Creek of diabetis, age, 80yrs.
        parents, ____ & ____ Harrow. born Augusta Co. occ. ____.
    consort of ____. info, Otho Gum, neighbor.

Harding, Eliz., WF, **d. 1 May** at Monterey of ____, age, 78yrs.
        parents, ____ & ____ Arbogast. born ____. occ. ____.
    consort of ____. info, Sallie Crummett, daughter.

Helmick, ____, WM, **d.** ____ Oct. on St. Creek of ____, age, 3mos, 3dys.
        parents, Harvey & Lucy Ann Helmick. born St. Creek.
    occ. ____. consort of ____. info, ____, father.

Hoover, Mary Ann, WF, **d. 1 July** at Doe Hill of dropsy, age, 75yrs.
        parents, Philip & Susan Eckard. born Pendleton Co. occ. ____.
    consort of ____. info, ____.

Halterman, Marg't. A., WF, **d. 28 June** on St. Creek of paralysis, age, 58yrs, 28dys.
        parents, Wm. & Mary Beverage. born Pendleton Co. occ. ____.
    consort of P. R. Eagle. info, P. R. Eagle,** husband.

Hiner, Benj., WM, **d. 25 Jan.** at McDowell of pyamae,* age, 88yrs, 6mos.
        parents, Harmon & Jemima Hiner. born Pendleton Co.
    occ. ____. consort of ____. info, J. J. Hiner, son.

Kincaid, Warwick, WM, **d. 15 Nov.** in Illinois of ____, age, 58yrs, 12dys.
        parents, Jno. D. & Sarah Kincaid. born Bath Co. occ. ____.
    consort of ____. info, L. B. Kincaid, brother.

---

* probably pyemia.
** see p. 215

Leach, J. C., WM, **d.** ____ **April** on B. P. Mt. of ____, age, 43yrs.
        parents, ____ **& Betsy Leach.** born Bull P. Mt. occ. ____.
        consort of Roxanna Leach. info, ____, wife.

Lamb, ____, WF, **d. 22 May** on Cow Past. of neuralgia, age, 86yrs.
        parents, ____ **&** ____ **Bright.** born ____. occ. ____.
        consort of ____. info, Jno. H. Armstrong, grandson.

Malcom, ____, WF, **d.** ____ **Feb.** at Monterey of ____, age, 2dys.
        parents, Crawf. & Mary E. Malcom. born near Monterey.
        occ. ____. consort of ____. info, ____, father.

Mackey, Chas. E., WM, **d.** ____ **Nov.** in Bath Co. of suicide, age, 23yrs, 7mos.
        parents, W. H. & Mary V. McGuffin. *[sic]* born Bath Co.
        occ. ____. consort of ____. info, ____, mother.

McCray, H. H., WM, **d.** ____ **Aug.** on Cow Pasture of the falling of a tree, age, 26yrs.
        parents, Rob't. & Polly McCray. born Shaw's Fork. occ. ____.
        consort of ____. info, ____, father.

McCoy, Julia A., WF, **d.** ____ **Aug.** on Bull Past. R. of dropsy, age, 33yrs, 2mos, 3dys.
        parents, Townson & ____ **Price.** born Bull Past. occ. ____.
        consort of ____. info, W. H. McCoy. info, ____, husband.

Miller, George W., WM, **d. 1 Feb.** at Franklin, W.Va. of consumption, age, 28yrs.
        parents, Wm. & Millie Miller. born Bull Past. occ. ____.
        consort of ____. info, ____, father.

Phelps, A. C., WM, **d.** ____ at Crabbottom of heart trouble, age, 85yrs.
        parents, ____ **&** ____ **Phelps.** born ____. occ. ____.
        consort of ____. info, ____.

Propst, J. J., WM, **d. 15 Nov.** on St. Creek of consumption, age, 57yrs, 6mos.
        parents, Henry & ____ **Propst.** born ____. occ. ____.
        consort of Eliza J. Propst. info, P. M. Propst, son.

Robertson, Emma, WF, **d. 1 Dec.** on Jackson's River of croup, age, 1yr.
        parents, Albert & Naomi Robertson. born ____. occ. ____.
        consort of ____. info, ____, mother.

Revercomb, Susan, WF, **d. 5 June** on Bull P. River of consumption, age, 56yrs.
        parents, Rob't. & Emily Lockridge. born Bull Past. occ. ____.
        consort of ____. info, A. J. Revercomb, son.

Revercomb, George B., WM, **d. ____ March** on Bull P. River of dropsy, age, 63yrs.
    parents, Geo. & Rebecca Revercomb. born Bath Co. occ. farmer.
consort of Sarah Revercomb. info, A. W. Revercomb, son.

Steuart, J. M., WM, **d. 13 Sep.** on Cow Past. River of gastric fever, age, 76yrs, 10mos.
    parents, Wm. & Betsy Steuart. born Bath Co. occ. farmer.
consort of ____. info, W. B. Steuart, son.

Swope, Marg't. M., WF, **d. 5 July** on Bull Past. River of dysentery, age, 85yrs.
    parents, Jno. & Marg't. Burns. born Bath Co. occ. ____.
consort of ____. info, Geo. B. Swope, son.

Shafier, George F., WM, **d. 26 March** at Meadow Dale of diphtheria,
    age, 15yrs, 1mo, 19dys. **parents, Jas. M. & Marg't. Shafier.**
born Meadow Dale. occ. ____. consort of ____.
info, ____, father.

Shafier, Effie, WF, **d. 28 Feb.** on Jackson's River of ____, age, 18dys.
    parents, M. O. & Hattie Shaffier. born Jackson's R. occ. ____.
consort of ____. info, ____, father.

Stahlnaker, Harrison, WM, **d. 9 Nov.** on Jacksdon's River of consumption, age, 33yrs.
    parents, ____ & Eliz. Botkin. born Bull Past. Mt. occ. miller.
consort of Joanna Stahlnaker. info, ____, wife.

Snyder, Anna, WF, **d. 24 Dec.** on Back Creek of childbirth, age, ____.
    parents, D. H. & Sarah Harold. born head of J. River. occ. ____.
consort of W. D. Snyder. info, ____, husband.

Snyder, Hazel F., WF, **d. 28 Dec.** at Crabbottom of whooping cough, age, 10mos, 15dys.
    parents, W. E. & Ludie Snyder. born Crabbottom. occ. ____.
consort of ____. info, ____, father.

Slaven, Mary, WF, **d. 2 Jan.** at Monterey of liver trouble, age, 54yrs.
    parents, Jas. H. & Alice Byrd. born ____. occ. ____.
consort of J. B. Slaven. info, ____, husband.

Simmons, Susan, WF, **d. 6 Sep.** at ____ of ____, age, ____.
    parents, ____ & ____. born ____. occ. ____. consort of ____.
info, ____.

Simmons, Louis, WM, **d. 11 March** near Monterey of ____, age, 80yrs.
    parents, ____ & ____. occ. ____. consort of ____.
info, ____.

Samples, E. S., WF, **d. ____ Oct.** at Crabbottom of fever, age, 43yrs.
       parents, Elijah & Harriet Samples. born St. Creek.
       occ. tanner. consort of ____ Samples. info, ____, neighbor.

Terry, Elizabeth, WF, **d. ____ April** on Back Creek of consumption, age, 56yrs.
       parents, Eli & Naomi Wilson. born Doe Hill. occ. ____.
       consort of ____. info, M. H. Corbett, brother-in-law.

Terry, Howard H., WM, **d. 9 Nov.** on Jackson's R. of diphtheria, age, 1yr, 1mo.
       parents, H. H. & Sally Terry. born Jackson's River. occ. ____.
       consort of ____. info, ____, father.

Totten, F. M., Rev., WM, **d. 15 March** at McDowell of ____, age, ____.
       parents, ____ & ____. born ____. occ. minister.
       consort of Sarah D. Totten. info, ____, neighbor.

Vanpelt, Allie, WF, **d. 24 Jan.** on Bull Past. of consumption, age, 33yrs.
       parents, Emmul & Marg't. Mitchell. born ____. occ. ____.
       consort of J. B. Vanpelt. info, ____, husband.

Waybright, ____, WM, **d. ____ Feb.** at Crabbottom of ____, age, 1mo.
       parents, Chas. S. & Maud Waybright. born Crabbottom.
       occ. ____. consort of ____. info, ____, father.

Waggy, Rachel, WF, **d. ____ April** at Crabbottom of fever, age, 60yrs.
       parents, ____ & ____. born ____. occ. ____. consort of ____.
       info, ____.

———
    Betty, 78
    Capt. M., 174
    Elizabeth Jane, 87
    James, 212
    Joseph, 193
    Josiah, 212
    Malinda, 212
    Martin, 212
    Matthew, 212
    Mary, 212
    Nancy, 212
    Norval, 212
    Lucy, 212
    Rachel, 211
    Roxanna, 86
    Saml., 211
    Sarah, 212
    W. A. C., 174

Alexander
    Henry E. E., 88
    J. W., 82
    James Steele, 82
    John W., 82, 88, 98
    Joseph, 83
    Nannie, 82, 88
    Nannie S., 98
    W. T., 165

Allen
    ———, 110
    D. C., 167
    Hannah, 1
    Reese, 110
    Rob., 110

Anderson
    ———, 215
    David W., 142
    Delia, 142
    Harriet, 76
    J. A., 142
    Jno., 76
    John, 215
    Mahala, 76
    Mahala Harriet, 76

Arbogast
    ———, 18, 155, 161, 196, 216
    A. B., 196
    A. F., 196
    A. P., 142, 189, 196
    A. W., 155
    Adam, 133
    Alcinda, 18
    Amanda, 155, 189
    Amanda M., 37
    Amelia, 189
    Amelia A., 142
    Arlie, 189
    Benj., 142
    Benj. S., 142
    Catherine, 15, 34, 87
    Charles C., 155
    Chas., 137, 145
    Cora A., 37
    Daniel, 21
    E. J., 174
    Eliz., 142
    Elizabeth, 104
    Elizth., 66
    Emanuel, 196
    Ephraim, 66
    Eunice, 174
    Geo., 161, 174
    George, 15
    Gracy A., 66
    H., 149
    Hannah, 34
    Henry, 66, 104, 142, 155, 174
    J. E., 149, 196
    J. W., 144, 155
    James, 18
    Jane, 149
    Jennie, 196
    Jno., 34, 196
    Jno. D., 149, 196
    Jno. W., 37, 155
    John W., 37
    Jonathan, 34
    Levi, 87, 142
    Lulu, 196
    M., 54
    Mary, 142, 149, 155
    Mary E., 37
    Mary J., 196
    Morgan B., 54
    Ollie, 196
    Robbie W., 155
    S., 54
    Sarah, 21, 133
    Sue, 149
    Susan, 196
    W. G., 149
    W. H. A., 174
    Wm. M., 207

Armstrong
    ———, 13, 23, 52, 70, 116, 135, 153, 182
    A. H., 51, 103, 182, 190
    Abel H., 68, 116
    Agnes, 68, 116, 182
    Allen, 25, 63, 80
    B., 127
    Barbara, 70, 88

Caroline, 103
Eleanor, 1
Eliz., 80
Ella Florence, 182
Emma C., 149
Esther, 126
Esther C., 25
Felix G., 92
Geo., 51, 57, 73
Geo. W., 80, 126
George, 80
Gideon, 51
Gilbert, 182
H., 121
Hanson, 1
Hudson, 121
J., 23
J. H., 92, 93
James A., 80
Jane, 63,
Jane E., 127
Jared, 51, 52, 63, 68, 93, 116, 182
Jared M., 80
Jas. C., 116
John, 63, 80
John E., 70, 88
John T., 61, 63, 182
Jno., 68
Jno. H., 217
Jno. M., 73, 126
Jno. W. A., 209
Josiah, 52, 53, 57
Louisa, 33
Louisa F., 16
M. A., 51
M. C., 127
M. M., 149
Mahlon, 16, 33
Martha, 52
Martha E., 25
Mary, 116, 135
Mary Ann, 190
Mary M., 92, 93
Matherial, 57
Nancy, 63, 68, 80, 182
Nancy J., 16, 190
Not Named, 96
Polly, 13, 51
Robert, 51
Rosa, 88
S., 51
S. E., 149, 153
S. J., 96
Sally, 73, 126
Saml., 13, 51
Saml. E., 23, 51

Samuel A., 121
Samuel E., 98
Sarah, 57, 68, 80
Sarina, 80
Savina, 23, 51
Susan, 116
W. H., 116, 182
Wm., 52, 68
Wm. H., 51, 96, 98

Ashby
Eyster Pence, 209
Atchinson
E. D., 121
May, 121
Baker
Howard, 143
Jonas, 143
Susan, 143
Ball
A. R., 93
Amos R., 57
Frances E., 57, 93
Wm. B., 57
Barkley
_____, 174
Calvin, 174
Catherine, 182
Geo., 174
H., 182
Henry, 182
Mary, 174
Bashaw
Cuthbert, 20
Beard
_____, 142, 190
Amanda, 160, 168
C., 160
Chas., 135, 142, 167
Chas. D., 190
Letitia, 135, 167
Lewis, 160, 168
Lillie, 135
Lou, 190
Patsy, 142, 160
Rose Ella, 167
Willie, 168
Beathe
_____, 66
Anna, 174
Crawford, 160
E. J., 36
Fannie, 198
James, 160, 198
Jas., 12, 45, 116, 174
Jas. A., 36, 45
Jas. M., 36

Jas. R., 140
Jno., 31
Jno. P., 66
John, 58
Jos., 36
Jos. A., 116
M., 45
M. J., 36
Margt., 12, 160, 174
Martha, 31, 58
Martha A., 66
Martha F., 58
Mary, 36, 116, 198
Mary A., 12
Mary M., 209
Peter H., 45
S. P., 116
Saml. W., 31
Samuel P., 174
Wm. C., 36

Benson
____, 192
Ada, 90
Adelaide, 155, 190
Alles S., 26
Annie, 155
Calvin Y., 90
Carrie G., 190
Chas. H., 111
Eddie, 90
Elizabeth, 103
Geo. H., 111
George H., 6, 16, 103
H., 47
Hamilton, 103
Harvey, 192
Jas., 202
Margt., 111
Mathias, 176, 202
Matthew, 168
Rebecca A., 26
Robert F., 90
S., 168
Susan, 176, 202
W. L. C., 111
W. W., 90, 155, 190, 202
Wm. W., 26

Beverage
____, 55, 118, 209, 215
Addison, 100
Amanda, 100
Andrew, 43
Annie M., 116
Charles E., 27
Eliz., 149
Elizabeth, 11

Frances, 100, 116
Geo., 24, 59
George, 24
Gertie May, 167
Hannah, 24, 59, 69, 135
Harvey, 27, 59
Henry, 69
J. C., 136
J. R., 167
Jas. C., 116
Jennie, 149
Jno., 11, 55, 58, 69, 73, 100, 118
Jno, Jr., 100
John, 58, 73, 84, 149, 215
Lucinda, 27, 59
M., 149
M. M., 167
Martin H., 58
Margaret, 84
Mary, 13, 58, 216
Mary E., 74
Mary J., 167
Mary M., 149
P., 43
Peter, 43
Polly, 215
Robert, 11, 58
Rufus, 24
S. C., 167
Sallie, 96
Susan, 58, 73
Thomas, 11, 149
Thos., 74, 215
Virgil, 149
W. A., 149, 215
Wesley, 96, 135
Wm., 13, 58, 216

Biby
Catherine, 215
J. P., 215

Bird
____, 21, 104, 127, 135, 149
A. W., 215
Aaron, 39
Adam, 90, 93
Allen, 149
Andrew H., 43
Anson G., 39
C. A., 39
Charlotte, 167
Chas. T., 202
Chas. W., 202
D. H., 39
David, 5, 202
David, Jr., 42
David H., 5, 39

E., 43
Eleanor, 5
Eliz., 5, 202, 215
Elizabeth, 90
Elizth., 93
Esther, 28
Eva J., 127
F. M., 167
Frances, 39
Frederick, 2
Geo., 104
Geo. A., 202
Geo. H., 202
Hester, 108, 160
Isabella, 42
J., 39, 41, 42, 143
J. W., 127
Jacob, 41
James, 58
James H., 90
Jesse F., 40
Jesse H., 127
Jno., 21, 22, 41, 42, 43, 90
Jno. T., 43
Jno. W., 182
John, 101
Lanty, 160
Laura J., 40
M., 41, 42, 143
M. J., 39
M. R., 135, 143
Martha E., 143
Mary, 43, 160
Mary J., 58
Matilda, 202
Melissa, 202
Mollie E., 182
Morgan S., 39
Nancy E., 28
Nancy M., 39
Nettie, 135
O. A., 160
Olive, 21
Otho M., 58
P. H., 39
Peter, 109, 167
Peter H., 58, 90
S., 39
S.A., 39
S. M., 40
S. R., 93
Sarah, 58, 90, 118, 133, 167
Sarah A., 28
Sarah Ann, 143
Sophia, 58, 90, 109, 127
Val, 39

Valentine, 28, 90, 93, 108
W. C., 118, 133
William, 82
William, Sr., 90
Wm., 58, 167
Wm. C., 40, 143

Bishop
Ella, 209
J. P., 195
Jas. L., 190
John, 63, 98
Lucy, 63
Lucy M., 195
Marguerite, 190
Mary, 98
Minnie M., 190
Sarah, 98
Sarah E., 190
V. B., 90

Black
Jas., 96
Martha, 96

Blackemore
_____, 101
Jno. L., 101

Blagg
_____, 53
Ab'm., 53
Abraham, 53
Alberta F., 80
Amanda J., 80
B. H., 202
Chas. H., 215
E., 53
Elizabeth, 53
Frances H., 58
H. J., 53
Henry J., 53
J., 53
James H., 58, 80, 88
Jane, 53
Jno., 53, 121
Jno., Jr., 53
Jno., Sr., 53, 88
John, 58
M., 53
Mary, 53, 58, 88, 121, 215
P., 53
Phebe, 53
S. E., 202
S. J., 215
Saml. H., 53
Wm., 53
Wm. H., 202

Blaine
 ____, 146
Bland
 Jas. A., 215
 Jonus, 131
 Lina, 131
Boner
 Addison, 66
Bonner
 A. E., 128
 Jno. A., 99
Botkin
 ____, 13, 52, 72, 103, 111, 135, 140, 149, 183, 218
 A. J., 135
 A. J., Jr., 135
 A. S., 196
 Andrew J., 21
 Annie D., 196
 B., 58
 Barbara, 6
 Charles W., 135
 Chas., 111
 Chas. W., 135
 Christina, 83
 Christine, 80
 Eli, 143
 Eli C., 147
 Eliz., 135, 218
 Eliz. L., 168
 Elizabeth, 88, 93, 103
 Elizth., 69
 Emily, 20
 Esther, 196
 G. L., 183
 Geo., 168
 Geo. W., 168
 Henry H., 135
 Isaac N., 13, 52
 J., 149, 177
 J. A., 93
 J. M., 215
 Jacob, 171
 Jacob T., 25
 James, 25, 183
 Jas. H., 168
 Jas. M., 190
 Jno., 20, 50, 68, 125, 135
 Jno. E., 190
 John L., 69
 Jos., 111
 Joseph, 83, 89, 135
 Laban, 50
 Lillie D., 168
 Lolo, 196
 M., 190
 Margaret, 20, 50, 83, 89
 Margt., 111
 Martin V., 83
 Mary, 68
 Mary A., 13
 Mary Susan, 88
 Matilda, 168
 Polly, 50, 52
 Robert, 88, 103
 Robt., 69, 88
 Ruhama, 190
 Saml., 6, 135
 Samuel, 6, 58
 Sarah, 135, 215
 Sarah J., 111
 Sarah M., 6
 Susan, 25
 W. W., 103
 Willie, 190
Boude
 Hattie, 190
 Jos. T., 190
 Sarah J., 190
Bowen
 Barbara, 127
 Dora Ellen, 127
 James E., 127
 Wm., 127
Bower
 Margt. J., 63
Bowers
 ____, 177
 Alzina, 25
 Barbara, 35, 58, 142
 Eliza, 202
 James F., 142
 Jno., 35, 177, 190
 Joseph, 35, 58
 Joseph, Jr., 34
 Lucy, 35
 Margaret, 25
 Margt., 25, 34
 Polly, 190
 Solomon, 35, 58
 W. H., 202
 Wm., 25, 34, 142
 Zetie F., 202
Bowyer
 Leonard, 22
 Mary J., 21
 Rachel, 22
 Sarah S. J., 21
 W. C., 21

Bradshaw
    ____, 64
    Eliza J., 45, 191
    Franklin, 25
    Isabella, 25
    J. B., 178
    Jas., 25
    Jno, 45, 191
    M. M., 208
    Mary, 178
    Robt. H., 45

Brantner
    Martha B., 27
    Saml., 13, 27
    Samuel, 13
    Sarah, 27
    Sarah J., 13
    Sarah M., 13

Brennaman
    ____, 142
    L. G., 142
    W. W., 142

Bright
    ____, 217
    Jacob, 121
    Jno., 166
    John, 121
    Margt., 121, 166
    Mary, 121

Briscoe
    ____, 168
    Isaac, 96, 120, 168, 182, 184
    J., 11
    Jacob, 11, 96
    Priscilla, 96, 120, 182, 184
    Sarah, 11

Brock
    C. A., 182
    Chas. A., 127
    Lizzie, 182
    Lizzie C., 127
    Mary L., 182

Brown
    ____, 47
    Ann, 135, 175
    Cynthia, 135, 182
    E., 47
    Elijah, 135
    Elizabeth, 8
    Elizth., 66
    J., 47
    James, 66
    Jno. W., 155
    Jos., 124
    M., 47
    Margaret, 1, 66
    Martha, 135
    Sam'l., 135
    Thomas, 8
    Thos., 8, 47, 66
    Thos. T., 135
    W. E., 135
    Winfield, 47

Bryant
    Chas. B., 143
    Clarence R., 117
    Frances, 143
    H. E., 117, 132, 143
    Mary F., 117
    Robt. C., 209

Bucher
    ____, 121
    David O., 117
    E. A., 117
    Emily A., 121
    J. D., 117, 121

Burk
    John, 76
    Sarah, 76

Burns
    Christina, 71
    Elizth., 95
    Hattie V., 127
    Jno., 218
    Joseph, 71
    Margt., 218
    P. S., 127
    Peter, 95
    Peter S., 127
    Ruhama, 127

Burtner
    Harriet, 206
    Sol, 206

Bussard
    Ann, 182
    Jesse A., 182
    Rachel, 182
    Sol, 182
    Wm. A., 182

Buzzard
    ____, 182
    A. W., 169
    D. N., 182
    J. A., 111
    L. A., 182
    N. A., 109
    Sarah, 169

Byers
    ____, 174
    Samuel, 174

Byrd
    ____, 155
    Alice, 16, 99, 190, 218
    Elizabeth, 149
    F. M., 96
    J. H., 155
    J. T., 149
    James H., 2, 3, 16, 75
    Jas. H., 16, 99, 190, 218
    Jno., 16
    Julia A., 96
    Lyddia, 75
    Mary, 155
    Rebecca, 16, 75
    William, 75

Calhoun
    ____, 106
    Aaron, 106
    Eph., 127
    Louisa, 127

Campbell
    ____, 117, 167
    A. J., 167
    A. Hanson, 155
    Alex, 108, 111, 117, 122
    Alexander, 155
    Alexr., 7
    Amanda, 101, 122
    Amos J., 87
    Ananais, 42
    Annie L., 167
    Austin W., 24
    Azanah P., 7
    B. B., 122
    Clarence, 66
    David H., 75
    E., 38
    Ed J., 127
    Edgar, 37
    Eliza, 75
    Elizabeth, 17
    Elizth., 37, 63
    Etta Jane, 64
    Filmore T., 108
    Georgia E., 87
    Gertrude, 117
    Isabel, 117
    Isabel W., 196
    Isabelle, 155
    J., 42
    J. N., 104
    James, 9, 83
    James B., 37
    James K., 87
    Jas. B., 122
    John, 87, 111
    L. E., 122
    L. R., 122
    Laura, 125
    Laura E., 196
    Lou, 127
    Louisa, 68
    Mar., 155
    Margaret J., 63
    Margt., 108, 111, 117, 122
    Margt. J., 64, 66
    Mary, 7, 104, 196
    Nancy, 83
    Newton, 66
    Newton A., 63, 64
    Not Named, 75, 87
    O. J., 191
    R., 127
    Rachel, 111
    Robert, 9
    Rollin, 117, 127
    S. B., 42
    Sallie, 87
    Sally, 111, 191
    Saml. B., 7, 27, 117
    Susan, 122, 126, 136
    Susan M., 24
    Thomas, 17, 24, 64
    Thos., 17, 24, 63, 66
    W. B., 196
    W. M., 104, 196
    W. P., 117
    William M., 108
    Wm. M., 9,
    Wm. T., 24

Capetoe
    ____, 149

Carichoff
    L. A., 153
    Stuart, 209

Caricoff
    L. A., 100, 168
    R. J., 100

Carlisle
    ____, 9
    Christopher, 9
    Eliza, 109
    Elizth., 73
    John, 9
    Jno., 73
    Margaret, 73
    Rachel, 9
    Robt., 109

Carpenter
    A. T., 185, 192
    C. R., 136
    Chas. R., 136
    Clifton C., 209
    D. W., 122, 168
    Eliz. F., 73
    Frances, 184
    Georgie E., 209
    Harmon B., 168
    Ivy W., 136
    J., 175
    J. M., 128
    Jared M., 73
    Jno., 175
    Jno. M., 25, 57
    M. S., 136
    Martha A., 25
    Martha S., 128
    Preston R., 122
    R., 57
    R. M., 57
    Reb., 175
    Rebecca, 25, 73, 128, 175
    Robert, 73
    Robt., 73, 128, 184
    S. J., 168
    Sarah J., 122
    Stanley W., 209
    Wm. W., 57

Carr
    Blaine, 209
    Geo., 128
    Harriett, 128
    J. D., 161
    Jas., 128

Carrol
    Chas., 198
    Jesse, 136

Carroll
    Charles, 32
    David, 136
    G. W., 183
    Geo. W., 183
    Harvey H., 59
    Jesse, 59,
    John D., 59
    Julia A., 122
    L. F., 59
    Lavina, 32
    Lillie F., 183
    Margaret, 136
    Mary, 32
    Wm., 32
    Wm. J., 122
    Wm. K., 32

Carson
    Mrs., 128

Carter
    ____, 168
    G. W., 100
    Maria, 100
    Minnie V., 168
    Nelson, 141
    Sophia, 141

Carty
    Benjamin, 78
    Cyrus, 78
    Jemima, 78

Carver
    F. H., 97, 128
    H. D., 128
    Joseph, 97
    Martha S., 97
    Mary M., 128
    N. S., 128
    Nancy F., 97

Chanler
    ____, 215

Chesnut
    Alice, 40
    Eliza, 40
    Eliza C., 28
    Elizi., 5
    Elizth., 29
    Jac. N., 40
    Jno., 28
    Jno. F., 29
    John F., 5
    Jos., 40
    Joseph D., 29
    Joseph G., 28
    Mary, 3
    N. J., 40
    Nancy, 28
    S. A., 40
    Thos. A., 5
    Virginia, 40
    Wm. G., 28, 40
    Wm. H., 40

Chew
    ____, 155, 161, 209, 215
    Annie Lou, 174
    Cassandra, 168, 183
    Christina, 168
    Christine, 193
    Christn., 26
    D. S., 128
    E., 193
    Eliz., 183
    Eze., 168
    Ezekiel, 26

G. E. M., 161
G. L., 174
G. Lee, 174
Geo., 155, 183
Geo. E. M., 215
Jesse, 6, 155, 161
Jno. H., 26
Jno. W., 34
Jonas, 59, 168
Jos., 128
Jos. L., 34
Joseph L., 34
Lavina, 26, 104
Lou, 174
Lucinda, 121, 215
Mar., 6
Milton E., 13
O. P., 168, 183
Polly, 34, 161, 215
Silas N., 6
Susan, 13, 26, 44, 128
Wm. M., 13

Chewning
_____, 79
Robt., 79

Church
E., 45
Eliza, 31, 34
Elizth., 34, 59
Jno., 31
Jos., 185
Joseph, 59
Mary, 59, 185
Mary E., 45
Wm., 31, 34, 45, 59

Claxton
_____, 175
Mary J., 175
William, 175

Cleek
_____, 186
Mathias, 186

Clendenen
_____, 149
Adam S., 64
C. R., 190
Cath., 190
Catherine, 22, 28, 64
J., 149
J. F., 190
J. M., 28
Jac. F., 104
Jacob, 22
Jno., 28, 190
John, 64, 149
Mary E., 104

Steuart H. A., 22

Clendennen
Charles, 82, 84, 87
Hulda, 84
Hulda H., 87
John, 82
Mary, 82, 84, 87
Not Named, 82

Clendinnen
Elizabeth, 75
Jacob F., 75
Not Named, 75

Clinedenst
Waldo, 209

Cobb
_____, 136, 155, 161, 168, 197
Emily C., 128
Eliz. A., 168
Jno. H., 128, 136
M., 155
Martha, 161, 197
Martha J., 168
S. A., 161, 168, 197
Sam, 161
Sam'l., 155
Susie, 168

Cobbs
_____, 9
E. A., 9
Jno. A., 9
John A., 9

Coil
Dorothy, 17
Jno., 17

Colaw
_____, 143
A. J., 93
A. N., 147, 174
Allen, 35, 59
Allie, 174
America, 63
Catherine C., 93
Catherine E., 18
Clara Elizth., 59
Cornelius, 196
Cyrus, 18
D., 121, 135, 161
D. E., 143, 197
Daniel, 161
Dan'l., 135
Dora Etta, 161
Elizabeth, 10, 84
George, 10, 84
Howard Milton, 63
J. M., 183
Jno. M., 183

Jonas, 63
Josie M., 183
Lee, 35
Lucinda, 18
Mary, 143
Mary E., 196
Mary M., 197
Mary Ruth, 197
Rob't. E. L., 121
Roxana, 35, 59
S. J., 161
Sarah, 135, 209
Sarah J., 121
W. E. Cameron, 135

Collins
Mc., 161
Mary, 161
W. H., 161

Cook
____, 68
Catherine, 115
Dr. J. R., 135
Jno., 68, 115
Jno. D., 147
Lucinda, 161
Mrs., 200
Paul, 44

Corbett
M. H., 219
Sallie J., 197
Victoria, 197
W. H., 197

Corrigan
Amanda, 104
Caroline, 104
Jas., 104, 111, 136, 143, 203

Coursey
____, 202
D. L., 202

Crickenberger
____, 197
J. F., 197

Cross
____, 168
Eliza J., 69
Jno. E., 69, 168
Patsy, 168

Crummet
Henry, 50
Jas., 100
Mary H., 117
Pollie, 100
S., 50
Sarah, 50
W. L., 117

Crummett
____, 136, 155, 191
Amanda, 128
Arlie, 203
Catherine, 155
Eli, 150
G. S., 136
Geo. F., 191
Geo. P., 140
Geo. R., 191
H. W., 128
Jacob, 136
L. E., 150
Martha, 202, 203
Minnie, 150
S. B., 202, 203
Sallie, 216
Sally, 191
Sarah, 128
Susan, 136

Cunningham
____, 174
E. M., 161
May M., 174
R. Stuart, 174
W. A., 159, 161

Curry
____, 188, 215
A., 40, 51, 56
Adam, 104
And., 215
Ben, 168
Benami, 90
E., 51
Edward E., 83
Eliz. A., 143
Hugh, 56
J., 168
James, 83, 215
Jas., 56, 136
Jennie, 136
John, 104, 168
M., 143
Mary, 90, 168
Mary Ann, 168
Medda, 40
Melissa, 51
Molly, 83
Not Named, 90
Phoebe, 104, 215
Rich., 215
Richd., 23
S., 40
W. H., 168

Dabney
    Adaline, 93
    Nancy, 93
    Tho., 93
    Thos., 93

Daggy
    Noah, 67
    Saml. B., 67
    Susannah, 67

Dalton
    Jacob, 80
    Rachel, 80
    Sarah, 80

Daugherty
    Fan, 136
    Fanny, 143
    Ida E., 143
    Lucretia Bell, 136
    Maggie, 136
    Mary E., 136
    Wm., 136, 143

Davenport
    _____, 169
    Adam, 169
    James, 169
    Mary, 169

Davis
    A. S. T., 93, 97, 150, 161, 175, 183
    E. J., 97, 150, 175
    Eliz. J., 183
    Elizabeth J., 161
    H. S., 12
    Harvey S., 12
    Harvey W., 3
    James H., 175
    James S., 59
    John L., 183
    Lewis, 16, 26, 31, 59, 67
    Lizzie P., 150
    Mr., 3
    Nancy, 12
    Not Named, 97
    Phebe C., 12
    Phoebe, 93
    Sarah, 26
    Sarah A., 16, 31, 59, 67
    Wm. P., 31

Dawson
    _____, 161
    Austin, 161
    F., 161
    Frances, 161
    Lewis, 197
    Millie, 197
    Morgan, 197

Deal
    Amos, 48
    Hannah, 48
    Jno., 48

Dear
    Anna, 101
    W. W., 101, 103, 104, 106, 108
    W. W., Dr., 101
    Wellington , Jr., 101

Delord
    John, 1

Dettimore
    _____, 156
    D. F., 156
    Esther, 156

Dettor
    Margaret, 17
    Joseph, 17

Dever
    _____, 81, 150, 183
    Annie, 122
    Cath., 183
    E., 39
    Eliza, 22, 39, 203
    Ewin, 36
    Francis, 81
    Jackson, 22
    Jasper, 191
    John, 22, 39
    John, Jr., 183
    Jno., 22, 39, 203
    Julia, 191
    Luke, 170
    Martha, 170
    Mary, 150
    Peggy, 39
    Sam'l G., 122
    Sam'l. Kent, 191
    Samuel G., 122

Devericks
    A. H., 205
    A. P., 83
    Allen, 33, 77
    Allen P., 117
    Allen H., 73, 209
    Henry C., 183
    Hester Ann, 73
    Jane, 33, 73
    Jno., 20, 33, 117, 137
    John, 33
    Louisa, 117
    Lucinda, 98
    Lucinda G., 77
    Lucinda T., 73
    M., 161
    Margaret, 20, 33

Margt., 73, 117
Mary, 33, 137
Mary A., 183
Mary E., 161
Naomi Jane, 77
Rachel, 83
T. M., 161, 172, 183
W. L., 161
William, 97
Wm., 73
Wm. M., 97

Dick
David, 8
Mary, 8

Dickenson
L. A., 161
L. S., 183, 203
Lida, 161
Lucy B., 183
Matie, 183, 203
Robt. L., 203

Dickson
_____, 209
C. A., 161
Collingwood, 161
H., 161
William, 161

Diehl
Amos, 191
Hannah, 191
Jno., 191

Douglass
_____, 77, 80, 152
Harriet, 80
James, 77
Jas., 52
M., 52
Magdalena, 77
Martin, 80
Nancy, 9, 165
Robt., 52
Sarah, 52
Thomas, 77
Thos., 52
W. M., 117
Wm., 9, 165

Doyle
_____, 104, 136, 143, 156
Admison W., 28
Amanda, 136
Ann, 25, 111, 129, 203
Arthur F., 143
Asa, 136
Catherine, 14
Eli, 28, 63
Eliza, 203
Elizth., 63
F. A., 104
Geo. W., 104
J. C., 63
James, 156
Jacob, 63
Jacob C., 14
Jacob J., 14
Jno., 14
Leona, 143
Lucy A., 14
M., 156
Margt., 63
Mary, 28
Melissa, 156
Mich., 129
Michael, 25, 111, 203
Sallie, 111
Sarah, 25
Sarah J., 104
Sarah M., 14
Willis, 136
Wm., 14

Dudley
Geo. D., 182

Dunlap
Archibald, 17
Julian, 17

Eagle
_____, 104, 118, 169
Benj. B., 9
Bessie T., 175
C., 44, 45
Chris., 118
Christian, 44, 45, 210
Enoch, 59, 183
Geo., 44, 45
H., 143
Harman H., 59
Harvey, 183
Hen., 169
Henrietta, 215
J., 44, 45
Jane, 44, 210
Jno. N., 96
Lizzie, 143
M. M., 204
Martha, 118
Martha C., 59
Martha J., 104
Martha M., 59
Not Named, 96
O. B., 183
Ora B., 183
P. R., 143, 169, 175, 215, 216
Patsy, 210

Phillip, 59
S. C., 104, 204, 210
S. C., Jr., 118
Sallie O., 59
Sarah, 9, 59
Saml. C., 20, 59
Samuel C., 59, 118
Susan, 59, 183
Virginia, 96

Eckard
_____, 188
Abr., 188
Job, 143, 203
Philip, 216
Preston, 143
Ruhama, 143
Susan, 216

Eddins
_____, 191
Florence, 191
J. T., 191
Jas. T., 191

Edins
J. T., 151

Elyard
_____, 143
Jacob, 143

Ervin
_____, 183
Addison, 145
Benj., 14, 183
Benja. C., 20
Betty, 145
D. W., 38
Deborah, 46
E. R., 38
E. W., 38
Ebeline E., 35
Edward, 104
Eliza, 104
Eliza H., 137
Elizabeth, 67, 104
Elizth., 38
Elizth. R., 38
Emma, 203
Frances, 20
Geo., 46
Geo. W., 104, 136, 137
J. D., 35
J. P., 38
Jared D., 35
Jarucia E., 14
Jno. P., 38, 67
John S., 215
John W., 104
Margaret, 104

Margaret A., 215
Marian K., 203
Mary, 136
Nancy, 14
Naomi, 104
Phebe, 38
R. A., 38
R. F., 143
R. N., 203
Robert P., 14
Robt., 38, 104
Robt. B., 143
Robt. N., 104, 146
Saml. R., 38
Sarah, 20, 143
Wm., 20, 104

Ervine
_____, 128, 150
Aug., 117, 128
Azinia V., 117
Benj., 108
Debora, 166
Della, 175
E., 150
E. V., 122, 209
Elizabeth, 197
Frances, 122
Francis, 150
Geo., 166
H. H., 175
James, 211
John, 122
John B., 108
Louisa, 117
Mary, 211
Nancy, 108, 150, 197
Rebecca, 197
Sally A., 210
Sarah A., 150
Thomas, 150
William B., 108
Willie, 175
Wm., 122, 150, 197

Erwin
Benj., 48
Edw., 156
Eliza, 156
Fanny, 48
Geo. W., 156
James, 78
S., 48
Wm., 48

Eureto
Hannah, 8
Thomas, 8

Euritt
    H., 48
    Nancy, 48
    Thos., 48

Eustis
    Lot, 74
    Phebe, 74

Evick
    ____, 191
    D., 150
    Dice, 117, 130, 150
    Hannah, 191
    Mary A., 150
    Sallie C., 117

Ewing
    ____, 125
    Wm., 125

Eye
    ____, 150, 156
    C. V., 117
    Caroline, 111
    Cora S., 117
    Cora Susan, 111
    Custie D., 117
    Curtis Deve, 111
    Elizabeth, 111
    Estille, 122
    Henry, 111, 156
    J. P., 150
    J. Pope, 150
    Jas. P., 122
    Jno., 156
    Mary, 122, 150
    P., 156
    S. H., 111, 117, 139

Fagan
    ____, 76, 144, 151
    Bundy, 144
    Mary, 151
    William, 76

Few
    ____, 150
    Sarah C., 117
    Stephen J., 117

Finlay
    E., 174
    Marion, 174

Fisher
    ____, 150
    Charles Harvey, 64
    J. L., 150
    James, 64
    Jas., 64
    Louisa, 64
    Sarah Ann, 64

Fleisher
    A. H., 101, 105, 156
    Adam H., 24, 156
    Andrew, 79, 105
    Austin, 197, 203
    B. E., 156
    Barbara, 8
    Benj., 8, 156, 188, 214
    Carrie S., 156
    Catherine, 79
    Chas. T., 191, 203
    Cora Lee, 67
    Eliza, 191
    Eliza J., 105
    Elizabeth, 17, 79, 105, 112
    Finney F., 191
    Geo. O., 100
    H. C., 144, 150, 169, 185, 188
    Hannah, 156
    Hannah P., 156
    Harry, 197
    Henry, 79
    Henry H., 17
    Henry J., 8, 67
    Irene E., 175
    J. A. F., 175
    Jas. A., 175
    Jno. S., 197
    Jno. W., 144
    John H., 8
    Joseph, 20
    Mary, 144, 197, 203
    Mary M., 150
    Orion, 112
    Rachel, 20, 101
    Rachel H., 24
    Rachel P., 20
    Sadie, 203
    Sallie, 203
    Sally, 214
    Sarah, 108, 188, 203
    Sarah Rebecca, 101
    Sol, 191
    Solomon, 13, 79, 105
    Wm. Olin, 150

Fleming
    Marg't., 122
    Margt L., 3
    W. C., 122
    W. W., 122
    Wm. W., 3, 76

Flesher
    Barbara, 77
    Barbara A., 67
    Benjamin, 78
    Hannah, 77

Henry, 77, 78
Henry A., 77
Henry J., 67
Nancy, 78
Thomas, 77

Floid
Ed M., 14
Edward M., 14
Polly M., 14
Virda A., 14

Floyd
Susan Izetta, 210

Folks
____, 78, 108
Adam, 41, 112
C., 41
Charles, 78
Chas. D., 56
Chas. H., 105
E., 41, 45
Geo., 104
Geo. A., 55
H., 41
Harriett, 108
J. L., 108
Jasper L., 108
Jno., 45
Jno. W., 15
L., 45
Levina, 45
M., 41, 55, 56
Malvina, 78
Margaret, 105
Margt., 104
Mary, 15, 104, 112
Nancy J., 104
Not Named, 78
R. D., 162
Rachel, 162
Ruby D., 162
Val., 55, 56
Valentine, 15, 55, 56, 104
Wm., 41
Wm. A., 45

Foster
David, 173
Phebe, 173

Foutess
Richard, 11

Fox
____, 93, 105, 144
A. H., 98
Asiriah, 30
C. H., 144
Chas., 197
Elizabeth, 97

Geo. W., 93
H., 30
Harriet, 191, 203
Isaac, 105
J. M., 30, 191, 203
J. W., 191
Jared M., 30
John, 93
M., 144
Margaret, 98, 197
Mary, 65
Michael, 93, 97
R. D., 176
W. H., 105
Wm. H., 65

Freeman
J. C., 118
Mary, 118
Sam'l., 118

Friel
____, 191
Amanda, 191
John, 80

Fry
Mary, 112
Rudolph, 112

Gaines
____, 122
Lossing, 122

Galford
James, 112
Jane, 112, 162
John, 162
Wm., 112

Gammon
Cyrus, 64
Jane, 64
Thos., 64

Gardner
Catherine, 112
Francis, 137
Frank, 112
Jno. H., 27
Naomi, 27
S. H., 27
Saml. H., 27
Tersy, 137

Gay
James W., 82
Paul, 130
Susan, 82
Susan H., 203

Gentry
Cornelia, 153
J., 153

Gibbs
_____, 120
Gibson
_____, 76, 137
Alice S., 76
Alice B., 88
Alice M., 112
Alice S., 204
Allice, 60
Charles, 88
E. A., 156
Jno. L., 76, 88, 109, 204
John L., 88, 112
Lillie W., 112
S. A., 156
Sally, 137, 156, 204
Saml., 60, 204
Sarah, 60
Willis, 204
Wm. D., 156
Gilbert
_____, 105
Fannie, 105
Huggard, 105
Gilkerson
Jas., 174
Mary, 174
Gillespie
_____, 169, 184, 203
Ashby, 129
Gay, 144, 184
J. A., 144, 184
James, 129
James E., 144
Jas., 203
Jas. A., 144, 184
Jennie, 169
Jennie G., 169
Rosie, 129
Theodore B., 169
Gillett
A. W., 191
Maggie I., 191
Gilmer
_____, 118
Alex., 118
S. A., 118
Gilmor
Jennie, 184
S. A., 184
Sallie, 184
Gilmore
_____, 175
Alex., 28
C. M., 175
Delila, 182
Jesse S., 28
Robt., 182
S., 28
S. L., 175
Sally, 28
Girard
A. M., 210
Cornelia, 210
Nellie Mina, 210
Given
Margt., 60
Robt., 60
Givens
David, 64
Milly, 64
Gladwell
Ellie, 169
Estaline, 86
Gracie, 169
W. L., 169
Warren L., 169
Godden
Isaac, 86
Mary, 86
Gordon
_____, 188
Geo., 93
Hannah, 188
Virginia, 93
Graham
_____, 73, 112, 116, 216
Christopher, 9, 19, 89
D. C., 210
Elizabeth, 73
Emma V., 210
Geo. W., 112
George T., 216
Jane, 9, 19, 89
Lyman H., 210
Susie, 216
Thomas, 73
Gray
_____, 189
James, 84
William C., 84
Greene
Margaret, 5
Gregory
Clara E., 184
Demy, 184, 186
Demy Cath., 176
Emma E., 184
J. F., 176, 184, 186
Jas., 176
Jesse, 177, 178
Joe, 184

M., 177
Malinda, 178
Mary A., 176
W. J., 176

Grey
_____, 192

Griffen
_____, 129, 156, 176
Ascola, 129
Ashby, 156
Calvin, 197
Eliza, 176
J. R., 197
Jesse, 156
John R., 216
Lucretia, 216
Martha, 201
Mollie, 197
Robt., 169
S., 169
Sarah C., 197
Sarah M., 197
W. C., 176
Wm., 169, 201

Griffin
_____, 184
Clark, 184
Eliza, 184
Jas. E., 56
Martha, 97
Mattie, 151
Naomi Frances, 64
R., 56
Robert H., 64
Robt. H., 64
Sarah M., 64
W., 151
William, 97, 151
Wm., 97
Wm. J., 56

Grimes
_____, 111
Arthur, 111

Grogg
_____, 150, 175
A., 44, 54
Adam, 10, 36
Allie, 216
C., 44, 54
Catherine, 54
Charles, 83
Charlotte, 10, 36
Christina, 67, 69
Emily, 83
H., 44, 175
Henry, 10, 67, 69
Henry, Sr., 175
James, 83
Jas. T., 54
Jno., 36, 175
John, 10, 67
Julia, 150
Margt., 203, 216
Martha J., 10
Nancy, 78
Not Named, 78
Philip, 36
Rebecca H., 54
S., 78
Saml., 203, 216
Samuel, 78
Sophia, 10
Wm. (of A.), 44
Wm. (of H.), 44

Grove
Hannah M., 21

Groves
David, 21
Genetta, 21
Sally, 129

Gum
_____, 151
---, ----nnie E., 60
A., 42, 148, 156, 175
A. D., 182, 184
A. F., 128, 169
Abisha R., 60
Abm., 14
Abm. W., 18
Abraham, 14, 41, 82, 108
Abraham R., 41
Abraham W., 18
Abrm., 41
Ad., 197
Adam, 17, 137, 169, 210
Adam F., 75
Adam L., 105
Addie E., 175
Agnes S., 60
Alice, 24, 112, 128, 175
Amos, 129, 156, 193
Anna, 108
Barbara, 210, 215
Betty E., 60
Charles W., 82
Chas. L. M., 184
Chas. W., 144
Cornelius, 60
Drusilla, 184
Elcy, 18
Eliz., 105
Eliza, 136

Elizabeth A., 29
Elliot, 60
Frank, 137
George W., 59
H. A., 175
Harry, 197
Isaac, 29, 37, 41, 60, 67, 210, 215
Isaac W., 175
J., 42, 175
James E., 29
James P., 129
Jane, 60, 67, 175
Jared W., 60
Jas. B., 41
Jenny, 184
Jesse McBride, 18
Jno., 24
Jno. E., 42, 106
Jno. E., Sr., 67
John, 2, 24, 59, 84, 128
Josiah, 42
L., 148
Leonard, 2, 108, 144
Leonard W., 60
Louisa, 129
Lucinda, 17, 137, 145
M., 41
Matil, 60
Margaret A., 18
Margt. C., 41
Martha, 37
Mary, 2, 14, 24, 29, 41, 60, 82, 193
Mary Ann, 60
Mary E., 41
Mary P. C., 14
Matilda, 42
McB., 42, 128, 175
McBride, 18, 24, 112, 175
N., 156
Nancy, 60, 184, 197
Nellie, 137
Not Named, 84
O. H., 112, 175
Omega, 156
Otho, 105, 136, 144, 184, 216
Patsy, 60
Peter, 60, 62, 63, 65, 136, 210, 215
Pollie, 108
Polly, 59, 169
Roger, 60, 112
Sallie, 105
Sally, 122, 129
Sarah, 60, 137
Susan, 17, 169, 210
Susan J., 75
Wm., 60, 197

Wm. H. P., 18

Gutshall
____, 184, 210
Charlie, 210
Elsie, 210
Emma V., 204
G. G., 169
Geo. G., 169
H., 175
H. C., 184
J. L., 184, 204
Jno., 183
Jno. L., 210
John, 184
Maggie, 204, 210
Maggie E., 184
Nannie, 210, 216
P. M., 216
Peter, 210
Rachel, 184
Rosie, 183, 184
Samilda Ann, 169
Virgil, 184
Wm., 184

Gwin
____, 128, 162, 176, 182, 185
Alcinda, 176
Andrew S., 44
Ann, 91
Blackburn, 80
D., 128
David, 19, 128, 129
Edith G., 71
Edna, 203
Eliz., 80
Eliz. A., 144
Eliza, 2
Eliza J., 128
Elizabeth, 47, 69, 112
Ellen, 79, 203
F. N., 112
Fannie B., 144
H. F., 44, 71
Hamilton, 32, 162
Harrison, 185
Houston F., 71
J., 44, 176
James, 25, 30, 69, 91
James K., 30
Jane, 25, 129, 144
Jane S., 71
Jas., 2, 30, 43, 79, 93
Jas. H., 203
Jim, 185
Jno., 162
John, 93

John C., 32
Joseph, 32, 69
M., 47, 156
Mahala, 30, 69, 74, 88, 91
Mamie, 176, 185
Margaret A., 47
Martha, 176, 185, 203
Mary, 4, 25, 32, 69, 74, 85
Morgan, 156
Moses, 7, 9, 69, 112, 144
Mrs., 9
Mrs. Morgan, 156
Nancy, 93, 109
O., 47
R., 43
Rachel, 2, 4, 32, 69, 79, 91, 93, 112, 129, 144
Robt., 74, 80, 85
Sally, 156
Samuel, 79
Sarah, 97, 129
W. A. B., 112
W. K., 144
Wm. A. B., 25, 86
Wm. K., 6, 25

Halterman
_____, 213
Adam, 213
Ambe S., 11
Barbara J., 79
Cora A., 211
Elizabeth, 11
Geo. A., 79
J. F., 185
Jeremiah, 79
Jno., 74
Joseph, 11, 79
Margaret, 176
Margt. A., 216
N. W., 211
P. H., 176
Perry C., 211
Sarah J., 185
Susan, 74

Hamilton
_____, 105
Alexander, 89
Charles, 18, 84
Chas., 105
D. C., 139
Dan'l. C., 105
E., 161
Elcy, 18
Hamey, 198
J. D., 161
Jas., 66

Jas. W., 56
Jno., 198
M. R., 139
Margaret, 198
Margt. R., 105
Musto, 56
Polly, 66
R., 46
Rebecca G., 5, 6, 26, 32, 46, 89
S., 56
T. A., 105
W. T., 198

Hammer
_____, 211
Balser, 38, 69
E., 38
E. A., 192, 211
Elizth., 69
Ella, 192
Geo., 93
George, 7
Leonard, 69
Nancy, 93
Saml., 211
Wm. Ashby, 192

Hansel
B., 57, 119, 204
Benami, 105
Chas., 105
Fanny, 71
J. H., 176
Jno. H., 71, 176
John H., 71
Margaret, 176
Margt., 71
Martha, 105
Mary, 57, 105, 118, 119
Matthew W., 57
Polly, 204

Harding
E. J., 97
Eliz., 216
James A., 97
Mary, 97
William, 97

Hardway
Elizabeth, 3

Harison
_____, 198
Geo., 198
Martha, 198

Harold
_____, 211
Cath., 211
D. H., 218
Danl., 67, 211

Eliz., 169
Hannah E., 67
L. A., 211
Miles, 211
Sarah, 67, 218

Harouff
C. H., 71
Christian H., 71
Cleminza, 211
Harriet, 71
V. F., 211

Harper
_____, 179
Leonard, 15
Phebe, 15

Harris
_____, 192
Ben, 192

Harrison
_____, 192
George, 192

Harrouff
C. H., 86
Susan Catherine, 86

Harrow
_____, 216
Morgan, 216
Nancy G., 97

Haslet
_____, 22
Robert, 22

Hatfield
_____, 165
Edw., 165

Hawley
_____, 186
J. M., 181, 186
Kate, 181, 186
Louis W., 181

Helmic
_____, 118,
Cora, 157, 162
Elizabeth, 162
G. W., 166
Isaac T., 123
Jascah, 118
John A., 157
John O., 162
Mahulda, 123
P., 123

Helmick
_____, 113, 137, 216
E. C., 7
Harvey, 216
Ida, 85
Lucy Ann, 216

M., 7
Malinda, 84, 85, 88
Nancy, 137, 144
Philip, 7, 84, 85, 88
Phillip, 85
Thos. H., 84

Helms
_____, 73, 144, 211
Betsy A., 74
Eliz. A., 73
J. S., 144
J. W., 109, 144
Jane, 74, 109, 211
Jas. A., 74
Jas. S., 73
John, 74
Mary, 144
Toody, 73

Herold
_____, 162
D., 162
E. M., 162

Hevener
_____, 112, 129, 137, 157, 176
Barbara, 91
Cath., 135
Catherine, 94, 112
Ed, 176
Ed H., 129, 130, 176
Eleanor, 10, 157
Ellen, 112
Emma, 156, 157
Geo. W., 127
George W., 5, 94
Glendy, 216
Henry, 162, 176
J., 156
J. B., 198
J. F., 198
J. G., 112, 162
J. P., 112, 137, 157, 162
J. R., 198
Jac., 54, 94
Jacob, 18, 42, 94, 135, 176
Jac. P., 99
Jacob P., 99
James Pinckney, 176
Jane, 5, 157, 198
Jno., 10, 157
Jno. H., 216
John, 149
Jonas, 156, 157
Jos., 105
Jos. H., 157, 176
Lavinia, 162, 176
Luemma V., 105

M., 54
M. C., 127
Malinda, 176
Mary, 42
Millie, 105
Mima, 198
N., 149
N. B., 99
Naomi, 70, 118, 157, 162, 176
Nora, 216
P., 129
Phebe, 157, 176
Phoebe, 112, 137
Rebecca, 198
W. W., 118
William, 91, 176
Wm., 5, 10, 91, 157, 162
Wm. D., 157

Hicklin
Eliz., 77, 105, 190
Elizabeth, 23
Geo., 77, 105, 190
Geo. H., 145
Geo. W., 77
George, 23
H. S., 145
Harvey, 23
Harvey H., 77
Henry, 90
Henry B., 77
Ida E., 145
James C., 105
Jane, 12, 23
Jas. C., 77
Jesse H., 105
Jno., 12, 23
Jno. S., 105, 125
John S., 77
July A., 90
Malinda, 105, 198
Martha, 105
Rebecca, 77
Sarah, 63
Stuart, 90
Viola J., 105

Hicks
_____, 192
Frances, 74
Jno., 74, 192
Lou, 192
Margaret, 176
Wm., 30, 176, 192

Hidy
_____, 113
Cath., 145
Catherine, 2, 93

Clifton, 185
Henry C., 90
J. B., 185
J. H., 113
Jac. H., 93
Jacob, 2, 145
Jas. B., 145, 185, 204
Jno., 34
Jno. A., 93
John A., 145
Laura V., 185
Martha, 93, 113
Matilda, 34, 145, 204
Not Named, 93
Sally, 90
Wm. J., 34

Hildebrand
_____, 144
Mag. A., 144
Rev. Thos., 144

Hilderbran
Sarah Jane, 86
Thomas, 86

Hill
Jacob J., 11
Lucy R. A., 11
S. C., 11

Hille
Henry, 195
M., 195

Hinegardner
_____, 198
Godlove, 198
H. B., 94
M. J., 94

Hiner
_____, 68, 112, 113, 123, 140, 144,
    160, 185, 198, 211
Alex., 109, 162, 169
Alexander, 85
Agnes, 63
Alex., 52
Andrew A., 64
Arch Mc., 123
B., 113, 123, 204
Benj., 176, 216
Benj. F., 112
Bennett, 169
Bernie Gay, 112
Bessie, 129
Caroline, 73, 185
Cath., 189
Catherine C., 73
Chas. D., 94
Chas. P., 50
Eliz., 80

Eliza J., 2
Eliza Jane, 60
Elmipa E. V., 91
Fanny, 123
Francis, 85
G. J., 123, 124
H., 52
Harman, 73
Harmon, 126, 216
Harmon A., 52, 60
Harriett, 85, 162, 169
Helen E., 123
Henry, 167
J., 151, 169
J. A., 198
J. B., 167
J. H., 167
J. J., 181, 186, 204, 216
J. O., 160
Jacob, 90, 211
Jane, 123, 162, 185
Janie, 160, 192
Jas., 50, 185
Jas. P., 185
Jemima, 126, 216
Jeremiah, 73
Jno., 43, 88
Jno. L., 192
John, 60, 64, 68, 85, 162
Jos., 123
Jos. A., 123, 129, 144, 185
Joseph, 50, 90
Joseph B., 151
Julia A., 185
Lucy, 129, 185
Lucy C., 123
Lucy E., 144
Lydia, 169
M. M., 50
Marg. A., 123
Margt., 90
Martha, 52
Mary, 88, 91, 113, 176
Mary A., 109, 204
Mary E., 112
May, 109
Nancy, 90
R. L., 198
Rachel, 43, 64
Ressie B., 185
Robt. K., 185
Rosie, 185
Ruth, 151, 167, 192
S. Brown, 109
Saml., 211
Sarah V., 94
Susan Jane, 80
U., 94
U. B., 94, 113
Verdalia, 185
Virginia, 113
W. H., 185
William, 2, 80, 109
Wm., 60, 91, 113, 123, 189

Hise
Annie B., 204
Clarence, 210
Ella V., 210
Ellen, 118, 204
Eva, 204
Fred, 204
Kenny, 118
Sam, 204
Sam'l., 118, 210

Hite
_____, 192
Allen, 109
Cecelia, 185
Cecilia, 109
Geo. W., 185
George W., 109
Harley W., 151
Isaac, 109
L., 151
Lee, 151
Lee F., 185, 192
Maggie, 151, 185, 192
Mary, 109
Susan, 109

Hively
Nancy, 123

Hodge
_____, 197
Chas. G., 157
Eliz. A., 73
Geo. H., 157
H. J., 157
Jas., 137
Jas. A., 73
Jno., 137
Mary, 137
Nova, 73
Wm., 137, 197

Hoffman
And., 137
Andy, 129, 131
Geo., 137
Henry, 129
Mary, 137
Mary S., 129

Holt
    Jno. E., 89
    Martha F., 71
    Martha I., 89
    Mary E., 89
    Minerva, 71
    Thos., 71
    Wm. F., 71

Homan
    Geo., 145
    Henry, 145
    Laura, 145

Hook
    _____, 51, 157
    B. T., 186
    D., 51
    Ella V., 129
    G. W., 157
    J. M., 51, 85
    Nancy, 186
    P. A., 157
    R. N., 129
    Robert S., 85
    Robt. N., 129
    Sallie V., 186
    Susan, 129

Hooks
    Adison, 32
    Geo. W., 32
    J. S., 32
    Mary, 32

Hoover
    _____, 118, 125, 127, 129
    Barbara, 18
    Cain, 54, 137
    Clara, 129, 137
    Eli, 80
    Geo., 129
    Hally, 125
    Henry, 127
    Jac., 54
    Jacob, 69
    Leah, 129
    M., 137
    Margt., 187
    Mary, 118, 129, 137
    Mary Ann, 216
    Mary E., 118
    N. C., 54
    Nannie, 129
    Rufus, 129
    S., 54
    S. W., 118
    Saml., 187
    Susan, 69, 80
    Wm., 18

Horn
    Elizabeth, 32
    Jeff, 32
    Jefferson, 32

Hott
    E. C., 176
    Jos., 176
    Jos. B., 176
    Rev. J. M., 176

Houdyshell
    Jno., 30
    Lidda, 30
    Rebecca E., 30

Houlihan
    Christina, 169
    Eze., 169
    M., 169
    M. F., 169
    Malinda, 104
    Margaret, 169
    Mich., 169

Howard
    Jno., 167
    Sarah, 167

Howdyshell
    Biddy, 94
    Jno. D., 94
    Jno. H., 94
    S. A., 94

Huff
    Boling, 71
    John T., 71
    Louisa C., 71

Hughs
    Margt., 156
    John, 156

Hull
    _____, 98, 108, 130, 204
    A., 41
    Adam, 27, 29, 37, 76, 93, 108
    Amanda, 75
    Amanda E., 96
    Amelia, 169
    Art., 204
    C. S., 98, 123, 130
    Camilla O., 192
    Cyrus S., 98
    E. J., 198
    Edw. H., 123
    Eliz., 36
    Eliza J., 90
    Elizth. M., 67
    Elizabeth, 36
    Elizabeth M., 67
    Ellen, 75, 98, 123
    Ellen E., 130

Ester, 93
Esther, 27, 29
F. K., 8, 27, 169
Felix, 67
Felix H., 36
Frederick K., 76
Geo. W., 52
Hester, 37, 76
J. N., 198
Jacob, 27, 37
Jacob N., 90
Jno., 29, 175
Jno. H., 192, 198
John, 75
John A., 41
John E. M., 75
John W., 169
Jos., 204
Joseph, 75
Julia A., 76
Luther, 204
M. H., 41
Mahala, 27, 37
Margaret, 29, 75
Mary E., 8
Matthew H., 71
Mgt., 175
Minnie A., 90
Morgan W., 8
Nora May, 211
Peter, 36, 52, 71
Rachel, 36, 52, 71
Renick M., 67
Robert, 29
Robert R., 75
Sally, 211
Sarah A., 52, 75
Sarah M., 169, 185
W. C., 96, 211

Hunklefoot
_____, 157
Henry, 157, 162

Hupman
_____, 71, 177
Annie B., 123, 170
Bob, 177
Geo. L., 204
Hettie, 191
J. W., 12
Jas. S., 71, 191
John, 60
John H., 71
Lillie F., 123
Lizzie C., 123
Louisa, 60
Mary, 60, 191

P. H., 105, 106, 123, 170
P. V., 191
Peter, 9, 60, 191
Pollie, 105
Rebecca, 12
Synthia, 71
Wm. Arthur, 170

Husk
T. J., 51

Jack
Barbara A., 92
Cain, 44
D., 44
David, 27, 69, 71
Harman, 44
Jacob, 24, 27, 145
John, 24, 71, 92, 145
Jno., 24, 198
L. S., 118
Levi, 92
M., 44
M. M., 145, 198
Margaret, 198
Mary, 27, 69, 71
Mary E., 118
Sarah, 24, 71, 92, 118, 145, 198

Jackson
_____, 157, 170, 187
A., 145
Alb., 177
Albert, 94, 137, 145, 157, 158, 159
Albert M., 145
Clay, 170
F., 157, 158
Frances, 157
George, 177
H., 157, 158
Henry, 157
Henry Clay, 157
James, 145
Lou A., 94
Mary, 94, 145, 177, 187
Mary J., 137
Not Named, 94
Sarah, 177
Whalen, 94
William, 158

Jenkins
Henry, 157
Nancy, 157
Oz, 157

Johns
Eliz. A., 170
J. W., 47, 170
Lucinda, 32, 47
M., 47

    Margaret, 32, 47
    Martha, 32
    Mary, 6, 32
    Mary A., 32
    Mary B., 137
    Saml., 32, 47
    Samuel, 32
    Sarah, 4
    W., 47
    Wm., 32, 47
    Wm. (of Jr.), 6
    Wm. W., 32, 47

Johnson
    James, 101
    Nancy J., 101

Johnston
    ____, 187, 191
    And., 211
    Ella, 211
    Jesse, 191
    Lulu, 211
    Saml., 187

Jones
    ____, 119
    A. J., 48
    Andrew J., 177
    Bell C., 119
    C. P., 211
    Caroline H., 33
    Carter M., 33
    Chas. P., 211
    D. H., 34, 48, 192
    Decatur H., 34, 48
    Dr., 113
    Dr. H. H., 113, 116, 177, 183, 204
    Effie, 123
    Elizth E., 48
    Emma, 192
    Gideon B., 83
    H. C., 48
    H. H., 80, 101, 102, 103, 106, 107, 108,
        181, 204
    Henry, 8
    Henry C., 8, 13, 57, 113
    J., 48
    J. A., 119
    Jane, 34, 48, 177, 192
    Jemima, 113
    Jemima J., 204
    Jno. A., 192
    Jno. M., 113
    Jno. Marvin, 211
    John W., 48
    Jos., 123, 170, 192
    Jos. Mondell, 170
    Joseph, 1, 77, 83, 151, 192
    Lilia F., 33
    Martha M., 13
    Martha O., 113
    Mary, 8, 9, 113, 177
    Mary A., 4, 33
    Mattie W., 211
    Sarah, 2, 77, 83, 123, 151, 170, 192
    Susan E., 34
    T. C., 192
    Thos., 8, 113, 177
    Thos. H., 48
    Victoria, 13, 113
    W. H., 192
    Wilbur K., 33
    William C., 1, 2
    Wm. C., 17, 33
    Wm. E., 33

Jordan
    A. J., 123
    Abraham, 48
    Andrew, 33
    Anne, 76
    Annie, 170
    Barbara Ann, 48
    E. M., 170
    Elizth., 49
    Geo. W., 48
    H. A., 170
    H. M., 71
    Harvey M., 71, 76
    Jno., 33, 76
    John, 48
    Lotta, 33
    Margart A., 76
    Margt., 170
    Mary E., 71, 76, 170
    N., 48, 49
    Nancy, 13, 48, 49, 123
    Nancy C., 49
    Peter, 13
    S. B., 162, 198
    S. E., 162
    Sampson, 13, 33, 48, 49, 117
    Sarah C., 71
    Sarah E., 198
    Wm. F., 48
    Zola Estelle, 198
    Zula C., 162

Joyce
    C. A., 130, 137
    Fanny, 130, 137
    Fanny G., 130
    Lulu J., 137

Judy
    Adam, 170
    Allen, 94
    Amanda J., 94
    Burke, 170
    M., 183
    Mollie, 170
    Sarah A., 183

Karicofe
    B. I., 109, 113
    Benj. I., 109
    Elvira, 113
    Maria Jane, 109
    Marietta, 113
    Mary, 109

Kayser
    _____, 106
    Henry, 106
    Jane, 106

Keer
    Wm., 20

Keishear
    Jacob, 19

Keister
    _____, 130, 151
    Ann, 130, 151
    Cammie V., 130
    Gracie, 130
    K. C., 130
    Marcilla, 130
    Martha, 130
    W. R., 130
    Wm. R., 90

Keller
    A., 44, 54
    Eline, 44
    M. L., 44

Kelley
    _____, 138
    A. J., 163, 177
    Chas. E., 109
    Eliza J., 109
    Gertie V., 163
    Jennetta, 177
    Mary, 138

Kelly
    _____, 130, 187
    A, J., 163
    Ann, 64
    Eliza, 113
    Eliza J., 64,
    J. W., 130
    Jennetta, 163
    Jno. A., 113
    Polly, 187
    Samelle, 130
    Wm. D., 64

Ker
    Jas. W., 119
    Sarah A., 119

Ketterman
    _____, 22
    Eley, 22
    Esau, 22, 61
    Esau A., 22, 61
    Flora A., 61
    Jane, 61

Keys
    Mary, 77
    Nichs., 77

Kile
    Elizth., 63

Killingsworth
    _____, 170, 205
    Jane, 12
    John, 12
    Mag., 170
    Margaret, 1
    Mary S., 12
    Sarah J., 4
    Thos., 205

Kincade
    Hannah, 75
    William, 75

Kincaid
    _____, 21, 199
    Amanda E., 23
    C. R., 162
    Charles, 23
    Charles L., 23
    Chas. L., 186
    Cynthia H., 94
    D. G., 138
    D. H., 204
    D. N., 94, 145, 162
    D. W., 199
    David, 145, 199
    David G., 204
    Edw. S., 204, 211
    Eliz., 206
    Elizabeth H., 94
    Elizth. H., 94
    Ferdinand, 19
    Floyd, 86
    H. H., 94, 177
    Harriett, 177
    J., 47
    J. M., 205
    James, 21
    Jno. D., 216
    L. B., 216

Lucinda, 204
M., 46
M. E., 162
Margaret, 19
Martha, 199, 204, 205
Mary, 138, 205
Mary A., 138
Matilda, 46
Mrs., 192
Nancy, 3, 23, 186, 199
Not Named, 94
Perry L., 94
Radie, 177
Robert A., 124
Sally, 145, 204
Sarah, 21, 211, 216
Sarah A., 145
T., 47
Theresa G., 124
Thomas, 204
Thos., 211
W. C., 94
Wm., 46

King
Margt. A., 68

Kinkaid
Charles, 61
Hetty H., 61
Mary, 61
William, 61

Kinkead
____, 151
Andrew, 45
Chas. L., 71
Cora, 99
D. G., 43
David G., 11
David H. A., 11
Elizabeth, 71
F. H. H., 106, 109
Gracey M., 71
H., 38
John J., 3
M. A., 43
Matilda, 71
Mary, 11, 106
Nancy, 71
Nancy J., 106, 109
P. H., 109
Peter H., 106
R. A., 99
Robt. A., 99
Theresa, 99
Thomas, 3
Thos., 106
Virginia E., 38

William, 151
Wm. F., 43
W. P., 38
Wm. P., 38, 71

Kinney
George, 2

Kiracofe
B. I., 123, 163
Geo., 53
Geo. M., 52, 53
J., 53
Lenora L., 163
M. E., 163
Margt. A., 52, 53
Mary E., 123
Turner J., 123

Kiracoff
Benj. I., 101
Mary E., 101

Kirby
____, 80
Almira, 80
Rebecca, 80

Kirkpatrick
____, 187
Adam B., 40
Geo. D., 40
J., 40, 162
John, 162, 187
N., 40
Nancy, 112, 162
Naomi J., 40

Kiter
James, 35

Kitz
Dorothy, 6

Knisely
Arthur Lee, 86
Geo. W., 86
Susan S., 86

Koogler
Eliza J., 211

Kramer
____, 138
Adam, 64
B., 5
Barbara, 24, 69, 138, 187
Conrad, 5, 24, 60, 64, 69, 138
Elizth., 64
Elizth. R., 60
Henry, 60
J. H., 187
Margaret E., 24
S. N., 138
Wellington, 5
Wm. F., 69

Kuglar
- Eliza J., 118
- Jno. G., 118

Kyer
- Bessemer, 163
- E., 163
- Elijah, 163
- Mary, 163

Lamb
- _____, 113, 151, 217
- Catherine, 77, 113
- E., 151
- E. J., 52
- Eliza J., 113
- Jno., 52, 113
- John, 77, 113
- Malinda, 113
- Mary L., 151
- Nathaniel, 113
- Peter F., 52
- Wm. H. H., 52

Lambert
- John, 65
- Polly, 65

Lane
- Harvey, 6
- John R., 6
- Lucinda, 6

Lantz
- _____, 193
- Benj., 37, 61
- Cyrus, 37, 65, 192
- Daniel, 61
- Dice, 162
- Elizth. M., 61
- George W., 37
- Jemima, 37
- Jemimah, 61
- Jonas, 1
- Joseph, 26, 193
- Levi, 203
- Mary Ann, 65
- R. D., 169
- Susan, 26
- Virginia, 192

Lautenschlager
- _____, 193
- J. W. F., 193
- Mariha, 193

Layne
- _____, 101
- J., 52
- Jos., 52
- Joseph, 101
- Mary, 119
- Polly, 101

Leach
- _____, 72, 199, 217
- Betsy, 217
- Catherine, 61, 72
- Henry S., 72
- J. C., 217
- J. S., 199
- James, 210
- Jane, 61
- Jno., 73
- John, 51, 61
- John T., 61
- Margt., 61, 73
- Roxanna, 217
- Sally, 210
- Susanna, 199

Lee
- _____, 124
- Eliz., 124, 170
- J., 170
- Jack, 170
- John H., 170
- Jno., 124

Lewis
- _____, 109, 151, 170
- A., 170
- Amanda, 170
- Ben, 170
- Ellen, 101, 109
- Emaline, 101, 124
- Frankie, 109
- Henry, 101, 124
- Jesse, 109
- Not Named, 101

Life
- Ann, 11
- Henry, 17
- Martin, 11

Lightner
- A., 39
- Adam, 22, 39, 114, 186
- Anthony, 114
- Augusta, 163
- Clevie R., 151
- Clevie Rachel, 163
- Eleanor, 39, 124
- Elenor, 186
- Ellen, 114
- G., 151
- Jane, 87, 138, 203
- Jno., 29, 130
- Jno. H., 39
- John, 203
- Mary D., 18
- Paul, 130
- R., 151

R. W., 163
Ro. W., 163
Susan, 114
Virginia, 130
Wm., 18
Wm. S., 124

Lindsay
[Ella], 211
Ella, 212
Ella M., 205
Jos., 205
Jos. W., 211, 212
Joseph, 205
Lillie, 205

Loche
Ellen, 186

Lockridge
_____, 124, 145, 199
A. R., 193
Amanda, 193
Clara, 163
D. E., 198, 201
David, 29
Eliza, 177
Emily, 170, 198, 217
Emma, 130, 205
Fanny, 163
G. H., 176
Grover C., 193
Hattie E., 138
J. J., 163
Jane H., 124
Julia, 205
Julia E., 205
L. A., 138, 145
Laura A., 145
Lidda, 28
Miss F., 170
Nancy, 95
Not Named, 86
Polly, 170, 177
Reese, 124
Robert, 5, 19
Robt., 64, 130, 170, 177, 198, 205, 217
Robt. C., 28
S. A., 138, 145, 205
Susan, 86
Susie, 199
W. H., 130
W. P. B., 124
William, 177
Wm., 86, 95
Wm. H., 28
Wm. Lee, 86

Long
Annie B. B., 109
Eliza M., 109
James C., 109

Losh
Hulda, 131
Jos., 131
Sarah, 177
Uriah, 177

Lough
_____, 177, 186
Christina, 213
Mrs., 177
Wm., 213

Lowman
_____, 124
Jacob, 124

Lowry
Mary, 95
Sarah, 95
Wm., 95

Lunsford
Jno., 53
John, 110
Josh, 163
Joshua, 53, 54
Mary, 54
N., 54
Naoma, 53
Naomi, 119, 163
Noah, 130
S., 53
S. A., 119
Sarah A., 119
Susan, 110
Tim, 130
Vallena, 130
Wm., 53, 54, 119
Wm. M., 119

Mackey
Chas. E., 217
Henry, 99
J. Wood, 186
Jno. H., 212
John H., 186
M. M., 99
M. V., 186
Mary M., 99
Mary V., 212
Nancy, 99
W. H., 186, 212, 217
Wm. H., 99

Madison
_____, 146
Thomas, 146

Malcom
_____ 81, 158, 171, 205, 212, 217
Ada, 205
Albert E., 158
Crawf., 205, 217
Crawford, 212
E. B., 212
Elick, 81
Elizabeth, 101
Etta, 212
Ferguson, 212
Frances, 81
Geo., 106
Geo. W., 89, 114
George, 81
Georgie, 114
J. M., 131
James, 81, 91
Jane, 80, 89, 91, 106, 114
Jane P., 131
Jas. P., 212
John, 8, 131
Leona E., 89
Lewis H., 114
M. V., 101, 158
Mary, 8
Mary E., 205, 217
Not Named, 101
Rachel, 91
Sarah, 114
Sarah M., 207
Sarahn, 200
Thos., 131
Virginia, 205
Walter, 106, 114

Malcomb
_____, 199
Ada, 199
Jane, 98
Jas. M., 126
Robert, 86
Wm., 98

Maloy
_____, 186
E. J., 186
P., 119
Patrick, 186
Susan J., 186

Marshall
_____, 95, 187
Charlie, 199
Chas. H., 89
Elizabeth, 97
Elizth. H., 95
F. J., 95
Jno. L., 186
John, 97
John L., 97
M., 187, 199
Mary, 89
Maude, 95
Nancy G., 186
Not Named, 89
Phebe, 22
S. M., 47
Saml. M., 23, 89, 97
Sarah E., 22
W., 199
W. N., 199
W. W., 95, 128
Wm., 22, 95

Masters
A. M., 77
Alan, 86
Andrew M., 77
Frederick, 86
Martha, 86
Mary M., 6
Mrs., 210
Robert C., 6
Sarah B., 77
Wm. Andrew, 86

Matheny
_____, 138
Abijah, 138
Araminta, 39
Brown S., 170
Daniel, 138
Edith, 138
Edw. L., 186
Frances, 34
J. C., 101, 138
J. G., 39
Jno. G., 28
Levi, 2, 22
Lizzie, 138
Lulu, 170
M. E., 166
M. J., 39
Margt., 101, 138
Martin M., 34
Mary, 22
Mary J., 186
Mrs., 145
R. L., 170
Reuben, 34
Saml. R., 39
Silas B., 2

Mauzy
_____, 114
D. L., 42
David, 69, 124

David L., 55, 71
Emma J., 99, 114
Geo. W., 99, 114
Geoff, 133
Georgie, 114
Gracie, 124
James C., 99
Jemima, 42
M., 42
M. C., 114
Michael, 124
Polly, 55, 71
Susan, 124
Whitfield, 55
Willis Whitfield, 114

Maxey
_____, 171
Sarah, 171

Maxsy
_____, 119
Peter, 119

May
Annie, 177
J. F., 177
Jacob, 24
Jas. F., 177
Jas. M., 24
Margaret J., 24
Rachel, 24
Reuben A., 24

McAllister
_____, 131, 138
Benj., 138
C. H., 131, 138
Chas. H., 131
Eliza, 131
John, 138
Mary, 138
Rob't. Cecil, 138
Sarah, 138

McCarty
Amanda K., 28
Catherine, 22
Jane, 28
Jestin, 28
John, 160
Justin, 22
Sarah, 160

McClintic
A., 124
A. B., 107, 146
Frank, 85
Jno. W., 146
Leah, 85
M. E., 146
Nancy, 146

Wm., 146

McClung
_____, 106
Ada W., 95
Frank W., 119
Jno., 94
L. M., 95, 99, 119, 131
Lewis M., 98
Mary, 94
Mor., 138, 139
Morrison, 106
Nannie V., 138
Reamer, 131
S. C., 119
Sally, 106, 138
Sudie, 131
Sue E., 95
Willie B., 119
Wm. M., 45

McCluster
Frank, 74, 96
Franklin, 1
Martin, 1
Susan, 74, 96

McCoy
_____, 53, 119
Addison, 120
And. J., 8
Benj., 8, 43
Cynthia, 8
Henry, 43
Julia A., 217
M. A., 43
Margaret, 8
Mary, 43, 120
Oliver, 119
W. H., 217

McCrae
Robert, 76

McCray
_____, 188, 199
Alex., 131
Cami Erdine, 131
Carrie, 146
Catherine, 61
Elizabeth, 51
H. H., 146, 205, 217
Jas. H., 131
Jos., 51
M., 51
Margaret, 61
Margt., 61
Mary, 131, 171
May, 177
Polly, 217
R. J., 177

Rebecca, 146, 205
Robert, 199
Robt., 171, 199, 217
Rodie R., 131
St. Clair, 51, 61
St. Clair, Jr, 61
Thomas, 61
Wm., 171

McDaniel
Mary E., 3
Mr., 3

McGlaughlin
_____, 124
A., 56
Ann, 13
E. A., 124, 177
James, 109
James M., 24
Jas. M., 24
Jane, 24
Jno., 13, 56
Kenton G., 177
Lizzie, 124
S., 56
Sarah, 56
Sarah C., 177

McGuffin
A. G., 163
A. G., Jr., 163
Eliza, 163
Elizabeth, 104
James, 163
Jas., 104
Mary V., 217
Nannie, 163

McLaughlin
Adam, 186
Isabel, 186

McLuain
C., 173
D., 173

McNett
W. H., 129

McNulty
Chas., 186
Danl., 41
David, 68
F., 41, 163, 186
Fanny, 163, 186
Frank, 163
J., 41
Jno., 186
Jno. S., Jr., 163
M., 41
Margt., 186

McQuain
_____, 47, 152
Hugh, 47
Jno., 47

Meadows
Jacob, 26, 52
N., 52
Nancy, 26
Phebe, 52
Thomas J., 26
Thos. J., 52

Meeks
Margt., 210
Wm., 210

Merrett
Elizth., 32
Jno., 32

Metheney
Elizabeth J., 91
Jacob C., 91
James Cecil, 91
John G., 91
Levi, 91
Mary, 91
Mary J., 91

Metheny
J. C., 99
Lizzie J., 99

Michael
D., 102
Dan'l T., 124
David, 33, 50, 69, 101
Delilah, 107
Eliz., 74, 77, 123
Elizabeth, 69
George, 33
Jared, 101
Jemima S., 124
Jno., 50, 69, 123
John, 69
John F., 74
John Franklin, 77
John H., 163
Jos., 163
Martha, 33, 50, 101
Mary Hester, 101
Nancy, 117
Peter, 5, 74, 77
Susan, 163

Middleton
Ellen, 97
Hezekiah, 97
Leonidas, 97

Miller
_____, 109, 151, 212
A. G., 38

Adam G., 69
Agnes, 109
Amanda, 124, 212
Amy, 151
Blanche, !51
G., 151
Geo., 69, 151
Geo. B., 124
George W., 217
Jno. A., 151
Mary, 69
Mary M., 38, 69
Millie, 217
Robt. S., 124
Sarah A., 69
Susan, 193
William B., 151
Wm., 109, 151, 193, 217

Minor
____, 76, 178, 193
Allen, 106, 158
Fred, 106, 158, 178, 193, 205
Israel, 76
Isrial, 81
Jennie F., 205
Jno., 178
Rachel, 81, 158, 178, 193, 205

Mitchell
Emmul., 219
Margt., 219

Moats
____, 171
A., 163
Amanda, 186
Harry D., 186
Henry C., 163
J., 163
Jas., 186
Jno. W., 171
Jonas, 212
Martha, 212
Nelia, 193
Sophia, 212
Wm., 193

Montgomery
____, 139
A., 139
Henry, 139

Moore
____, 138
Jno., 138

More
Mary, 29

Morton
Ed., 33
Ed D., 23

Edwd. D., 33
James, 20
Jas., 23
Jno. T., 23
Margaret E., 33
Mary J., 20
Robert B., 20
Sarah, 20, 23, 33

Mowry
____, 69
Matilda J., 69
Saml., 69

Moyers
____, 119
James, 32
Lucinda, 163
Martin, 73, 83, 119
Nickson S., 32
Rachel, 32
S., 163
Saml., 32, 83
Samuel, 163
Sarah, 73, 83

Mozingo
Cath., 6
Louisa E., 6
Robt., 6
Wm. H., 6

Mulinax
Christina, 72
Elizth., 65
Geo., 65
Wm., 72

Mullenax
____, 137, 206
A., 145
Charity, 21
Christina, 193
Edward, 106
G. W., 171
Geo. W., 206
George, 99
H., 131, 140, 141, 150, 162, 166, 180,
    181, 191
Henry, 137, 139, 144
J., 180
J. K., 131
James K., 158
Jas. K., 131
Mary, 206
Nancy, 131
Oliver, 193
S. E., 171
Saml., 21
Sarah, 99, 158
Susan, 131

W., 158
Walter W., 171
Winnie F., 106
Wm., 131, 137, 145

Mullinax
H., 55
Hannah, 15
Jac., 55
Jacob, 15
Jno., 15
John H., 55
R., 55
Rachl., 55

Murphy
_____, 139
Jno., 19
John, 51, 139
Mary, 19, 51
S., 51
Sarah, 139

Neil
Della Gertrude, 139
Jemima, 139
S. M., 139

Nelson
_____, 195
Wm., 195

Newlin
Fan, 132

Newman
_____, 67, 114
A. T., 171
Claude D., 212
Jacob, 158, 164, 196, 212
Jas. C., 67
Jno. S., 105, 118, 119
L., 158
Leonard, 164
Louisa M., 67
M., 158, 164
Malinda, 171, 196, 212
Myrtie, 212
P. T., 95
Phoebe, 114
S., 114, 158, 212
Salisbury, 114
Sarah E, 95, 119

Nicholas
_____, 99, 210
Annie, 23
Catherine, 65, 72, 99
Catherine J., 4
Eliz. J., 186
Eliza J., 114
Eliz'th. J., 99
F., 178
Floyd, 164
Francis, 65, 72, 99
Geo., 65
Geo. A., 114, 164, 186
H., 178
H. B., 99, 124
Henry, 72, 99
Jane, 23, 72
Jas. M., 186
Jas. N., 205
Laura, 205
Mary, 65
Mattie B., 124
Nela C., 205
Phebe J., 164, 186
R., 178
Robt., 114
Sarah, 99
Sol., 23, 114, 186
Solomon, 72, 124
Susie, 178
Wally C., 99

Nicholis
Francis, 199
Henry, 199
Kate, 199

Noel
_____, 158
Elizabeth, 21
Jno., 21
Mary, 158
Mary E., 21
Mollie L., 158
R., 158
Wm. J., 13, 21

Norman
Ella, 99
Henry, 99

Northern
_____, 139
Sarah, 139

Oaks
Jno., 19
Malinda, 19, 65, 146
Thomas, 19
Thos., 65
Wm. R., 19
Wm. Rufus, 65

Orville
_____, 192

Pack
Jno., 34

Page
Emma S., 47
J. W., 47
Joel, 27

M., 47
Malvina J., 47
Mary J., 27

Parmer
____, 171, 193
Ann, 193
C. K., 171
Christian, 139
David, 139
Ernest, 205
Ida, 205
J. H., 139
Jane, 139
Julia, 171
Mary K., 139
Saml., 193
W. S., 205

Patterson
E. J., 114
Edna, 114
Frank, 205
H. M., 111, 114
Hy M., 114
J. H., 14
Jessie, 205
Mrs., 41
Rachel, 205
Rebecca A., 14

Peck
Abra., 128
Abraham, 2, 11
Andrew, 2
Ann, 11
Annie, 206
Bine, 139
Caroline, 139
Catherine, 88
E., 55
Elizabeth, 55
Enos, 55
Henry, 88
Hulda, 55
Jacob, 11, 206
Jno., 34, 55
M. M., 206
Mary M., 206
Morgan, 34
Mortie, 139
S., 55
Susan, 34, 128

Pence
____, 188
Angeline, 35
Mary, 35
R., 35
Reuben, 35

Peninger
____, 204

Penniger
Henry, 171
Polly, 171

Peterson
____, 171
C. S., 178
C. W., 132
Chas. W., 125, 132, 171
D. H., 206
Ella V., 178
Hattie M., 206
Maggie, 125
Mary, 125, 132, 171
W., 171
Willie May, 132

Phelps
____, 217
A. C., 217

Pleasants
____, 114, 178
Anthony, 77, 89, 114
Charlie, 114
Chas., 178
Emily J., 89
Jane, 146
John, 146
Mahala, 77
Sarah, 77
Venus, 89
Wm., 146

Porter
Helen N. C., 152
Lillie, 152
S. A., 138, 152, 203

Potter
____, 199
Mathew, 199
Vergie Bell, 199

Powers
Margaret, 85
Wm., 85

Pray
Elizabeth, 74, 88
John, 74, 88

Price
____, 47, 217
Caroline, 125, 132
Jane, 68
Lillie, 132
Lillie E., 125
T., 125, 132
Townsend, 68, 125
Townson, 71, 217
Wm., 47

Prit
    _____, 152
    Bell, 152
    Sally, 152

Pritt
    _____, 193
    Almira, 99
    Charlotte S., 99
    J. H., 199
    Jno. C., 99
    Mary Alice, 199
    N. M., 199
    Taylor, 193

Propst
    _____, 164, 217
    Bella Morgan, 132
    Daniel, 132
    E., 132
    Eliz., 119
    Eliza J., 217
    Eman., 206
    Emmanuel, 111, 132
    Geo. J., 86
    H., 152
    Henry, 86, 152, 164, 217
    J. J., 217
    J. M., 164
    James K., 164
    Jas., 200
    Jas. K., 132
    L. D., 164
    Leonard, 119
    M., 132
    Mary, 132
    Mary M., 206
    Nancy, 72, 86, 164, 200
    Nancy E., 152
    P. M., 217
    S. J., 164
    Sarah J., 164

Pruitt
    Almira, 114
    Bishop Marvin, 114
    Jas. C., 114

Puffenbarger
    _____, 76, 106, 206, 207
    A. J., 206
    Adam, 206
    Amanda S., 68
    Ambrose H., 68
    And., 193
    Barsillis McNear, 82
    Birta Alice, 82
    C. L., 158
    Christian, 83
    Elijah, 68
    Eliza, 206
    Elizth., 37
    Elmer C., 158
    Gracie A., 193
    Joel, 82
    Job, 37
    Jonas, 82
    Martha, 37
    Naomi, 106
    Peter, 206
    S. E., 76
    Sarah E., 82
    Solomon, 76

Puffenberger
    A. J., 164
    And., 212, 213
    C. L., 212
    Chas. Emory, 164
    E., 164
    Eliz. B., 212, 213
    Elizabeth, 19
    Job, 19
    Sarah, 19
    Sarah S., 212

Pullin
    _____, 110, 132, 146, 206
    A., 158
    A. M., 174, 205, 206
    Annie, 132, 164
    Annis, 139, 146, 152, 158
    B. H., 113
    Balser H., 26, 81
    Cameron, 158
    Catherine, 26
    Cora, 146
    F., 52
    Fr., 37
    Francis, 26
    Georgie, 139
    H., 152,
    H. B., 119, 187
    H. M., 70, 119, 164, 188, 193
    Henrietta, 152
    Henry, 26, 31, 65
    Henry B., 81
    Henry H., 187
    Icy, 152
    Isaac H., 193
    Isy, 146
    J. E. C., 171
    J. H., 102, 110
    James, 158, 164
    Jane, 26, 65, 74, 110, 134
    Jerry, 132, 139, 146, 152, 158, 164
    Jesse, 26
    Jesse B. M., 61

Jno., 132, 146, 158
Jno. E. C., 67
Jno. H., 31, 36
John, 139, 171
John S., 61
L. C., 171
Loftus, 26, 37, 52, 74, 205
Louisa, 146, 158, 160
Lydia, 119
Lydia V., 187
M. A., 193
M. M., 205, 206
Margaret, 1
Maggie B., 119
Maggie L., 102
Martha, 81
Mary, 134
Mary A., 164
Mollie, 139
Mrs. R. C., 134
Nancy, 61, 90, 171
Rachel J., 70
Robt. C., 65
S., 152, 165
S. E., 25, 37, 52
S. H., 152
Sallie, 119, 146
Sally, 168
Sarah, 31, 70, 165
Sarah A., 67
Sarah E., 70
Saml., 25, 26, 31, 36, 52, 70, 168
Saml. B., 187
Saml. S., 25, 37, 70
Samuel J., 164
Susan, 70, 74, 102
Susan E., 37
Theodore N., 25
Thos., 26, 65, 74, 110, 134
W. R., 146
Willis, 152

Quidore
_____, 132
Ella, 119
H., 119
H. R., 132
L. L..., 100, 101, 102, 106, 107, 119, 132

Ralston
_____, 102, 146, 178, 194
Ann, 146
Annie, 200
C., 160
Conrad, 140
D. C., 146
Dollie B., 147

Dolly B., 172
Eliza, 172
Fanny, 146, 188
Indiana F., 102
James A., 146
Janie, 178
Jas. A., 205
Jemima, 146
Jesse Leroy, 140
Jno., 102, 124, 140
John, 194
Josiah, 132, 146
Luke E., 147
Malinda, 132
Mrs. John, 194
Nancy, 124, 140
Nannie, 140
R. M., 147
S., 146
S. A., 188
S. R. M., 97, 172
Saml., 146, 172, 200
Samuel, 200
Urania, 97
W., 178

Ranson
John, 81
Margaret, 81

Ratcliff
_____, 125
Andrew, 125
Arch., 152
Betsy, 177
E., 152
E. A., 152
Eliz., 113
Jno., 113, 152, 177

Rauch
David, 25
Joseph, 25
Lucinda, 25

Raugh
Ann, 19
Peter, 19

Reed
_____, 110, 115
Alex., 115
Alexr., 11
James, 11
James P., 115
John W., 110
Mahala, 110
Margt., 115
Mary, 11
Thos., 70

Reid
    ____, 140
    Lloyd, 140

Revercomb
    A. J., 217
    A. W., 218
    G., 178
    G. B., 201
    Geo., 46, 62, 218
    George, 62
    George B., 218
    Jacob A., 62
    Jno. R., 178
    John R., 110
    Mrs. S. R., 178
    Reb., 178
    Rebecca, 62, 218
    Sarah, 218
    Susan, 110, 178, 217
    Susan R., 110

Rexrode
    ____, 8, 22, 65, 125, 139, 158, 178, 182, 187, 200, 207
    Adam, 1, 74, 164
    Alcinda, 173
    Ambrose, 206
    Amos, 6
    And., 118
    Andrew, 17, 200
    Annie V., 164
    B., 199
    Barbara, 6, 22, 35, 178, 187, 213
    Barbara A., 61
    Benj., 6, 18, 22, 71, 147, 213
    Bertie L., 200
    Caroline M., 187
    Cath., 181, 206
    Catherine, 91, 115
    Chris, 207
    Christian, 111
    Conrad, 91, 181
    Daniel, 125
    Danl. H., 22, 213
    E. A., 164
    E. K., 213
    Edna, 99
    Eldridge, 194
    Eleanor, 54, 147
    Eliza, 206, 214
    Elizabeth, 74, 97
    Esau, 214
    G. K., 99
    G. M., 178, 187
    Gertie, 125
    Geo., 200, 206
    Geo. A., 147, 206
    Geo. K., 99, 125
    Geo. M., 178
    George F., 61
    H., 158
    H. B., 210, 215
    Henry A., 6
    Hez., 187
    J., 178
    J. L., 178
    J. M., 97, 110
    Jacob, 6
    James, 200
    Jess, 171
    Jesse, 6
    Jno., 35, 74, 132, 139, 147, 173, 200
    Jno. L., 187
    Jno. M., 74, 115, 164, 206
    Jno. R., 139
    John, 4, 65, 132
    John L., 4
    John R., 139
    Joseph, 61, 206
    Josephine, 187
    L., 35, 153, 159
    Lavinia, 152, 153
    Leah, 111
    Leonard, 152, 153
    Leond., 35
    Louisa, 200
    M., 153
    Margaret, 6, 74
    Margt., 35
    Martha J., 187, 213
    Mary, 147, 206
    Mary A., 17, 200
    Mary J., 164
    Mary S., 132
    Michael, 8, 158
    Minor, 187
    N. C., 121
    Nellie, 96, 106
    Nicholas, 91
    O. F., 132, 206
    Pearley C., 178
    Rebecca, 171
    Rebecca J., 139
    Robert T., 17
    Ruth, 206
    S. F., 194
    Saml., 72, 132, 199, 200
    Saml. C., 187
    Samuel, 125
    Sarah, 8, 18, 61, 206
    Sarah A., 125
    Sarah E., 152
    Sarah J., 99, 125, 206

Sidney, 65, 74, 132
Sol., 54, 139
Solomon, 96, 106
Susan, 72, 132
V. J., 213
Virginia C., 206
W., 164
W. A., 194
W. C., 130, 206
W. P., 164
W. T., 206
Wash, 181
Willie A., 213
Wm., 181, 182
Wm. A., 159

Reynolds
Alice Gray, 77
Bettie, 164
Dosia, 164
Eliz., 77, 81
Ida, 152
Jno., 35
John, 164
Louisa, 152
S. J., 152, 164
Sarah, 35
Steph. J., 77
Stephen J., 77, 81
W. Scott, 81
William H. H., 81
Wm., 152

Rider
Estie, 200
Geo. W., 152
Jacob M., 199
Jas. K., 152
Jno., 200
Jno. L., 200
Mary, 152
Mary Gracie, 200
Nancy, 152
Susan, 199

Rimer
Elizabeth, 55
Thos., 55

Rivercomb
____, 99
George, 99

Robertson
____, 12, 152, 172, 178, 188
Albert, 217
And. J., 56
C. R., 194
Clara, 178
Emma, 217
G. A., 178
Geo., 172, 178
Geo. A., 172, 178
J., 152
Jas., 132
Jess, 188
Jesse, 12, 30, 132, 152
Julia, 188
Lavinia, 194
Lucinda, 12, 30
M., 56
Martha, 132
Mary A., 56
Naomi, 217
Polly, 197
W., 30
Walter, 30
Wm., 56, 132, 188, 197

Robinson
Alcinda, 89
Jesse, 89, 102
Lucinda, 102
Magdalina E., 89
Martha J., 95
Mary A., 95

Rodgers
____, 167, 172, 188, 204
Fany, 68
Gordon, 68
Harriet, 127, 188
Harriet W., 68
Henr., 172
Jno., 159
Laura M., 172
Lizzie, 167
Mary, 159
Milburn, 159
Nelson, 74, 188
Reuben, 68, 127
Robt. M., 188
Sarinah, 74
W. G., 127

Rogers
Mary, 19
Wm. L., 19
Wm. L. D., 19

Ross
Jno. M., 197
Parthenia, 197

Rough
Delila, 46
George, 27
George A., 7
Isabella, 46
J., 7
Jno., 46
Joseph, 27

L., 7
Lucinda, 27
Sally, 27
Ruckman
____, 200
Anna, 158
Anna H., 68
D. V., 26, 70, 158
David V., 26, 67, 68
Glenn, 213
Margt., 70
Mary, 67
Mary C., 68
Nancy, 200
Ora F., 213
S. T., 200
Saml., 67, 70
Saml. T., 213
Samuel H., 158
Thomas, 200
Ursula, 213
Wm., 200
Ruff
____, 125
A. W., 125
Lelia, 125
Ruleman
Christian W., 8
Henry, 8
S., 52
Sarah, 8
Rusmisel
Eliz. E., 74
Estalene, 81
Harmon H., 74
Jno., 74
Jno. J., 74
John J., 81
Malissa C., 81
Miami Augusta, 81
Rutherford
____, 72
Elizth., 72
John E., 72
Jno. E., 72
Ryder
____, 122, 213
Carl, 164
Estie L., 213
Geo. B., 183
J., 164
Jas., 164
Jas. K., 194
Jno. L., 213
Sarah, 164
Sarah J., 194
Thomas, 194
Wm. J., 122
Rymer
Amanda, 85
Anne, 106
Anthony, 81, 97
Elizabeth, 24
Ellen, 24
Geo., 95
Geo. W., 167
George, 7, 24
M., 167
Margt., 95
Martha J., 7
Sarah, 7
Susan, 81
T., 55
Thomas, 24
Thos., 106
Thos. J., 24, 85
Samples
A. M., 173
E., 159, 165
E. S., 218
Elijah, 79, 159, 165, 173, 218
H., 159
Harriett, 165, 173, 218
Jno. H., 173
John, 79
John H., 213
Ruhama, 213
Sarah, 79
Thomas J., 159
Scott
____, 140, 141, 159, 166, 173
Agg., 166
James, 159
John, 98, 167
Lizzie, 140, 141
Mag., 173
Mary, 98
Not Named, 98
Seebert
Catherine, 28
Jacob, 28
Seig
Bolling L., 133
F. V., 133
Jas. M., 133
S. B., 133
Seiver
Frederick, 97
Henry S., 37
J. W., 37
James W., 91, 97
Jas. S., 54

Jas. W., 37, 54
M. K., 54
Margaret, 97
Martha, 133
Martha K., 37, 91
Martha R., 97
Robt. M., 37

Sennite
____, 179
A., 179
Abel, 179
Sarah, 179

Seybert
____, 115
And., 110
Andrew, 36
C., 57
Cath., 147, 185
Catherine, 188
Eliza., 110
H. H., 126, 172
Henry, 13, 37, 62, 126, 172
Jac., 57, 185
Jacob, 13, 36, 37, 57, 108, 147, 172
John W., 110
Leah, 36
Lucinda, 62, 126
Mary, 13, 36, 37, 147, 172
Mary S., 57
Rachel, 13
William, 62
Zeb., 115

Shafier
Effie, 218
George F., 218
Hattie, 218
Jas. M., 218
M. O., 218
Margt., 136, 218

Sharp
Betsy, 68
Betty, 31
Daniel K., 31
Elizab., 23
Elizth., 63
John, 23, 31, 64, 68
Jno., 23
Mary K., 31
Rice, 31

Sheffer
____, 159, 179
Bertie, 179
D. A., 120
E., 159
Eliz., 159
Geo. W., 159

Jno. W., 120
Jos., 179
Maggie G., 120
Sarah, 120

Shelton
E. M., 102
S. C., 102

Sheridan
Elizabeth, 11
Elizth., 56
Francis, 11

Shineberry
Jas., 43

Shinneberry
Jacob, 70
Margt., 70
Sally, 70

Shiplett
____, 96
Cora B., 96
Jno. M., 96

Shough
J., 190
Leah, 190

Shrader
Jane, 87
Martha, 87

Shumate
____, 179
A. A., 132, 213
Aug., 132, 179
Augustus, 179
Bettie, 132
Chas., 179
Chas. T., 188
Eliz., 188
Elizabeth, 179
J. L., 135
Jane, 179
Mary E., 213
Mollie C., 213

Sims
Katy, 89
Silas, 89

Simmons
____, 10, 43, 92, 140, 162, 173, 179, 201, 213
A., 43, 179
Ad., 179
Addison, 213
Almeda, 206
And., 179
Anne Grace, 200
Betty, 102, 173
C., 207
Carrie Etta, 140

Cath., 165
Charles J., 98
Charley, 141
Chris, 200, 207, 213, 215
Christ., 96
Christian, 33, 96, 98
Cora E., 140
David, 103
E., 153
E. A., 165
Edw., 207
Eli, 153
Eliza., 110
Eliz., 179
Eliz. A., 165
Floyd, 207
Geo. A., 33
Geo. W., 153
Granville, 153, 173
Grover C., 207
Hannah, 140, 141
Harriet, 179
Harvey, 165
J., 154, 179
J. E., 173
J. S., 201
J. W., 43
Jas., 206, 212
Jasper, 179, 206
Jno., 10, 140, 153
Jno. S., 102
Jno. W., 165
John, 5, 10, 110
John A., 140
John S., 110
L., 153, 154, 165, 167
Lafe, 126, 214
Laney, 33
Leah, 103
Lewis, 165, 207, 213
Lottie, 213
Louis, 218
Lucinda, 10
Luella, 110
Luther E., 126
M., 154, 165, 179
M. A., 140
M. E., 207
M. J., 140
Magdalen, 125
Malinda, 5, 207
Margaret, 78, 82
Margt., 153
Mark, 95, 140, 163
Martha E., 102
Minie, 201

Mordecai, 179
Mrs. W. H., 153
Nellie P., 213
Not Named, 96
Polly, 165
R., 43
Rebecca, 153, 207
Robt. Lee, 165
Rodie, 133
Ruhama, 213
Sally, 98, 140, 163, 200
Sally M., 207
Sam'l., 140
Sarah, 95, 96
Sarah A., 72
Sarah F., 43
Sarah M., 207
Sol D., 207
Susan, 179, 218
Susie, 126
T., 165
Tacy, 133
W. G., 92, 141
W. H., 133, 185, 187, 201, 213
Wash, 207
Wesley, 140
William, 78, 82, 95
Wm., 43
Wm. G., 92, 207
Wm. H., 92

Sipe
Catherine, 165
J., 165
Maggie S., 98
Mary A., 98
William A., 98
Wm. A., 98

Sipes
Alice C., 25
John E., 25
Jno. E., 25
Mary A., 25

Siple
Conrad, 50
Joel, 13
Marg., 13
Margaret, 13, 50
Martha, 13

Siples
Amanda, 188
Jos., 188
Mary M., 188

Sirams
Sally, 140

Siron
 ____, 153, 159, 207
 A. C., 159
 E., 52, 153
 Elizabeth, 200
 Elizth., 52
 Hester, 87
 J., 122, 126, 132
 J. M., 153, 159
 Jacob, 23, 51, 52, 87
 Jane, 16
 Jno., 52, 101
 Jno. M., 126
 Joel W., 207
 John, 87
 Jonathan, 70, 153, 207
 Joseph, 16
 Julia, 52
 L., 52
 Lavina, 23
 Levina, 87
 Martha, 59
 Martha J., 23
 Mary J., 126
 Nancy, 101
 Sarah J., 159
 Thomas L., 16
 Tilden, 126

Sitlington
 ____, 165
 Barbara, 72
 Elizabeth, 90
 Elizth., 72
 Henrietta, 125
 Jno., 15, 90, 165
 John, 72
 Margt., 72
 Mary Ann, 17
 Nancy, 98
 R., 105, 125
 Robert, 72, 165
 Robt., 72, 90, 98, 125

Slave
 ____, 7, 26, 29, 46
 Adaline, 32
 Adam, 18
 Alice, 9
 Amanda, 15
 Andrew, 19, 26
 Betta, 15
 Bill, 31, 42
 Catherine, 17
 Charles, 13
 Charlotte, 16, 19
 Clarke, 27, 42
 Eliza, 29
 Ellen, 46
 Ellis, 46
 Emaline, 37
 Emiline, 28
 Estaline, 32
 Geo. Washington, 38
 Grace, 36
 Hannah, 7
 Harriet, 24
 Henry, 46
 Hiram, 16
 Israel, 25
 James, 7
 James M., 9
 John Letcher, 6
 Lucinda, 13, 38
 Lucy, 16, 56
 Madora, 15
 Mahala, 15
 Margaret, 47
 Martha Brown, 58
 Mary A., 6
 Milla, 13
 Moses, 45
 Nancy, 36
 Nancy Jane, 45
 Pegga, 30
 Philip, 5
 Rachel, 6, 46
 Rachel Ann, 46
 Ru, 32
 Sally, 57
 Samuel Brown, 58
 Sarah, 5, 13
 Sarah E., 17
 Sylvester, 29
 William, 5
 Wood, 58
 Zechariah, 26

Slaven
 Alice V., 41
 Becca A., 14
 Bexe, 24
 Chas., 196
 E., 41
 Edmonia, 137
 Edwin, 17
 Eleanor, 70
 Elizabeth, 100
 Elizth., 70
 Emma, 130, 133
 Gracie Dare, 102
 H., 179
 H. H., 214
 H. S., 179
 Helen A., 92

Isabel, 124
Isabella, 17, 100
J. B., 92, 218
Jacob, 41, 70
Jacob O., 14
James, 3, 7
Jesse, 102
Jesse B., 14, 70, 92
John, 70
John B., 5
Lizzie M., 179
Lucy J., 92
Margaret, 17
Mary, 102, 218
Mary & child, 3
Mary H., 92
Mary P., 14, 70
Maud, 179
Rebecca, 133
Reuben, 14, 24, 100
S. C., 100, 214
Sarah, 214
Steuart, 17, 100,
Stuart, 124
Thos. H., 17

Sloat
____, 107
A. H., 107

Smily
John W., 79
Sarah A., 79

Smith
____, 72, 102, 107, 125, 133, 147, 170, 194, 206, 207, 215
Barbara, 8
Bessie, 188
Cath., 166
Catherine, 8
Chas., 188
Christina, 8, 72
D., 125, 133
Eliza & child, 5
Fannie, 122
G. A., 166
Hannah, 72
Henry, 8
James, 27, 72
Jemima J., 125
Jno., 8
Jno. W., 211
Jos., 77
Joseph, 77, 147
Laura, 207
Magdalene, 77
Malinda, 107
Martha, 125, 133

Nancy, 27
Orfie, 206
Rebecca, 72, 107
Sam, 171
Saml., 207
Sarah, 188
Sarah A., 166
Sidney, 77
Susan, 102
W., 119

Snyder
____, 72, 147, 153, 154, 179, 200 214
Abe, 153
Alice, 133
Amanda, 54
Amos, 76
Anna, 218
C. C., 115, 147
Calvin, 82, 200
Caroline, 200
Chas. P., 147
D., 54
David, 82, 154, 200
E., 41
Edgar N., 179
Elizabeth, 74, 91
Elizth., 41
G. W., 103
Geo. H., 188
Geo. W., 188, 207
H., 54
Hannah, 54
Hazel F., 218
Isabella, 70
J., 41
J. L., 100
James L., 100
Jas. R., 74
Jennie, 100
Jno., 41, 74, 200
John, 91
Jos. T., 172, 179
Judi, 172
Louisa, 82, 115, 147
Lucinda, 38
Ludie, 179, 218
Mary, 70, 72, 153
Mary A., 207
Mattie, 188
Mollie, 147
Olive, 82
Polly, 38, 188, 207
Ratie, 172
S., 41
Sally, 38

Sally M., 207
Saml., 38, 70, 72, 207
Samuel, 70
Sidney, 72
Susan, 76
T. J., 147
W. D., 218
W. E., 133, 179, 207, 218
William D., 115
Willie G., 100
Zudie, 179

Sorrel
M., 156
T., 156

Somers
Aggie, 102
Agnes, 102
Sam'l., 102
Susan, 102
Wm. W., 102

Sommers
Hatti, 91
Jane, 61
M., 42
Paul, 93
S., 42
Saml., 42,
Susan A., 91
W. M., 42
Wm. M., 42, 65, 91
Wm. T., 91

Spencer
Frances, 18
George W., 18
Jno. H., 18

Splaun
Daniel, 115
Dan'l., 115
M. J., 115
Marg't., 115

Splawn
_____, 141
Daniel, 141
Mary J., 141

Sponaugle
_____, 172
Amos, 172
Mary, 172
Pat, 172
Polly, 172
Rachel, 172, 207
W. J., 172

Spriggs
_____, 172
A., 165
Allen, 165, 172

Gertie, 172
Howard, 165
Millie, 172
Mollie, 165
Mollie B., 165

Sproul
Ann, 111
Jno., 111

Sprouse
_____, 11
Lucy, 11
Jacob, 11

Stahlnaker
Harrison, 218
Joanna, 218

Stanton
_____, 147, 199
Amanda, 147
James, 106
Jas., 148
Mary, 106

Stephens
Robt., 25

Stephenson
_____, 88, 128, 141, 194
A., 26, 29, 147
A. C., 43, 81, 207
A. F., 100, 141
A. T., 102, 151, 173, 199, 201
Adam, 5, 10, 26, 159, 194
Alvaretta, 55
Asgil, 81
Augustus T., 102
Brad, 194
C. L., 140
Clement, 81
D., 30
David, 19, 30, 85, 100
E. J., 55
Eliza, 140
Eliza J., 65
Elizabeth, 3
Emma V., 10
G. E., 102
Georgie E., 102, 173
Harriet E., 43
Hester R., 85
Jane, 5, 19, 100, 147, 159
James, 14
James B., 23
Jas., 14, 23
Jno., 19, 128, 140, 147, 159
John, 100, 194
John W., 147
L. H., 88, 155, 159
L. W., 173

Laura, 194
Lina V., 141
Lucinda, 14, 23
Luella H., 14
Mary L., 88
Mary T., 43
Nancy, 15, 140
O. A., 194
S. E., 56, 57
Sally, 194
Sarah C., 10, 194
Susan, 159
Susan E., 19
Sarah E., 15
V., 43
V. C., 207
Virginia, 55, 62
Virginia C., 81
W., 57
Wash A., 57
Washington, 19, 65
Wm., 5, 15, 55, 65, 140, 194

Sterrett
    S. W., 109

Steuart
    _____, 153, 189, 201
    Almira, 115
    Annie E., 189
    Barbara A., 46
    Betsy, 218
    Car., 120
    Caroline, 65, 120, 124
    Catherine, 115
    Charles, 9, 12
    Charles W., 62
    Chas., 12. 62, 207
    Coleman, 115
    Cynthia, 30, 36
    Ed., 25
    Ed M., 15
    Edw., 120, 124
    Edward, 12, 25
    Edward M., 15
    Edwd., 65
    Eliz., 12
    Eliza, 15
    Elizabeth, 16, 19
    Elizth., 62
    Geo. E., 189
    Geo. H., 103
    George, 62
    Gilson, 16
    Hannah, 12, 120
    Harriett, 36
    Henrietta, 153
    Henry C., 65
    Hulda, 15
    Isabella, 12
    J., 45, 46
    J. M., 46, 218
    J. W., 12, 36, 45
    Jacintha, 19
    Jacinthia, 12, 15
    Jac., 36
    Jacob, 12, 19, 30
    Jacob W., 12, 15, 19
    James, 16, 105, 106
    Jane, 16, 120, 125
    Jared M., 46
    Jas., 12, 120
    Jas. A., 91
    Jno., 45, 120, 201
    Jno. B., 16
    Jno. E., 120
    Jno. M., 201
    Joanna S., 46
    John, 12, 153
    John B., 7
    M. V., 153
    Maggie, 201
    Margaret, 16, 106
    Margt., 105
    Mary J., 16
    Mary S., 102
    Mrs. S. J., 182
    Nancy, 115
    P. H., 89, 102
    P. K., 125
    Peachy, 63
    Robt. A., 106
    Robt. E., 115
    St. C., 120
    Sally, 153
    Sam'l., 115, 153
    Tericy, 62
    Thercey, 9
    Theresa, 207
    Thomas, 12
    Thos. G., 124
    W. B., 153, 218
    Warwick, 19
    Wm., 125, 153, 218
    Wm. B., 16
    Wm. R., 16, 19, 62

Steward
    Ferdinand, 62

Stewart
    Annie, 172
    Geo. E., 172
    Maggie, 172

Stinespring
    ____, 147
    Mrs., 147

Stone
    ____, 42, 147, 165, 187, 207
    A., 165
    Annie, 194
    D. C., 187, 207
    Dan'l., 147
    E., 165
    Fannie, 107
    Jemima, 173
    Jno. A., 173, 194
    Joel, 78
    John A., 173
    Malinda, 107
    Mary, 78, 147
    Mary E., 214
    Polly, 194
    Saml., 214
    Sol., 147, 194
    Solomon, 78, 107

Strathy
    W., 127

Straughan
    ____, 159
    Jno. J., 159

Strickler
    E. M., 17
    J. P., 17
    Jacob P., 17
    Mary B., 17

Stuart
    ____, 83, 180
    Caroline, 165
    Charles, 83
    David G., 86
    E. J., 83, 170
    Edward, 83
    Etta, 177
    Jacob W., 7, 86
    James, 86
    John B., 5, 86
    M. V., 177
    Margaret, 86
    Sinthia Ann, 86
    T. G., 165, 180
    Wm. R., 86

Suddarth
    B. F., 91
    Susan, 91

Sullenberger
    ____, 133
    Don, 139
    Sam'l., 110

Sutton
    ____, 198
    Allie, 126
    Ellen, 198
    Geo. M., 126
    George M., 84
    John H., 84
    Lucinda, 126
    Lucinda J., 84

Swadley
    ____, 118, 206
    A. F., 179
    Henry, 118
    Margt., 179, 206
    Phebe, 179
    Will, 179
    Wm., 179, 206

Swecker
    Ambrose, 115
    Benj., 4, 21, 115, 194
    Benjamin, 4, 78
    Betsy, 115
    Cain, 4
    Cecilia, 10
    Celia, 27
    Celia F., 194
    Clara D., 200
    D. W., 194
    David W., 10, 27
    E., 194
    Elizabeth, 21, 78
    Estelle, 200
    Geo., 200, 201
    Geo. E., 194, 200
    J. C., 168
    Jeremy, 4
    John Hannan, 10
    Levi, 4
    Nathaniel, 21
    Polly, 115
    Robert W., 200
    Saml. C. E., 27

Swoope
    B. R., 52

Swope
    Esther, 165
    Geo. B., 218
    Henry, 165
    M. M., 165
    Margt. M., 218
    Peter, 73, 165

Tallman
    ____, 133
    Ben, 133
    Elizth., 71
    Jas., 71

Taylor
    ____, 154
    Fannie, 107
    G. W., 154
    Geo. P., 141
    Geo. W., 141, 154
    Jemma, 196
    Mary, 154
    Mary J., 141
    Mary Jane, 154
    Wm., 196
    Wm. H., 107

Terrell
    J. H. P., 201
    M., 201
    O. H. P., 201

Terry
    ____, 173, 208
    A. J., 189, 214
    Alex., 173
    Carrie, 78
    Cassa, 70
    D. G., 173
    Eli Orten, 107
    Eliz., 120
    Eliz. M., 107
    Elizabeth, 219
    H. H., 219
    Howard H., 219
    Hy M., 107
    Irene, 189, 214
    J. M., 56
    James, 78
    Jas., 120, 173
    Jas. M., 56
    Mary, 173
    Mollie B., 208
    N. M., 120
    Nancy, 78
    Sally, 219
    Sarah, 120
    Sarah M., 70
    Thos. K., 187
    W. W., 208
    Warrick, 70
    Warwick, 78
    Wm. C., 189
    Wm. H., 214

Tewning
    Albert, 89
    Mary H., 89
    Robt. E., 89

Tharp
    ____, 70
    Amos, 70

Thompson
    Flavius J., 56
    M., 56
    Margaret, 30
    Wm. S., 15, 30, 56

Tidd
    Amanda, 173
    Geo. W., 173

Todd
    ____, 180
    C., 159
    Cath., 166
    J., 166
    Jno., 142, 159, 166, 180
    John, 148
    Maggie, 166
    Maggie I., 159
    Nathan F., 180

Tolly
    ____, 195, 208
    Ada E., 195
    Mary, 195, 208
    W. H., 195, 208

Tomlinson
    H. M., 108
    H. M., Mrs., 107
    Henry, 75
    Hulda, 75
    Zachariah, 75

Tompkins
    ____, 65
    Jane, 65
    Sarah A., 65

Totten
    ____, 219
    F. M., 195
    Rev. F. M., 219
    Sarah D., 219

Townsend
    ____, 57, 148
    Alice, 154, 180
    Alice H., 173
    Darius, 154
    G. W., 148, 154
    Jas. B., 141
    Jno., 28, 39, 141, 173
    John, 194
    Kinney, 28, 39
    Louisa, 148
    Mary, 28, 141, 173, 194
    Mary Ann, 39
    Pinckney, 180
    R., 57
    Robert, 194
    Ruhama, 141
    S., 57

    W., 180
    W. T., 173
    Wash, 173, 180
    Wm., 57

Tracy
    _____, 159, 180
    Betty, 173
    J., 159
    Jno., 159, 173
    John, 173, 180
    Mary, 173
    Mrs., 159

Trainer
    _____, 207
    Mary A., 207
    Margt., 207
    Mich., 148, 207, 215
    Rachel, 148, 215

Trent
    Beverly, 144

Trimble
    _____, 10, 154, 180
    Alley, 154
    C., 44
    Catherine, 107
    Elizth., 36
    G. W., 44
    H. I., 120
    I. H., 148
    Harvey, 36
    J., 154
    James, 10, 44, 107, 154
    James A., 36
    Jas. A., 189
    Jno., 44
    John, 58
    John Z., 148
    K., 154
    Kenton, 154
    Lucy H., 189
    Lucy J., 120
    M., 154
    M. M., 189
    Martha, 180
    Mary J., 107
    Mat., 148
    Mollie, 154
    R., 153
    Sarah, 15
    William, 107
    Wm., 15, 180

Trumbo
    And., 171
    Mary, 171

Trumbull
    Andrew, 67
    Mary R., 67

Tucker
    _____, 161

Turner
    _____, 56, 154, 160, 194, 195
    Alex., 148
    Ann, 79
    Emma, 160
    F., 141, 154
    Fanny, 148, 154
    Frank, 141, 148
    Frances, 79
    G., 160
    G. R., 159
    G. W., 160
    Geo., 148
    Geo. W., 160
    H., 159
    Hattie, 159
    Hettie, 148
    M. A., 56
    M. B., 201
    Mary, 79, 194
    Mary J., 201
    Mathias, 79, 195
    Pollie, 160
    Rachel, 141
    St. Clair, 56
    Sam'l., 148
    Sam'l G., 160
    Sus., 169
    Suse, 194, 195
    Susan, 56, 115
    Wm., 194

Valentine
    Bolir, 75
    Elizabeth, 75
    J. C., 75
    Jasper, 75

Vance
    _____, 35
    A., 54
    Alcinda, 22, 54
    B., 45
    Benj., 180, 201
    Charles H., 22
    Christian, 22
    Dorcas, 201
    Eliza, 45
    Geo., 35, 45, 157
    George, 22, 35, 201
    H., 180
    Hannah, 201
    Helen, 102, 214

Jennie, 102
Margaret J., 45
Mary E., 45
S. M., 45
Samuel, 3
Sarah, 22
Susan, 35
Susan M., 22, 35
Wellington, 45
W. H., 102, 180, 214
William, 180
Willie M., 214
Wm. H., 22, 54

Vandevender
_____, 112, 127, 208
Catherine, 180
G., 180
Geo., 180, 208
J. E., 208

Vanpelt
Allie, 219
J. B., 219

Varner
_____, 100, 120, 126, 180
A. L., 96
Adam L., 84
Andrew, 34
Ann, 11, 155
Anna, 68
Annie, 110
B., 141, 172
Benj., 97, 115, 141
Benjamin, 78
Betsy, 107
C., 115
Cath., 202
Catherine, 201
D., 44
Daniel, 110
Danl., 43, 115
David, 44, 68, 120, 155
Eliz., 80, 126, 141
H. L., 43
Harvy F., 34
Henry, 100, 107, 126
J. K., 155, 180
Jacob, 100
Jas., 202
Jno. H., 201
John A., 110, 115
Jos., 43
Joseph, 6, 8, 11, 34, 35
Joseph S., 35
Louisa, 166
Lucy, 120
Luthenia, 100

M., 43, 44, 110
M. C., 96
M. H., 43
Margt., 110, 115
Martha J., 44
Mary, 8, 11, 34, 35, 102, 214
Mary C., 166
Mary E., 84
Mary R., 115
Mary S., 34
Morgan, 8
Not Named, 96
Peter, 11, 68, 110, 155
Phillip, 80
Reb., 180
S., 166
S. C., 141
Sam, 113
Sam'l., 115
Samuel, 120, 166
Sarah, 102, 155
Sarah K., 35
Susannah, 44
William H., 110
Wm., 102, 201
Wm. H., 35, 110

Vint
Ardenia, 97
E., 47
Elizabeth, 72
Esau, 72
John, 195
Joseph, 97
M. J., 189
Martha Ann, 195
Wm., 72, 189

Wade
_____, 18, 107, 127, 180, 181, 201
A. O., 11, 201
Abr., 180, 181
Abra., 181
Abraham, 98, 108, 110, 180
Adella, 11, 201
Adella C., 66
Alex., 166
Annie P., 208
Anson O., 11, 66, 87
C., 39
Cath., 22, 28
Catherine, 66, 214
Charles, 66
Chas., 22, 28, 39, 66, 122
D. B., 181
E. A., 150
E. E., 180
Electa E., 22

Elizabeth, 82
Emma, 208
Emma E., 11
How., 214
Howard, 107
Isaac N., 39
Isabella, 7
J. W., 120
Jas. S., 127, 133, 166
Jas. W., 60, 120, 214
Jno., 201
Jno. M., 135, 138
Jno. V. B., 18
John, 7, 87, 181
John Thomas, 66
Joseph G., 110
Katie, 122
M. C., 181
Mahala, 18
Mahala C., 181
Mariah, 108
Mary, 98
Mary A., 107
Mary C., 180, 181
Mary E., 166
Matilda, 7
Matilda M., 66
Nancy, 110
Otho, 82, 127, 214
Paul A., 28
Rachel, 181
Sarah A., 133
Sidney, 208
Sophia, 120
Sophia N., 120
Stuart, 7
W. A., 201
Wm. Boon, 108

Waggoner
_____, 154, 195, 208
Barb., 27
Barbara, 7, 26, 62, 63
Benj. A., 7
Catherine, 62
Eleanor, 74
Elener, 85
Eliz., 7
Henry, 26, 27, 62, 63
Iriah, 84
Isaac, 85
J. B., 116, 169
J. S., 154
Jacob, 7, 63
James M., 84
Jane, 63
Jesse, 63

Jno. A., 208
Jno. B., 74, 85
John B., 195
Joseph, 7, 62
Lena, 208
Luella, 84
Lucinda, 27
Not Named, 85
Sampson, 7
Sol., 84, 195
Solomon, 27, 154
Una, 85, 195

Waggy
_____, 116, 132
Ab., 132
Abm., 23
Abraham, 23, 30
Abr., 55
Abrm., 30
Crawford, 30
J., 29
Jacob, 29
Lavina, 29
Mahala, 23
Mariah, 29
Michie B., 116
Noah, 86
Rachel, 219
S., 55
Susan, 23, 30, 55, 86
Wm., 55
Wm. C., 29

Wallace
_____, 118
Math., 163
Sally, 163

Wamsley
C. A., 208
Christian, 208
Jacob, 208

Waugh
Elizabeth, 109
John, 109

Waybright
_____, 54, 141, 154, 180, 195, 214, 219
Ad., 195
Annette M., 173
Ben, 115
Cath., 72
Chas. S., 214, 219
Cordelia, 195
D. J., 108
David, 54
E. A., 54
Ella, 141
Ellen, 98

Florence, 173
Geo. W., 98, 173
Isaac S., 121
Jennie, 108, 154
Jno., 54, 115
John, 108, 154
Lucinda, 121
M., 181
Mary, 121, 154, 195
Maud, 219
Maude, 214
Michael, 72
Miles, 180
Molly, 108
Morgan, 121
N., 98, 141
Nick, 141
Not Named, 98
Peter, 103, 121
Pollie, 115
R., 181
S. S., 108, 154, 170, 195, 202
Sam'l. S., 108
Sarah J., 180
Susan, 103
Viola, 108
Wm., 115, 121

Weeks
____, 167, 189
A. J., 154
Jno. H., 103
John, 154
Mattie E., 189
Nancy, 103, 154, 167
Susan, 154
W. H., 189

Weese
Arthur, 202
Christina, 202
Harmon, 202

Weiland
Christina, 21
Mary M., 21
Thomas, 21
Thos., 21

Whistleman
____, 49, 142, 148
Artella, 134
Betty, 133
Danl., 49
Geo., 49, 50, 142, 148
Geo. A., 134
Jain, 49, 50
Jas. H., 134
Jno., 49, 133, 134
Lavina, 134

S., 49
Sarah, 50
Susan, 133, 134
Wm., 50

White
____, 66
Allen, 66
Eliz., 94
Eliza, 201
Harman, 68
Henry, 15
Jac., 94
Jacob, 79, 201
Jno., 176, 201
John, 79
Judson P., 68
Louisa C., 15
Mary M., 68
Matilda, 201
Phebe, 65, 66
Sabina, 15
Susan, 79, 176
Thos., 66

Whitecotton
S., 162

Whitelaw
Alexander, 17, 79
Earnest J., 92
Lucy, 17, 79, 92
N. A., 79, 92
Nicholas A., 17

Whitmer
Elizabeth, 88
John, 88

Wiley
____, 107
A. T., 120, 175
E., 56
Eliza J., 56
Elizabeth, 3
Jas., 2, 3
Jno., 56
John, 3, 110
M. F., 129
Nancy, 2, 3
Priscilla, 120, 175
R., 56
Robert, 2
Robt. C., 56
S., 56
Susan, 2, 110

Wilfong
____, 50
Barbara, 121
Caroline, 116
Charlotte, 100, 141

D., 100, 141
Daniel, 141, 166
E., 35, 50, 166
Eli, 55
Elias, 35, 121, 166
Elias, Sr., 103
Eliz., 141
Elizabeth, 103
Emanuel, 50, 100
Henry, 103
Jacob, 166
Jonas, 116, 154
Jos., 50
Joseph, 35, 55
L., 50
Lydia, 50
M., 166
Mary, 121
Mary C., 166
Matilda, 100
Naomi, 166
Robt. L., 116
Sabina, 35, 55, 103, 154
Samuel, 121
Walter A., 116
Willie P., 116

Williams
_____, 120, 126, 189
Ashley, 133
C. J., 120, 189
Chas. J., 120, 189
Christian, 120
E., 42
Elizth., 31
Erasmus, 126
Florence May, 81
Ida, 120, 189
Jas. W., 42
Jno. S., 120
Margaret, 31
Margt. F., 42
Mary, 23, 133
Minnie F., 85
Narsy, 120
Nellie, 181, 189
Otho G., 120
P. D., 31, 42
Price, 181
Pricie, 189
Rosie, 133
Sarah J., 81, 85
T., 23
Thomas J., 81
Thos., 23
Thos. J., 85
W. H., 181, 189

Wills
_____, 95
Lula, 201
Madge, 201
Mary Eliza, 201
W. P., 201
W. W., 95

Wilson
_____, 23, 92, 107, 148, 166, 167, 190
A., 47
A. E., 103, 121, 134
Abr., 166
Alex, 134
B., 122
Barbara, 166
Caroline, 51
Charles W., 83
Clara B., 134
Clara J., 134
E., 52
E. R. V., 133, 134
Eli, 12, 20, 181, 219
Eli H., 16, 20
Elick, 80
Elizabeth, 3, 20, 88
ERV, 89
Geo. N., 195
Geo. Rosser, 195
George Anna, 62
H. H., 214
H. W., 23
Hamilton, 62, 167
Henry, 81, 83, 87, 166
Henry W., 23
Isaac B., 12
J., 166
J. G., 47
Jane, 98
Jane A., 83
Jas., 52, 74
Jno., 134, 137
John, 72, 166, 214
John B., 83
John G., 87
John M., 12
Jonathan, 107
Jos., 62
Josephine, 167
Kenny B., 133
Laura, 166
Leze, 148
Lucy, 89
Lucy S., 126
M., 51, 154
Maggie, 107, 174

Manda, 87
Maoma, 12, 16, 20
Margaret, 83
Margaret A., 103
Margaret H., 87
Margt. M., 23
Martha, 134
Martha A., 16, 20
Martha E., 16
Mary, 6, 83, 92, 134, 214
Mary E., 166
Mary F., 92
Mary J., 195
Mary Margaret, 89
Matilda, 181
Matilda J., 62
Nancy, 122
Naomi, 121, 181, 219
Not Named, 89
O., 121, 125, 126, 174
Olin Dice, 134
Osborne, 74, 88
Phebe, 74
Presley, 83
S., 47, 190
S. L., 195
Saml., 51
Sam'l. Boyd, 103
Saml. L., 62
Samuel, 3, 92
Sarah M., 16, 20
Susan, 89, 134
Susan A., 133
Theo., 92
Thomas, 89
V. A. Alice, 62
W. E., 195
W. J. J., 134
Wesley, 154
William, 83
Wm., 6, 16, 20, 56, 92, 214
Wm. Henry, 87
Wm. J., 51
Wm. Shelton, 195

Wimer
    _____, 108, 142, 160, 166, 174, 180, 181, 208, 214
Amanda, 174
Ambe, 202
Ambi, 208
C., 103
C. E., 180, 181
Catherine, 10, 160, 166
Charlie C., 202
Cor., 142, 174
E., 55, 121
E. B., 174, 180, 181
Em., 181
Eman., 181
Ephraim, 121
Fannie G., 174
Henry, 10
Jos., 108
Joseph, 76
L. J., 208
Lee J., 208
Lelia May, 121
Margt. A., 76
Margt. Ann, 54
Martha, 121
Mathew, 208
Nathan, 72
P., 160
Philip, 54, 160, 166
Rachel A., 214
Ruhama, 72
Rumsey Smithson, 103
S. W., 174
Sally, 108
Sidney, 181
Susan, 103, 142, 174, 202, 208
Susan C., 55
Virginia F., 208
Wm., 55

Wine
    _____, 49
Barbara, 49
Geo., 49, 50
Geo. W., 49
John, 49
Jos. M., 49
Mary Ann, 49
Solomon, 49
Susannah, 49

Wise
    _____, 107, 141, 142
Elizabeth, 66
Jehu, 107
Jonathan, 66
Lewis, 141
Michael, 66, 107
Michl., 66
Minnie, 142

Wolf
    _____, 189
D., 181
Danl., 181
Evelyn, 181
Jno., 30, 181
Josiah, 10
Lewis Franklin, 181
Margaret, 30

    Margt., 181
    Martenella, 10
    Mary, 181
    Sarah E., 10
    Susan, 181, 189
    Wm. W., 30

Wood
    Jas. N., 198

Wooddell
    Eliza, 83
    John, 83
    Martha, 83
    Mary, 108
    Sarah, 83
    Wm., 108

Woodell
    Eliza, 214
    Eliza A., 214
    H. I., 214
    Jno., 214

Wooden
    _____, 116
    Jonathan, 116

Woodle
    _____, 53
    M., 53
    Wm., 53

Woods
    _____, 107, 126
    Chas. P., 148
    D., 29
    David B., 62
    Elvira A., 148
    James, 1, 29, 110
    James M., 92, 110
    Jas., 196
    Jas. M., 126
    Jno., 29
    Jno. A., 29
    Jno. Willie, 148
    John, 62, 79
    Lillie G., 202
    Lucy, 148, 202
    Lucy E., 208
    M. L., 29
    Martha, 1
    Mary, 11, 29, 62, 116, 196
    Mary Jewell, 208
    Mary S., 126
    Maude B., 148
    N. B., 112, 116, 148, 202, 208
    Not Named, 92
    Peter, 79
    Polly, 1
    Rachel, 79
    Robbie B., 148
    Saml., 11, 29
    Sarah, 92, 110
    T. J., 29, 148

Wright
    A. L., 103
    A. T., 95, 107, 120
    Albert C., 31
    Allie, 96, 196
    Annie E., 195
    Christopher G, 2
    Corda J., 103
    E., 30, 31
    Elisha, 12, 30, 31
    Eliz., 94
    Elvina, 2
    Frances, 195
    George, 12
    J. R. L., 96
    James, 6, 19, 32, 89, 95, 98
    Jas., 195, 196
    L. D. C., 95
    L. E., 195
    L. G., 95
    Lorra T., 31
    Louisa, 30
    Nancy, 12, 30, 31, 94, 107
    Robert, 19, 198
    Robt, 2, 107
    S. A., 95
    Susan, 2, 19, 103, 198

Young
    Ellen, 89
    M., 48
    P., 48

Zickafoose
    _____, 79

www.ingramcontent.com/pod-product-compliance
Lightning Source LLC
Chambersburg PA
CBHW081347230426
43667CB00017B/2754